The Spirit of the Age

The Spirit of the Age

Victorian Essays

Edited by

Gertrude Himmelfarb

Yale University Press

New Haven and London

Published with assistance from the Louis Stern Memorial Fund.
Copyright © 2007 by Yale University
Introduction and editorial apparatus
copyright © 2007 by Gertrude Himmelfarb

Set in Adobe Garamond type by Keystone Typesetting, Inc., Orwigsburg, Pennsylvania.
Printed in the United States of America by Sheridan Books, Ann Arbor, Michigan.

Library of Congress Control Number: 2007925376
ISBN: 978-0-300-12330-2

A catalogue record for this book is available from the British Library.

The paper in this book meets the guidelines for permanence and durability of the Committee on
Production Guidelines for Book Longevity of the Council on Library Resources.

10 9 8 7 6 5 4 3 2 1

Contents

Mid-Victorian England

Late Victorian England

Introduction

I The Spirit of the Age

In 1831, at the age of twenty-five, John Stuart Mill published a series of essays (anonymously, as was the custom) in the radical weekly the *Examiner,* under the title "The Spirit of the Age." The opening sentences of the first essay commented on the title: "The 'spirit of the age' is in some measure a novel expression. I do not believe that it is to be met with in any work exceeding fifty years in antiquity."

It was not, in fact, an altogether novel expression at the time. It was the title of a book by the well-known writer William Hazlitt.[1] Like Mill's essays, those in *The Spirit of the Age* originated in a periodical, the *New Monthly,* but unlike Mill's, they were reissued almost immediately as a volume in 1825. Mill's failure to mention it is all the more odd because the leading essay was on Jeremy Bentham, a subject that had been at the heart of his own extraordinary education and of the "crisis," as he called it, brought on by that education, from

1. William Hazlitt, *The Spirit of the Age: Or Contemporary Portraits* (1825). The phrase also appears, capitalized, in the opening sentence of the second essay in this volume, on Godwin: "The Spirit of the Age was never more fully shown than in its treatment of this writer. . . . " Had Mill read back issues of the *Examiner* (in which his own essays appeared), he might have come across a reference by Hazlitt, in 1816, to a book in German published in 1805, *Der Geist der Zeit.* In 1820, Hazlitt used that phrase, in the English translation, in an article in the *London Magazine.* (Editorial note to "The Spirit of the Age," in Mill, *Newspaper Writings,* ed. Ann P. Robson and John M. Robson [Toronto, 1986], I, 228.)

which he was only then beginning to recover—thanks to two of the other subjects in that volume, Wordsworth and Coleridge.

Long before Hazlitt, and long before those "fifty years" mentioned by Mill, the expression "spirit of the age" appeared in another essay that Mill may have read.[2] Almost a century earlier, in an uncommon burst of exuberance, David Hume had written: "The spirit of the age affects all the arts, and the minds of men being once roused from their lethargy and put into a fermentation turn themselves on all sides and carry improvements into every art and science. Profound ignorance is totally banished, and men enjoy the privilege of rational creatures to think as well as to act, to cultivate the pleasures of the mind as well as those of the body." Hume did not use the word *Enlightenment* (it was not yet in currency in 1741 when he was writing), but it was clearly the age of the Enlightenment he was celebrating, when material progress went hand in hand with moral progress, when the "mechanical" and "liberal" arts were complementary, each requiring the other for its "perfection," when "philosophers and politicians, renowned generals and poets," lived happily beside the "skillful weavers and ship carpenters," who partook of the same spirit and furthered the same arts.[3]

If Mill had read and remembered that essay, he would have been struck by the contrast between Hume's "spirit of the age" and his own. Unlike Hume's orderly and harmonious age, Mill's was an "age of transition," of "intellectual anarchy," when "mankind have outgrown old institutions and old doctrines, and have not yet acquired new ones," when the "march of intellect" was bandied about mindlessly, when people learned to "reason more" but not to "reason better," when the "increase of discussion" led to the "diffusion of superficial knowledge" but not of wisdom or virtue. Eventually, this transitional state should give way to a "natural state," the "virtuous and best-instructed of the nation" acquiring a "worldly power" commensurate with their moral and intellectual power, and society resuming its "onward progress."[4] But Mill gave no indication of when or how that would come about; nor did he express any confidence that it would.

In his *Autobiography,* Mill dismissed his own essays as "lumbering in style" and so "ill-timed" that they "missed fire altogether." Their only effect, he said, was that they caught the attention of Thomas Carlyle, then living in seclusion

2. Mill was thoroughly familiar with Hume's work. At the age of seven, under the tutelage of his father, he had read the whole of Hume's *History of England.* Eight years later he read a volume of his essays, although perhaps not that containing the essay alluding to the "spirit of the age."

3. David Hume, "Of Refinement in the Arts," in *Political Essays* ([1741–42] New York, 1953), pp. 123–24. (In the original edition, this essay was titled "Of Luxury.")

4. See below, pp. 51ff.

in Scotland, who saw in them, he later told Mill, the makings of "a new Mystic." They were the first hint, Carlyle said, that "the age was not the best of all possible ages."[5] The first hint, that is, apart from his own writings, for he himself had expressed similar sentiments two years earlier in the *Edinburgh Review.* There is no mention in Mill's letters or autobiography of Carlyle's essay "Signs of the Times," although the *Edinburgh Review* was certainly one of the journals he read (and to which he later contributed). Mill's "age of transition" echoes Carlyle's "mechanical age," when all that had seemed to be "fixed and immutable, deep as the foundations of the world," was vanishing, to be replaced by "machinery" that pervaded not only the "external and physical" aspects of life but the "internal and spiritual" as well.[6]

Carlyle and Mill were hardly alone in this diagnosis of their time. Lytton Bulwer confirmed it in his *England and the English* in 1833. Carlyle had little respect for Bulwer, a popular writer whose dandyish character he parodied in *Sartor Resartus* (which had just appeared in *Fraser's Magazine*), but he thought better of him after reading, on the strong recommendation of Mill, Bulwer's new book.[7] In his account of "the intellectual spirit of the time," Bulwer delivered a eulogy of Byron that was, in effect, a eulogy of his age. While neither Mill nor Carlyle shared his enthusiasm for Byron (Mill had earlier participated in a debate in which he allied himself with Wordsworth against Byron), they did agree that the death of Byron signified a death of poetry, a triumph of the spirit of utility over imagination and sentiment. "When Byron passed away," Bulwer wrote, "the feeling he had represented craved utterance no more. With a sign we turned to the actual and practical career of life: we awoke from the morbid, the passionate, the dreaming, 'the moonlight and the dimness of the mind,' and by a natural reaction addressed ourselves to the active and daily objects which lay before us."[8]

5. *Autobiography of John Stuart Mill,* ed. John Jacob Coss (New York, 1924), p. 122; *The Earlier Letters of John Stuart Mill, 1812–1848,* ed. Francis E. Mineka (Toronto, 1963), in *Collected Works,* I, 86 (letter of Mill to John Sterling, Oct. 20–22, 1831).

6. See below, pp. 34ff. About the same time that Mill's essays were appearing in the *Examiner,* Carlyle returned to the theme in the *Edinburgh Review,* using a different metaphor to characterize the mechanical age: "The whole Life of Society must now be carried on by drugs: doctor after doctor appears with his nostrum, of Cooperative Societies, Universal Suffrage, Cottage-and-Cow systems, Repression of Population, Vote by Ballot." (Thomas Carlyle, "Characteristics," *Edinburgh Review,* December 1831, reprinted in *Critical and Miscellaneous Essays* [London, 1891], IV, 19.)

7. Mill thought so well of it that he contributed to it (anonymously) an appendix on Bentham and utilitarianism, a prelude to his longer critique five years later.

8. Edward Lytton Bulwer, *England and the English,* ed. Standish Meacham ([1833] Chicago, 1970), p. 286. (Bulwer is better known as Edward Bulwer-Lytton, the name he assumed when he became a baronet and succeeded to his estate.) For a later perspective on

To Carlyle, the tragedy of the age was that it was "at once destitute of faith and terrified at scepticism."[9] To Bulwer, it was the end of the "romantic age" and the beginning of a bleak utilitarianism. To Mill it was an age of "intellectual anarchy," when the old virtues and moral authorities had died and new ones had not yet been born. Yet there was another aspect to the age that belied these dire diagnoses. So far from being "destitute of faith," it was buoyed up by the Evangelical spirit that was the heir of Methodism. The French historian Elie Halévy, in his classic work on Victorian England, made much of the Methodist revival that had started in England early in the eighteenth century and was very much alive a century and more later. What was distinctive about this revival, and what made it a powerful social as well as a religious force, was the fact that it was also a moral revival. Methodism brought religion to the aid of morality, giving religious sanction to such prosaic virtues as work, responsibility, charity, and fraternity. This ethic soon permeated all denominations and classes, the working classes being drawn to the Methodists (who left the Church of England after the death of John Wesley), while the middle and upper classes remained, as Evangelicals, within the established church.

Methodism was, from the beginning, a social as well as an individual ethic. "Christianity," Wesley announced, "is essentially a social religion. To turn it into a solitary religion is indeed to destroy it."[10] In accord with that dictum, he established, among other things, a poorhouse, a soup-kitchen, a dispensary for the poor, and a fund for the unemployed. So, too, the Evangelical campaign for a "moral reformation" was more than a prescription of individual behavior (for the rich as well as the poor). It was also a call for a social reformation. In that spirit, William Wilberforce, an ardent Evangelical and energetic member of Parliament, led the antislavery movement that culminated in 1833, a month after his death, in the passage of the act abolishing slavery in the British empire. That same year, thanks to the efforts of another Evangelical, Lord Shaftesbury, a factory act was passed limiting child labor. These were followed by other measures—health, sanitation, housing, education—which made this (in the

---

Byron, commenting on the distance England had come from that romantic age, see John Morley, "Byron," *Fortnightly Review,* December 1870, reprinted in Morley, *Nineteenth-Century Essays,* ed. Peter Stansky (Chicago, 1970), pp. 3–31.

A generation of remarkable poets died about the same time: Keats in 1821, Shelley in 1822, Byron in 1824, Blake in 1827, Coleridge in 1834. Only Wordsworth survived to the ripe age of eighty in 1850.

9. Carlyle, "Sir Walter Scott," *London and Westminster Review,* January 1838, in *Critical and Miscellaneous Essays,* VI, 46.

10. Quoted in Robert F. Wearmouth, *Methodism and the Working-Class Movements of England, 1800–1850* (London, 1937), p. 160.

titles of two influential books on this period) an "Age of Reform," an "Age of Improvement."[11]

To Carlyle, these legislative reforms were evidence of the incorrigibly utilitarian character of the age, mechanical attempts to cope with spiritual problems. In fact, they were brought about by the combined efforts of Evangelicals and utilitarians—and Evangelicals perhaps more than utilitarians. The philosophy of the two could not have been more discordant. Where Evangelicalism derived its ethical and social imperatives from religion and morality (a religiously suffused morality), utilitarianism was a purely secular and pragmatic philosophy; the calculus of pleasure and pain that determined the individual's self-interest was presumed also to determine the public interest, "the greatest happiness of the greatest number." Yet this odd couple, Evangelicalism and utilitarianism, so far from operating at cross purposes, managed to cooperate in pursuit of the same social ends.

For Halévy, it was this social ethic, in conjunction with its unique political institutions, that contributed to "the miracle of modern England," the fact that England survived the whole of the nineteenth century without succumbing to the revolutions that erupted on the Continent. The sources of that ethic, to be sure, became muted and diluted in the course of time. The historian Thomas Macaulay, son of the prominent Evangelical Zachary Macaulay, was conspicuously lacking in the religious fervor of his father, but he retained enough of his spirit to criticize utilitarianism for thinking that a secular ethic could be sustained without the "ought" that only Christianity could provide. So too, John Stuart Mill, having initially rebelled against the utilitarianism of his father, later produced a revised version of the pleasure-pain calculus by incorporating duty into the category of pleasure and the pangs of conscience into that of pain. Eventually, he even came to appreciate the social role of religion in general and of Christianity in particular, extolling Jesus as "a morally perfect Being," "a standard of excellence and a model for imitation," "the pattern of perfection for humanity."[12]

If Mill refused to reprint "The Spirit of the Age" a quarter of a century later, it was not only because the essays were no longer consonant with his own views, but also because they no longer represented the spirit of that later time. The "Victorian age" (the word *Victorian* itself did not come into usage until 1851) was long and varied, a series of "ages," reflecting a host of changes—

11. E. L. Woodward, *The Age of Reform, 1815–1870* (Oxford, 1938); Asa Briggs, *The Age of Improvement, 1783–1867* (London, 1959).

12. John Stuart Mill, "Theism," in *Essays on Ethics, Religion and Society* (in *Collected Works*), ed. J. M. Robson (Toronto, 1969), pp. 486–87.

industrial, economic, political, social, and, not least, intellectual. To accommodate those changes, historians have divided the age in three periods: early, mid-, and late Victorian.

By common consent, early Victorian England predates the reign of Victoria—"Victorianism before Victoria," one historian has dubbed it.[13] Carlyle's "Signs of the Times" and Mill's "Spirit of the Age" clearly warrant the term *Victorian,* although the first antedates the queen's ascension to the throne by eight years, the latter by six. It was in the reign of her predecessor, William IV, that one of the most notable events of the period occurred, the Reform Bill of 1832, which extended the franchise to the middle classes—an act that is often thought to initiate "early Victorian England." For Carlyle the ominous "signs of the times" had appeared even earlier under George IV, with the acts giving greater liberties to Dissenters and emancipating Catholics. (Had he been writing two years later, he might have cited Macaulay's essay proposing the emancipation of Jews.)

Some of the anxieties and forebodings expressed by Carlyle and Mill in those early years persisted after Victoria came to the throne. The sense of a society in transition or, worse, in disarray—not only in a state of "intellectual anarchy," as Mill saw it, but of social anarchy—seemed to be confirmed by the Chartist "uprising" in 1839, the bad harvests and unemployment that gave the following decade the name of the "Hungry Forties," the agitation for home rule in Ireland exacerbated by a depression far more severe than that in England, the unsettling effects of railways (the first started operation in 1830), and all the other anxieties accompanying a rapidly industrialized and urbanized society.

In retrospect, some of these events seem less cataclysmic than they appeared to be at the time. The Chartist movement consisted of sporadic, easily suppressed local riots, concluding in 1848 in a thoroughly peaceful convention and demonstration. Moreover, the Charter itself, a demand for manhood suffrage and other minor parliamentary reforms, was hardly revolutionary, certainly not by comparison with the revolutions on the Continent. Yet it was not only

13. Briggs, *Age of Improvement,* p. 72. For the varied dating of this early period, see, for example, the *Wellesley Index to Victorian Periodicals* (Toronto, 1965–88), which takes as its starting date 1824 when the *Westminster Review,* "a major vehicle of new ideas," was founded (I, xix). The *Norton Anthology of English Literature,* ed. M. H. Abrams (7th ed., 1999), dates the Victorian age from 1830, as do *The Victorians and After, 1830–1914,* ed. Edith Batho and Bonamy Dobree (New York, 1938), and *Early Victorian England, 1830–65,* ed. G. M. Young (Oxford, 1989). The opening item in *The Portable Victorian Reader,* ed. Gordon S. Haight (New York, 1972), is a letter by Macaulay dated June 24, 1831. And 1832 is the starting date of J. F. C. Harrison, *The Early Victorians, 1832–51* (London, 1971).

the hyperbolic Carlyle who saw in Chartism evidence of the "bitter discontent of the Working Classes," a "condition and disposition" that were "ominous"; his pamphlet "Chartism," published in 1839, had as its epigraph the proverb "It never smokes but there is a fire."[14] Disraeli also gave Chartism a prominent role in his novel *Sybil* in 1845, the heroine's father being an ardent Chartist who complains of the "degradation of the people," people "nearer the condition of brutes than they had been at any time since the Conquest."[15] Neither Carlyle nor Disraeli agreed with the Chartists' political solution to that problem, but they did share a concern with the problem itself—"the condition-of-England question," as Carlyle put it ("England" being a euphemism for "the people," "the working classes," "the poor").

Disraeli later, although not convincingly, claimed credit for that phrase, "the condition-of-England question." But he did unquestionably coin another, "the two nations," which was the subtitle of *Sybil*. Those two nations, the rich and the poor, his protagonist explained, were "as ignorant of each other's habits, thoughts, and feelings, as if they were dwellers in different zones, or inhabitants of different planets; who are formed by different breeding, are fed by different food, are ordered by different manners, and are not governed by the same laws."[16] Other writers picked up the theme and responded to the challenge, Dickens in his novels as well as his journal, *Household Words*, and Henry Mayhew in his articles on "London Labour and the London Poor" in the *Morning Chronicle*. In different ways, they helped bridge the gap between the nations by bringing the poor into the consciousness—a sympathetic consciousness—of the reading public. The Victorians, acutely aware of the significant differences within the working classes, always pluralized that term; it was "working classes," never "working class."[17] Dickens and Mayhew went further, humanizing and individualizing them, portraying them in all their variety and peculiarity—not as a social problem, still less as a political threat, but as human beings pursuing their trades (often rather odd ones), living out their lives (often precariously), and coping with private and familial problems not al-

14. Carlyle, "Chartism," in *English and Other Critical Essays* (London: J. M. Dent, n.d.), p. 165.
15. Benjamin Disraeli, *Sybil, or the Two Nations* ([1845] Penguin ed., London, 1954), p. 170.
16. Ibid., pp. 72–73.
17. Later, in *Culture and Anarchy* (1868), Matthew Arnold singularized "working class" as well as "middle class." But for the most part, until well into the century, the English pluralized both terms. Engels, imposing upon the English his own Marxist perspective, used the singular in *Die Lage der arbeitenden Klasse in England*, published in Germany in 1845; the English translation (in America in 1887 and in England five years later) appeared under the title *The Condition of the Working Class in England in 1844*.

together unlike those of their social superiors. The nations remained as far apart as ever—further apart, in many respects—but the consciousness of the other nation, the "recognition of the other," as Hegel would say, was a new and defining feature of early Victorian England.

If the Reform Bill of 1832 marked the beginning of early Victorian England, the Great Exhibition of 1851, housed in the spectacular Crystal Palace in Hyde Park, may be said to have inaugurated mid-Victorian England.[18] With the Chartist Convention only three years earlier a bare memory, and the "Hungry Forties" dissipated by an economic boom, people flocked to this dramatic glass and iron structure and its equally impressive displays. Six million people in the course of its six-month existence paid the admission fee of a shilling or five shillings on weekends. It also spawned a voluminous literature, starting with Tennyson's paean published in the *Times* on opening day—"A palace as for fairy Prince,/A rare pavilion, such as man/Saw never since mankind began"—to the "Exhibition Hymn" by the popular versifier Martin Tupper, which was translated into thirty languages and put to music by Sebastian Wesley (the grandson of Charles Wesley, one of the founders of Methodism).[19] At home and abroad, the Exhibition appeared as a triumphal demonstration of England's industrial ingenuity and superiority. And it testified to something else as well: a political and social stability that was seen as the precondition of economic progress. While the Continent was still suffering the aftermaths of the political revolutions of 1848, England congratulated itself on having achieved an industrial revolution surpassing that of any other country, without anything resembling a political revolution—indeed, having emerged to enjoy an agreeable sense of well-being, an "Age of Equipoise," as one historian put it.[20]

The sense of equipoise, of balance and equanimity, informs one of the most

18. The dating of this middle period is as various as that of the early one. W. L. Burn defines it as 1852–67 (*The Age of Equipoise: A Study of the Mid-Victorian Generation* [London, 1964]); the *Norton Anthology*, 1848–70; Asa Briggs, 1851 to the mid- or late 1870s (introduction to *Victorian England*, ed. G. M. Young [London, 1999], p. xv); Geoffrey Best, 1851–1875 (*Mid-Victorian Britain* [New York, 1972]); K. Theodore Hoppen, 1846–86 (*The Mid-Victorian Generation* [Oxford, 1998]). The confusion about the end-date of the middle period is compounded by the opening date of a book on the following period; J. F. C. Harrison, *Late Victorian Britain* (London, 1990) opens on the cover with 1875 and on the title page with 1870.

19. Asa Briggs, *Iron Bridge to Crystal Palace: Impact and Images of the Industrial Revolution* (London, 1979), p. 165.

20. Burn, *The Age of Equipoise.* Burn's account is more nuanced and complicated than the title suggests; indeed, at times it almost seems ironic. For a discussion of this influential book, see Martin Hewitt, ed., *An Age of Equipoise?* (Aldershot, Eng., 2000).

thoughtful books of the time, Walter Bagehot's *The English Constitution*. It is interesting that it should have been an economist (the founder of the journal the *Economist*), who wrote that political treatise. Published serially from 1865 and as a book in 1867, it is an astute account of a polity in which history, law, precedent, and convention, with all their contradictions and anomalies, came together to provide the basis for an orderly society and a progressive economy. In an earlier series of articles, Bagehot had set the tone for that book by making a virtue out of what intellectuals regarded as a vice. "Dullness is our line," he said, "as cleverness is that of the French."[21] There was no better reminder of England's stability than the comparison with France's volatility.

Yet mid-Victorian England was neither as dull as Bagehot suggested nor as tranquil as the "age of equipoise" implies. It had its times of troubles: the Crimean War and bank crisis in the 1850s, the Fenian conspiracy and occasional strikes and riots in the following decade. But these were less momentous than they have sometimes been made out to be. The Hyde Park "riot," for example, provoked by the rejection by the House of Lords of a Liberal reform bill, resulted in little more than broken railings and trampled flower beds. Yet according to one eminent historian: "It is scarcely too much to say that the fall of the park railings did for England in July 1866 what the fall of the Bastille did for France in July 1789."[22] What that riot did, in fact, was to prepare the way for the peaceful passage of another reform bill the following year, this by the Conservatives.

The truly momentous events in this period were not crises or riots but books and ideas. The year 1859 saw the publication of two seminal works of modern times, Darwin's *Origin of the Species* and Mill's *On Liberty*. Both were intellectual triumphs, instantly recognized as the classics they have remained. And both were the subject of serious debate, raising the most compelling questions about religion and science, the individual and society, above all, the very nature of man. What is truly remarkable is that these controversies were assimilated into the culture with relative ease. Darwinism did not cause nearly as much spiritual turmoil as some clerics predicted; indeed, some quickly came to terms with it, assigning evolution and revelation to separate realms where they might complement rather than conflict with each other. Nor did Mill's liberalism prove to be quite the threat to traditional values that some conservatives feared; although the doctrine itself had radical implications, suggesting something like an absolute concept of liberty, it was generally inter-

21. See below, p. 149.
22. J. Dover Wilson, introduction to Matthew Arnold, *Culture and Anarchy* (Cambridge, 1957), p. xxvi.

preted more moderately, as an accommodation to principles and practices that were already widely accepted.

For late Victorian England there is no obvious label or starting point.[23] The Reform Act of 1867, which enfranchised most of the working classes, might qualify, except that some version of this reform had been anticipated; the only surprise was the extent and the sponsor of the franchise (the Conservatives rather than the Liberals). Or the Education Act of 1870, which expanded elementary education for a populace that had recently been admitted into the political order. Or the agricultural depression of 1873, which spilled over into the economy as a whole, lingering for much of the century and acquiring the dubious distinction of being known as the "Great Depression." Or the *fin-de-siècle* spirit that began to appear in the 1880s, which heralded the end of the Victorian age.

Although not easily characterized or dated, the period was unquestionably distinctive; no one would have confused it with an age of equipoise. Yet some issues raised in the earlier period persisted, in more exacerbated forms. By overzealous evolutionists like Herbert Spencer, Darwin's theory was extended from biology to society and morality, prompting T. H. Huxley, Darwin's most ardent disciple, to protest that so far from being a guide to ethics, the evolutionary process was the very antithesis of the ethical process. So, too, Mill's theory of liberty, designed to promote individuality, variety, and "experiments in living," was taken by *fin-de-siècle* bohemians to endorse experiments in "decadence," as they proudly called it, which Mill would surely have deplored.

What Mill did approve of was the burgeoning feminist movement led by Millicent Fawcett, inspired by the amendment Mill had introduced (in his brief period in Parliament) to the Reform Bill of 1867, substituting the word *person* for *man,* thus giving women the suffrage on the same basis as men. It was this principle, that women—as individuals, not as a collectivity— should enjoy the same rights and liberties as men, that governed Fawcett's position not only on the suffrage but on other issues as well. Thus she opposed factory laws restricting the hours and kinds of work for women, because they singled out women as a group, limiting their freedom as individuals (and limiting the freedom of trade in general); and she supported a bill abolishing penalties for

23. See note 18. The closing dates of the books on the mid-Victorian period correspond to the opening dates of the late Victorian period. And the termination of the late period generally coincides with the queen's death in January 1901. But even here there are some exceptions. Jonathan Rose, *The Edwardian Temperament* (Athens, Ohio, 1986), has as its subtitle *1895–1919,* suggesting that late Victorian England concluded half a dozen years before Victoria's death.

the breach of promise of marriage, on the grounds that the breach-of-promise law, so far from protecting women and strengthening marriage, was demeaning to both. Her mode of feminism, like Mill's, was well within the framework of Victorian liberalism and Victorian values.[24]

Other distinguished women kept well apart from the women's suffrage movement. George Eliot, for example, who played a prominent part in the founding of Girton College at Cambridge (Fawcett later helped found Newnham College) and whose unconventional relationship with George Lewes seemed to make her a natural ally of the feminists, surprised them by refusing to support Mill's amendment. Precisely because a woman had "the worse share in existence," she explained, there was all the more reason for a "sublimer resignation" on her part and a "more regenerating tenderness" on the man's part.[25] Half-a-dozen other novelists, including Mrs. Gaskell, Charlotte Brontë, and Elizabeth Barrett Browning, also declined to sign a petition for the suffrage. When Mill personally asked Florence Nightingale to join a committee for the suffrage, she refused, saying that other reforms, such as giving women control over their own property, were more important and would be jeopardized if they became the subject of political partisanship. She herself, she assured him, never felt the need for the vote. (She did later join the committee, but only reluctantly, and she never played an active part it it.)

Mrs. Humphrey Ward, whose enormously successful novel *Robert Elsmere* challenging religious orthodoxy had just been published, wrote "An Appeal against Female Suffrage," which appeared in the *Nineteenth Century* in June 1889. That manifesto was signed by more than a hundred well-known women, including, most remarkably, the socialist Beatrice Potter (later Mrs. Sidney Webb). While she did not want, Potter explained in her diary, to preserve "the old regimen of economic and personal dependence," neither did she want to endanger the special virtues of women as mothers and wives. That diary entry might have been written by the most proper Victorian lady: "Surely it is enough to have half the human race straining every nerve to outrun their fellows in the race for subsistence or power. Surely we need some human beings who will watch and pray, who will observe and inspire, and, above all, who will guard and love all who are weak, unfit or distressed. Is there not a special service of woman, as there is a special service of man?"[26]

24. She was an able assistant to her blind husband, Henry Fawcett, the professor of political economy at Cambridge and a Liberal member of Parliament, who was an orthodox proponent of laissez-faire. She herself wrote articles and books on economics.
25. *The George Eliot Letters,* ed. Gordon S. Haight (New Haven, 1975), IV, 364 (May 14, 1867).
26. *The Diary of Beatrice Webb,* ed. Norman Mackenzie and Jeanne Mackenzie (Cambridge, Mass., 1983), II, 53–54 (July 25, 1894).

Beatrice Potter was not the only socialist to remain incorrigibly Victorian. Other English socialists appeared to have more in common with their non-socialist compatriots than with socialists on the Continent. "We are all socialists now," proclaimed Sir William Harcourt, a Liberal member of Parliament, in 1888, a sentiment echoed (perhaps cynically) in 1895 by the Prince of Wales.[27] Although Karl Marx lived and died in London, he had few English associates or disciples. The two Marxist sects, the Social Democratic Federation and the Socialist League, were small and ineffectual. Among the other varieties of socialists were reformist Fabians like the Webbs, Christian socialists like Charles Kingsley, aesthetic socialists like Morris and Ruskin, even Tory socialists modeling themselves on Disraeli. As often as not, the label "socialist" was used loosely to connote any social reform, any measure of state intervention, any degree of "collectivism" (a word that came into currency in the 1880s), any concern with "the social problem" or, as Carlyle had earlier put it, "the condition-of-England question."

The Reverend Samuel Barnett, the founder of Toynbee Hall in 1884, defined "practicable socialism" as including the poor law, the education act, the Irish land acts, the housing act, and the libraries act. Sidney Webb cited these and other reforms as evidence of the "unconscious socialism" that had already, he was confident, set England on the path to a full-fledged socialism.[28] Webb proved to be wrong about that; England—Victorian England, at any rate—managed to be reformist without being socialist. But his remarks do point to a curiosity of the Victorian age: even in the earlier periods, now regarded as the heyday of laissez-faire, that doctrine was more often honored in the breach than the observance. More curious still was the number of eminent Victorians, not socialists, starting with Carlyle and going on to Dickens, Disraeli, Arnold, and numerous others, who did not honor that doctrine at all, indeed, who vigorously denied and disputed it.

It is also interesting that two of the wittiest and seemingly most irreverent of the late Victorian writers should have been socialists, although of different varieties. George Bernard Shaw joined the Fabian Society in 1884 soon after it was founded (even before Webb had), played an active part in the society, and was a contributor to its most important publication, *Fabian Essays,* in 1889. Two years later, Oscar Wilde, in his essay "The Soul of Man under Socialism," refuted that mode of socialism by proposing one of quite a different order, less collectivist, less economic-oriented, one designed, he said, to liberate not merely the body but the soul of man.

27. Gertrude Himmelfarb, *Poverty and Compassion: The Moral Imagination of the Late Victorians* (New York, 1991), p. 309.
28. Ibid., pp. 309ff.

The true radicalism of this late Victorian period—a moral rather than political radicalism—is associated with those self-styled "decadents" Aubrey Beardsley and Max Beerbohm, and with the magazine the *Yellow Book,* which took its name from the French yellow paperback novels that were thought to be especially salacious. The first issue, in April 1894, included contributions by such eminently respectable figures as the novelist Henry James, the president of the Royal Academy, and an Eton schoolmaster. The only parts of the journal that were at all provocative were a poem alluding to an encounter with a prostitute, a facetious piece by Beerbohm on cosmetics that professed to find artifice superior to nature, and the cover by Beardsley of an aged prostitute initiating a young one into the trade. For all its notoriety, however, the journal lasted only three years, and its successor, the *Savoy,* was even more short-lived, folding within one year.

Oscar Wilde is often identified with the *Yellow Book* although he never wrote for it, having had a falling out with Beardsley earlier.[29] Before he was overwhelmed by the scandal of his trial and imprisonment, Wilde's plays, while irreverent and satirical, were by no means immoral, let alone decadent. In a sense, they validated Victorian values even as they seemed to mock them. The title of his best-known play, "The Importance of Being Earnest," is ironic and yet affirmative. After a series of intricate and convoluted deceptions center-ing on the name Earnest, the plot resolves itself with the two couples appro-priately paired under their proper names (one of which is indeed Ernest), pre-paring to live happily together in wedded bliss—an appropriate Victorian denouement to a classical comedy of errors. At one point, a young woman rebukes the young man who has been engaging in the subterfuge: "I hope you have not been leading a double life, pretending to be wicked and being really good all the time. That would be hypocrisy."[30] "Being really good"—that is surely a peculiarly Victorian version of hypocrisy.

What was truly ironic was not the play itself but Wilde's personal situation at the time. On February 18, 1895, four days after the very successful opening of the play, the Marquess of Queensberry (the father of Lord Alfred Douglas, with whom Wilde was having an affair) issued the insult that led to Wilde's trial, conviction, and imprisonment. Five years later, on his deathbed, Wilde re-ceived the last rites of the Catholic Church—as a penitent, not a convert (he was a Catholic by birth). Two years before that, and only a year after the closing

29. When Wilde was arrested in 1895, he was reported to be carrying a copy of the *Yellow Book.* The publishers, fearful of a scandal, made a scapegoat of Beardsley and dismissed him from the journal. In fact, Wilde was carrying a yellow paperback French novel.
30. Oscar Wilde, *The Importance of Being Earnest and Related Writings,* ed. Joseph Bristow (London, 1992), p. 52.

of the *Yellow Book,* Beardsley, a convert, had done the same on his deathbed—a curious finale to this episode of "decadence."[31]

Before Wilde had dramatized "The Importance of Being Earnest," George Bernard Shaw had played with the same theme in his novel *An Unsocial Socialist,* which appeared serially in 1884 in the socialist journal *To-Day.* Shaw's heroine playfully proposes marriage to the hero, which the latter promptly accepts, leading to the following exchange: "You do not suppose I was in earnest, do you?" "Undoubtedly I do. *I* am in earnest." "Take care," she warns him, "I may change my mind and be in earnest, too; and then how will you feel, Mr. Trefusis?"[32] In the end, after further complications of mind and heart, they are, in all earnestness, engaged to marry. A similar plot unfolds in Shaw's play "John Bull's Other Island," with the hero protesting when the young woman doesn't take his professions of love seriously. "Stop laughing," he says, "I am in earnest—in English earnest. When I say a thing like that to a woman, I mean it."[33]

"In English earnest"—if there is one word that is common to the whole of the Victorian age, it is earnestness—the religious earnestness of the early period transmuted into a moral and intellectual earnestness. In a critical yet surprisingly sympathetic, even generous essay on Voltaire written in 1829, a few months before "Signs of the Times," Carlyle noted the "one deficiency" in Voltaire's character: "his inborn levity of nature, his entire want of Earnestness."[34] For Carlyle's generation, the want of Earnestness (capitalized) was the French vice. A later generation—Shaw and Wilde, most notably—made a virtue of vice by enlisting levity in the service of earnestness, thus preserving the spirit as well as the sobriety of the Victorian ethic.

This Victorian ethic, however, is not that commonly associated with the word *Victorian.* Today that word more often conjures up ideas of prudery, propriety, and hypocrisy—not the hypocrisy of being good while pretending to be bad, but being bad while pretending to be good. We are reminded of Gladstone, the Grand Old Liberal, also known as the Grand Old Moralist, who recorded in his diary his lapses into pornographic fantasies, for which he punished himself (or indulged himself) by flagellation—*le vice anglais,* the

31. Or not so curious. A surprising number of the *fin-de-siècle* aesthetes and "decadents" found refuge in Catholicism. After Wilde took up with Douglas, Wilde's earlier lover, the poet John Gray (the model for *Dorian Gray*), not only converted to Catholicism but took orders and became a priest. Douglas himself took the last rites upon his deathbed in 1945.
32. George Bernard Shaw, *An Unsocial Socialist* ([1884] London, 1991), p. 222.
33. Shaw, *John Bull's Other Island* ([1907] New York, 1913), p. 50.
34. Carlyle, "Voltaire," *Foreign Review,* April 1829, in *Critical and Miscellaneous Essays,* II, p. 133.

French dubbed it. Or we have images of piano legs modestly sheathed in pantaloons—a practice more common, in fact, in America than in England. Or we recall the Bowdlerized editions of Shakespeare and other works produced for the moral edification of the masses. "Much nonsense about 'the Victorians,'" G. M. Young wryly commented, "is dissipated by the reflection that it was the French Government that prosecuted *Madame Bovary.*"[35]

Much nonsense about the Victorians may also be dissipated by an examination of the periodical literature, which reveals a vigor and variety of opinion, a spirited questioning of received wisdom, a contentiousness and provocativeness that belie the stereotypical images of conformity and complacency. Apart from some taboo sexual words, the Victorians were remarkably forthright. Carlyle and Mill, longtime friends, did not hesitate to air their differences in public, and they did so with a notable lack of reserve. Carlyle's essay "Occasional Discourse on the Negro Question," published in *Fraser's Magazine* in December 1849, was followed by a vigorous rebuttal by Mill in the next issue, which in turn provoked Carlyle to expand upon his essay and issue it as a pamphlet with the deliberately provocative title "Occasional Discourse on the Nigger Question." (In England even then the word was regarded as offensive.) Nor did Matthew Arnold mince words when he entitled his essay in *Cornhill Magazine* (later a chapter in *Culture and Anarchy*) "Barbarians, Philistines, Populace"—hardly endearing terms for the aristocracy, the middle class, and the working class. Nor was Charles Kingsley reticent when he launched his attack on Newman in *Macmillan's Magazine* in January 1864 (taking the occasion of a review on quite another subject): "Truth for its own sake had never been a virtue with the Roman clergy. Father Newman informs us that it need not be, and on the whole ought not to be."[36] Those words were widely quoted in the press and were the occasion for the weekly pamphlets by Newman that made up the *Apologia Pro Vita Sua.*

Nor were the Victorians more discreet about the personal lives of their eminences. "How delicate, decent is English Biography, bless its mealy mouth." So Carlyle wrote in 1838 reviewing the biography of Sir Walter Scott by John Lockhart, who had been criticized for recounting some unsavory details about the novelist's life. Defending Lockhart, Carlyle sarcastically derided those who complained that he had been too "communicative," "indiscreet," failing to observe the "sanctities of private life."[37] It is ironic that Carlyle's own biographer, James Anthony Froude, should later have quoted this passage in the

---

35. G. M. Young, *Portrait of an Age* ([1936] New York, 1954), p. 43n.
36. Quoted in Wilfrid Ward, *The Life of John Henry Cardinal Newman* (London, 1912), II, 1.
37. Carlyle, "Sir Walter Scott," in *Critical and Miscellaneous Essays,* VI, 27.

preface to his own work to disarm the criticism he anticipated for revealing some unflattering aspects of Carlyle's marital life. The Victorian biographers, it is evident, at least the best of them, were not nearly as mealy-mouthed as Carlyle thought.

Nor did the political leaders conform to the image of the proper politician or statesman. It is remarkable that Disraeli should have reached the eminence he did—a Jew by birth (and conspicuously by name), a dandy by temperament, and a novelist by avocation. (He wrote the last of his dozen novels at the age of seventy-six, after completing his second administration.) Or Gladstone—a scholar and theologian manqué, the author of a three-volume work on Homer and other books and countless essays on religion, classical literature, and history. (His correspondence on church and religion alone occupies two good-sized volumes.) Nor were the novelists and journalists, even at their most inventive and satirical, without their earnest side. Dickens's bizarre characters bore an uncanny resemblance to the real people portrayed by Mayhew. Thackeray's parodies of the varieties of snobs came uncomfortably close to portraits of real persons. And *Punch's* irreverence, directed as much against lords and ladies as valets and servants, was as effective a form of social commentary as the more sober pronouncements of an *Edinburgh* reviewer.

Above all what the Victorians were earnest about was morality. Visiting England in the 1860s and early 1870s, the French philosopher and man of letters Hippolyte Taine contrasted the "English Mind" with the French, much to the credit of the French. Whereas a Frenchman enjoyed ideas for their own sake, an Englishman was interested in them only for their utility.

> The inside of an Englishman's head can be very fairly compared to a Murray's Guide: a great many facts, but few ideas; a great deal of exact and useful information, statistics, figures, reliable and detailed maps, short and dry historical notes, useful and moral tips by way of preface, no all-inclusive vision, and no relish of good writing. . . . The average English writer, although very well informed, has limited vision. Nothing is more rare than to find, among these people, a free and wide ranging play of intelligence in a soaring, far-seeing mind. . . . Excepting two or three, there are hardly any English writers who make their readers think.[38]

Several pages later, however, Taine modified this damning portrait: "When we praise [!] this taste for facts in the English we should remember that it is a question of moral as well as physical facts: they are zealous observers of the inner as well as the outwardly manifest life." Toward the end of the essay, after

---

38. Hippolyte Taine, *Notes on England* (London, 1957), pp. 242, 248–49. (The book was published in serial parts in France in 1860–70. This essay probably dates from 1870.)

quoting a poem by Elizabeth Barrett Browning, Taine arrived at a quite different estimate of the English. "The more I dwell upon this conformation of the English mind, this habit of turning in upon the self, this primacy of the moral being, this need to perceive that moral self first of all, and thereafter to see all nature through him, the nearer do I come to understanding the strong and manifold roots of that poem, their religion." This, in turn, reminded him of the advice Thomas Arnold gave to a person tortured by doubts: "Begin by looking at every thing from the moral point of view, and you will end by believing in God."[39]

Thomas Arnold's "God" was a surrogate for morality. For many other Victorians morality was a surrogate for God. When Darwin was asked what he himself believed in, he replied that the idea of God was "beyond the scope of man's intellect," but that man's obligation remained what it had always been: to "do his duty."[40] Leslie Stephen, after abandoning the effort to derive an ethic from Darwinism, confessed: "I now believe in nothing, but I do not the less believe in morality. . . . I mean to live and die like a gentleman if possible."[41] George Eliot, when asked how morality could subsist in the absence of religious faith (a proper question to put to the translator of Spinoza, Feuerbach, and David Strauss), is reported to have said that God was "inconceivable," immortality "unbelievable," but duty none the less "peremptory and absolute."[42] It was of the "little moralistic females à la Eliot" that Nietzsche wrote, in 1888:

> They are rid of the Christian God and now believe all the more firmly that they must cling to Christian morality. . . . In England one must rehabilitate oneself after every little emancipation from theology by showing in a veritably awe-inspiring manner what a moral fanatic one is. That is the penance they pay there. We others hold otherwise. When one gives up the Christian faith, one pulls the right to Christian morality out from under one's feet.

For Nietzsche, the effort to retain morality without Christianity proved that the English, even the nonbelieving English, had not liberated themselves from Christianity; on the contrary, they were still subject to the "dominion" of Christianity—and thus of Christian ethics. "For the English," he concluded, "morality is not yet a problem."[43]

39. Ibid., pp. 252, 271, 276.
40. Charles Darwin, *Life and Letters,* ed. Francis Darwin (London, 1887), I, 307 (April 2, 1873).
41. F. W. Maitland, *Life and Letters of Leslie Stephen* (London, 1906), pp. 144–45.
42. Basil Willey, *Nineteenth Century Studies* (London, 1949), p. 204.
43. Nietzsche, *Twilight of the Idols* in *The Portable Nietzsche,* ed. Walter Kaufmann (Penguin ed., London, 1976), pp. 515–16.

Nietzsche was quite right. Morality was not a problem for the Victorians—not even for those *fin-de-siècle* Victorians who were still Victorian in spirit (and, thus, in Nietzsche's sense, still Christian), whatever their professions of belief or unbelief. The Victorian "spirit of the age" somehow transcended the disputes over religion, as it also transcended the disputes over science (Darwinism, most notably), politics (liberalism and conservatism), and the other ideological challenges confronting it (socialism, feminism, aestheticism, even decadence). This, too, was the "miracle of modern England," a spirit capacious enough to accept the new and resilient enough to do so without abandoning the old.

II The Essay as Genre

The Victorians did not invent the essay form, but they did master and perfect it. Introducing a volume of essays spanning several centuries, John Gross paid tribute to the Victorians: "An anthology that was limited to a single decade of the Victorian age, perhaps even a single year, would still be able to draw on work of outstanding scope and quality."[44] In 1881, Leslie Stephen, himself a prolific essayist, recalled the essays published in the renowned *Spectator* in the early eighteenth century. They were written, he wrote, "by gentlemen for ladies—that is, for persons disposed to sit at gentlemen's feet, . . . who have hitherto been limited to an intellectual diet of decent devotional works or of plays and romances"; the journal lay "on the table by the side of the morning dish of chocolate." The essays of his own time, he was pleased to report, were very different in nature and meant for a very different audience. "They are serious discussions of important questions, where a man puts a whole system of philosophy into a dozen pages." "The present day," he exulted, "is not merely favourable to essay-writing but a very paradise for essayists."[45]

That paradise had its origin early in the century with the founding of three great quarterlies, each with a distinctive political coloration: the Whig *Edinburgh Review* in 1802, the Tory *Quarterly Review* in 1809, and the radical (in the Benthamite sense) *Westminster Review* in 1824. The *Edinburgh Review* was the model for the others, although its early years were not altogether promising, largely because of the all too many contributions by the editor, Francis Jeffrey (notorious for the opening words of his review of Wordsworth's "The Excursion": "This will never do").[46] Yet it attracted attention from the beginning and many of its early articles are still memorable. The inaugural issue contained the

---

44. *The Oxford Book of Essays,* ed. John Gross (Oxford, 1992), p. xxi.
45. Leslie Stephen, "The Essayists" (*Cornhill Magazine*, 1881), in Stephen, *Men, Books, and Mountains,* ed. S. O. A. Ullman (London, 1956), pp. 58, 65.
46. Another essay by Stephen is sharply critical of the early *Edinburgh Review:* "The First Edinburgh Reviewers" (1878), in Stephen, *Hours in a Library* (London, 1892), II, pp. 241–69.

first essay in England calling for the abolition of the slave trade, and later issues, supporting Catholic emancipation, the French Enlightenment, and other progressive causes, were sufficiently provocative to inspire the Tories to found a rival in the *Quarterly Review.* Even under Jeffrey's editorship, it managed to attract some of the most interesting writers of the time: Thomas Malthus, Walter Scott, James Mill, William Hazlitt, Thomas Arnold, Thomas Carlyle, and, most notably, T. B. Macaulay (who contributed eight articles between 1825 and 1829). And it drew readers from all over the country; although edited and published in Edinburgh, more than half its copies were sold in London.

The essays in each *Review* were just that: reviews of a book or several books, or of a lecture, an essay, a pamphlet, a journal, or even the text of a bill in Parliament. There had been book-review journals before that, but they were little more than booksellers' organs, brief notices of new publications. The new quarterlies contained long reflective, critical essays, often using the book as the pretext for an excursion into the subject at large. If the essay was the special forte of Victorian England, the review was the distinctive form of the essay, especially in the first half of the century.

Carlyle, who was himself a frequent contributor to the *Edinburgh* and other quarterlies, found the review format too constricting for his purposes. His "Signs of the Times," in the June 1829 issue of the *Edinburgh* (the last edited by Jeffrey), was a rare instance in that journal of an essay that was not a review. Two years later, in another essay in the same journal—this time a genuine review—Carlyle criticized the genre itself: "Far be it from us to disparage our own craft, whereby we have our living! Only we must note these things: that Reviewing spreads with strange vigour; that such a man as Byron reckons the Reviewer and the Poet equal; that at the last Leipzig Fair, there was advertised a Review of Reviews. By and by it will be found that all Literature has become one boundless self-devouring Review."[47]

Almost a quarter of a century later, Walter Bagehot, writing about the early *Edinburgh Review,* focused upon the same peculiar phenomenon: "the review-like-essay and the essay-like-review." "Review writing," he found, "is one of the features of modern literature. Many able men really give themselves up to it." He, too, thought it a sign of the times, but for different reasons from Carlyle's. Where Carlyle saw it as further evidence of the diseased self-consciousness that

47. Thomas Carlyle, "Characteristics" (*Edinburgh Review,* April 1831), in Carlyle, *Critical and Miscellaneous Essays,* IV, p. 22. I am indebted to John Gross for pointing me to this essay in his splendid book, *The Rise and Fall of the Man of Letters* (New York, 1969), p. 1. Carlyle's comments are echoed today by critics of postmodernism, who complain that literary theory has replaced literature itself as the subject of study, that the critic (that is, the reviewer) has usurped the authority of the poet, and that his "reading" of the poem is given more weight than the poem itself.

afflicted all aspects of modern life, Bagehot looked upon it as a natural and inevitable "transition from ancient writing to modern." Instead of studying and annotating the ancient masters, he said, modern reviewers read and discussed modern writers. And they did so casually, cursorily, reflecting the spirit of modern literature itself, as well as the democratic spirit of the times.

> On politics, on religion, on all less important topics still more, every one thinks himself competent to think,—in some casual manner does think,—to the best of our means must be taught to think rightly. . . . We must speak to the many so that they will listen,— that they will like to listen,—that they will understand. . . . The modern man must be told what to think,—shortly, no doubt,—but he *must* be told it. The essay-like criticism of modern times is about the length which he likes. The *Edinburgh Review,* which began the system, may be said to be, in this country, the commencement on large topics of suitable views for sensible persons.[48]

In describing this new mode of literature, Bagehot introduced the image that later historians have adopted. The essay was the perfect vehicle for the "railway age"—a slight, ephemeral, sensible bit of literature for impatient, transient, sensible people. "Everything about it is temporary and fragmentary. Look at a railway stall; you see books of every colour . . . , on every subject, in every style . . . —but all small. People take their literature in morsels, as they take sandwiches on a journey."[49]

In fact, of course, the essay-review long predated the railway age. The *Edinburgh,* the archetype of the quarterly review, was founded in 1802 and the two others followed, well before the first railway line started operation in 1830. But the image is deceptive for another reason. "Morsels" to be consumed like sandwiches on the train? Bagehot's own essay, which appeared in the first issue of the *National Review* in 1855 (a journal coedited by Bagehot himself), was thirty pages long, and many essays in the early as well as later issues of the *Edinburgh,* as in the other quarterlies, were longer and weightier. Carlyle's essay in the *Edinburgh* criticizing the review format ran to thirty-eight pages, and his others were considerably longer: sixty-five pages for Boswell's *Life of Johnson* in *Fraser's Magazine* in 1832, sixty for Lockhart's biography of Scott in the *London and Westminster Review* in 1838. Many years later, Leslie Stephen, decrying the trivial essays in the eighteenth-century *Spectator,* described that of his own

48. Walter Bagehot, "The First Edinburgh Reviewers" (*National Review,* October 1855), in Bagehot, *Collected Works,* ed. Norman St John-Stevas (Cambridge, Mass., 1965), I, pp. 309–13. (Bagehot, like Stephen later, was critical of Jeffrey, as well as of Sydney Smith, another major contributor to the early issues.)
49. Ibid., p. 310.

time, "where a man puts a whole system of philosophy into a dozen pages." A
dozen pages? The essay in which he made that point ran to almost thirty pages,
and most of those reprinted in his collections of essays were longer.[50] These
were hardly the casual, fragmentary reading matter conjured up by the "railway
age" image.

One of the most memorable essays in the *Edinburgh* was Macaulay's review
in 1837 of a sixteen-volume edition of Bacon's works. That "review" occupied
105 pages in the journal (somewhat more than that in editions of his works).
Even for Macaulay, the length took some explaining. His first essay for the
Edinburgh Review (on Milton, written at the age of twenty-five) was forty-five
pages long; three years later, his review of a book on the constitutional history
of England ran to seventy-five pages. His present subject, he told the editor,
was so vast that he could have made it twice as long. Macvey Napier consulted
his predecessor and was reassured. "What mortal," Jeffrey replied, "could ever
dream of cutting out the least particle of this precious work, to make it fit better
into your *Review*? It would be worse than paring down the Pitt diamond to fit
the old setting of a dowager's ring." Perhaps, Jeffrey suggested (mixing his
metaphors), that "rich repast" might be served in two courses in successive
issues.[51] In fact, Napier chose to publish it in its entirety in a single issue.

Macaulay's essay on Bacon is remembered today because it was as derisive of
him as a person and politician—cold-hearted and mean-spirited, corrupt and
venal—as it was extravagant in praise of his philosophy—practical, progressive,
and beneficial, unlike that of the ancient philosophers who did nothing to
alleviate the conditions of mankind. It was this dismissal of the ancients that
prompted Matthew Arnold to call Macaulay "the great apostle of the Philistines."[52] But the essay is also memorable because it tells us something else
about the spirit of the age: about a journal like the *Edinburgh* that would
commission a review of the collected works of Bacon; about the author of the
review who, if he did not read all of those sixteen volumes, read enough to
write about them at such length (from India, moreover, where, as a member of
the Supreme Council of the East India Company, he was busy reforming the
Indian system of education and legal code); and, not least, about the "general
reader," as Stephen described him (Bagehot's "sensible person"), who was expected to read an essay on that subject, at that length, by an anonymous

50. These are the page-lengths of the essays reprinted in volume form. They closely
approximate the length in the journals.
51. G. Otto Trevelyan, *The Life and Letters of Lord Macaulay* (New York, 1875), I, 398
(Jeffrey to Napier, May 2, 1837).
52. Matthew Arnold, *Lectures and Essays in Criticism,* ed. R. H. Super (Ann Arbor, Mich.,
1962), p. 210.

author. (Anonymity was the convention in most of the periodicals, especially in the earlier periods, although to the more knowing, Macaulay's inimitable style made him immediately identifiable.)[53]

The review essay, on the model initiated by the *Edinburgh,* was the most distinctive form of the essay, particularly in early Victorian England. But there were other essays that were not reviews, published in journals called magazines, which were monthlies or weeklies rather than quarterlies and included fiction as well, often serialized novels that attracted more readers than the essays. They also had the advantage of being much cheaper than the quarterlies. Where the latter cost as much as six shillings, the monthlies—*Fraser's Magazine, Macmillan's Magazine, Cornhill Magazine*—cost two shillings sixpence or less, and the weeklies—*Examiner, Spectator, Athenaeum, Household Words*—sixpence or twopence. The first issue of *Cornhill* in January 1860, containing installments of novels by Trollope and Thackeray as well as essays by G. H. Lewes, Leigh Hunt, and others, sold 120,000 copies at one shilling; circulation dropped to 84,000 in the following two years and to 25,000 in the next decade. The misnamed *Fortnightly Review* (misnamed because it retained the name *Fortnightly* even after it became a monthly and because it was as much a magazine as a review) sold 14,000 copies at two shillings sixpence. The first issue of Dickens's weekly, *Household Words,* priced at twopence, sold 100,000 copies; later issues averaged 40,000. Even the figures for the more costly quarterlies are impressive. In their heyday, the *Edinburgh* and *Quarterly* sold 12,000 to 14,000 copies each (a figure that compares favorably with comparable journals in the United States today, in a population almost twenty times that of England at the time). The readership of all the periodicals was obviously far greater than the circulation figures, each issue being read by several people at home and by many more in the coffee shops that provided periodical fare as well as refreshments.

It is also impressive to recall how many books originated as essays or reviews in journals. That Victorian novels were often published serially, in magazines

---

53. The *Fortnightly Review,* started in 1869, was the first serious journal to sign its reviews. But many others persisted in the practice of anonymity well into the following century. (The *Times Literary Supplement* did not start signing its reviews until 1975!) But within the literary circle, the identity of the authors was often recognized. And anonymity was abandoned, of course, when the essays were republished in volume form, sometimes soon after their appearance in the reviews.

For the authorship of the articles, scholars are greatly indebted to Walter E. Houghton, editor of the five-volume *Wellesley Index to Victorian Periodicals, 1824–1900* (Toronto, 1965–88), and to the Research Society for Victorian Periodicals, which sponsors the *Victorian Periodicals Review.*

or in separately printed parts, is well known. Less well known is the fact that some of the most important nonfiction works were also published serially: Bagehot's *English Constitution* and *Physics and Politics* (in the *Fortnightly*); Arnold's *Culture and Anarchy* and Ruskin's *Unto This Last* (in *Cornhill*); Mill's *Utilitarianism* and Carlyle's *Sartor Resartus* (in *Fraser's*); Newman's *Apologia* (in weekly parts) and Carlyle's *Latter-Day Pamphlets* (in monthly parts); Cobbett's *Rural Rides* (in the *Political Register*).

The importance of the essay as a genre is also evident from the willingness of so many eminent writers to serve as editors or publishers of the journals. For a time, George Eliot edited (her official title was assistant editor) the *Westminster Review;* Mill the *London and Westminster Review;* Trollope *St. Paul's Magazine;* Acton the *Rambler* and *Home and Foreign Review;* Newman the *British Critic* and, briefly, the *Rambler;* Dickens *Bentley's Miscellany, Household Words,* and *All the Year Round;* Thackeray the *Cornhill Magazine,* G. H. Lewes the *Cornhill,* the *Leader* and, briefly, the *Fortnightly Review;* Bagehot the *Inquirer,* the *National Review,* and the *Economist;* John Morley the *Fortnightly;* Disraeli *The Press* (which he owned and sold only when he became prime minister). None of these periodicals was subsidized, as many of their equivalents are today. All were profitable for the owners (or were sold or closed if not) and paid their contributors as well as their editors. In 1860, *Cornhill* paid Trollope £2,000 for one serial and Eliot £10,000 for another.[54]

These journals—"quality journals," we would now say—were part of a larger popular culture that was extraordinarily vital and varied. The sheer quantity of publications is formidable. In the decade of the 1820s, 100 new journals were founded; in the 1860s, 170; in the 1870s, 140. (In the single year of 1859, when *Macmillan's Magazine* was started, 114 other periodicals were founded in London alone.) Many were short-lived, but others survived for long periods, some into the next century. The circulation figures of the more successful ones are equally remarkable: 200,000 copies of the weekly *Penny Magazine,* founded in 1832 by the Society for the Diffusion of Useful Knowledge and discontinued in 1845 when the circulation fell to 40,000; 500,000 copies of the *London Journal,* founded in 1845 and specializing in the more melodramatic kind of fiction ("low" fiction, the Victorians called it); 250,000 copies of the *Family Herald,* another weekly started at about the same time, which featured fiction of a more

54. In 1860, the pound was worth about $11. Thus Trollope received about $22,000 and Eliot $110,000. It has been estimated that a pound, in terms of purchasing power, would be the equivalent of about $100 today, which makes Trollope's £2,000 worth about $200,000 and Eliot's £10,000 about $1,000,000. These are, of course, very rough equivalents. They do indicate, however, that the sums were, by any standard, exceedingly generous. (See George P. Landow and James Skipper, "Wages, the Cost of Living, Contemporary Equivalents to Victorian Money," www.VictorianWeb.org.)

edifying character. In 1858, Wilkie Collins (Dickens's friend, whose novels were published in *All the Year Round*) estimated that the audience for all the week-lies was at least 3 million. And then there were the daily newspapers: in 1829, seven morning and six evening papers in London alone, selling at the consider-able price of fivepence. (The price fell to a penny or half-penny after the repeal of the newspaper tax in 1855.)[55] All these figures must be put in the context of the population. Of the 18 million people in England and Wales in 1851, 11.5 million were over the age of fourteen, one-third or one-fourth of whom were illiterate or barely literate, leaving an adult reading public of about 8 million. (The inclusion of Scotland would raise the literacy quotient.)[56]

In a thoroughly class-conscious society ("class-ridden," it might be said invidiously), contemporaries had no trouble distinguishing between the qual-ity journals and the popular ones. The former were read almost exclusively by the middle classes, who constituted about 20 percent of the population in mid-century and 30 percent by the end of the century. And the authors of the essays, with few exceptions, were of the same class. They were more learned, gifted, and articulate than their readers, but not because they were aristocratic by birth, privileged by wealth, or even specially trained by education. They were not, for the most part and for much of the century, university graduates.[57] This was the great virtue of the Victorian essays at their best. They were serious and learned, even scholarly, without being pedantic or abstruse. They were accessi-ble to a relatively large audience because they were written by nonacademics for nonacademics, in a common language and reflecting common values.

55. A common laborer in London in the mid-1860s earned about 3s.9d a day, an artisan (bricklayer or carpenter) 6s.6d., an engineer 7s.6d. A poor vicar might earn as little as £1 a week. Fivepence a day for a newspaper was thus a considerable sum. (See James Skipper and George P. Landow, "Wages and Cost of Living in the Victorian Era," www.Victorian Web.org.)
56. Among the excellent sources for this subject, in addition to John Gross, *The Rise and Fall of the Man of Letters* (see n. 47 above), are Amy Cruse, *The Victorians and Their Reading* (Boston, 1935); John Clive, *Scotch Reviewers: The Edinburgh Review, 1802–1815* (London, 1957); Walter Graham, *English Literary Periodicals* (New York, 1930); Richard D. Altick, *The English Common Reader: A Social History of the Mass Reading Public, 1800–1900* (Chicago, 1957); R. K. Webb, *The British Working Class Reader, 1790–1848* (London, 1955); T. W. Heyck, *The Transformation of Intellectual Life in Victorian England* (London, 1982).
57. During the first half of the century, the universities commanded little respect. Teaching was perfunctory and the intellectual level of the professors was often sadly deficient. The total student body of all the colleges in Cambridge and Oxford in the 1850s ranged from 2,400 to 3,100; the total number of entering freshmen was about 800. Only later in the century, after the universities had been reformed, did the *Saturday Review* begin to draw many of its authors (although not most of its readers) from Oxford and Cambridge.

The authors were referred to as "men of letters," a term that did not have the belletristic connotation it now has. (Or the sexist implication; the term was understood to be generic, including women.) Today they would be called intellectuals—a noun that came into general usage only in the 1870s (although the adjective had long been familiar). Then, as now, the man of letters *cum* intellectual had an equivocal role in the culture, as a representative and purveyor of the "spirit of the age" and at the same time as a critic of it. In his 1840 lecture "The Hero as Man of Letters," Carlyle identified the man of letters as "the man of intellect," who performed the same function in modern times as the prophet of old but who now all too often exhibited the "spiritual paralysis," the fatal "skepticism" that was the blight of the age.[58] The title of the essay was ironic; Carlyle's hero, the man of letters, was something of an antihero.

A dozen years later Newman was even more derisive of intellectuals and the periodicals that nurtured them.

> An intellectual man, as the world now conceives of him, is one who is full of "views" on all subjects of philosophy, on all matters of the day. It is almost thought a disgrace not to have a view at a moment's notice on any question from the Personal Advent to the cholera or mesmerism. This is owing in great measure to the necessities of periodical literature, now so much in request. Every quarter of a year, every month, every day, there must be a supply, for the gratification of the public, of new and luminous theories on the subjects of religion, foreign politics, home politics, civil economy. . . . The very nature of periodical literature, broken into small wholes, and demanded punctually to an hour, involves this extempore philosophy.[59]

Yet Newman's own life and work belie that critique, for he himself was not only an eminent intellectual ("man of letters" is too bland for his severe cast of mind) but also a frequent contributor to periodicals. One of his earliest writings, on Aristotle's *Poetics,* was published in the *London Review* in 1829, and others followed in the 1830s and 1840s in the *British Magazine* and *British Critic.* His important essay "Prospects of the Anglican Church," a coda to *Tracts for the Times,* appeared in 1839 in the *British Critic,* of which he was then an editor. He continued to write for journals—the *Atlantis,* the *Rambler,* the *Month*—even after his dismissive remarks about them, and he thought well

58. Thomas Carlyle, *Heroes, Hero Worship and the Heroic in History* ([1841] New York: A. L. Burt, n.d.), pp. 200–201. The lectures were delivered in 1840; the book was published the following year.
59. John Henry Newman, *On the Scope and Nature of University Education* ([1852] London, 1955), pp. xxxix–xli.

enough of those essays to reprint them in 1872 in the three volumes of his
Historical Sketches.

From his exalted vantage point, Newman could look down on the periodical literature of his time. Some of it was indeed "railway literature," trivial
essays for busy people. But some of it, indeed, a good deal of it, was not at all
trivial. Bagehot, with his instinct for—and his respect for—the "sensible persons" who read those journals, had a surer grasp of the culture inhabited by
them. "There is as yet no Act of Parliament," he wrote, "compelling a *bona fide*
traveller to read. If you wish him to read, you must make reading pleasant. You
must give him short views, and clear sentences."[60] "Short" and "clear"—to a
reader today that hardly seems to characterize Macaulay's lengthy essays and
his prose with its elaborate antitheses, or Carlyle's often densely allusive, almost
baroque style. Yet both men had a substantial readership, and not only among
the well educated.[61] And not only when the essays first appeared between the
loose covers of the journal, but afterward as well, in the form of volumes.
"From Eton and Harrow down to an elementary school in St. Gile's or Bethnal
Green," John Morley wrote in 1881, "Macaulay's *Essays* are a textbook."[62]

"If you wish him to read . . . "—to the modern reader, Bagehot's comments
sound condescending and derogatory. But this was his deliberately provocative
mode of speech. Just as he praised, not criticized, English politicians for making "dull" speeches on "dull" issues, so he praised "sensible persons" for having
the good common sense not to be clever—that is, too clever by half. The
sensible reading public he had in mind included the middle classes who only a
generation earlier had acquired the suffrage and been admitted to the political
nation, as well as the literate, skilled, and socially mobile working classes who
had demonstrated their will in the Chartist movement and who would, a
generation hence, receive the vote and become fully accredited members of the
nation. The essays may not have been "short" and "clear" by present-day
standards, but they were by comparison with formidable full-length (often
multivolume) books. And the journals in which they appeared were not only
cheaper than books but also more accessible and inviting.

60. Bagehot, "The First Edinburgh Reviewers," p. 311.
61. A man living on the outskirts of Manchester invited his poorer neighbors to his house
every evening after work and read the whole of Macaulay's *History of England* to them.
After the last reading, one of them moved a vote of thanks to the author "for having
written a history that working men can understand"—a motion reported to Macaulay
who was much moved by it. So, too, Carlyle was pleased to receive a letter from a Scottish
weaver thanking him for the enlightenment his *French Revolution* brought him and his
friends. (See G. Otto Trevelyan, *The Life and Letters of Lord Macaulay* [New York, 1875], II,
207; Cruse, *The Victorians and Their Reading,* pp. 127.)
62. Cruse, *The Victorians and Their Reading,* p. 295.

Eventually, many of these essays did appear in book form, either as a series on the same subject (like Bagehot's *English Constitution* or Arnold's *Culture and Anarchy*) or in collections of the author's essays (and almost every author had one or more such collections). But even then, they retained the unique quality of the essay form, much as the great novels of the time retained the dramatic quality that came from their initial part-publication. The essay, even a substantial one, conveyed its ideas with an immediacy and vigor lacking in a book. In that shorter form, arguments were sharpened and controversy was heightened, so that the reader entered more readily into the mind and spirit of an author more knowledgeable and thoughtful than himself.[63]

The historian W. L. Burn described all generalizations about Victorian England (including, presumably, his own "Age of Equipoise") as instances of "selective Victorianism."[64] The essays in the present volume are selective in a somewhat different sense, intended to illustrate "a spirit of the age" that was varied and complex, self-critical more often than self-satisfied, opinionated and controversial, reflecting ideas, beliefs, and dispositions that shaped Victorian England as surely as the political, social, economic, and other events of the time, a spirit that at the end of the century, as at the beginning, was recognizably "Victorian."

Two apologies are in order. First, my use of "England" and "English" in this introduction, rather than "Britain" and "British." This conforms to the contemporary usage, which located even so patently a Scottish journal as the *Edinburgh Review* in the sphere of "Victorian England." In a volume of essays by Victorians about Victorians, it would be anachronistic and intrusive to speak of "Britain" while they habitually spoke of "England."

More dubious is my temerity in doing what a Victorian editor might not have done—cutting some of the essays. Having made such a point of the Victorian tolerance for lengthy essays, I am uncomfortably aware of the irony of my abridging them. I wish I could say, of Mill's almost fifty-page "Spirit of

---

63. It was this quality that may account for the later experiences of two young readers of Macaulay's essays. Lord Rosebery, the distinguished Liberal statesman, recalled coming by chance upon those books in the family library when he was eleven years old. Falling "at once under the wand of the enchanter," he began with the essay on Milton and read on through the three volumes, not understanding everything, he said, but delighting in it all. "To that book I owe all the ambitions and aspirations I have ever indulged in." The Tory statesman Lord Balfour also remembered reading the essays as a boy and being entranced by Macaulay's style and "dialectics." "He supplied much of the mental nourishment I desired in the exact form that best suited my very youthful appetite." Cruse, *The Victorians and Their Reading*, p. 296.
64. W. L. Burn, *The Age of Equipoise: A Study of the Mid-Victorian Generation* (London, 1964), p. 8.

the Age," as Lord Jeffrey said of Macaulay's hundred-odd-page essay on Bacon, that I would not dream of cutting "the least particle of this precious work." Yet I have cut Mill, judiciously, I hope, as I have several other long essays, not to make them more readable but only to make room for more essays. (The cuts are indicated by ellipses within brackets.) It is the limitation of space that also accounts for the omission of other worthy essays. And other notable Victorians are absent—Darwin, for example—because they were not essayists.

I hope I have succeeded in doing what John Gross said could be done: creating an anthology that brings together essays of "outstanding scope and quality" which illuminate the spirit of a memorable age.

Early Victorian England

THOMAS CARLYLE (1795–1881)

Signs of the Times (1829)

*T*his essay appeared in the last issue of the Edinburgh Review *edited by Francis Jeffrey; it was one of the few essays in the journal that was not a review. In a mischievous mood, perhaps prompted by his resignation, Jeffrey invited Carlyle's critique of the progressive, utilitarian philosophy that the journal normally espoused. Taking his title from St. Matthew's gospel, Carlyle set himself against the "spirit of the age," thus becoming part of the dissident temper that was itself expressive of the spirit of the age.*

Carlyle suspected that with the retirement of Jeffrey, his essays would no longer be welcome in the Edinburgh Review. *Instead, Jeffrey's successor, Macvey Napier, was pleased to publish, two years later, another essay by Carlyle, "Characteristics" (ostensibly a review of two works of philosophy, one in German), in which Carlyle elaborated upon some themes introduced in "Signs of the Times": the "false action" that is the fruit of "false speculation," the "diseased self-consciousness" of man's internal as well as external world, the "cunningly-devised 'Constitution'" that passes as progress.* [1]

The willingness of such good Whigs as Jeffrey and Napier to publish essays so subversive of their principles and of their journal is itself a "sign of the times." So is the remarkable tolerance displayed by these editors, and even more, by their readers, of the style in which Carlyle communicated his displeasure—passionate, dense,

Thomas Carlyle (1795–1881), "Signs of the Times," *Edinburgh Review,* June 1829. Reprinted in Thomas Carlyle, *Critical and Miscellaneous Essays* (London, 1899), II, 56–82.

1. Carlyle, *Critical and Miscellaneous Essays,* IV, 19, 37.

heavily and often obscurely allusive, making no attempt to ingratiate himself with his readers or to placate them. (In a later work, Sartor Resartus, *he delivered his message in the guise of a tract by a German professor, replete with German words and references.) Carlyle was in the classic tradition of the prophet. And it was as such, as a prophet, that he was read and respected by the Victorians whom he so severely chastised.*

I t is no very good symptom either of nations or individuals, that they deal much in vatication. Happy men are full of the present, for its bounty suffices them; and wise men also, for its duties engage them. Our grand business undoubtedly is, not to *see* what lies dimly at a distance, but to *do* what lies clearly at hand.

> Know'st thou *Yesterday,* its aim and reason;
> Work'st thou well *Today,* for worthy things?
> Calmly wait the *Morrow's* hidden season,
> Need'st not fear what hap soe'er it brings.

But man's "large discourse of reason" *will* look "before and after"; and, impatient of the "ignorant present time," will indulge in anticipation far more than profits him. Seldom can the unhappy be persuaded that the evil of the day is sufficient for it; and the ambitious will not be content with present splendour, but paints yet more glorious triumphs, on the cloud-curtain of the future.

The case, however, is still worse with nations. For here the prophets are not one, but many; and each incites and confirms the other; so that the fatidical fury spreads wider and wider, till at last even Saul must join in it. For there is still a real magic in the action and reaction of minds on one another. The casual deliration of a few becomes, by this mysterious reverberation, the frenzy of many; men lose the use, not only of their understandings, but of their bodily senses; while the most obdurate unbelieving hearts melt, like the rest, in the furnace where all are cast as victims and as fuel. It is grievous to think, that this noble omnipotence of Sympathy has been so rarely the Aaron's-rod of Truth and Virtue, and so often the Enchanter's-rod of Wickedness and Folly! No solitary miscreant, scarcely any solitary maniac, would venture on such actions and imaginations, as large communities of sane men have, in such circumstances, entertained as sound wisdom. Witness long scenes of the French Revolution, in these late times! Levity is no protection against such visitations, nor the utmost earnestness of character. The New-England Puritan burns witches, wrestles for months with the horrors of Satan's invisible world, and all ghastly phantasms, the daily and hourly precursors of the Last Day; then suddenly bethinks him that he is frantic, weeps bitterly, prays contritely, and the history of that gloomy season lies behind him like a frightful dream.

Old England too has had her share of such frenzies and panics; though happily, like other old maladies, they have grown milder of late: and since the days of Titus Oates have mostly passed without loss of men's lives; or indeed without much other loss than that of reason, for the time, in the sufferers. In this mitigated form, however, the distemper is of pretty regular recurrence; and may be reckoned on at intervals, like other natural visitations; so that reasonable men deal with it, as the Londoners do with their fogs,—go cautiously out into the groping crowd, and patiently carry lanterns at noon; knowing, by a well-grounded faith, that the sun is still in existence, and will one day reappear. How often have we heard, for the last fifty years, that the country was wrecked, and fast sinking; whereas, up to this date, the country is entire and afloat! The "State in Danger" is a condition of things, which we have witnessed a hundred times; and as for the Church, it has seldom been out of "danger" since we can remember it.

All men are aware that the present is a crisis of this sort; and why it has become so. The repeal of the Test Acts, and then of the Catholic disabilities, has struck many of their admirers with an indescribable astonishment. Those things seemed fixed and immovable; deep as the foundations of the world; and lo, in a moment they have vanished, and their place knows them no more! Our worthy friends mistook the slumbering Leviathan for an island; often as they had been assured, that Intolerance was, and could be nothing but a Monster; and so, mooring under the lee, they had anchored comfortably in his scaly rind, thinking to take good cheer; as for some space they did. But now their Leviathan has suddenly dived under; and they can no longer be fastened in the stream of time; but must drift forward on it, even like the rest of the world: no very appalling fate, we think, could they but understand it; which, however, they will not yet, for a season. Their little island is gone; sunk deep amid confused eddies; and what is left worth caring for in the universe? What is it to them that the great continents of the earth are still standing; and the pole-star and all our loadstars, in the heavens, still shining and eternal? Their cherished little haven is gone, and they will not be comforted! And therefore, day after day, in all manner of periodical or perennial publications, the most lugubrious predictions are sent forth. The King has virtually abdicated; the Church is a widow, without jointure; public principle is gone; private honesty is going; society, in short, is fast falling in pieces; and a time of unmixed evil is come on us.

At such a period, it was to be expected that the rage of prophecy should be more than usually excited. Accordingly, the Millennarians have come forth on the right hand, and the Millites on the left. The Fifth-monarchy men prophesy from the Bible, and the Utilitarians from Bentham. The one announces that the last of the seals is to be opened, positively, in the year 1860; and the other assures us that "the greatest-happiness principle" is to make a heaven of earth, in a still shorter time. We know these symptoms too well, to think it necessary or safe to interfere with them. Time and the hours will bring relief to all parties. The grand encourager of Delphic or other noises is—the Echo. Left to themselves, they will the sooner dissipate, and die away in space.

Meanwhile, we too admit that the present is an important time; as all present time necessarily is. The poorest Day that passes over us is the conflux of two Eternities; it is made up of currents that issue from the remotest Past, and flow onwards into the remotest Future. We were wise indeed, could we discern truly the signs of our own time; and by knowledge of its wants and advantages, wisely adjust our own position in it. Let us, instead of gazing idly into the obscure distance, look calmly around us, for a little, on the perplexed scene where we stand. Perhaps, on a more serious inspection, something of its perplexity will disappear, some of its distinctive characters and deeper tendencies more clearly reveal themselves; whereby our own relations to it, our own true aims and endeavours in it, may also become clearer.

Were we required to characterise this age of ours by any single epithet, we should be tempted to call it, not an Heroical, Devotional, Philosophical, or Moral Age, but, above all others, the Mechanical Age. It is the Age of Machinery, in every outward and inward sense of that word; the age which, with its whole undivided might, forwards, teaches and practises the great art of adapting means to ends. Nothing is now done directly, or by hand; all is by rule and calculated contrivance. For the simplest operation, some helps and accompaniments, some cunning abbreviating process is in readiness. Our old modes of exertion are all discredited, and thrown aside. On every hand, the living artisan is driven from his workshop, to make room for a speedier, inanimate one. The shuttle drops from the fingers of the weaver, and falls into iron fingers that ply it faster. The sailor furls his sail, and lays down his oar; and bids a strong, unwearied servant, on vaporous wings, bear him through the waters. Men have crossed oceans by steam; the Birmingham Fire-king has visited the fabulous East; and the genius of the Cape, were there any Camoens now to sing it, has again been alarmed, and with far stranger thunders than Gamas. There is no end to machinery. Even the horse is stripped of his harness, and finds a fleet fire-horse yoked in his stead. Nay, we have an artist that hatches chickens by steam; the very brood-hen is to be superseded! For all earthly, and for some unearthly purposes, we have machines and mechanic furtherances; for mincing our cabbages; for casting us into magnetic sleep. We remove mountains, and make seas our smooth highway; nothing can resist us. We war with rude Nature; and, by our resistless engines, come off always victorious, and loaded with spoils.

What wonderful accessions have thus been made, and are still making, to the physical power of mankind; how much better fed, clothed, lodged and, in all outward respects, accommodated men now are, or might be, by a given quantity of labour, is a grateful reflection which forces itself on every one. What changes, too, this addition of power is introducing into the Social System; how wealth has more and more increased, and at the same time gathered itself more and more into masses, strangely altering the old relations, and increasing the distance between the rich and the poor, will be a question for Political Economists, and a much more complex and important one than any they have yet engaged with.

But leaving these matters for the present, let us observe how the mechanical genius of our time has diffused itself into quite other provinces. Not the external and physical alone is now managed by machinery, but the internal and spiritual also. Here too nothing follows its spontaneous course, nothing is left to be accomplished by old natural methods. Everything has its cunningly devised implements, its preestablished apparatus; it is not done by hand, but by machinery. Thus we have machines for Education: Lancastrian machines; Hamiltonian machines; monitors, maps and emblems. Instruction, that mysterious communing of Wisdom with Ignorance, is no longer an indefinable tentative process, requiring a study of individual aptitudes, and a perpetual variation of means and methods, to attain the same end; but a secure, universal, straightforward business, to be conducted in the gross, by proper mechanism, with such intellect as comes to hand. Then, we have Religious machines, of all imaginable varieties; the Bible-Society, professing a far higher and heavenly structure, is found, on inquiry, to be altogether an earthly contrivance: supported by collection of moneys, by fomenting of vanities, by puffing, intrigue and chicane; a machine for converting the Heathen. It is the same in all other departments. Has any man, or any society of men, a truth to speak, a piece of spiritual work to do; they can nowise proceed at once and with the mere natural organs, but must first call a public meeting, appoint committees, issue prospectuses, eat a public dinner; in a word, construct or borrow machinery, wherewith to speak it and do it. Without machinery they were hopeless, helpless; a colony of Hindoo weavers squatting in the heart of Lancashire. Mark, too, how every machine must have its moving power, in some of the great currents of society; every little sect among us, Unitarians, Utilitarians, Anabaptists, Phrenologists, must have its Periodical, its monthly or quarterly Magazine;—hanging out, like its windmill, into the *popularis aura,* to grind meal for the society.

With individuals, in like manner, natural strength avails little. No individual now hopes to accomplish the poorest enterprise single-handed and without mechanical aids; he must make interest with some existing corporation, and till his field with their oxen. In these days, more emphatically than ever, "to live, signifies to unite with a party, or to make one." Philosophy, Science, Art, Literature, all depend on machinery. No Newton, by silent meditation, now discovers the system of the world from the falling of an apple; but some quite other than Newton stands in his Museum, his Scientific Institution, and behind whole batteries of retorts, digesters, and galvanic piles imperatively "interrogates Nature,"—who, however, shows no haste to answer. In defect of Raphaels, and Angelos, and Mozarts, we have Royal Academies of Painting, Sculpture, Music; whereby the languishing spirit of Art may be strengthened, as by the more generous diet of a Public Kitchen. Literature, too, has its Paternoster-row mechanism, its Trade-dinners, its Editorial conclaves, and huge subterranean, puffing bellows; so that books are not only printed, but, in a great measure, written and sold, by machinery.

National culture, spiritual benefit of all sorts, is under the same management. No Queen Christina, in these times, needs to send for her Descartes; no King Frederick for his Voltaire, and painfully nourish him with pensions and flattery: any sovereign of taste, who wishes to enlighten his people, has only to impose a new tax, and with the proceeds establish Philosophic Institutes. Hence the Royal and Imperial Societies, the Bibliothèques, Glyptothèques, Technothèques, which front us in all capital cities; like so many well-finished hives, to which it is expected the stray agencies of Wisdom will swarm of their own accord, and hive and make honey. In like manner, among ourselves, when it is thought that religion is declining, we have only to vote half-a-million's worth of bricks and mortar, and build new churches. In Ireland it seems they have gone still farther, having actually established a "Penny-a-week Purgatory-Society"! Thus does the Genius of Mechanism stand by to help us in all difficulties and emergencies, and with his iron back bears all our burdens.

These things, which we state lightly enough here, are yet of deep import, and indicate a mighty change in our whole manner of existence. For the same habit regulates not our modes of action alone, but our modes of thought and feeling. Men are grown mechanical in head and in heart, as well as in hand. They have lost faith in individual endeavour, and in natural force, of any kind. Not for internal perfection, but for external combinations and arrangements, for institutions, constitutions,—for Mechanism of one sort or other, do they hope and struggle. Their whole efforts, attachments, opinions, turn on mechanism, and are of a mechanical character.

We may trace this tendency in all the great manifestations of our time; in its intellectual aspect, the studies it most favours and its manner of conducting them; in its practical aspects, its politics, arts, religion, morals; in the whole sources, and throughout the whole currents, of its spiritual, no less than its material activity.

Consider, for example, the state of Science generally, in Europe, at this period. It is admitted, on all sides, that the Metaphysical and Moral Sciences are falling into decay, while the Physical are engrossing, every day, more respect and attention. In most of the European nations there is now no such thing as a Science of Mind; only more or less advancement in the general science, or the special sciences, of matter. The French were the first to desert Metaphysics; and though they have lately affected to revive their school, it has yet no signs of vitality. The land of Malebranche, Pascal, Descartes and Fénelon, has now only its Cousins and Villemains; while, in the department of Physics, it reckons far other names. Among ourselves, the Philosophy of Mind, after a rickety infancy, which never reached the vigour of manhood, fell suddenly into decay, languished and finally died out, with its last amiable cultivator, Professor Stewart. In no nation but Germany has any decisive effort been made in psychological science; not to speak of any decisive result. The science of the age, in short, is physical, chemical, physiological; in all shapes mechanical. Our favourite Mathematics, the highly prized exponent of all these other sciences, has also become more and more mechanical. Excellence in what is called its higher departments depends less on natural genius than on acquired expertness in wielding its machinery. Without undervaluing the wonderful results which a Lagrange or Laplace educes by means of it, we may remark, that their calculus, differential and integral, is little else than a more cunningly-constructed arithmetical mill; where the factors being put in, are, as it were, ground into the true product, under cover, and without other effort on our part than steady turning of the handle. We have more Mathematics than ever; but less Mathesis. Archimedes and Plato could not have read the *Mécanique Céleste;* but neither would the whole French Institute see aught in that saying, "God geometrises!" but a sentimental rodomontade.

Nay, our whole Metaphysics itself, from Locke's time downwards, has been physical; not a spiritual philosophy, but a material one. The singular estimation in which his Essay was so long held as a scientific work (an estimation grounded, indeed, on the estimable character of the man) will one day be thought a curious indication of the spirit of these times. His whole doctrine is mechanical, in its aim and origin, in its method and its results. It is not a philosophy of the mind: it is a mere discussion concerning the origin of our consciousness, or ideas, or whatever else they are called; a genetic history of what we see *in* the mind. The grand secrets of Necessity and Freewill, of the Mind's vital or non-vital dependence on Matter, of our mysterious relations to Time and Space, to God, to the Universe, are not, in the faintest degree touched on in these inquiries; and seem not to have the smallest connexion with them.

[. . .]

This condition of the two great departments of knowledge,—the outward, cultivated exclusively on mechanical principles; the inward, finally abandoned, because, cultivated on such principles, it is found to yield no result,—sufficiently indicates the intellectual bias of our time, its all-pervading disposition towards that line of inquiry. In fact, an inward persuasion has long been diffusing itself, and now and then even comes to utterance, That, except the external, there are no true sciences; that to the inward world (if there be any) our only conceivable road is through the outward; that, in short, what cannot be investigated and understood mechanically, cannot be investigated and understood at all. We advert the more particularly to these intellectual propensities, as to prominent symptoms of our age, because Opinion is at all times doubly related to Action, first as cause, then as effect; and the speculative tendency of any age will therefore give us, on the whole, the best indications of its practical tendency.

Nowhere, for example, is the deep, almost exclusive faith we have in Mechanism more visible than in the Politics of this time. Civil government does by its nature include much that is mechanical, and must be treated accordingly. We term it indeed, in ordinary language, the Machine of Society, and talk of it as the grand working wheel from which all private machines must derive, or to which they must adapt, their movements. Considered merely as a metaphor, all this is well enough; but here, as in so many other cases, the "foam hardens itself into a shell," and the shadow we have wantonly evoked stands terrible before us and will not depart at our bidding. Government includes much also that is not mechanical, and cannot be treated mechanically; of which latter truth, as appears to us, the political speculations and exertions of our time are taking less and less cognisance.

Nay, in the very outset, we might note the mighty interest taken in *mere political arrangements,* as itself the sign of a mechanical age. The whole discontent of Europe takes this direction. The deep, strong cry of all civilised nations,—a cry which, every one now sees, must and will be answered, is: Give us a reform of Government! A good structure of legislation, a proper check upon the executive, a wise arrangement of the judiciary, is *all* that is wanting for human happiness. The Philosopher of this age is not a Socrates, a Plato, a Hooker, or Taylor, who inculcates on men the necessity and infinite worth of moral goodness, the great truth that our happiness depends on the mind which is within us, and not on the circumstances which are without us; but a Smith, a De Lolme, a Bentham, who chiefly inculcates the reverse of this,—that our happiness depends entirely on external circumstances; nay, that the strength and dignity of the mind within us is itself the creature and consequence of these. Were the laws, the government, in good order, all were well with us; the rest would care for itself! Dissentients from this opinion, expressed or implied, are now rarely to be met with; widely and angrily as men differ in its application, the principle is admitted by all.

Equally mechanical, and of equal simplicity, are the methods proposed by both parties for completing or securing this all-sufficient perfection of arrangement. It is no longer the moral, religious, spiritual condition of the people that is our concern, but their physical, practical, economical condition, as regulated by public laws. Thus is the Body-politic more than ever worshipped and tendered; but the Soul-politic less than ever. Love of country, in any high or generous sense, in any other than an almost animal sense, or mere habit, has little importance attached to it in such reforms, or in the opposition shown them. Men are to be guided only by their self-interests. Good government is a good balancing of these; and, except a keen eye and appetite for self-interest, requires no virtue in any quarter. To both parties it is emphatically a machine: to the discontented, a "taxing-machine"; to the contented, a "machine for securing property." Its duties and its faults are not those of a father, but of an active parish-constable.

Thus it is by the mere condition of the machine, by preserving it untouched, or else by reconstructing it, and oiling it anew, that man's salvation as a social being is to be ensured and indefinitely promoted. Contrive the fabric of law aright, and without farther effort on your part, that divine spirit of Freedom, which all hearts venerate and long for, will of herself come to inhabit it; and under her healing wings every noxious influence will wither, every good and salutary one more and more expand. Nay, so devoted are we to this principle, and at the same time so curiously mechanical, that a new trade, specially grounded on it, has arisen among us, under the name of "Codification," or codemaking in the abstract; whereby any people, for a reasonable consideration, may be accommodated with a patent code;—more easily than curious individuals with patent breeches, for the people does *not* need to be measured first.

To us who live in the midst of all this, and see continually the faith, hope and practice of every one founded on Mechanism of one kind or other, it is apt to seem quite natural, and as if it could never have been otherwise. Nevertheless, if we recollect or reflect a little, we shall find both that it has been, and might again be otherwise. The domain of Mechanism,—meaning thereby political, ecclesiastical or other outward establishments,—was once considered as embracing, and we are persuaded can at any time embrace, but a limited portion of man's interests, and by no means the highest portion.

To speak a little pedantically, there is a science of *Dynamics* in man's fortunes and nature, as well as of *Mechanics*. There is a science which treats of, and practically addresses, the primary, unmodified forces and energies of man, the mysterious springs of Love, and Fear, and Wonder, of Enthusiasm, Poetry, Religion, all which have a truly vital and *infinite* character; as well as a science which practically addresses the finite, modified developments of these, when they take the shape of immediate "motives," as hope of reward, or as fear of punishment.

Now it is certain, that in former times the wise men, the enlightened lovers of their kind, who appeared generally as Moralists, Poets or Priests, did, without neglecting the Mechanical province, deal chiefly with the Dynamical; applying themselves chiefly to regulate, increase and purify the inward primary powers of man; and fancying that herein lay the main difficulty, and the best service they could undertake. But a wide difference is manifest in our age. For the wise men, who now appear as Political Philosophers, deal exclusively with the Mechanical province; and occupying themselves in counting-up and estimating men's motives, strive by curious checking and balancing, and other adjustments of Profit and Loss, to guide them to their true advantage: while, unfortunately, those same "motives" are so innumerable, and so variable in every individual, that no really useful conclusion can ever be drawn from their enumeration. But though Mechanism, wisely contrived, has done much for a man in a social and moral point of view, we cannot be persuaded that it has ever been the chief source of his worth or happiness. Consider the great elements of human enjoyment, the attainments and possessions that exalt man's life to its present height, and see what part of these he owes to institutions, to Mechanism of any kind; and what to the instinctive, unbounded force, which Nature herself lent him, and still continues to him. Shall we say, for example, that Science and Art are indebted principally to the founders of Schools and Universities? Did not Science originate rather, and gain advancement, in the obscure closets of the Roger Bacons, Keplers, Newtons; in the workshops of the Fausts and the Watts; wherever, and in what guise soever Nature, from the first times downwards, had sent a gifted spirit upon the earth? Again, were Homer and Shakspeare members of any beneficed guild, or made Poets by means of it? Were Painting and Sculpture created by forethought, brought into the world by institutions for that end? No; Science and Art have, from first to last, been the free gift of Nature; an unsolicited, unexpected gift; often even a fatal one. These things rose up, as it were, by spontaneous growth, in the free soil and sunshine of Nature. They were not planted or grafted, nor even greatly multiplied or improved by the culture or manuring of institutions. Generally speaking, they have derived only partial help from these; often enough have suffered damage. They made constitutions for themselves. They originated in the Dynamical nature of man, not in his Mechanical nature.

Or, to take an infinitely higher instance, that of the Christian Religion, which, under every theory of it, in the believing or unbelieving mind, must ever be regarded as the crowning glory, or rather the life and soul, of our whole modern culture: How did Christianity arise and spread abroad among men? Was it by institutions, and establishments and well-arranged systems of mechanism? Not so; on the contrary, in all past and existing institutions for those ends, its divine spirit has invariably been found to languish and decay. It arose in the mystic deeps of man's soul; and was spread abroad by the "preaching of the word," by simple, altogether natural and individual efforts; and flew, like hallowed fire, from heart to heart, till all were purified and illuminated by it; and its heavenly light shone, as it still shines, and (as sun or star) will ever shine, through the whole dark destinies of man. Here again was no Mechanism; man's highest attainment was accomplished Dynamically, not Mechanically.

Nay, we will venture to say, that no high attainment, not even any far-extending movement among men, was ever accomplished otherwise. Strange as it may seem, if we read History with any degree of thoughtfulness, we shall find that the checks and balances of Profit and Loss have never been the grand agents with men; that they have never been roused into deep, thorough, all-pervading efforts by any computable prospect of Profit and Loss, for any visible, finite object; but always for some invisible and infinite one. The Crusades took their rise in Religion; their visible object was, commercially speaking, worth nothing. It was the boundless Invisible world that was laid bare in the imaginations of those men; and in its burning light, the visible shrunk as a scroll. Not mechanical, nor produced by mechanical means, was this vast movement. No dining at Freemasons' Tavern, with the other long train of modern machinery; no cunning reconciliation of "vested interests," was required here: only the passionate voice of one man, the rapt soul looking through the eyes of one man; and rugged, steel-clad Europe trembled beneath his words, and followed him whither he listed. In later ages it was still the same. The Reformation had an invisible, mystic and ideal aim; the result was indeed to be embodied in external things; but its spirit, its worth, was internal, invisible, infinite. Our English Revolution too originated in Religion. Men did battle, in those old days, not for Purse-sake, but for Conscience-sake. Nay, in our own days, it is no way different. The French Revolution itself had something higher in it than cheap bread and a Habeas-corpus act. Here too was an Idea; a Dynamic, not a Mechanic force. It was a struggle, though a blind and at last an insane one, for the infinite, divine nature of Right, of Freedom, of Country.

Thus does man, in every age, vindicate, consciously or unconsciously, his celestial birthright. Thus does Nature hold on her wondrous, unquestionable course; and all our systems and theories are but so many froth-eddies or sand-banks, which from time to time she casts up, and washes away. When we can drain the Ocean into mill-ponds, and bottle-up the Force of Gravity, to be sold by retail, in gas jars; then may we hope to comprehend the infinitudes of man's soul under formulas of Profit and Loss; and rule over this too, as over a patent engine, by checks, and valves, and balances.

Nay, even with regard to Government itself, can it be necessary to remind any one that Freedom, without which indeed all spiritual life is impossible, depends on infinitely more complex influences than either the extension or the curtailment of the "democratic interest"? Who is there that, "taking the high *priori* road," shall point out what these influences are; what deep, subtle, inextricably entangled influences they have been and may be? For man is not the creature and product of Mechanism; but, in a far truer sense, its creator and producer: it is the noble People that makes the noble Government; rather than conversely. On the whole, Institutions are much; but they are not all. The freest and highest spirits of the world have often been found under strange outward circumstances: Saint Paul and his brother Apostles were politically slaves; Epictetus was personally one. Again, forget the influences of Chivalry and Religion, and ask: What countries produced Columbus and Las Casas? Or, descending from virtue and heroism to mere energy and spiritual talent: Cortes, Pizarro, Alba, Ximenes? The Spaniards of the sixteenth century were indisputably the noblest nation of Europe: yet they had the Inquisition and Philip II. They have the same government at this day; and are the lowest nation. The Dutch too have retained their old constitution; but no Siege of Leyden, no William the Silent, not even as Egmont or De Witt any longer appears among them. With ourselves also, where much has changed, effect has nowise followed cause as it should have done: two centuries ago, the Commons Speaker addressed Queen Elizabeth on bended knees, happy that the virago's foot did not even smite him; yet the people were then governed, not by a Castlereagh, but by a Burghley; they had their Shakspeare and Philip Sidney, where we have our Sheridan Knowles and Beau Brummel.

These and the like facts are so familiar, the truths which they preach so obvious, and have in all past times been so universally believed and acted on, that we should almost feel ashamed for repeating them; were it not that, on every hand, the memory of them seems to have passed away, or at best died into a faint tradition, of no value as a practical principle. To judge by the loud clamour of our Constitution-builders, Statists, Economists, directors, creators, reformers of Public Societies; in a word, all manner of Mechanists, from the Cartwright up to the Code-maker; and by the nearly total silence of all Preachers and Teachers who should give a voice to Poetry, Religion and Morality, we might fancy either that man's Dynamical nature was, to all spiritual intents, extinct, or else so perfected that nothing more was to be made of it by the old means; and henceforth only in his Mechanical contrivances did any hope exist for him.

To define the limits of these two departments of man's activity, which work into one another, and by means of one another, so intricately and inseparably, were by its nature an impossible attempt. Their relative importance, even to the wisest mind, will vary in different times, according to the special wants and dispositions of those times. Meanwhile, it seems clear enough that only in the right coordination of the two, and the vigorous forwarding of *both*, does our true line of action lie. Undue cultivation of the inward or Dynamical province leads to idle, visionary, impracticable courses, and, especially in rude eras, to Superstition and Fanaticism, with their long train of baleful and well-known evils. Undue cultivation of the outward, again, though less immediately preju-dicial, and even for the time productive of many palpable benefits, must, in the long-run, by destroying Moral Force, which is the parent of all other Force, prove not less certainly, and perhaps still more hopelessly, pernicious. This, we take it, is the grand characteristic of our age. By our skill in Mechanism, it has come to pass, that in the management of external things we excel all other ages; while in whatever respects the pure moral nature, in true dignity of soul and character, we are perhaps inferior to most civilised ages.

In fact, if we look deeper, we shall find that this faith in Mechanism has now struck its roots down into man's most intimate, primary sources of conviction; and is thence sending up, over his whole life and activity, innumerable stems,— fruit-bearing and poison-bearing. The truth is, men have lost their belief in the Invisible, and believe, and hope, and work only in the Visible; or, to speak it in other words: This is not a Religious age. Only the material, the immediately practical, not the divine and spiritual, is important to us. The infinite, abso-lute character of Virtue has passed into a finite, conditional one; it is no longer a worship of the Beautiful and Good; but a calculation of the Prof-itable. Worship, indeed, in any sense, is not recognised among us, or is me-chanically explained into Fear of pain, or Hope of pleasure. Our true Deity is Mechanism. It has subdued external Nature for us, and we think it will do all other things. We are Giants in physical power: in a deeper than metaphorical sense, we are Titans, that strive, by heaping mountain on mountain, to con-quer Heaven also.

The strong Mechanical character, so visible in the spiritual pursuits and methods of this age, may be traced much farther into the condition and prevailing disposition of our spiritual nature itself. Consider, for example, the general fashion of Intellect in this era. Intellect, the power man has of knowing and believing, is now nearly synonymous with Logic, or the mere power of arranging and communicating. Its implement is not Meditation, but Argument. "Cause and effect" is almost the only category under which we look at, and work with, all Nature. Our first question with regard to any object is not, What is it? but, How is it? We are no longer instinctively driven to apprehend, and lay to heart, what is Good and Lovely, but rather to inquire, as onlookers, how it is produced, whence it comes, whither it goes. Our favourite Philosophers have no love and no hatred; they stand among us not to do, nor to create anything, but as a sort of Logic-mills, to grind out the true causes and effects of all that is done and created. To the eye of a Smith, a Hume or a Constant, all is well that works quietly. An Order of Ignatius Loyola, a Presbyterianism of John Knox, a Wickliffe or a Henry the Eighth, are simply so many mechanical phenomena, caused or causing.

The *Euphuist* of our day differs much from his pleasant predecessors. An intellectual dapperling of these times boasts chiefly of his irresistible perspicacity, his "dwelling in the daylight of truth," and so forth; which, on examination, turns out to be a dwelling in the *rush*-light of "closet-logic," and a deep unconsciousness that there is any other light to dwell in or any other objects to survey with it. Wonder, indeed, is, on all hands, dying out: it is the sign of uncultivation to wonder. Speak to any small man of a high, majestic Reformation, of a high majestic Luther; and forthwith he sets about "accounting" for it; how the "circumstances of the time" called for such a character, and found him, we suppose, standing girt and road-ready, to do its errand; how the "circumstances of the time" created, fashioned, floated him quietly along into the result; how, in short, this small man, had he been there, could have performed the like himself! For it is the "force of circumstances" that does everything; the force of one man can do nothing. Now all this is grounded on little more than a metaphor. We figure Society as a "Machine," and that mind is opposed to mind, as body is to body; whereby two, or at most ten, little minds must be stronger than one great mind. Notable absurdity! For the plain truth, very plain, we think is, that minds are opposed to minds in quite a different way; and *one* man that has a higher Wisdom, a hitherto unknown spiritual Truth in him, is stronger, not than ten men that have it not, or than ten thousand, but than *all* men that have it not; and stands among them with a quite ethereal, angelic power, as with a sword out of Heaven's own armory, sky-tempered, which no buckler, and no tower of brass, will finally withstand.

But to us, in these times, such considerations rarely occur. We enjoy, we see nothing by direct vision; but only by reflection, and in anatomical dismemberment. Like Sir Hudibras, for every Why we must have a Wherefore. We have our little *theory* on all human and divine things. Poetry, the workings of genius itself, which in all times, with one or another meaning, has been called Inspiration, and held to be mysterious and inscrutable, is no longer without its scientific exposition. The building of the lofty rhyme is like any other masonry or bricklaying: we have theories of its rise, height, decline and fall,—which latter, it would seem, is now near, among all people. Of our "Theories of Taste," as they are called, wherein the deep, infinite, unspeakable Love of Wisdom and Beauty, which dwells in all men, is "explained," made mechanically visible, from "Association" and the like, why should we say anything? Hume has written us a "Natural History of Religion"; in which one Natural History all the rest are included. Strangely too does the general feeling coincide with Hume's in this wonderful problem; for whether his "Natural History" be the right one or not, that Religion must have a Natural History, all of us, cleric and laic, seem to be agreed. He indeed regards it as a Disease, we again as Health; so far there is a difference; but in our first principle we are at one.

To what extent theological Unbelief, we mean intellectual dissent from the Church, in its view of Holy Writ, prevails at this day, would be a highly important, were it not, under any circumstances, an almost impossible inquiry. But the Unbelief, which is of a still more fundamental character, every man may see prevailing, with scarcely any but the faintest contradiction, all around him; even in the Pulpit itself. Religion in most countries, more or less in every country, is no longer what it was, and should be,—a thousand-voiced psalm from the heart of Man to his invisible Father, the fountain of all Goodness, Beauty, Truth, and revealed in every revelation of these; but for the most part, a wise prudential feeling grounded on mere calculation; a matter, as all others now are, of Expediency and Utility; whereby some smaller quantum of earthly enjoyment may be exchanged for a far larger quantum of celestial enjoyment. Thus Religion too is Profit, a working for wages; not Reverence, but vulgar Hope or Fear. Many, we know, very many we hope, are still religious in a far different sense; were it not so, our case were too desperate: but to witness that such is the temper of the times, we take any calm observant man, who agrees or disagrees in our feeling on the matter, and ask him whether our *view* of it is not in general well-founded.

Literature too, if we consider it, gives similar testimony. At no former era has Literature, the printed communication of Thought, been of such importance as it is now. We often hear that the Church is in danger; and truly so it is,—in a danger it seems not to know of: for, with its tithes in the most perfect safety, its functions are becoming more and more superseded. The true Church of England, at this moment, lies in the Editors of its Newspapers. These preach to the people daily, weekly; admonishing kings themselves; advising peace or war, with an authority which only the first Reformers, and a long-past class of Popes, were possessed of; inflicting moral censure; imparting moral encouragement, consolation, edification; in all ways diligently "administering the Discipline of the Church." It may be said too, that in private disposition the new Preachers somewhat resemble the Mendicant Friars of old times: outwardly full of holy zeal; inwardly not without stratagem, and hunger for terrestrial things. But omitting this class, and the boundless host of watery personages who pipe, as they are able, on so many scrannel straws, let us look at the higher regions of Literature, where, if anywhere, the pure melodies of Poesy and Wisdom should be heard. Of natural talent there is no deficiency: one or two richly-endowed individuals even give us a superiority in this respect. But what is the song they sing? Is it a tone of the Memnon Statue, breathing music as the *light* first touches it? A "liquid wisdom," disclosing to our sense the deep, infinite harmonies of Nature and man's soul? Alas, no! It is not a matin or vesper hymn to the Spirit of Beauty, but a fierce clashing of cymbals, and shouting of multitudes, as children pass through the fire to Moloch! Poetry itself has no eye for the Invisible. Beauty is no longer the god it worships, but some brute image of Strength; which we may call an idol, for true Strength is one and the same with Beauty, and its worship also is a hymn. The meek, silent Light can mould, create and purify all Nature; but the loud Whirlwind, the sign and product of Disunion, of Weakness, passes on, and is forgotten. How widely this veneration for the physically Strongest has spread itself through Literature, any one may judge who reads either criticism or poem. We praise a work, not as "true," but as "strong"; our highest praise is that it has "affected" us, has "terrified" us. All this, it has been well observed, is the "maximum of the Barbarous," the symptom, not of vigorous refinement, but of luxurious corruption. It speaks much, too, for men's indestructible love of truth, that nothing of this kind will abide with them; that even the talent of a Byron cannot permanently seduce us into idol-worship; that he too, with all his wild siren charming, already begins to be disregarded and forgotten.

Again, with respect to our Moral condition: here also he who runs may read that the same physical, mechanical influences are everywhere busy. For the "superior morality," of which we hear so much, we too would desire to be thankful: at the same time, it were but blindness to deny that this "superior morality" is properly rather an "inferior criminality," produced not by greater love of Virtue, but by greater perfection of Police; and of that far subtler and stronger Police, called Public Opinion. This last watches over us with its Argus eyes more keenly than ever; but the "inward eye" seems heavy with sleep. Of any belief in invisible, divine things, we find as few traces in our Morality as elsewhere. It is by tangible, material considerations that we are guided, not by inward and spiritual. Self-denial, the parent of all virtue, in any true sense of that word, has perhaps seldom been rarer: so rare is it, that the most, even in their abstract speculations, regard its existence as a chimera. Virtue is Pleasure, is Profit; no celestial, but an earthly thing. Virtuous men, Philanthropists,

Martyrs are happy accidents; their "taste" lies the right way! In all senses, we worship and follow after Power; which may be called a physical pursuit. No man now loves Truth, as Truth must be loved, with an infinite love; but only with a finite love, and as it were *par amours*. Nay, properly speaking, he does not *believe* and know it, but only "*thinks*" it, and that "there is every probability!" He preaches it aloud, and rushes courageously forth with it,—if there is a multitude huzzaing at his back; yet ever keeps looking over his shoulder, and the instant the huzzaing languishes, he too stops short.

In fact, what morality we have takes the shape of Ambition, of "Honour": beyond money and money's worth, our only rational blessedness is Popularity. It were but a fool's trick to die for conscience. Only for "character," by duel, or in case of extremity, by suicide, is the wise man bound to die. By arguing on the "force of circumstances," we have argued away all force from ourselves; and stand leashed together, uniform in dress and movement, like the rowers of some boundless galley. This and that may be right and true; *but* we must not do it. Wonderful "Force of Public Opinion"! We must act and walk in all points as it prescribes; follow the traffic it bids us, realise the sum of money, the degree of "influence" it expects of us, *or* we shall be lightly esteemed; certain mouthfuls of articulate wind will be blown at us, and this what mortal courage can front? Thus, while civil liberty is more and more secured to us, our moral liberty is all but lost. Practically considered, our creed is Fatalism; and, free in hand and foot, we are shackled in heart and soul with far straiter than feudal chains. Truly may we say, with the Philosopher, "the deep meaning of the Laws of Mechanism lies heavy on us"; and in the closet, in the marketplace, in the temple, by the social hearth, encumbers the whole movements of our mind, and over our noblest faculties is spreading a nightmare sleep.

These dark features, we are aware, belong more or less to other ages, as well as to ours. This faith in Mechanism, in the all-importance of physical things, is in every age the common refuge of Weakness and blind Discontent; of all who believe, as many will ever do, that man's true good lies without him, not within. We are aware also, that, as applied to ourselves in all their aggravation, they form but half a picture; that in the whole picture there are bright lights as well as gloomy shadows. If we here dwell chiefly on the latter, let us not be blamed: it is in general more profitable to reckon up our defects than to boast of our attainments.

Neither, with all these evils more or less clearly before us, have we at any time despaired of the fortunes of society. Despair, or even despondency, in that respect, appears to us, in all cases, a groundless feeling. We have a faith in the imperishable dignity of man; in the high vocation to which, throughout his earthly history, he has been appointed. However it may be with individual nations, whatever melancholic speculators may assert, it seems a well-ascertained fact, that in all times, reckoning even from those of the Heraclides and Pelasgi, the happiness and greatness of mankind at large have been continually progressive. Doubtless this age also is advancing. Its very unrest, its ceaseless activity, its discontent contains matter of promise. Knowledge, education are opening the eyes of the humblest; are increasing the number of thinking minds without limit. This is as it should be; for not in turning back, not in resisting, but only in resolutely struggling forward, does our life consist.

Nay, after all, our spiritual maladies are but of Opinion; we are but fettered by chains of our own forging, and which ourselves also can rend asunder. This deep, paralysed subjection to physical objects comes not from Nature, but from our own unwise mode of *viewing* Nature. Neither can we understand that man wants, at this hour, any faculty of heart, soul or body, that ever belonged to him. "He, who has been born, has been a First Man"; has had lying before his young eyes, and as yet unhardened into scientific shapes, a world as plastic, infinite, divine, as lay before the eyes of Adam himself. If Mechanism, like some glass bell, encircles and imprisons us; if the soul looks forth on a fair heavenly country which it cannot reach, and pines, and in its scanty atmosphere is ready to perish,—yet the bell is but of glass; "one bold stroke to break the bell in pieces, and thou art delivered!" Not the invisible world is wanting, for it dwells in man's soul, and this last is still here. Are the solemn temples, in which the Divinity was once visibly revealed among us, crumbling away? We can repair them, we can rebuild them. The wisdom, the heroic worth of our forefathers, which we have lost, we can recover. That admiration of old nobleness, which now so often shows itself as a faint *dilettantism,* will one day become a generous emulation, and man may again be all that he has been, and more than he has been. Nor are these the mere daydreams of fancy; they are clear possibilities; nay, in this time they are even assuming the character of hopes. Indications we do see in other countries and in our own, signs infinitely cheering to us, that Mechanism is not always to be our hard taskmaster, but one day to be our pliant, all-ministering servant; that a new and brighter spiritual era is slowly evolving itself for all men. But on these things our present course forbids us to enter.

Meanwhile, that great outward changes are in progress can be doubtful to no one. The time is sick and out of joint. Many things have reached their height; and it is a wise adage that tells us, "the darkest hour is nearest the dawn." Wherever we can gather indication of the public thought, whether from printed books, as in France or Germany, or from Carbonari rebellions and other political tumults, as in Spain, Portugal, Italy and Greece, the voice it utters is the same. The thinking minds of all nations call for change. There is a deep-lying struggle in the whole fabric of society; a boundless grinding collision of the New with the Old. The French Revolution, as is now visible enough, was not the parent of this mighty movement, but its offspring. Those two hostile influences, which always exist in human things, and on the constant intercommunion of which depends their health and safety, had lain in separate masses, accumulating through generations, and France was the scene of their fiercest explosion; but the final issue was not unfolded in that country: nay, it is not yet anywhere unfolded. Political freedom is hitherto the object of these efforts; but they will not and cannot stop there. It is towards a higher freedom than mere freedom from oppression by his fellow-mortal, that man dimly aims. Of this higher, heavenly freedom, which is "man's reasonable service," all his noble institutions, his faithful endeavours and loftiest attainments, are but the body, and more and more approximated emblem.

On the whole, as this wondrous planet, Earth, is journeying with its fellows through infinite Space, so are the wondrous destinies embarked on it journeying through infinite Time, under a higher guidance than ours. For the present, as our astronomy informs us, its path lies towards *Hercules,* the constellation of *Physical Power:* but that is not our most pressing concern. Go where it will, the deep Heaven will be around it. Therein let us have hope and sure faith. To reform a world, to reform a nation, no wise man will undertake; and all but foolish men know, that the only solid, though a far slower reformation, is what each begins and perfects on *himself.*

JOHN STUART MILL (1806–73)

The Spirit of the Age (1831)

*T*he five essays in this series were not reprinted in Mill's lifetime. In his Autobiography, *written in the mid-1850s, Mill spoke disparagingly of them as*
"lumbering in style" and "ill-timed."[1] *In the preface to the two-volume collection of*
his essays, Dissertations and Discussions, *published in 1859, he repeated this*
criticism, adding that some essays were excluded either because they were of little or
ephemeral value or because "any utility they may have possessed has since been
superseded by other and more mature writings of the author."[2] *The last proviso was*
especially pertinent to "The Spirit of the Age."

The year 1859 saw the publication of not only Dissertations and Discussions
but also On Liberty, *which was diametrically opposed to "The Spirit of the Age."*
Where On Liberty *made the freedom of discussion an absolute good, the precondi-*
tion for the emergence of truth, "The Spirit of the Age" regarded the freedom of
discussion as one of the unfortunate characteristics of a transitional age, a time
when "every dabbler . . . thinks his opinion as good as another's," when those
engaged in discussion were often "in no degree fitted" to do so and had not the "right
means of understanding" to discover or appreciate truth. Similarly, where On
Liberty *decried any authority that would stand in the way of the individual's*

John Stuart Mill (1806–73), "The Spirit of the Age," *Examiner,* January 6–May 29, 1831.
Reprinted in John Stuart Mill, *Essays on Politics and Culture,* ed. Gertrude Himmelfarb
(New York, 1962), pp. 3–50.

1. See Introduction, p. 2, above.

2. *Dissertations and Discussions: Political, Philosophical, and Historical* (London, 1859),
pp. iii–lv.

liberty to think and discuss, "The Spirit of the Age" looked upon authority—"the authority of the best-instructed," of "more cultivated minds"—as "the ultimate sanction" of reason and of a "natural state" of society.

It is no wonder that Mill chose not to reprint "The Spirit of the Age." Yet these essays not only are crucial to an understanding of Mill's intellectual development but also help put On Liberty *in perspective—in the perspective of social as well as intellectual history. So far from being "ill-timed," they were expressive of a "spirit of the age" shared (as the introduction suggests) by some of the most perceptive and influential thinkers of the time.*[3]

I

The "spirit of the age" is in some measure a novel expression. I do not believe that it is to be met with in any work exceeding fifty years in antiquity. The idea of comparing one's own age with former ages, or with our notion of those which are yet to come, had occurred to philosophers; but it never before was itself the dominant idea of any age.

It is an idea essentially belonging to an age of change. Before men begin to think much and long on the peculiarities of their own times, they must have begun to think that those times are, or are destined to be, distinguished in a very remarkable manner from the times which preceded them. Mankind are then divided, into those who are still what they were, and those who have changed: into the men of the present age, and the men of the past. To the former, the spirit of the age is a subject of exultation; to the latter, of terror; to both, of eager and anxious interest. The wisdom of ancestors, and the march of intellect, are bandied from mouth to mouth; each phrase originally an expression of respect and homage, each ultimately usurped by the partisans of the opposite catch-word, and in the bitterness of their spirit, turned into the sarcastic jibe of hatred and insult.

The present times possess this character. A change has taken place in the human mind; a change which, being effected by insensible gradations, and without noise, had already proceeded far before it was generally perceived. When the fact disclosed itself, thousands awoke as from a dream. They knew not what processes had been going on in the minds of others, or even in their own, until the change began to invade outward objects; and it became clear that those were indeed new men, who insisted upon being governed in a new way.

---

3. Mill is the only writer represented in this volume by two essays; the other essay dates from the same year as *On Liberty*. Mill's preeminent position in Victorian England might alone warrant this double representation, but it also puts Mill himself in proper perspective.

But mankind are now conscious of their new position. The conviction is already not far from being universal, that the times are pregnant with change; and that the nineteenth century will be known to posterity as the era of one of the greatest revolutions of which history has preserved the remembrance, in the human mind, and in the whole constitution of human society. Even the religious world teems with new interpretations of the Prophecies, foreboding mighty changes near at hand. It is felt that men are henceforth to be held together by new ties, and separated by new barriers; for the ancient bonds will now no longer unite, nor the ancient boundaries confine. Those men who carry their eyes in the back of their heads and can see no other portion of the destined track of humanity than that which it has already travelled, imagine that because the old ties are severed mankind henceforth are not to be connected by any ties at all; and hence their affliction, and their awful warnings. For proof of this assertion, I may refer to the gloomiest book ever written by a cheerful man—Southey's "Colloquies on the Progress and Prospects of Society"; a very curious and not uninstructive exhibition of one of the points of view from which the spirit of the age may be contemplated. They who prefer the ravings of a party politician to the musings of a recluse, may consult a late article in Blackwood's Magazine, under the same title which I have prefixed to this paper. For the reverse of the picture, we have only to look into any popular newspaper or review.

Amidst all this indiscriminate eulogy and abuse, these undistinguishing hopes and fears, it seems to be a very fit subject for philosophical inquiry, what the spirit of the age really is; and how or wherein it differs from the spirit of any other age. The subject is deeply important: for, whatever we may think or affect to think of the present age, we cannot get out of it; we must suffer with its sufferings, and enjoy with its enjoyments; we must share in its lot, and, to be either useful or at ease, we must even partake its character. No man whose good qualities were mainly those of another age, ever had much influence on his own. And since every age contains in itself the germ of all future ages as surely as the acorn contains the future forest, a knowledge of our own age is the fountain of prophecy—the only key to the history of posterity. It is only in the present that we can know the future; it is only through the present that it is in our power to influence that which is to come.

Yet, because our own age is *familiar* to us, we are presumed, if I may judge from appearances, to know it by nature. A statesman, for example, if it be required of him to have studied any thing at all (which, however, is more than I would venture to affirm) is supposed to have studied history—which is at best the spirit of ages long past, and more often the mere inanimate carcass without the spirit: but is it ever asked (or to whom does the question ever occur?) whether he understands his own age? Yet that also is history, and the most important part of history, and the only part which a man may know and understand, with absolute certainty, by using the proper means. He may learn in a morning's walk through London more of the history of England during the nineteenth century, than all the professed English histories in existence will tell him concerning the other eighteen: for, the obvious and universal facts, which every one sees and no one is astonished at, it seldom occurs to any one to place upon record; and posterity, if it learn the rule, learns it, generally, from the notice bestowed by contemporaries on some accidental exception. Yet are politicians and philosophers perpetually exhorted to judge of the present by the past, when the present alone affords a fund of materials for judging, richer than the whole stores of the past, and far more accessible.

But it is unadvisable to dwell longer on this topic, lest we should be deemed studiously to exaggerate that want, which we desire that the reader should think ourselves qualified to supply. It were better, without further preamble, to enter upon the subject, and be tried by our ideas themselves, rather than by the need of them.

The first of the leading peculiarities of the present age is, that it is an age of transition. Mankind have outgrown old institutions and old doctrines, and have not yet acquired new ones. When we say outgrown, we intend to prejudge nothing. A man may not be either better or happier at six-and-twenty, than he was at six years of age: but the same jacket which fitted him then, will not fit him now.

The prominent trait just indicated in the character of the present age, was obvious a few years ago only to the more discerning: at present it forces itself upon the most inobservant. Much might be said, and shall be said on a fitting occasion, of the mode in which the old order of things has become unsuited to the state of society and of the human mind. But when almost every nation on the continent of Europe has achieved, or is in the course of rapidly achieving, a change in its form of government; when our own country, at all former times the most attached in Europe to its old institutions, proclaims almost with one voice that they are vicious both in the outline and in the details, and that they *shall* be renovated, and purified, and made fit for civilized man, we may assume that a part of the effects of the cause just now pointed out, speak sufficiently loudly for themselves. To him who can reflect, even these are but indications which tell of a more vital and radical change. Not only, in the conviction of almost all men, things as they are, are wrong—but, according to that same conviction, it is not by remaining in the old ways that they can be set right. Society demands, and anticipates, not merely a new machine, but a machine constructed in another manner. Mankind will not be led by their old maxims, nor by their old guides; and they will not choose either their opinions or their guides as they have done heretofore. The ancient constitutional texts were formerly spells which would call forth or allay the spirit of the English people at pleasure: what has become of the charm? Who can hope to sway the minds of the public by the old maxims of law, or commerce, or foreign policy, or ecclesiastical policy? Whose feelings are now roused by the mottoes and watch-words of Whig and Tory? And what Whig or Tory could command ten followers in the warfare of politics by the weight of his own personal authority? Nay, what landlord could call forth his tenants, or what manufacturer his men? Do the poor respect the rich, or adopt their sentiments? Do the young respect the old, or adopt their sentiments? Of the feelings of our ancestors it may almost be said that we retain only such as are the natural and necessary growth of a state of human society, however constituted; and I only adopt the energetic expression of a member of the House of Commons, less than two years ago, in saying of the young men, even of that rank in society, that they are ready to advertise for opinions.

Since the facts are so manifest, there is the more chance that a few reflections on their causes, and on their probable consequences, will receive whatever portion of the reader's attention they may happen to deserve.

With respect, then, to the discredit into which old institutions and old doctrines have fallen, I may premise, that this discredit is, in my opinion, perfectly deserved. Having said this, I may perhaps hope, that no perverse interpretation will be put upon the remainder of my observations, in case some of them should not be quite so conformable to the sentiments of the day as my commencement might give reason to expect. The best guide is not he who, when people are in the right path, merely praises it, but he who shows them the pitfalls and the precipices by which it is endangered; and of which, as long as they were in the wrong road, it was not so necessary that they should be warned.

There is one very easy, and very pleasant way of accounting for this general departure from the modes of thinking of our ancestors: so easy, indeed, and so pleasant, especially to the hearer, as to be very convenient to such writers for hire or for applause, as address themselves not to the men of the age that is gone by, but to the men of the age which has commenced. This explanation is that which ascribes the altered state of opinion and feeling to the growth of the human understanding. According to this doctrine, we reject the sophisms and prejudices which misled the uncultivated minds of our ancestors, because we have learnt too much, and have become too wise, to be imposed upon by such sophisms and such prejudices. It is our knowledge and our sagacity which keep us free from these gross errors. We have now risen to the capacity of perceiving our true interests; and it is no longer in the power of impostors and charlatans to deceive us.

I am unable to adopt this theory. Though a firm believer in the improvement of the age, I do not believe that its improvement has been of this kind. The grand achievement of the present age is the *diffusion* of *superficial* knowledge; and that surely is no trifle, to have been accomplished by a single generation. The persons who are in possession of knowledge adequate to the formation of sound opinions by their own lights, form also a constantly increasing number, but hitherto at all times a small one. It would be carrying the notion of the march of intellect too far, to suppose that an average man of the present day is superior to the greatest men of the beginning of the eighteenth century; yet they *held* many opinions which we are fast renouncing. The intellect of the age, therefore, is not the cause which we are in search of. I do not perceive that, in the mental training which has been received by the immense majority of the reading and thinking part of my countrymen, or in the kind of knowledge and other intellectual aliment which has been supplied to them, there is any thing likely to render them much less accessible to the influence of imposture and charlatanerie than there ever was. The Dr. Eadys still dupe the lower classes, the St. John Longs the higher: and it would not be difficult to produce the political and literary antitypes of both. Neither do I see, in such observations as I am able to make upon my cotemporaries, evidence that they have any principle within them which renders them much less liable now than at any former period to be misled by sophisms and prejudices. All I see is, that the opinions which have been transmitted to them from their ancestors, are not the kind of sophisms and prejudices which are fitted to possess any considerable ascendancy in their altered frame of mind. And I am rather inclined to account for this fact in a manner not reflecting such extraordinarily great honour upon the times we live in; as would result from the theory by which all is ascribed to the superior expansion of our understandings.

The intellectual tendencies of the age, considered both on the favourable and on the unfavourable side, it will be necessary, in the prosecution of the present design, to review and analyse in some detail. For the present it may be enough to remark, that it is seldom safe to ground a positive estimate of a character upon mere negatives: and that the faults or the prejudices, which a person, or an age, or a nation *has not*, go but a very little way with a wise man towards forming a high opinion of them. A person may be without a single prejudice, and yet utterly unfit for every purpose in nature. To have erroneous convictions is one evil; but to have no strong or deep-rooted convictions at all, is an enormous one. Before I compliment either a man or a generation upon having got rid of their prejudices, I require to know what they have substituted in lieu of them.

Now, it is self-evident that no fixed opinions have yet generally established themselves in the place of those which we have abandoned; that no new doctrines, philosophical or social, as yet command, or appear likely soon to command, an assent at all comparable in unanimity to that which the ancient doctrines could boast of while they continued in vogue. So long as this intellectual anarchy shall endure, we may be warranted in believing that we are in a fair way to become wiser than our forefathers; but it would be premature to affirm that we are already wiser. We have not yet advanced beyond the unsettled state, in which the mind is, when it has recently found itself out in a grievous error, and has not yet satisfied itself of the truth. The men of the present day rather incline to an opinion than embrace it; few, except the very penetrating, or the very presumptuous, have full confidence in their own convictions. This is not a state of health, but, at the best, of convalescence. It is a necessary stage in the progress of civilization, but it is attended with numerous evils; as one part of a road may be rougher or more dangerous than another, although every step brings the traveller nearer to his desired end.

Not increase of wisdom, but a cause of the reality of which we are better assured, may serve to account for the decay of prejudices; and this is, increase of discussion. Men may not reason, better, concerning the great questions in which human nature is interested, but they reason more. Large subjects are discussed more, and longer, and by more minds. Discussion has penetrated deeper into society; and if no greater numbers than before have attained the higher degrees of intelligence, fewer grovel in that state of abject stupidity, which can only co-exist with utter apathy and sluggishness.

The progress which we have made, is precisely that sort of progress which increase of discussion suffices to produce, whether it be attended with increase of wisdom or no. To discuss, and to question established opinions, are merely two phrases for the same thing. When all opinions are questioned, it is in time found out what are those which will not bear a close examination. Ancient doctrines are then put upon their proofs; and those which were originally errors, or have become so by change of circumstances, are thrown aside. Discussion does this. It is by discussion, also, that true opinions are discovered and diffused. But this is not so certain a consequence of it as the weakening of error. To be rationally assured that a given doctrine is *true,* it is often necessary to examine and weigh an immense variety of facts. One single well-established fact, clearly irreconcilable with a doctrine, is sufficient to prove that it is *false.* Nay, opinions often upset themselves by their own incoherence; and the impossibility of their being well-founded may admit of being brought home to a mind not possessed of so much as one positive truth. All the inconsistencies of an opinion with itself, with obvious facts, or even with other prejudices, discussion evolves and makes manifest: and indeed this mode of refutation, requiring less study and less real knowledge than any other, is better suited to the inclination of most disputants. But the moment, and the mood of mind, in which men break loose from an error, is not, except in natures very happily constituted, the most favourable to those mental processes which are necessary to the investigation of truth. What led them wrong at first, was generally nothing else but the incapacity of seeing more than one thing at a time; and that incapacity is apt to stick to them when they have turned their eyes in an altered direction. They usually resolve that the new light which has broken in upon them shall be the sole light; and they wilfully and passionately blew out the ancient lamp, which, though it did not show them what they now see, served very well to enlighten the objects in its immediate neighbourhood. Whether men adhere to old opinions or adopt new ones, they have in general an invincible propensity to split the truth, and take half, or less than half of it; and a habit of erecting their quills and bristling up like a porcupine against any one who brings them the other half, as if he were attempting to deprive them of the portion which they have.

I am far from denying, that, besides getting rid of error, we are also continually enlarging the stock of positive truth. In physical science and art, this is too manifest to be called in question; and in the moral and social sciences, I believe it to be as undeniably true. The wisest men in every age generally surpass in wisdom the wisest of any preceding age, because the wisest men possess and profit by the constantly increasing accumulation of the ideas of all ages: but the multitude (by which I mean the majority of all ranks) have the ideas of their own age, and no others: and if the multitude of one age are nearer to the truth than the multitude of another, it is only in so far as they are guided and influenced by the authority of the wisest among them.

This is connected with certain points which, as it appears to me, have not been sufficiently adverted to by many of those who hold, in common with me, the doctrine of the indefinite progressiveness of the human mind; but which must be understood, in order correctly to appreciate the character of the present age, as an age of moral and political transition. These, therefore, I shall attempt to enforce and illustrate in the next paper.

II

I have said that the present age is an age of transition: I shall now attempt to point out one of the most important consequences of this fact. In all other conditions of mankind, the uninstructed have faith in the instructed. In an age of transition, the divisions among the instructed nullify their authority, and the uninstructed lose their faith in them. The multitude are without a guide; and society is exposed to all the errors and dangers which are to be expected when persons who have never studied any branch of knowledge comprehensively and as a whole attempt to judge for themselves upon particular parts of it.

That this is the condition we are really in, I may spare myself the trouble of attempting to prove: it has become so habitual, that the only difficulty to be anticipated is in persuading any one that this is not our natural state, and that it is consistent with any good wishes towards the human species, to pray that we may come safely out of it. The longer any one observes and meditates, the more clearly he will see, that even wise men are apt to mistake the almanack of the year for a treatise on chronology; and as in an age of transition the source of all improvement is the exercise of private judgment, no wonder that mankind should attach themselves to that, as to the ultimate refuge, the last and only resource of humanity. In like manner, if a caravan of travelers had long been journeying in an unknown country under a blind guide, with what earnestness would the wiser among them exhort the remainder to use their own eyes, and with what disfavour would any one be listened to who should insist upon the difficulty of finding their way, and the necessity of procuring a guide after all. He would be told with warmth, that they had hitherto missed their way solely from the fatal weakness of allowing themselves to be guided, and that they never should reach their journey's end until each man dared to think and see for himself. And it would perhaps be added (with a smile of contempt), that if he were sincere in doubting the capacity of his fellow-travellers to see their way, he might prove his sincerity by presenting each person with a pair of spectacles, by means whereof their powers of vision might be strengthened, and, all indistinctness removed.

The men of the past, are those who continue to insist upon our still adhering to the blind guide. The men of the present, are those who bid each man look about for himself, with or without the promise of spectacles to assist him.

While these two contending parties are measuring their sophistries against one another, the man who is capable of other ideas than those of his age, has an example in the present state of physical science, and in the manner in which men shape their thoughts and their actions within its sphere, of what is to be hoped for and laboured for in all other departments of human knowledge; and what, beyond all possibility of doubt, will one day be attained.

We never hear of the right of private judgment in physical science; yet it exists; for what is there to prevent any one from denying every proposition in natural philosophy, if he be so minded? The physical sciences however have been brought to so advanced a stage of improvement by a series of great men, and the methods by which they are cultivated so entirely preclude the possibility of material error when due pains are taken to arrive at the truth, that all persons who have studied those subjects have come to a nearly unanimous agreement upon them. Some minor differences doubtless exist; there are points on which the opinion of the scientific world is not finally made up. But these are mostly questions rather of curiosity than of use, and it is seldom attempted to thrust them into undue importance, nor to remove them, by way of appeal from the tribunal of the specially instructed to that of the public at large. The compact mass of authority thus created overawes the minds of the uninformed: and if here and there a wrong-headed individual, like Sir Richard Phillips, impugns Newton's discoveries, and revives the long-forgotten sophisms of the Cartesians, he is not regarded. Yet the fallacies which at one time enthralled the subtlest understandings, might find, we suspect, in the present day, some intellects scarcely strong enough to resist them: but no one dares to stand up against the scientific world, until he too has qualified himself to be named as a man of science: and no one does this without being forced, by irresistible evidence, to adopt the received opinion. The physical sciences, therefore, (speaking of them generally) are continually *growing*, but never *changing*: in every age they receive indeed mighty improvements, but for them the age of transition is past.

It is almost unnecessary to remark in how very different a condition from this, are the sciences which are conversant with the moral nature and social condition of man. In those sciences, this imposing unanimity among all who have studied the subject does not exist; and every dabbler, consequently, thinks his opinion as good as another's. Any man who has eyes and ears shall be judge whether, in point of fact, a person who has never studied politics, for instance, or political economy systematically, regards himself as any-way precluded thereby from promulgating with the most unbounded assurance the crudest opinions, and taxing men who have made those sciences the occupation of a laborious life, with the most contemptible ignorance and imbecility. It is rather the person who *has* studied the subject systematically that is regarded as disqualified. He is a *theorist:* and the word which expresses the highest and noblest effort of human intelligence is turned into a bye-word of derision. People pride themselves upon taking a "plain, matter-of-fact" view of a subject. I once heard of a book entitled "Plain Politics for Plain People." I well remember the remark of an able man on that occasion: "What would be thought of a work with such a title as this, Plain Mathematics for Plain People?" The parallel is most accurate. The nature of the evidence on which these two sciences rest, is different, but both are systems of connected truth: there are very few of the practical questions of either, which can be discussed with profit unless the parties are agreed on a great number of preliminary questions: and accordingly, most of the political discussions which one hears and reads are not unlike what one would expect if the binomial theorem were propounded for argument in a debating society none of whose members had completely made up their minds upon the Rule of Three. Men enter upon a subject with minds in no degree fitted, by previous acquirements, to understand and appreciate the true arguments: yet they lay the blame on the arguments, not on themselves: truth, they think, is under a peremptory obligation of being intelligible to them, whether they take the right means of understanding it or no. Every mode of judging, except from first appearances, is scouted as false refinement. If there were a party among philosophers who still held to the opinion that the sun moves round the earth, can any one doubt on which side of the question the vulgar would be? What terms could express their contempt for those who maintained the contrary! Men form their opinions according to natural shrewdness, without any of the advantages of study. Here and there a hard-headed man, who sees farther into a mill-stone than his neighbours, and takes it into his head that thinking on a subject is one way of understanding it, excogitates an entire science, and publishes his volume; in utter unconsciousness of the fact, that a tithe of his discoveries were known a century ago, and the remainder (supposing them not too absurd to have occurred to anybody before) have been refuted in any year which you can mention, from that time to the present.

This is the state we are in; and the question is, how we are to get out of it. As I am unable to take the view of this matter which will probably occur to most persons as being the most simple and natural, I shall state in the first instance what this is, and my reasons for dissenting from it.

A large portion of the talking and writing common in the present day, respecting the instruction of the people, and the diffusion of knowledge, appears to me to conceal, under loose and vague generalities, notions at bottom altogether fallacious and visionary.

I go, perhaps, still further than most of those to whose language I so strongly object, in the expectations which I entertain of vast improvements in the social condition of man, from the growth of intelligence among the body of the people; and I yield to no one in the degree of intelligence of which I believe them to be capable. But I do not believe that, along with this intelligence, they will ever have sufficient opportunities of study and experience, to become themselves familiarly conversant with all the inquiries which lead to the truths by which it is good that they should regulate their conduct, and to receive into their own minds the whole of the evidence from which those truths have been collected, and which is necessary for their establishment. If I thought all this indispensable, I should despair of human nature. As long as the day consists but of twenty-four hours, and the age of man extends but to threescore and ten, so long (unless we expect improvements in the arts of production sufficient to restore the golden age) the great majority of mankind will need the far greater part of their time and exertions for procuring their daily bread. Some few remarkable individuals will attain great eminence under every conceivable disadvantage; but for men in general, the principal field for the exercise and display of their intellectual faculties is, and ever will be, no other than their own particular calling or occupation. This does not place any limit to their possible intelligence; since the mode of learning, and the mode of practising, that occupation itself, might be made one of the most valuable of all exercises of intelligence: especially when, in all the occupations in which man is a mere machine, his agency is so rapidly becoming superseded by real machinery. But what sets no limit to the *powers* of the mass of mankind, nevertheless limits greatly their possible *acquirements*. Those persons whom the circumstances of society, and their own position in it, permit to dedicate themselves to the investigation and study of physical, moral, and social truths, as their peculiar calling, can alone be expected to make the evidences of such truths a subject of profound meditation, and to make themselves thorough masters of the philo- sophical grounds of those opinions of which it is desirable that all should be firmly *persuaded,* but which they alone can entirely and philosophically *know.* The remainder of mankind must, and, except in periods of transition like the present, always do, take the far greater part of their opinions on all extensive subjects upon the authority of those who have studied them.

It does not follow that all men are not to inquire and investigate. The only complaint is, that most of them are precluded by the nature of things from ever inquiring and investigating enough. It is right that they should acquaint them- selves with the evidence of the truths which are presented to them, to the utmost extent of each man's intellects, leisure, and inclination. Though a man may never be able to understand Laplace, that is no reason he should not read Euclid. But it by no means follows that Euclid is a blunderer, or an arrant knave, because a man who begins at the forty-seventh proposition cannot understand it: and even he who begins at the beginning, and is stopped by the *pons asinorum,* is very much in the wrong if he swears he will navigate his vessel himself, and not trust to the nonsensical calculations of mathematical land- lubbers. Let him learn what he can, and as well as he can—still however bearing in mind, that there are others who probably know much with which he not only is unacquainted, but of the evidence of which, in the existing state of his knowledge, it is impossible that he should be a competent judge.

It is no answer to what has just been observed, to say that the grounds of the most important moral and political truths are simple and obvious, intelligible to persons of the most limited faculties, with moderate study and attention; that all mankind, therefore, may master the evidences, and none need take the doctrines upon trust. The matter of fact upon which this objection proceeds, is happily true. The proofs of the moral and social truths of greatest importance to mankind, are few, brief, and easily intelligible; and happy will be the day on which these shall begin to be circulated among the people, instead of second- rate treatises on the Polarization of Light, and on the Rigidity of Cordage. But, in the first place, it is not every one—and there is no one at a very early period of life—who has had sufficient experience of mankind in general, and has sufficiently reflected upon what passes in his own mind, to be able to appreciate the force of the reasons when laid before him. There is, however, a great number of important truths, especially in Political Economy, to which, from the particular nature of the evidence on which they rest, this difficulty does not apply. The proofs of these truths may be brought down to the level of even the uninformed multitude, with the most complete success. But, when all is done, there still remains something which they must always and inevitably take upon trust: and this is, that the arguments really *are* as conclusive as they appear; that there exist no considerations relevant to the subject which have been kept back from them; that every objection which can suggest itself has been duly examined by competent judges, and found immaterial. It is easy to say that the truth of certain propositions is obvious to *common sense.* It may be so: but how am I assured that the conclusions of common sense are confirmed by accurate knowledge? Judging by common sense is merely another phrase for judging by first appearances; and every one who has mixed among mankind with any capacity for observing them, knows that the men who place implicit faith in their own common sense are, without any exception, the most wrong-headed, and impracticable persons with whom he has ever had to deal. The maxim of pursuing truth without being biassed by authority, does not state the question fairly; there is no person who does not prefer truth to authority—for authority is only appealed to as a voucher for truth. The real question, to be determined by each man's own judgment, is, whether most confidence is due in the particular case, to his own understanding, or to the opinion of his authority? It is therefore obvious, that there are some persons in whom disregard of authority is a virtue, and others in whom it is both an absurdity and a vice. The presumptuous man needs authority to restrain him from error: the modest man needs it to strengthen him in the right. What truths, for example, can be more obvious, or can rest upon considerations more simple and familiar, than the first principles of morality? Yet we know that extremely ingenious things may be said in opposition to the plainest of them—things which the most highly-instructed men, though never for a single moment misled by them, have had no small difficulty in satisfactorily answering. Is it to be imagined that if these sophisms had been referred to the verdict of the half-instructed—and we cannot expect the majority of every class to be any thing more—the solution of the fallacy would always have been found and understood? notwithstanding which, the fallacy would not, it is most probable, have made the slightest impression upon them:—and why? Because the judgment of the multitude would have told them, that their own judgment was not a decision in the last resort; because the conviction of their understandings going along with the moral truth, was sanctioned by the authority of the best-informed; and the objection, though insoluble by their own understandings, was not supported but contradicted by the same imposing authority. But if you once persuade an ignorant or a half-instructed person, that he ought to assert his liberty of thought, discard all authority, and—I do not say *use* his own judgment, for that he never can do too much—but *trust* solely to his own judgment, and receive or reject opinions according to his own views of the evidence;—if, in short, you teach to all the lesson of *indifferency,* so earnestly, and with such admirable effect, inculcated by Locke upon *students,* for whom alone that great man wrote, the merest trifle will suffice to unsettle and perplex their minds. There is not a truth in the whole range of human affairs, however obvious and simple, the evidence of which an ingenious and artful sophist may not succeed in rendering doubtful to minds not very highly cultivated, if those minds insist upon judging of all things exclusively by their own lights. The presumptuous man will dogmatize, and rush headlong into opinions, always shallow, and as often wrong as right; the man who sets only the just value upon his own moderate powers, will scarcely ever feel more than a half-conviction. You may prevail on them to repudiate the authority of the best-instructed, but each will full surely be a mere slave to the authority of the person next to him, who has greatest facilities for continually forcing upon his attention considerations favourable to the conclusion he himself wishes to be drawn.

It is, therefore, one of the necessary conditions of humanity, that the major-ity must either have wrong opinions, or no fixed opinions, or must place the degree of reliance warranted by reason, in the authority of those who have made moral and social philosophy their peculiar study. It is right that every man should attempt to understand his interest and his duty. It is right that he should follow his reason as far as his reason will carry him, and cultivate the faculty as highly as possible. But reason itself will teach most men that they must, in the last resort, fall back upon the authority of still more cultivated minds, as the ultimate sanction of the convictions of their reason itself.

But where is the authority which commands this confidence, or deserves it? Nowhere: and here we see the peculiar character, and at the same time the peculiar inconvenience, of a period of moral and social transition. At all other periods there exists a large body of received doctrine, covering nearly the whole field of the moral relations of man, and which no one thinks of questioning, backed as it is by the authority of all, or nearly all, persons, supposed to possess knowledge enough to qualify them for giving an opinion on the subject. This state of things does not now exist in the civilized world—except, indeed, to a certain limited extent in the United States of America. The progress of inquiry has brought to light the insufficiency of the ancient doctrines; but those who have made the investigation of social truths their occupation, have not yet sanctioned any new body of doctrine with their unanimous, or nearly unan-imous, consent. The true opinion is recommended to the public by no greater weight of authority than hundreds of false opinions; and, even at this day, to find any thing like a united body of grave and commanding authority, we must revert to the doctrines from which the progressiveness of the human mind, or, as it is more popularly called, the improvement of the age, has set us free.

In the mean time, as the old doctrines have gone out, and the new ones have not yet come in, every one must judge for himself as he best may. Learn, and think for yourself, is reasonable advice for the day: but let not the business of the day be so done as to prejudice the work of the morrow. "Les supériorités morales," to use the words of Fiévée, "finiront par s'entendre"; the first men of the age will one day join hands and be agreed: and then there is no power in itself, on earth or in hell, capable of withstanding them.

But ere this can happen there must be a change in the whole framework of society, as at present constituted. Worldly power must pass from the hands of the stationary part of mankind into those of the progressive part. There must be a moral and social revolution, which shall, indeed, take away no men's lives or property, but which shall leave to no man one fraction of unearned distinction or unearned importance.

That man cannot achieve his destiny but through such a transformation, and that it will and *shall* be effected, is the conclusion of every man who can *feel the wants of his own age,* without hankering after past ages. Those who may read these papers, and in particular the next succeeding one, will find there an attempt, how far successful others must judge, to set forth the grounds of this belief.

For mankind to change their institutions while their minds are unsettled, without fixed principles, and unable to trust either themselves or other people, is, indeed, a fearful thing. But a bad way is often the best, to get out of a bad position. Let us place our trust for the future, not in the wisdom of mankind, but in something far surer—the force of circumstances—which makes men see that, when it is near at hand, which they could not foresee when it was at a distance, and which so often and so unexpectedly makes the right course, in a moment of emergency, at once the easiest and the most obvious.

III

The affairs of mankind, or of any of those smaller political societies which we call nations, are always either in one or the other of two states, one of them in its nature durable, the other essentially transitory. The former of these we may term the *natural* state, the latter the *transitional.*

Society may be said to be in its *natural* state, when worldly power, and moral influence, are habitually and undisputedly exercised by the fittest persons whom the existing state of society affords. Or, to be more explicit; when on the one hand, the temporal, or, as the French would say, the *material* interests of the community, are managed by those of its members who possess the greatest capacity for such management; and on the other hand, those whose opinions the people follow, whose feelings they imbibe, and who practically and by common consent, perform, no matter under what original title, the office of thinking for the people, are persons better qualified than any others whom the civilization of the age and country affords, to think and judge rightly and usefully.

In these circumstances the people, although they may at times be unhappy and consequently discontented, habitually acquiesce in the laws and institutions which they live under, and seek for relief through those institutions and not in defiance of them. Individual ambition struggles to ascend by no other paths than those which the law recognizes and allows. The ruling powers have no immediate interest in counteracting the progress of civilization; society is either stationary, or moves onward solely in those directions in which its progress brings it into no collision with the established order of things.

Society may be said to be in its *transitional* state, when it contains other persons fitter for worldly power and moral influence than those who have hitherto enjoyed them: when worldly power, and the greatest existing capacity for worldly affairs, are no longer united but severed; and when the authority which sets the opinions and forms the feelings of those who are not accustomed to think for themselves, does not exist at all, or, existing, resides anywhere but in the most cultivated intellects, and the most exalted characters, of the age.

When this is the posture of affairs, society has either entered or is on the point of entering into a state in which there are no established doctrines; in which the world of opinions is a mere chaos; and in which, as to worldly affairs, whosoever is dissatisfied with any thing or for any reason, flies at once to an alteration in the conditions of worldly power, as a means for obtaining something which would remove what he deems the cause of his dissatisfaction. And this continues until a moral and social revolution (or it may be, a series of such) has replaced worldly power and moral influence in the hands of the most competent: when society is once more in its natural state, and resumes its onward progress, at the point where it was stopped before by the social system which it has shivered.

It is the object of the present paper, and of that by which it will be immediately followed, to demonstrate, that the changes in the visible structure of society which are manifestly approaching, and which so many anticipate with dread, and so many with hope of a nature far different from that which I feel, are the means by which we are to be carried through our present transitional state, and the human mind is to resume its quiet and regular onward course; a course as undisturbed by convulsions or anarchy, either in the political or in the moral world, as in the best times heretofore, but far more favoured than any former period in respect to the means of rapid advancement, and less impeded by the effect of counteracting forces.

To begin with the conditions of worldly power.

There are two states of society, differing in other respects, but agreeing in this, that worldly power is habitually exercised by the fittest men. One is, when the holders of power are purposely selected for their fitness. The other is, when the circumstances of society are such, that the possession of power of itself calls forth the qualifications for its exercise, in a greater degree than they can be acquired by any other persons in that state of society.

The former state was exemplified in the best constituted republics of antiquity, and is now realized in the United States of America: the latter prevailed throughout most of the nations of Europe in the middle ages.

In the best of the ancient republics all offices, political or military, which were supposed to require peculiar abilities, were conferred upon those who, in the opinion of the best judges, the educated gentlemen of the country (for such the free citizens of Athens, and, in its best times, of Rome, essentially were) possessed the greatest personal qualifications for administering the affairs of the state, and would administer them according to the best ideas of their age. With how much wisdom the choice was usually made, is evidenced in the case of Athens, by the extraordinary series of great men by whom the affairs of that little commonwealth were successively managed, and who made it the source of light and civilization to the world, and the most inspiring and elevating example which history has yet produced, of how much human nature is capable. In the case of Rome, the same fact is as certainly demonstrated, by the steady unintermitted progress of that community from the smallest beginnings to the highest prosperity and power.

In the United States, where those who are called to power, are so by the general voice of the whole people, experience equally testifies to the admirable good sense with which the highest offices have been bestowed. At every election of a President, without exception, the people's choice has fallen on the person whom, as all impartial observers must admit, every circumstance that the people knew, pointed out as the fittest; nor is it possible to name one person preeminently qualified for the office, who has not, if he was a candidate, obtained it. In the only two cases in which subsequent experience did not confirm the people's judgment, they corrected the error on the very first lawful opportunity.

But supposing that, in communities constituted like the United States, the holders of power were not really, as in fact they are, the most qualified persons; they are at least those whom the people imagine to be so. The people, consequently, are satisfied with their institutions, and with their rulers; and feel no disposition to lay the blame of their private ills upon the existing order of society, nor to seek the improvement of their circumstances by any means which are repugnant to that order.

In addition to these instances, where the management of the affairs of the community is in the fittest hands because those hands are deliberately selected and put in charge of it there is another class of cases, in which power is not assigned to him who is already the fittest, but has a strong tendency to render that person the fittest to whom it is assigned. The extreme case of this state of society is that of a Highland clan: and all other small societies of barbarous people are in the main similar. The chief of a clan is despotic, so far as custom and opinion and habit can render him so. He is not selected for any qualities of his, for his office is in all cases hereditary. But he is bred to it, and practised in it from his youth upwards; while every other member of the community is bred to, and practised in, something else, and has no opportunity of training himself to that. The position, moreover, of the society itself, does not admit of the chief's being utterly destitute of the necessary qualifications for leading the clan in battle, and guiding them in council. It is the condition of his existence and theirs, that he should be capable of maintaining himself in circumstances of considerable difficulty. As men generally contrive to acquire the faculties which they cannot possibly do without, the head of a clan is scarcely ever absolutely unfit for governing: the clansmen are fit for executing, and sometimes for advising, but seldom for commanding. The leader, therefore, is still the fittest, or at the least as fit as any one else: and the essential character of a natural state of society is realised, for the people have confidence in those who manage their affairs.

Between these two states of society, that in which capacity raises men to power, and that in which power calls forth their capacity, there is this important difference, that the former state does not contain in itself the seeds of its own dissolution. A society which is directed by its most capable members, wheresoever they are to be found, may doubtless come to an end, as is shown by many instances, but at least its dissolution is never the direct consequence of its own organization, since every new intellectual power which grows up, takes its natural place in the existing social order, and is not obliged to break it in pieces in order to make itself way. But when the possession of power is guaranteed to particular persons independently of their capacity, those persons may be the fittest to-day and the most incapable tomorrow: and these social arrangements are exposed to certain destruction, from every cause which raises up in the society itself, fitter persons for power than those who possess it. For although mankind, in all ages except those of transition, are ever ready to obey and love those whom they recognize as better able to govern them, than they are to govern themselves, it is not in human nature to yield a willing obedience to men whom you think no wiser than yourself, especially when you are told by those whom you do think wiser, that they would govern you in a different manner. Unless therefore this state of society be so constituted as to prevent altogether the progress of civilization, that progress always ultimately over-throws it—the tendency of civilization being on the one hand, to render some of those who are excluded from power, fitter and fitter for it, and on the other hand (in a way hereafter to be explained) to render the monopolizers of power, actually less fit for it than they were originally.

Now, the proposition which I am about to prove is, that the above is a correct account of the process which has been going on for a considerable length of time in modern Europe:—that the qualification for power has been, and is, anything rather than fitness for it, either real or presumed: that nevertheless the holders of power, for a long time, possessed, from the necessary circumstances of society, greater fitness for it than was possessed by any other persons at that time; which fitness they have for some time been losing while others through the advancement of civilization have been gaining it, until power, and fitness for power, have altogether ceased to correspond: and that this is one great cause, so far as political circumstances are concerned, of the general dissatisfaction with the present order of society, and the unsettled state of political opinion.

From the earliest periods of the nations of modern Europe, all worldly power has belonged to one particular class, the wealthy class. For many centuries the only wealth was land, and the only wealthy were the territorial aristocracy. At a later period, landed wealth ceased to be so greatly engrossed by a few noble families, and manufacturing and commercial wealth grew by little and little into large masses. Worldly power, under which expression I include all direct influence over the worldly affairs of the community, became proportionably diffused. It then belonged to two classes, but to them exclusively, the landed gentry, and the monied class; and in their hands it still remains.

For many ages these were felt by all to be the proper depositories of power, because they possessed, on the average, such qualifications for it as no other members of the community, in the then state of civilization, could rationally hope to acquire. It cannot, for example, be imagined that the villeins or serfs, or even the smaller freeholders, in those ages in which nothing was to be learnt from books, but all from practice and experience, could be so fit for commanding the nation in battle, or deliberating on its affairs in council, as those who had been taught to look to these as their appointed functions and occupations, who had been trained to fitness for them in every way which was suggested by the conceptions of those times, and who from constant practice, possessed at least the same kind of superiority in their business which an experienced workman possesses over one who has never handled a tool.

It is not pretended that the barons were in themselves very fit for power, or that they did not use it very ill; they did so, as history testifies, to a frightful extent: not that I agree in one-half of all that is said in their disparagement by many who, if cotemporary with them, would most probably have admired them, having no standard of approbation but the ideas of their own age. But those may be in themselves very unfit, than whom, nevertheless, an uncivilized age affords none fitter: and power, which is not accountable to those interested in its being properly employed, is likely to be abused, even though it be held by the most capable persons, not in a rude age only, but in the most highly civilized one. This is one of those principles which being true in all states and in all situations in which man has been found, or in which we can rationally expect to find him, must be allowed the paramount importance which is due to it, whatever be the state of society that we are considering. This may not always have been duly adverted to by the historical school of politicians (by whom, be it understood, I mean the really profound and philosophic inquirers into history in France and Germany, not the Plausibles, who in our own land of shallowness and charlatanerie, babble about induction without having ever considered what it is, relying on that rhetoric which is defined by Plato as the art of appearing profoundly versed in a subject to those who know nothing at all about it). I say, those who have endeavoured to erect an inductive philosophy of history, may be charged with having taken insufficient account of the qualities in which mankind in all ages and nations are alike, their attention being unduly engrossed by the differences; but there is an error on the other side, to which those are peculiarly liable, who build their philosophy of politics upon what they term the universal principles of human nature. Such persons often form their judgments, in particular cases, as if, because there are universal principles of human nature, they imagined that all are such which they find to be true universally of the people of their own age and country. They should consider that if there are some tendencies of human nature, and some of the circumstances by which man is surrounded, which are the same in all ages and countries, these never form the whole of the tendencies, or of the circumstances, which exist in any particular age or country: each possesses, along with those invariable tendencies, others which are changeable, and peculiarly its own; and in no age, as civilization advances, are the prevailing tendencies exactly the same as in the preceding age, nor do those tendencies act under precisely the same combination of external circumstances.

We must not therefore (as some may be apt to do,) blame the people of the middle ages for not having sought securities against the irresponsible power of their rulers; persuading ourselves that in those or in any times, popular institutions might exist, if the many had sense to perceive their utility, and spirit to demand them. To find fault with our ancestors for not having annual parliaments, universal suffrage, and vote by ballot, would be like quarrelling with the Greeks and Romans for not using steam navigation, when we know it is so safe and expeditious; which would be, in short, simply finding fault with the third century before Christ for not being the eighteenth century after. It was necessary that many other things should be thought and done, before, according to the laws of human affairs, it was possible that steam navigation should be thought of. Human nature must proceed step by step, in politics as well as in physics. The people of the middle ages knew very well, whether they were oppressed or not; and the opinion of the many, added to the fear of vengeance from some injured individual, acted in a certain, though doubtless by no means a sufficient, extent, as a restraint upon oppression. For any more effectual restraint than this, society was not yet ripe. To have thrown off their masters, and taken others, would have been to buy a still worse government at the price of a convulsion: to contrive, establish, and work the machine of a responsible government, was an impossibility in the then state of the human mind. Though the idea had been conceived, it could not have been realized. Several antecedent stages in civilization had previously to be passed through. An insurrection of the peasants against their feudal lords, could, in the nature of things, have only been, what it actually was, a Jacquerie: for any more rational effort there was needed a power of self-restraint for the purpose of union, and a confidence in each other, which they are not to be blamed for not having, since it could only be the slow result of a habit of acting in concert for other purposes, which, in an extensive country, can only co-exist with a high state of civilization. So soon as any portion of the people did acquire this habit of acting together, they did seek better political securities, and obtained them: witness the rise of the free cities, and corporations, all over Europe. The people therefore of the middle ages had as good a government as the circumstances of the middle ages admitted; their affairs were less badly managed, in that bad age, by their masters, than they could have managed them for themselves. The army of Godefroi de Bouillon in the first crusade, was not quite so efficient an instrument of warfare as that of the Duke of Wellington, in 1815: but it was considerably more so than that of Peter the Hermit, which preceded it.

From these remarks it will be seen how greatly I differ, at once from those, who seeing the institutions of our ancestors to be bad for us, imagine that they were bad for those for whom they were made, and from those who ridiculously invoke the wisdom of our ancestors as authority for institutions which in substance are now totally different, howsoever they may be the same in form. The institutions of our ancestors served passably well for our ancestors, and that from no wisdom of theirs; but from a cause to which, I am afraid, nearly all the good institutions which have ever existed, owed their origin, namely the force of circumstances: but the possessors of power in the present day are not the natural successors of the possessors of power in that day. They may show a valid title to inherit the property, perhaps, of the ancient Barons; but political power descends, as will be found in the long run, by a different law.

It is not necessary for me to point out that until a comparatively recent period, none but the wealthy, and even, I might say, the hereditarily wealthy, had it in their power to acquire the intelligence, the knowledge, and the habits, which are necessary to qualify a man, in any tolerable degree, for managing the affairs of his country. It is not necessary for me to show that this is no longer the case, nor what are the circumstances which have changed it: the improvement in the arts of life, giving ease and comfort to great numbers not possessed of the degree of wealth which confers political power: the increase of reading: the diffusion of elementary education: the increase of the town-population, which brings masses of men together, and accustoms them to examine and discuss important subjects with one another; and various other causes, which are known to every body. All this, however, is nothing more than the acquisition by other people in an inferior degree, of a few of the advantages which have always been within the reach of the higher classes, in a much greater degree: and if the higher classes had profited as they might have done by these advantages, and had kept their station in the vanguard of the march of improvement, they would not only at this moment have been sure to retain in their hands all the powers of government, subject perhaps to severer conditions of responsibility, but might possibly even have continued for a considerable time longer to retain them on the same footing as at present. For ample experience has proved that mankind (who, however prone they may be, in periods of transition, to even groundless suspicion and distrust, are as strongly addicted at all other times to the opposite extreme of blind and boundless confidence), will bear even great excesses of abused power, from those whom they recognize as fitter to hold the reins of government than themselves.

But the higher classes, instead of advancing, have retrograded in all the higher qualities of mind. In the humanizing effects of civilization they have indeed partaken, and, to some extent, in the diffusion of superficial knowledge, and are so far superior to their predecessors: but those predecessors were braced and nerved by the invigorating atmosphere of a barbarous age, and had all the virtues of a strong will and an energetic active mind, which their descendants are destitute of. For these qualities were not the fruits of an enlightened education skilfully pointed to that end, but of the peculiar position of the holders of power; and that position is no longer the same.

All is not absolutely unfounded in the notion we imbibe at school, from the modern writers on the decline of the ancient commonwealths, that luxury deadens and enervates the mind. It is true that these writers (whose opinion, truly, was the result of no process of thought in their own imitative souls, but a faint impression left by a ray of the stoic philosophy of Greece and Rome themselves, refracted or bent out of its direction by the muddy medium through which it had passed) were wrong in laying it down as a principle that pleasure enervates; as if pleasure, only to be earned by labour and won by heroic deeds, ever did or ever could enervate the mind of any one. What really enervates, is the secure and unquestioned possession, without any exertion, of all those things, to gain which, mankind in general are wont to exert themselves. This secure and lazy possession, the higher classes have now for some generations enjoyed; their predecessors in the same station and privileges did not enjoy it.

Who, for example, that looks over the catalogue of the Kings who have reigned in Europe for the last two centuries, would not conclude, from that and the nature of the case combined, that the station of a hereditary king was the very most unfavourable to be found in this sublunary world, for the acquisition of any talents for governing? Is not the incapacity of the monarch allowed for, as an inevitable inconvenience, even by the most strenuous supporters of monarchy; represented at best as an evil susceptible of palliation, and preventing other evils far more fatal? From the beginning of the eighteenth century it has passed into a philosophic truism, that kings are generally unfit to govern, and likely even to delegate their power not to statesmen, but to favourites, unless forced to choose those Ministers whom the public voice recommends to them. Yet this maxim is far from being borne out by history. A decided majority of all the kings of England previous to the Revolution, will be found to have been men who, in every endowment belonging to their age, might be compared to the best men in it. The same may be said of the Emperors of Germany, and even of the Kings of France, of Spain, the Dukes of Burgundy, and so on. Would you know why? Think of Edward the Second and Richard the Second. In that turbulent age, no rank or station rendered the situation of a man without considerable personal endowments, a secure one. If the king possessed eminent talents, he might be nearly absolute: if he was a slave to ease and dissipation, not only his importance was absolutely null, but his throne and his life itself were constantly in danger. The Barons stood no less in need of mental energy and ability. Power, though not earned by capacity, might be greatly increased by it, and could not be retained or enjoyed without it. The possessor of power was not in the situation of one who is rewarded without exertion, but of one who feels a great prize within his grasp, and is stimulated to every effort necessary to make it securely his own.

But the virtues which insecurity calls forth, ceased with insecurity itself. In a civilized age, though it may be difficult to *get,* it is very easy to *keep:* if a man does not earn what he gets before he gets it, he has little motive to earn it thereafter. The greater the power a man has upon these terms, the less he is likely to deserve it. Accordingly, as Mr. Hallam has remarked, Great Britain has had since WILLIAM III. no monarch of more than ordinary personal endowments; nor will she ever more, unless the chapter of accidents should open at a page inscribed with very singular characters. We may add, that the House of Peers has produced, since the same epoch, hardly any remarkable men; though some such have, from time to time, been aggregated to the order. As soon as these facts became manifest, it was easy to see a termination to hereditary monarchy and hereditary aristocracy: for we never shall again return to the age of violence and insecurity, when men were forced, whatever might be their taste for incapacity, to become men of talents in spite of themselves: and mankind will not always consent to allow a fat elderly gentleman to fill the first place, without insisting upon his doing something to deserve it. I do not undertake to say in what particular year hereditary distinctions will be abolished, nor do I say that I would vote for their abolition, if it were proposed now, in the existing state of society and opinion: but to the philosopher, who contemplates the past and future fortunes of mankind as one series, and who counts a generation or two for no more in marking the changes of the moral, than an age or two in those of the physical world, the ultimate fate of such distinctions is already decided.

There was an intermediate stage in the history of our own island, in which it was yet a question whether the Crown should share in the government of the country as the master of the aristocracy, or only as the first and most powerful of its members. Though the progress of civilization had given to the gentry of England, personal security independently of honourable exertion, it had not yet given them undisputed power. They were nothing, except through the Parliament, and the Parliament as yet, was nothing, except through their energy and talents. The great names by which the seventeenth century of English history has been immortalized, belonged almost without an exception to the same class which now possesses the governing power. What a contrast! Think, good heavens! that Sir John Elliot, and John Hampden, and Sir John Colepepper, and Sir Thomas Wentworth, were *country gentlemen*—and think who are the parliamentary leaders of that class in our own day: a Knatchbull, a Bankes, a Gooch, a Lethbridge! Think even of the most respectable names among the English landholders of our time, such as Lord Wharncliffe, or Mr. Coke. The remainder of the great politicians of that age, the Bacons, the Cecils, the Walsinghams, the Seldens, the Iretons, the Pyms, the Cokes, were mostly lawyers. But what lawyers, and how strikingly distinguished, as well by their origin as by the range of their faculties and acquirements, from our successful Barristers, our Sugdens and Copleys! They were almost to a man, the younger or even the elder sons of the first families among the English gentry: who studied the law as being what it then in some degree was, a liberal profession, a pursuit fit for a gentleman, and not for a mere drudge; exercising at least the higher faculties, by the comprehension of principles, (though frequently absurd ones), not the mere memory, by the heaping together of unconnected details: and who studied it chiefly that it might serve them in fulfilling the exalted mission, to which they were called by an ambition justly to be called noble, since it required of them great sacrifices, and could be gratified only by the accomplishment of what was then nearest to their country's weal.

Applied to these men, the expression, natural leaders of the people, has some meaning: and then and then only it was that our institutions worked well, for they made this country the nurse of more that is exalted in sentiment, and expansive and profound in thought, than has been produced by all other countries in the modern world taken together, until a recent period. The whole of their effect is now the direct contrary—to degrade our morals, and to narrow and blunt our understandings: nor shall we ever be what we might be, nor even what we once were, until our institutions are adapted to the present state of civilization, and made compatible with the future progress of the human mind. But this will, I trust, more clearly appear, when, in the next paper, the historical survey which I have here taken of the conditions of worldly power, shall also have been taken of the conditions of moral influence.

IV

It has been stated, in the preceding paper, that the conditions which confer worldly power are still, amidst all changes of circumstances, the same as in the middle ages—namely, the possession of wealth, or the being employed and trusted by the wealthy. In the middle ages, this form of government might have been approved, even by a philosopher, if a philosopher had been possible in those ages: not, surely, for its intrinsic excellence; not because mankind enjoyed, or could have enjoyed, the blessings of good government under it: but there are states of society in which we must not seek for a good government, but for the least bad one. It is part of the inevitable lot of mankind, that when they themselves are in a backward state of civilization, they are unsusceptible of being well governed.

But, now, mankind are capable of being better governed than the wealthy classes have ever heretofore governed them: while those classes, instead of having improved, have actually retrograded in capacity for government. The abuses of their power have not diminished, though now showing themselves no otherwise than in forms compatible with the mildness of modern manners, and being of that kind which provokes contempt, mingled with resentment, rather than terror and hatred, as of yore.

Such of the above propositions as required illustration appearing to have sufficiently received it in the foregoing paper, I proceed to take a similar survey of the changes which mankind have undergone in respect to the conditions on which moral influence, or power over the minds of mankind, is dependent.

These are three distinguishable sources of moral influence:—eminent wisdom and virtue, real or supposed; the power of addressing mankind in the name of religion; and, finally, worldly power.

It is not necessary to illustrate the manner in which superiority of wisdom and virtue, or in which religion, pre-engages men's minds with the opinions and feelings in favour of which those authorities declare themselves. It is equally superfluous to insist upon the influence exercised over the minds of men by worldly power. The tendency of the human mind to the worship of power, is well understood. It is matter of common complaint, that even the Supreme Being is adored by an immense majority as the Almighty, not as the All-good; as he who can destroy, not as he who has blessed. It is a familiar fact, that the vulgar, in all parts of the world, have in general little or no rule of conduct or of opinion, but to do as their betters do, and to think as their betters think: and this very word *betters,* is a speaking proof of the fact which we allege—meaning, as it does, not their *wisers,* or their *honesters,* but their *richers,* and those placed in authority over them.

All persons, from the most ignorant to the most instructed, from the most stupid to the most intelligent, have their minds more or less under the dominion of one or other, or all, of the influences which have just been mentioned. All bow down, with a submission more or less implicit, to the authority of superior minds, or of the interpreters of the divine will, or of their superiors in rank and station.

When an opinion is sanctioned by all these authorities, or by any one of them, the others not opposing, it becomes the received opinion. At all periods of history in which there has existed a general agreement among these three authorities, there have existed *received doctrines:* a phrase the sense of which is now almost forgotten. The most marked character of such periods is a firm confidence in inherited opinions. Men cleave with a strong and fervent faith to the doctrine which they have imbibed from their infancy: though in conduct they be tempted to swerve from it, the belief remains in their hearts, fixed and immoveable, and has an irresistible hold upon the consciences of all good men. When, on the contrary, the three authorities are divided among themselves, or against each other, a violent conflict rages among opposing doctrines, until one or other prevails, or until mankind settle down into a state of general uncertainty and scepticism. At present, we are in a mixed state; some fight fiercely under their several banners, and these chiefly the least instructed; while the others (those few excepted who have strength to stand by themselves) are blown about by every breath, having no steady opinion—or at least no deep-rooted conviction that their opinion is true.

Society, therefore, has its natural state, and its transitional state, with respect to moral influence as well as to worldly power. Let us bestow a few words upon the natural state, and upon the nature of those varieties of the social order in which it has hitherto been realized.

It is in states of society in which the holders of power are chosen by the people (or by the most highly civilized portion of the people) for their supposed fitness, that we should most expect to find the three authorities acting together, and giving their sanction to the same doctrines. As men are raised to worldly power for their supposed wisdom and virtue, two of the three sources of moral influence are united in the same individuals. And although the rulers of such societies, being the creatures of the people's choice, have not, *qua* rulers, that ascendancy over the minds of the people, which power obtained and held independently of their will, commonly possesses; nevertheless, the station to which they are elevated gives them greater opportunities of rendering their wisdom and their virtue visible, while it also fixes the outward stamp of general recognition upon that merit, which would otherwise operate upon each mind only in proportion to its confidence in its own power of discriminating the most worthy.

Accordingly, in the best-constituted commonwealths of the ancient world, this unity of moral influence did to a very great degree exist. And in the great popular government of our own times, it exists with respect to the general doctrines of the constitution, and many maxims of national policy, and the list of received doctrines is increasing as rapidly as the differences of opinion among the persons possessing moral influence will allow.

[. . .]

V

[. . .]

For many centuries, undivided moral influence over the nations of Europe, the unquestioned privilege of forming the opinions and feelings of the Christian world, was enjoyed, and most efficiently exercised by the Catholic clergy. Their word inspired in the rest of mankind the most fervent faith. It not only absolutely excluded doubt, but caused the doubter to be regarded with sentiments of profound abhorrence, which moralists had never succeeded in inspiring for the most revolting of crimes. It is certainly possible to feel perfectly sure of an opinion, without believing that whosoever doubts it will be damned, and should be burnt: and this last is by no means one of those peculiarities of a natural state of society which I am at all anxious to see restored. But the deep earnest feeling of firm and unwavering conviction, which, it pre-supposes, we may, without being unreasonable, lament that it was impossible, and could not *but* be impossible, in the intellectual anarchy of a general revolution in opinion, to transfer unimpaired to the truth.

The priesthood did not claim a right to dictate to mankind, either in belief or practice, beyond the province of religion and morals, but the political interests of mankind came not the less within their pale, because they seldom assumed the authority to regulate those concerns by specific precepts. They gave the sanction of their irresistible authority to one comprehensive rule, that which enjoined unlimited obedience to the temporal sovereign: an obligation from which they absolved the conscience of the believer, only when the sovereign disputed their authority within their peculiar province: and in that case they were invariably triumphant, like all those to whom it is given to call forth the moral sentiments of mankind in all their energy, against the inducements of mere physical hopes and fears.

The Catholic clergy, at the time when they possessed this undisputed authority in matters of conscience and belief, were, in point of fact, the fittest persons who *could* have possessed it—the then state of society, in respect of moral influence, answers to the description of a *natural* state.

Now, when we consider for how long a period the Catholic clergy were the only members of the European community who could even read; that they were the sole depositaries of all the treasures of thought, and reservoirs of intellectual delight, handed down to us from the ancients; that the sanctity of their persons permitted to them alone, among nations of semibarbarians, the tranquil pursuit of peaceful occupations and studies; that, howsoever defective the morality which they taught, they had at least a mission for curbing the unruly passions of mankind, and teaching them to set a value upon a distant end, paramount to immediate temptations, and to prize gratifications consisting of mental feelings above bodily sensation; that, situate in the position of the rivals to the temporal sovereign, drafted chiefly from the inferior classes of society, from men who otherwise would have been serfs, and the most lowly among them all having the road open before him, even to the papal chair, they had the strongest motives to avail themselves of the means afforded by Christianity, for inculcating the natural equality of mankind, the superiority of love and sacrifice above mere courage and bodily prowess, of menacing the great with the only terrors to which they were accessible, and speaking to their consciences in the name of the only superior whom they acknowledged, in behalf of the low. Reflecting on these things, I cannot persuade myself to doubt that the ascendancy of the Catholic clergy was to be desired, for that day, even by the philosopher; and that it has been a potent cause, if even it was not an indispensable condition, of the present civilization of Europe. Nor is this an apology for the vices of the Catholic religion: those vices were great and flagrant, and there was no natural connection between them; and the more civilizing and humanizing features in which all that there was of good in it resided. We may regret that the influence of the priesthood was not super-seded by a better influence: but when in those days did any such influence exist?

I conclude, therefore, that, during a part of the middle ages, not only worldly power, as already shown, but moral influence also, was indisputedly exercised by the most competent persons; and that the conditions of a natural state of society were then fully realized.

But the age of transition arrived. A time came when that which had over-matched and borne down the strongest obstacles to improvement, became itself incompatible with improvement. Mankind outgrew their religion, and that, too, at a period when they had not yet outgrown their government, because the texture of the latter was more yielding, and could be stretched. We all know how lamentably effectual an instrument the influence of the Catholic priesthood then became, for restraining that expansion of the human intellect, which could not any longer consist with their ascendancy, or with the belief of the doctrines which they taught.

The more advanced communities of Europe succeeded, after a terrific strug-gle, in effecting their total or partial emancipation: in some, the Reformation achieved a victory—in others, a toleration; while, by a fate unhappily too common, the flame which had been kindled where the pile awaited the spark, spread into countries where the materials were not yet sufficiently prepared; and instead of burning down the hateful edifice, it consumed all that existed capable of nourishing itself, and was extinguished. The germs of civilization to come were scorched up and destroyed; the hierarchy reigned stronger than ever, amidst the intellectual solitude which it had made: and the countries which were thus denuded of the means of further advancement, fell back into barbarism irretrievable—except by foreign conquest. Such is the inevitable end, when, unhappily, changes to which the spirit of the age is favourable, can be successfully resisted. Civilization becomes the terror of the ruling powers, and that they may retain their seat, it must be their deliberate endeavour to barbar-ize mankind. There has been, since that day, one such attempt, and only one, which has had a momentary success: it was that of a man in whom all the evil influences of his age were concentered with an intensity and energy truly terrific, less tempered by any of its good influences than could appear possible in the times in which he lived—I need scarcely say that I refer to Napoleon.

May his abortive effort to uncivilize human nature, to uncultivate the mind of man, and turn it into a desolate waste, be the last!

[. . .]

I have already adverted to the decline of the higher classes in active talent, as they became enervated by lazy enjoyment. In the same ratio in which they have advanced in humanity and refinement, they have fallen off in energy of intellect and strength of will. Many of them were formerly versed in business: and into the hands of such, the remainder committed the management of the nation's affairs. Now, the men of hereditary wealth are mostly inexperienced in business, and unfit for it. Many of them formerly knew life and the world: but their knowledge of life is now little more than the knowledge of two or three hundred families, with whom they are accustomed to associate; and it may be safely asserted, that not even a fellow of a college is more ignorant of the world, or more grossly mistakes the signs of the times, than an English nobleman. Their very opinions,—which, before they had passed into aphorisms, were the result of choice, and something like an act of the intelligence,—are now merely hereditary. Their minds were once active—they are now passive: they once generated impressions—they now merely take them. What are now their political maxims? Traditional texts, relating, directly or indirectly, to the privileges of their order, and to the exclusive fitness of men of their own sort for governing. What is their public virtue? Attachment to these texts, and to the prosperity and grandeur of England, on condition that she shall never swerve from them; idolatry of certain abstractions, called church constitution, agriculture, trade, and others: by dint of which they have gradually contrived, in a manner, to exclude from their minds the very idea of their living and breathing fellow-citizens, as the subjects of moral obligation in their capacity of rulers. They love their country as Bonaparte loved his army—for whose glory he felt the most ardent zeal, at a time when all the men who composed it, one with another, were killed off every two or three years. They do not love England as one loves human beings, but as a man loves his house or his acres.

Being such persons as has now been described, and being at last completely found out by the more intelligent, they no longer retain sufficient moral influence to give, as heretofore, vogue and currency to their opinions. But they retain—and the possessors of worldly power must always retain—enough of that influence, to prevent any opinions, which they do not acknowledge, from passing into received doctrines. They must, therefore, be divested of the monopoly of worldly power, ere the most virtuous and best-instructed of the nation will acquire that ascendancy over the opinions and feelings of the rest, by which alone England can emerge from this crisis of transition, and enter once again into a natural state of society.

[. . .]

T. B. MACAULAY (1800–59)

Civil Disabilities of the Jews (1831)

*T*his essay is an expanded version of a speech—his maiden speech—Macaulay delivered in Parliament the preceding year. It is remarkable that he chose this issue, a protest against the exclusion of Jews from Parliament, as his subject on this memorable occasion, rather than the larger issue of parliamentary reform, which had already been raised and might have made for a more dramatic entry into the House. (In fact, his speeches on the Reform Bill in 1832 immediately established him as an important figure in the House and a great parliamentary orator.) Macaulay continued to speak in favor of later bills supporting the admission of Jews to Parliament, to no avail. When Lord Russell, in 1853, asked him to propose a resolution to that effect, he refused, objecting that only a bill would do. "I really cannot consent," he told Russell, "to perform a rhetorical exercise on the subject of religious liberty for the amusement of the ladies."[1] Five years later, a bill admitting Jews was finally passed, but by then Macaulay had retired from Parliament.

Long before that, however, Jews had been admitted to municipal office, and a Jew became Lord Mayor of London three years before he could have sat in Parliament. On July 16, 1858, Lionel de Rothschild took the oath "So help me, Jehovah" (in place of "on the truth faith of a Christian") that permitted him to take his seat as the first Jewish member of Parliament.

T. B. Macaulay (1800–59), "Civil Disabilities of the Jews," *Edinburgh Review,* January 1831. Reprinted in *The Works of Lord Macaulay* (London, 1898), VIII, 1–17.

1. Macaulay to Russell, June 19, 1853, in the Rothschild Archives.

T he distinguished member of the House of Commons who, towards the close of the late Parliament, brought forward a proposition for the relief of the Jews, has given notice of his intention to renew it. The force of reason, in the last session, carried the measure through one stage, in spite of the opposition of power. Reason and power are now on the same side; and we have little doubt that they will conjointly achieve a decisive victory. In order to contribute our share to the success of just principles, we propose to pass in review, as rapidly as possible, some of the arguments, or phrases claiming to be arguments, which have been employed to vindicate a system full of absurdity and injustice.

The constitution, it is said, is essentially Christian; and therefore to admit Jews to office is to destroy the constitution. Nor is the Jew injured by being excluded from political power. For no man has any right to power. A man has a right to his property; a man has a right to be protected from personal injury. These rights the law allows to the Jew; and with these rights it would be atrocious to interfere. But it is a mere matter of favour to admit any man to political power; and no man can justly complain that he is shut out from it.

We cannot but admire the ingenuity of this contrivance for shifting the burden of the proof from those to whom it properly belongs, and who would, we suspect, find it rather cumbersome. Surely no Christian can deny that every human being has a right to be allowed every gratification which produces no harm to others, and to be spared every mortification which produces no good to others. Is it not a source of mortification to a class of men that they are excluded from political power? If it be, they have, on Christian principles, a right to be freed from that mortification, unless it can be shown that their exclusion is necessary for the averting of some greater evil. The presumption is evidently in favour of toleration. It is for the prosecutor to make out his case.

The strange argument which we are considering would prove too much even for those who advance it. If no man has a right to political power, then neither Jew nor Gentile has such a right. The whole foundation of government is taken away. But if government be taken away, the property and the persons of men are insecure; and it is acknowledged that men have a right to their property and to personal security. If it be right that the property of men should be protected, and if this can only be done by means of government, then it must be right that government should exist. Now there cannot be government unless some person or persons possess political power. Therefore it is right that some person or persons should possess political power. That is to say, some person or persons must have a right to political power.

It is because men are not in the habit of considering what the end of government is, that Catholic disabilities and Jewish disabilities have been suffered to exist so long. We hear of essentially Protestant governments and essentially Christian governments, words which mean just as much as essentially Protestant cookery, or essentially Christian horsemanship. Government exists for the purpose of keeping the peace, for the purpose of compelling us to settle our disputes by arbitration instead of settling them by blows, for the purpose of compelling us to supply our wants by industry instead of supplying them by rapine. This is the only operation for which the machinery of government is peculiarly adapted, the only operation which wise governments ever propose to themselves as their chief object. If there is any class of people who are not interested, or who do not think themselves interested, in the security of property and the maintenance of order, that class ought to have no share of the powers which exist for the purpose of securing property and maintaining order. But why a man should be less fit to exercise those powers because he wears a beard, because he does not eat ham, because he goes to the synagogue on Saturdays instead of going to the church on Sundays, we cannot conceive.

The points of difference between Christianity and Judaism have very much to do with a man's fitness to be a bishop or a rabbi. But they have no more to do with his fitness to be a magistrate, a legislator, or a minister of finance, than with his fitness to be a cobbler. Nobody has ever thought of compelling cobblers to make any declaration on the true faith of a Christian. Any man would rather have his shoes mended by a heretical cobbler than by a person who had subscribed all the thirty-nine articles, but had never handled an awl. Men act thus, not because they are indifferent to religion, but because they do not see what religion has to do with the mending of their shoes. Yet religion has as much to do with the mending of shoes as with the budget and the army estimates. We have surely had several signal proofs within the last twenty years that a very good Christian may be a very bad Chancellor of the Exchequer. But it would be monstrous, say the persecutors, that Jews should legislate for a Christian community. This is a palpable misrepresentation. What is proposed is, not that the Jews should legislate for a Christian community, but that a legislature composed of Christians and Jews should legislate for a community composed of Christians and Jews. On nine hundred and ninety-nine questions out of a thousand, on all questions of police, of finance, of civil and criminal law, of foreign policy, the Jew, as a Jew, has no interest hostile to that of the Christian, or even to that of the Churchman. On questions relating to the ecclesiastical establishment, the Jew and the Churchman may differ. But they cannot differ more widely than the Catholic and the Churchman, or the Independent and the Churchman. The principle that Churchmen ought to monopolise the whole power of the state would at least have an intelligible meaning. The principle that Christians ought to monopolise it has no meaning at all. For no question connected with the ecclesiastical institutions of the country can possibly come before Parliament, with respect to which there will not be as wide a difference between Christians as there can be between any Christian and any Jew.

In fact, the Jews are not now excluded from political power. They possess it; and as long as they are allowed to accumulate large fortunes, they must possess it. The distinction which is sometimes made between civil privileges and political power is a distinction without a difference. Privileges are power. Civil and political are synonymous words, the one derived from the Latin, the other from the Greek. Nor is this mere verbal quibbling. If we look for a moment at the facts of the case, we shall see that the things are inseparable, or rather identical.

That a Jew should be a judge in a Christian country would be most shocking. But he may be a juryman. He may try issues of fact; and no harm is done. But if he should be suffered to try issues of law, there is an end of the constitution. He may sit in a box plainly dressed, and return verdicts. But that he should sit on the bench in a black gown and white wig, and grant new trials, would be an abomination not to be thought of among baptised people. The distinction is certainly most philosophical.

What power in civilised society is so great as that of the creditor over the debtor? If we take this away from the Jew, we take away from him the security of his property. If we leave it to him, we leave to him a power more despotic by far than that of the king and all his cabinet.

It would be impious to let a Jew sit in Parliament. But a Jew may make money; and money may make members of Parliament. Gattan and Old Sarum may be the property of a Hebrew. An elector of Penryn will take ten pounds from Shylock rather than nine pounds nineteen shillings and eleven pence three farthings from Antonio. To this no objection is made. That a Jew should possess the substance of legislative power, that he should command eight votes on every division as if he were the great Duke of Newcastle himself, is exactly as it should be. But that he should pass the bar and sit down on those mysterious cushions of green leather, that he should cry "hear" and "order," and talk about being on his legs, and being, for one, free to say this and to say that, would be a profanation sufficient to bring ruin on the country.

That a Jew should be privy-councillor to a Christian king would be an eternal disgrace to the nation. But the Jew may govern the money-market, and the money-market may govern the world. The minister may be in doubt as to his scheme of finance till he has been closeted with the Jew. A congress of sovereigns may be forced to summon the Jew to their assistance. The scrawl of the Jew on the back of a piece of paper may be worth more than the royal word of three kings, or the national faith of three new American republics. But that he should put Right Honourable before his name would be the most frightful of national calamities.

It was in this way that some of our politicians reasoned about the Irish Catholics. The Catholics ought to have no political power. The sun of England is set for ever if the Catholics exercise political power. Give the Catholics every thing else; but keep political power from them. These wise men did not see that when every thing else had been given, political power had been given. They continued to repeat their cuckoo song, when it was no longer a question whether Catholics should have political power or not, when a Catholic Association bearded the Parliament, when a Catholic Agitator exercised infinitely more authority than the Lord Lieutenant.

If it is our duty as Christians to exclude the Jews from political power, it must be our duty to treat them as our ancestors treated them, to murder them, and banish them, and rob them. For in that way, and in that way alone, can we really deprive them of political power. If we do not adopt this course, we may take away the shadow, but we must leave them the substance. We may do enough to pain and irritate them; but we shall not do enough to secure ourselves from danger, if danger really exists. Where wealth is, there power must inevitably be.

The English Jews, we are told, are not Englishmen. They are a separate people, living locally in this island, but living morally and politically in communion with their brethren who are scattered over all the world. An English Jew looks on a Dutch or a Portuguese Jew as his countryman, and on an English Christian as a stranger. This want of patriotic feeling, it is said, renders a Jew unfit to exercise political functions.

The argument has in it something plausible; but a close examination shows it to be quite unsound. Even if the alleged facts are admitted, still the Jews are not the only people who have preferred their sect to their country. The feeling of patriotism, when society is in a healthful state, springs up, by a natural and inevitable association, in the minds of citizens who know that they owe all their comforts and pleasures to the bond which unites them in one community. But, under a partial and oppressive government, these associations cannot acquire that strength which they have in a better state of things. Men are compelled to seek from their party that protection which they ought to receive from their country, and they, by a natural consequence, transfer to their party that affection which they would otherwise have felt for their country. The Huguenots of France called in the help of England against their Catholic Kings. The Catholics of France called in the help of Spain against a Huguenot King. Would it be fair to infer, that at present the French Protestants would wish to see their religion made dominant by the help of a Prussian or English army? Surely not. And why is it that they are not willing, as they formerly were willing, to sacrifice the interests of their country to the interests of their religious persuasion? The reason is obvious: they were persecuted then, and are not persecuted now. The English Puritans, under Charles the First, prevailed on the Scotch to invade England. Do the Protestant Dissenters of our time wish to see the Church put down by an invasion of foreign Calvinists? If not, to what cause are we to attribute the change? Surely to this, that the Protestant Dissenters are far better treated now than in the seventeenth century. Some of the most illustrious public men that England ever produced were inclined to take refuge from the tyranny of Laud in North America. Was this because Presbyterians and Independents are incapable of loving their country? But it is idle to multiply instances. Nothing is so offensive to a man who knows any thing of history or of human nature as to hear those who exercise the powers of government accuse any sect of foreign attachments. If there be any proposition universally true in politics it is this, that foreign attachments are the fruit of domestic misrule. It has always been the trick of bigots to make their subjects miserable at home, and then to complain that they look for relief abroad; to divide society, and to wonder that it is not united; to govern as if a section of the state were the whole, and to censure the other sections of the state for their want of patriotic spirit. If the Jews have not felt towards England like children, it is because she has treated them like a step-mother. There is no feeling which more certainly developes itself in the minds of men living under tolerably good government than the feeling of patriotism. Since the beginning of the world, there never was any nation, or any large portion of any nation, not cruelly oppressed, which was wholly destitute of that feeling. To make it therefore ground of accusation against a class of men, that they are not patriotic, is the most vulgar legerdemain of sophistry. It is the logic which the wolf employs against the lamb. It is to accuse the mouth of the stream of poisoning the source.

If the English Jews really felt a deadly hatred to England, if the weekly prayer of their synagogues were that all the curses denounced by Ezekiel on Tyre and Egypt might fall on London, if, in their solemn feasts, they called down blessings on those who should dash our children to pieces on the stones, still, we say, their hatred to their countrymen would not be more intense than that which sects of Christians have often borne to each other. But in fact the feeling of the Jews is not such. It is precisely what, in the situation in which they are placed, we should expect it to be. They are treated far better than the French Protestants were treated in the sixteenth and seventeenth centuries, or than our Puritans were treated in the time of Laud. They, therefore, have no rancour against the government or against their countrymen. It will not be denied that they are far better affected to the state than the followers of Coligni or Vane. But they are not so well treated as the dissenting sects of Christians are now treated in England; and on this account, and, we firmly believe, on this account alone, they have a more exclusive spirit. Till we have carried the experiment farther, we are not entitled to conclude that they cannot be made Englishmen altogether. The statesman who treats them as aliens, and then abuses them for not entertaining all the feelings of natives, is as unreasonable as the tyrant who punished their fathers for not making bricks without straw.

Rulers must not be suffered thus to absolve themselves of their solemn responsibility. It does not lie in their mouths to say that a sect is not patriotic. It is their business to make it patriotic. History and reason clearly indicate the means. The English Jews are, as far as we can see, precisely what our government has made them. They are precisely what any sect, what any class of men, treated as they have been treated, would have been. If all the red-haired people in Europe had, during centuries, been outraged and oppressed, banished from this place, imprisoned in that, deprived of their money, deprived of their teeth, convicted of the most improbable crimes on the feeblest evidence, dragged at horses' tails, hanged, tortured, burned alive, if, when manners became milder, they had still been subject to debasing restrictions and exposed to vulgar insults, locked up in particular streets in some countries, pelted and ducked by the rabble in others, excluded everywhere from magistracies and honours, what would be the patriotism of gentlemen with red hair? And if, under such circumstances, a proposition were made for admitting red-haired men to office, how striking a speech might an eloquent admirer of our old institutions deliver against so revolutionary a measure! "These men," he might say, "scarcely consider themselves as Englishmen. They think a red-haired Frenchman or a red-haired German more closely connected with them than a man with brown hair born in their own parish. If a foreign sovereign patronises red hair, they love him better than their own native king. They are not Englishmen: they cannot be Englishmen: nature has forbidden it: experience proves it to be impossible. Right to political power they have none; for no man has a right to political power. Let them enjoy personal security; let their property be under the protection of the law. But if they ask for leave to exercise power over a community of which they are only half members, a community the constitution of which is essentially dark-haired, let us answer them in the words of our wise ancestors, *Nolumus leges Angliæ mutari.*"

But, it is said, the Scriptures declare that the Jews are to be restored to their own country; and the whole nation looks forward to that restoration. They are, therefore, not so deeply interested as others in the prosperity of England. It is not their home, but merely the place of their sojourn, the house of their bondage. This argument which first appeared in the Times newspaper, and which has attracted a degree of attention proportioned not so much to its own intrinsic force as to the general talent with which that journal is conducted, belongs to a class of sophisms by which the most hateful persecutions may easily be justified. To charge men with practical consequences which they themselves deny is disingenuous in controversy: it is atrocious in government. The doctrine of predestination, in the opinion of many people, tends to make those who hold it utterly immoral. And certainly it would seem that a man who believes his eternal destiny to be already irrevocably fixed is likely to indulge his passions without restraint and to neglect his religious duties. If he is an heir of wrath, his exertions must be unavailing. If he is pre-ordained to life, they must be superfluous. But would it be wise to punish every man who holds the higher doctrines of Calvinism, as if he had actually committed all those crimes which we know some Antinomians to have committed? Assuredly not. The fact notoriously is that there are many Calvinists as moral in their conduct as any Arminian, and many Arminians as loose as any Calvinist.

It is altogether impossible to reason from the opinions which a man professes to his feelings and his actions; and in fact no person is ever such a fool as to reason thus, except when he wants a pretext for persecuting his neighbours. A Christian is commanded, under the strongest sanctions, to be just in all his dealings. Yet to how many of the twenty-four millions of professing Christians in these islands would any man in his senses lend a thousand pounds without security? A man who should act, for one day, on the supposition that all the people about him were influenced by the religion which they professed, would find himself ruined before night; and no man ever does act on that supposition in any of the ordinary concerns of life, in borrowing, in lending, in buying, or in selling. But when any of our fellow creatures are to be oppressed, the case is different. Then we represent those motives which we know to be so feeble for good as omnipotent for evil. Then we lay to the charge of our victims all the vices and follies to which their doctrines, however remotely, seem to tend. We forget that the same weakness, the same laxity, the same disposition to prefer the present to the future, which make men worse than a good religion, make them better than a bad one.

It was in this way that our ancestors reasoned, and that some people in our own time still reason, about the Catholics. A Papist believes himself bound to obey the pope. The pope has issued a bull deposing Queen Elizabeth. Therefore every Papist will treat her grace as an usurper. Therefore every Papist is a traitor. Therefore every Papist ought to be hanged, drawn, and quartered. To this logic we owe some of the most hateful laws that ever disgraced our history. Surely the answer lies on the surface. The Church of Rome may have commanded these men to treat the queen as an usurper. But she has commanded them to do many other things which they have never done. She enjoins her priests to observe strict purity. You are always taunting them with their licentiousness. She commands all her followers to fast often, to be charitable to the poor, to take no interest for money, to fight no duels, to see no plays. Do they obey these injunctions? If it be the fact that very few of them strictly observe her precepts, when her precepts are opposed to their passions and interests, may not loyalty, may not humanity, may not the love of ease, may not the fear of death, be sufficient to prevent them from executing those wicked orders which she has issued against the sovereign of England? When we know that many of these people do not care enough for their religion to go without beef on a Friday for it, why should we think that they will run the risk of being racked and hanged for it?

People are now reasoning about the Jews as our fathers reasoned about the Papists. The law which is inscribed on the walls of the synagogues prohibits covetousness. But if we were to say that a Jew mortgagee would not foreclose because God had commanded him not to covet his neighbour's house, everybody would think us out of our wits. Yet it passes for an argument to say that a Jew will take no interest in the prosperity of the country in which he lives, that he will not care how bad its laws and police may be, how heavily it may be taxed, how often it may be conquered and given up to spoil, because God has promised that, by some unknown means, and at some undetermined time, perhaps ten thousand years hence, the Jews shall migrate to Palestine. Is not this the most profound ignorance of human nature? Do we not know that what is remote and indefinite affects men far less than what is near and certain? The argument too applies to Christians as strongly as to Jews. The Christian believes as well as the Jew, that at some future period the present order of things will come to an end. Nay, many Christians believe that the Messiah will shortly establish a kingdom on the earth, and reign visibly over all its inhabitants. Whether this doctrine be orthodox or not we shall not here inquire. The number of people who hold it is very much greater than the number of Jews residing in England. Many of those who hold it are distinguished by rank, wealth, and ability. It is preached from pulpits, both of the Scottish and of the English church. Noblemen and members of Parliament have written in defence of it. Now wherein does this doctrine differ, as far as its political tendency is concerned, from the doctrine of the Jews? If a Jew is unfit to legislate for us because he believes that he or his remote descendants will be removed to Palestine, can we safely open the House of Commons to a fifth-monarchy man, who expects that, before this generation shall pass away, all the kingdoms of the earth will be swallowed up in one divine empire?

Does a Jew engage less eagerly than a Christian in any competition which the law leaves open to him? Is he less active and regular in his business than his neighbours? Does he furnish his house meanly, because he is a pilgrim and sojourner in the land? Does the expectation of being restored to the country of his fathers make him insensible to the fluctuations of the stock exchange? Does he, in arranging his private affairs, ever take into the account the chance of his migrating to Palestine? If not, why are we to suppose that feelings which never influence his dealings as a merchant, or his dispositions as a testator, will acquire a boundless influence over him as soon as he becomes a magistrate or a legislator?

There is another argument which we would not willingly treat with levity, and which yet we scarcely know how to treat seriously. Scripture, it is said, is full of terrible denunciations against the Jews. It is foretold that they are to be wanderers. Is it then right to give them a home? It is foretold that they are to be oppressed. Can we with propriety suffer them to be rulers? To admit them to the rights of citizens is manifestly to insult the Divine oracles.

We allow that to falsify a prophecy inspired by Divine Wisdom would be a most atrocious crime. It is, therefore, a happy circumstance for our frail species, that it is a crime which no man can possibly commit. If we admit the Jews to seats in Parliament, we shall, by so doing, prove that the prophecies in question, whatever they may mean, do not mean that the Jews shall be excluded from Parliament.

In fact it is already clear that the prophecies do not bear the meaning put upon them by the respectable persons whom we are now answering. In France and in the United States the Jews are already admitted to all the rights of citizens. A prophecy, therefore, which should mean that the Jews would never, during the course of their wanderings, be admitted to all the rights of citizens in the places of their sojourn, would be a false prophecy. This, therefore, is not the meaning of the prophecies of Scripture.

But we protest altogether against the practice of confounding prophecy with precept, of setting up predictions which are often obscure against a morality which is always clear. If actions are to be considered as just and good merely because they have been predicted, what action was ever more laudable than that crime which our bigots are now, at the end of eighteen centuries, urging us to avenge on the Jews, that crime which made the earth shake, and blotted out the sun from heaven? The same reasoning which is now employed to vindicate the disabilities imposed on our Hebrew countrymen will equally vindicate the kiss of Judas and the judgment of Pilate. "The Son of man goeth, as it is written of him; but woe to that man by whom the Son of man is betrayed." And woe to those who, in any age or in any country, disobey his benevolent commands under pretence of accomplishing his predictions. If this argument justifies the laws now existing against the Jews, it justifies equally all the cruelties which have ever been committed against them, the sweeping edicts of banishment and confiscation, the dungeon, the rack, and the slow fire. How can we excuse ourselves for leaving property to people who are to "serve their enemies in hunger, and in thirst, and in nakedness, and in want of all things"; for giving protection to the persons of those who are to "fear day and night, and to have none assurance of their life"; for not seizing on the children of a race whose "sons and daughters are to be given unto another people"?

We have not so learned the doctrines of Him who commanded us to love our neighbor as ourselves, and who, when He was called upon to explain what He meant by a neighbour, selected as an example a heretic and an alien. Last year, we remember, it was represented by a pious writer in the John Bull newspaper, and by some other equally fervid Christians, as a monstrous indecency, that the measure for the relief of the Jews should be brought forward in Passion week. One of these humorists ironically recommended that it should be read a second time on Good Friday. We should have had no objection; nor do we believe that the day could be commemorated in a more worthy manner. We know of no day fitter for terminating long hostilities, and repairing cruel wrongs, than the day on which the religion of mercy was founded. We know of no day fitter for blotting out from the statute-book the last traces of intolerance than the day on which the spirit of intolerance produced the foulest of all judicial murders, the day on which the list of the victims of intolerance, that noble list wherein Socrates and More are enrolled, was glorified by a yet greater and holier name.

W. M. THACKERAY (1811–63)

The Snobs of England, by One of Themselves (1846–47)

*A*part from providing light relief after the solemnities of Carlyle, Mill, and
Macaulay, these essays help refute another stereotype: that the Victorians were
incorrigibly humorless. Punch, *which started publication in 1841, delivered its
weekly dose of satire and comedy (about politics and politicians, servants and
domestic mishaps), accompanied by egregious puns and inimitable cartoons, to
about 40,000 paying readers by the mid-1850s. Thackeray, one of the magazine's
founders, a member of the staff for several years, and a prolific contributor, made his
reputation as a journalist with his year-long series "The Snobs of England, by One
of Themselves." This series was coming to an end just as the monthly parts of* Vanity
Fair *began to appear. That novel proved to be his first and most enduring literary
success. But the articles in* Punch *have their claim to fame, bringing into the
language that indispensable concept, the snob. The word had appeared before; the*
Oxford English Dictionary *has a citation from 1831 that distinguishes between
"nobs" and "snobs," the former (deriving from "nobles") being the real thing, the
latter (possibly a corruption of "snab," the slang term for a cobbler's boy) being the
vulgar imitation. It was Thackeray, however, who gave the word a currency and
potency it had not previously had.*

Although most readers of Punch *responded enthusiastically to the articles, there
were the predictable critics: radicals who objected to his frivolous attitude toward*

W. M. Thackeray (1811–63), "The Snobs of England, by One of Themselves," *Punch,*
February 28, 1846 to February 27, 1847. Reprinted in Thackeray, *The Book of Snobs,* ed.
John Sutherland (New York, 1978), pp. 7–10, 14–17, 52–55, 64–66, 203–7.

serious problems in society, and conservatives to his irreverent treatment of the eminent figures and established institutions of society. Behind that frivolity and irreverence, however, there lurked a powerful moral sensibility, a caustic wit that penetrated to the heart of Victorian mores and conventions, leaving no stratum of society untouched. He was especially caustic about "Literary Snobs," a species, he pointed out, with which he was intimately familiar.

The Snob Socially Considered

T here are relative and positive Snobs. I mean by positive, such persons as are Snobs everywhere, in all companies, from morning till night, from youth to the grave, being by Nature endowed with Snobbishness—and others who are Snobs only in certain circumstances and relations of life.

For instance: I once knew a man [. . .] who, dining in my company at the Europa coffee-house, (opposite the Grand Opera, and, as everybody knows, the only decent place for dining at Naples,) ate peas with the assistance of his knife. He was a person with whose society I was greatly pleased at first—indeed, we had met in the crater of Mount Vesuvius, and were subsequently robbed and held to ransom by brigands in Calabria, which is nothing to the purpose—a man of great powers, excellent heart, and varied information; but I had never before seen him with a dish of peas, and his conduct in regard to them caused me the deepest pain.

After having seen him thus publicly comport himself, but one course was open to me—to cut his acquaintance. I commissioned a mutual friend (the HONOURABLE POLY ANTHUS) to break the matter to this gentleman as delicately as possible, and to say that painful circumstances—in no wise affecting MR. MARROWFAT's honour, or my esteem for him—had occurred, which obliged me to forego my intimacy with him; and accordingly we met, and gave each other the cut direct that night at the DUCHESS OF MONTE FIASCO's ball.

Everybody at Naples remarked the separation of the DAMON and PYTHIAS—indeed, MARROWFAT had saved my life more than once—but, as an English gentleman, what was I to do?

My dear friend was, in this instance, the Snob *relative*. It is not snobbish of persons of rank of any other nation to employ their knife in the manner alluded to. I have seen MONTE FIASCO clean his trencher with his knife, and every Principe in company doing likewise. I have seen, at the hospitable board of H.I.H. the GRAND DUCHESS STEPHANIE OF BADEN—(who, if these humble lines should come under her Imperial eyes, is besought to remember graciously the most devoted of her servants)—I have seen, I say, the Hereditary Princess of Potztausend-Donnerwetter (that serenely-beautiful woman!) use her knife in lieu of a fork or spoon; I have seen her almost swallow it, by Jove! like Ramo Samee, the Indian juggler. And did I blench? Did my estimation for the Princess diminish? No, lovely Amalia! One of the truest passions that ever was inspired by woman was raised in this bosom by that lady. Beautiful one! long, long may the knife carry food to those lips! the reddest and loveliest in the world!

The cause of my quarrel with Marrowfat I never breathed to mortal soul for four years. We met in the halls of the aristocracy—our friends and relatives. We jostled each other in the dance or at the board; but the estrangement continued, and seemed irrevocable, until the fourth of June, last year.

We met at Sir George Golloper's. We were placed he on the right, your humble servant on the left of the admirable Lady G. Peas formed part of the banquet—ducks and green peas. I trembled as I saw Marrowfat helped, and turned away sickening, lest I should behold the weapon darting down his horrid jaws.

What was my astonishment, what my delight when I saw him use his fork like any other Christian! He did not administer the cold steel once. Old times rushed back upon me—the remembrance of old services—his rescuing me from the brigands—his gallant conduct in the affair with the Countess Dei Spinachi—his lending me the 1700*l.* I almost burst into tears with joy—my voice trembled with emotion. "Frank, my boy!" I exclaimed, "Frank Marrowfat, my dear fellow! a glass of wine!"

Blushing—deeply moved—almost as tremulous as I was myself, Frank answered, "*George, shall it be Hock or Madeira?*" I could have hugged him to my heart but for the presence of the company. Little did Lady Golloper know what was the cause of the emotion which sent the duckling I was carving into her Ladyship's pink satin lap. The most good-natured of women pardoned the error, and the butler removed the bird.

We have been the closest friends ever since, nor, of course, has Frank repeated his odious habit. He acquired it at a country school, where they cultivated peas, and only used two-pronged forks, and it was only by living on the continent, where the usage of the four-prong is general, that he lost the horrible custom.

In this point—and in this only—I confess myself a member of the Silver Fork School, and if this tale induce but one reader of *Punch* to pause, to examine in his own mind solemnly, and ask, "Do I or do I not eat peas with a knife?"—to see the ruin which may fall upon himself by continuing the practice, or his family by beholding the example, these lines will not have been written in vain. And now, whatever other authors may be who contribute to this miscellany, I flatter myself Silk Buckingham will at least say that *I* am a moral man.

By the way, as some readers are dull of comprehension, I may as well say what the moral of this history *is*. The moral is this—Society having ordained certain customs, men are bound to obey the law of society, and conform to its harmless orders.

If I should go to the British and Foreign Institute (and Heaven forbid I should go under any pretext or in any costume whatever)—if I should go to one of the tea-parties in a dressing-gown and slippers, and not in the usual attire of a gentleman, viz., pumps, a gold-waistcoat, a crush hat, a sham frill, and a white chocker—I should be insulting society, and *eating peas with my knife*. Let the porters of the Institute hustle out the individual who shall so offend. Such an offender is, as regards society, a most emphatical and refractory SNOB. It has its code and police as well as governments, and he must conform who would profit by the decrees set forth for the common comfort.

I am naturally averse to egotism, and hate self-laudation consumedly; but I can't help relating here a circumstance illustrative of the point in question, in which I must think I acted with considerable prudence.

Being at Constantinople a few years since—(on a delicate mission)—the Russians were playing a double game, between ourselves, and it became necessary on our part to employ an *extra negotiator*. LECKERBISS PASHA of Roumelia, then Chief Galeongee of the Porte, gave a diplomatic banquet at his summer palace at Bujukdere. I was on the left of the Galeongee; and the Russian agent COUNT DE DIDDLOFF on his dexter side. DIDDLOFF is a dandy who would die of a rose in aromatic pain; he had tried to have me assassinated three times in the course of the negotiation: but of course we were friends in public, and saluted each other in the most cordial and charming manner.

The Galeongee is—or was, alas! for a bow-string has done for him—a staunch supporter of the old school of Turkish politics. We dined with our fingers, and had flaps of bread for plates; the only innovation he admitted was the use of European liquors, in which he indulged with great gusto. He was an enormous eater. Amongst the dishes a very large one was placed before him of a lamb dressed in its wool, stuffed with prunes, garlic, assafœtida, capsicums, and other condiments, the most abominable mixture that ever mortal smelt or tasted. The Galeongee ate of this hugely; and pursuing the Eastern fashion, insisted on helping his friends right and left, and when he came to a particularly spicy morsel, would push it with his own hands into his guests' very mouths.

I never shall forget the look of poor DIDDLOFF, when his Excellency, rolling up a large quantity of this into a ball and exclaiming, "Buk Buk" (it is very good), administered the horrible bolus to DIDDLOFF. The Russian's eyes rolled dreadfully as he received it; he swallowed it with a grimace that I thought must precede a convulsion, and seizing a bottle next him, which he thought was

Sauterne, but which turned out to be French brandy, he swallowed nearly a pint before he knew his error. It finished him; he was carried away from the dining room almost dead, and laid out to cool in a summer-house on the Bosphorus.

When it came to my turn, I took down the condiment with a smile, said Bismillah, licked my lips with easy gratification, and when the next dish was served, made up a ball myself so dexterously, and popped it down the old Galeongee's mouth with so much grace, that his heart was won. Russia was put out of Court at once, *and the treaty of* Kabobanople *was signed.* As for DIDD-LOFF, all was over with *him,* he was recalled to St. Petersburg, and SIR RODERIC MURCHISON saw him, under the No. 3967, working in the Ural mines.

The moral of this tale I need not say, is that there are many disagreeable things in society which you are bound to take down, and to do so with a smiling face.

The Influence of the Aristocracy on Snobs

Last Sunday week, being at church in this city, and the service just ended, I heard two Snobs conversing about the Parson. One was asking the other who the clergyman was? "He is Mr. So-and-so," the second Snob answered, "domestic chaplain to the Earl of What-d'ye-call'um." "Oh, IS HE?" said the first Snob, with a tone of indescribable satisfaction.—The parson's orthodoxy and identity were at once settled in this Snob's mind. He knew no more about the Earl than about the Chaplain, but he took the latter's character upon the authority of the former; and went home quite contented with his reverence, like a little truckling Snob.

This incident gave me more matter for reflection even than the sermon; and wonderment at the extent and prevalence of Lord-olatry in this country. What could it matter to Snob whether his Reverence were chaplain to his Lordship or not? What Peerage-worship there is all through this free country! How we are all implicated in it, and more or less down on our knees.—And with regard to the great subject on hand, I think that the influence of the Peerage upon Snobbishness has been more remarkable than that of any other institution. The increase, encouragement, and maintenance of Snobs are among the "priceless services," as LORD JOHN RUSSELL says, which we owe to the nobility.

It can't be otherwise. A man becomes enormously rich, or he jobs successfully in the aid of a minister, or he wins a great battle, or executes a treaty, or is a clever lawyer, who makes a multitude of fees and ascends the bench; and the country rewards him for ever with a gold coronet (with more or less balls or leaves) and a title, and a rank as legislator. "Your merits are so great," says the nation, "that your children shall be allowed to reign over us, in a manner. It does not in the least matter that your eldest son be a fool: we think your services so remarkable, that he shall have the reversion of your honours when death vacates your noble shoes. If you are poor we will give you such a sum of money as shall enable you and the eldest-born of your race for ever to live in fat and splendour. It is our wish that there should be a race set apart in this happy country, who shall hold the first rank, have the first prizes and chances in all government jobs and patronages. We cannot make all your dear children Peers—that would make Peerage common and crowd the house of Lords uncomfortably—but the young ones shall have everything a Government can give: they shall get the pick of all the places: they shall be Captains and Lieutenant-Colonels at nineteen, when hoary-headed old lieutenants are spending thirty years at drill: they shall command ships at one-and-twenty, and veterans who fought before they were born. And as we are eminently a free people, and in order to encourage all men to do their duty, we say to any man of any rank—get enormously rich, make immense fees as a lawyer, or great speeches, or distinguish yourself and win battles—and you, even you, shall come into the privileged class, and your children shall reign naturally over ours."

How can we help Snobbishness, with such a prodigious national institution erected for its worship? How can we help cringing to Lords? Flesh and blood can't do otherwise. What man can withstand this prodigious temptation? Inspired by what is called a noble emulation, some people grasp at honours and win them; others, too weak or mean, blindly admire and grovel before those who have gained them; others, not being able to acquire them, furiously hate, abuse, and envy. There are only a few bland and not-in-the-least-conceited philosophers, who can behold the state of society, viz., Toadyism, organised:— base Man-and-Mammon worship, instituted by command of law:—SNOB-BISHNESS, in a word, perpetuated, and mark the phenomenon calmly. And of these calm moralists, is there one I wonder whose heart would not throb with pleasure if he could be seen walking arm-in-arm with a couple of Dukes down Pall Mall? No: it is impossible, in our condition of society, not to be sometimes a Snob.

On one side it encourages the Commoner to be snobbishly mean: and the noble to be snobbishly arrogant. When a noble Marchioness writes in her travels about the hard necessity under which steamboat travellers labour of being brought into contact "with all sorts and conditions of people," implying that a fellowship with God's creatures is disagreeable to her Ladyship, who is their superior:—when, I say, the MARCHIONESS OF LONDONDERRY writes in this fashion, we must consider that out of her natural heart it would have been impossible for any woman to have had such a sentiment; but that the habit of truckling and cringing, which all who surround her have adopted towards this beautiful and magnificent lady,—this proprietor of so many black and other diamonds, has really induced her to believe that she is the superior of the world in general; and that people are not to associate with her except awfully at a distance. I recollect being once at the City of Grand Cairo, through which a European Royal Prince was passing India-wards. One night at the inn there was a great disturbance: a man had drowned himself in the well hard by: all the inhabitants of the hotel came bustling into the Court, and amongst others your humble servant, who asked of a certain young man the reason of the disturbance. How was I to know that this young gent. was a Prince? He had not his crown and sceptre on; he was dressed in a white jacket and felt hat: but he looked surprised at anybody speaking to him: answered an unintelligible monosyllable, and—*beckoned his Aide-de-Camp to come and speak to me.* It is our fault, not that of the great, that they should fancy themselves so far above us. If you *will* fling yourself under the wheels, Juggernaut will go over you, depend upon it; and if you and I, my dear friend, had Kotoo performed before us every day,—found people whenever we appeared grovelling in slavish adoration, we should drop into the airs of superiority quite naturally, and accept the greatness with which the world insisted upon endowing us.

Here is an instance out of LORD LONDONDERRY's travels, of that calm, good-natured, undoubting way in which a great man accepts the homage of his inferiors. After making some profound and ingenious remarks about the town of Brussels, his Lordship says:—"Staying some days at the Hotel de Belle Vue— a greatly overrated establishment, and not nearly so comfortable as the Hotel de France—I made acquaintance with DR. L—, the physician of the mission. He was desirous of doing the honour of the place to me, and he ordered for us a *dîner en gourmand* at the chief restaurateur's, maintaining it surpassed the Rocher at Paris. Six or eight partook of the entertainment, and we all agreed it was infinitely inferior to the Paris display, and much more extravagant. So much for the copy."

And so much for the gentleman who gave the dinner. DR. L—, desirous to do his Lordship "the honour of the place," feasts him with the best victuals money can procure—and my lord finds the entertainment extravagant and inferior. Extravagant! it was not extravagant to *him;*—Inferior! MR. L—did his best to satisfy those noble jaws, and my lord receives the entertainment, and dismisses the giver with a rebuke. It is like a three-tailed Pasha grumbling about an unsatisfactory bucksheesh.

But how should it be otherwise in a country where Lord-olatry is part of our creed, and our children are brought up to respect the Peerage as the Englishman's second Bible?

On Clerical Snobs

Among the varieties of the Snob Clerical, the University Snob and the Scholastic Snob ought never to be forgotten; they form a very strong battalion in the black-coated army.

The wisdom of our ancestors (which I admire more and more every day) seemed to have determined that the education of youth was so paltry and unimportant a matter, that almost any man, armed with a birch and a regulation cassock and degree, might undertake the charge; and many an honest country gentleman may be found to the present day, who takes very good care to have a character with his butler when he engages him, and will not purchase a horse without the strongest warranty and the closest inspection; but sends off his son, young JOHN THOMAS, to school without asking any questions about the Schoolmaster, and places the lad at Switchester College, under DOCTOR BLOCK, because he (the good old English gentleman) had been at Switchester, under DOCTOR BUZWIG, forty years ago.

We have a love for all little boys at school; for many scores of thousands of them read and love *Punch:*—may he never write a word that shall not be honest and fit for them to read! He will not have his young friends to be Snobs in the future, or to be bullied by Snobs, or given over to such to be educated. Our connexion with the youth at the Universities is very close and affectionate. The candid undergraduate is our friend. The pompous old College DON trembles in his common room, lest we should attack him and show him up as a Snob.

When Railroads were threatening to invade the land which they have since conquered, it may be recollected what a shrieking and outcry the authorities of Oxford and Eton made, lest the iron abominations should come near those seats of pure learning, and tempt the British youth astray. The supplications were in vain; the railroad is in upon them, and the Old-World institutions are doomed. I felt charmed to read in the papers the other day a most veracious puffing advertisement, headed, "TO COLLEGE AND BACK FOR FIVE SHILLINGS." "The College Gardens (it said) will be thrown open on this occasion; the College youths will perform a regatta; the Chapel of King's College will have its celebrated music";—and all for five shillings! The Goths have got into Rome; NAPOLEON STEPHENSON draws his republican lines round the sacred old cities; and the ecclesiastical big-wigs, who garrison them, must prepare to lay down key and crosier before the iron conqueror.

If you consider, dear reader, what profound Snobbishness the University system produced, you will allow that it is time to attack some of those feudal middle-age superstitions. If you go down for five shillings to look at the "College Youths," you may see one sneaking down the court without a tassel to his cap; another with a gold or silver fringe to his velvet trencher; a third lad with a master's gown and hat, walking at ease over the sacred College grass-plats, which common men must not tread on.

He may do it, because he is a nobleman. Because a lad is a lord, the University gives him a degree at the end of two years, which another is seven in acquiring. Because he is a lord, he has no call to go through an examination. Any man who has not been to College and back for five shillings, would not believe in such distinctions in a place of education, so absurd and monstrous do they seem to be.

The lads with gold and silver lace are sons of rich gentlemen, and called Fellow Commoners; they are privileged to feed better than the pensioners, and to have wine with their victuals, which the latter can only get in their rooms.

The unlucky boys who have no tassels to their caps, are called sizars—*servitors* at Oxford,—(a very pretty and gentlemanlike title). A distinction is made in their clothes because they are poor; for which reason they wear a badge of poverty, and are not allowed to take their meals with their fellow-students.

When this wicked and shameful distinction was set up, it was of a piece with all the rest—a part of the brutal, unchristian, blundering feudal system. Distinctions of rank were then so strongly insisted upon, that it would have been thought blasphemy to doubt them, as blasphemous as it is in parts of the United States now, for a nigger to set up as the equal of a white man. A ruffian like HENRY VIII. talked as gravely about the divine powers vested in him, as if he had been an inspired prophet. A wretch like JAMES I. not only believed himself a particular sanctity, but other people believed him. Government regulated the length of a merchant's shoes as well as meddled with his trade, prices, exports, machinery. It thought itself justified in roasting a man for his religion, or pulling a Jew's teeth out if he did not pay a contribution, or ordered him to dress in a yellow gabardine, and locked him in a particular quarter.

Now a merchant may wear what boots he pleases, and has pretty nearly acquired the privilege of buying and selling without the Government laying its paws upon the bargain. The stake for heretics is gone; the pillory is taken down; Bishops are even found lifting up their voices against the remains of persecution, and ready to do away with the last Catholic Disabilities. SIR ROBERT PEEL, though he wished it ever so much, has no power over MR. BENJAMIN DISRAELI's grinders, or any means of violently handling that gentleman's jaw. Jews are not called upon to wear badges: on the contrary, they may live in Piccadilly, or the Minories, according to fancy; they may dress like Christians, and do so sometimes in a most elegant and fashionable manner.

Why is the poor College servitor to wear that name and that badge still? Because Universities are the last places into which Reform penetrates. But now that she can go to College and back for five shillings, let her travel down thither.

On Literary Snobs

What will he say about Literary Snobs? has been a question, I make no doubt, often asked by the public. How can he let off his own profession? Will that truculent and unsparing monster, who attacks the nobility, the clergy, the army, and the ladies indiscriminately, hesitate when the turn comes to *égorger* his own flesh and blood?

My dear and excellent querist, whom does the Schoolmaster flog so resolutely as his own son? Didn't Brutus chop his offspring's head off? You have a very bad opinion indeed of the present state of Literature and of literary men, if you fancy that any one of us would hesitate to stick a knife into his neighbour penman, if the latter's death could do the state any service.

But the fact is, that in the literary profession THERE ARE NO SNOBS. Look round at the whole body of British men of letters, and I defy you to point out among them a single instance of vulgarity, or envy, or assumption.

Men and women, as far as I have known them, they are all modest in their demeanour, elegant in their manners, spotless in their lives, and honourable in their conduct to the world and to each other. You *may*, occasionally, it is true, hear one literary man abusing his brother; but why? Not in the least out of malice; not at all from envy; merely from a sense of truth and public duty. Suppose, for instance, I good-naturedly point out a blemish in my friend *Mr. Punch's* person, and say *Mr. P.* has a hump-back, and his nose and chin are more crooked than those features in the Apollo or Antinous, which we are accustomed to consider as our standards of beauty; does this argue malice on my part towards *Mr. Punch?* Not in the least. It is the critic's duty to point out defects as well as merits, and he invariably does this duty with the utmost gentleness and candour.

An intelligent foreigner's testimony about our manners is always worth having, and I think, in this respect, the work of an eminent American, Mr. N. P. Willis, is eminently valuable and impartial. In his "History of Ernest Clay," a crack Magazine writer, the reader will get an exact account of the life of a popular man of letters in England. He is always the great lion of society.

He takes the *pas* of Dukes and Earls; all the nobility crowd to see him: I forget how many Baronesses and Duchesses fall in love with him. But on this subject let us hold our tongues. Modesty forbids that we should reveal the names of the heart-broken Countesses and dear Marchionesses who are pining for every one of the contributors in this periodical.

If anybody wants to know how intimately authors are connected with the fashionable world, they have but to read the genteel novels. What refinement and delicacy pervades the works of Mrs. Barnaby! What delightful good company do you meet with in Mrs. Armytage! She seldom introduces you to anybody under a Marquis! I don't know anything more delicious than the pictures of genteel life in *Ten Thousand a Year,* except perhaps the *Young Duke,* and *Coningsby.* There's a modest grace about *them,* and an air of easy high fashion, which only belongs to blood, my dear Sir—to true blood.

And what linguists many of our writers are! LADY BULWER, LADY LONDONDERRY, SIR EDWARD himself—they write the French language with a luxurious elegance and ease, which sets them far above their continental rivals, of whom not one (except PAUL DE KOCK), knows a word of English.

And what Briton can read without enjoyment the works of JAMES, so admirable for terseness; and the playful humour and dazzling off-hand lightness of AINSWORTH? among other humorists, one might glance at a JERROLD, the chivalrous advocate of Toryism and Church and State; an àBECKETT, with a lightsome pen, but a savage earnestness of purpose; a JEAMES, whose pure style, and wit unmingled with buffoonery, was relished by a congenial public.

Speaking of critics, perhaps there never was a review that has done so much for literature as the admirable *Quarterly.* It has its prejudices, to be sure, as which of us have not? It goes out of its way to abuse a great man, or lays mercilessly on to such pretenders as KEATS and TENNYSON; but on the other hand, it is the friend of all young authors, and has marked and nurtured all the rising talent of the country. It is loved by everybody. There, again, is *Blackwood's Magazine*—conspicuous for modest elegance and amiable satire; that Review never passes the bounds of politeness in a joke. It is the arbiter of manners; and, while gently exposing the foibles of Londoners (for whom the *beaux esprits* of Edinburgh entertain a justifiable contempt), it is never coarse in its fun. The fiery enthusiasm of the *Athenaeum* is well known; and the bitter wit of the too difficult *Literary Gazette.* The *Examiner* is perhaps too timid, and the *Spectator* too boisterous in its praise—but who can carp at these minor faults? No, no; the critics of England and the authors of England are unrivalled as a body; and hence it becomes impossible for us to find fault with them.

Above all, I never knew a man of letters *ashamed of his profession.* Those who know us, know what an affectionate and brotherly spirit there is among us all. Sometimes one of us rises in the world; we never attack him or sneer at him under those circumstances, but rejoice to a man at his success. If JONES dines with a lord, SMITH never says JONES is a courtier and cringer. Nor, on the other hand, does JONES, who is in the habit of frequenting the society of great people, give himself any airs on account of the company he keeps; but will leave a Duke's arm in Pall Mall to come over and speak to poor BROWN, the young penny-a-liner.

That sense of equality and fraternity amongst Authors has always struck me as one of the most amiable characteristics of the class. It is because we know and respect each other, that the world respects us so much; that we hold such a good position in society, and demean ourselves so irreproachably when there.

Literary persons are held in such esteem by the nation, that about two of them have been absolutely invited to Court during the present reign; and it is probable that towards the end of the season, one or two will be asked to dinner by SIR ROBERT PEEL.

They are such favourites with the public, that they are continually obliged to have their pictures taken and published; and one or two could be pointed out, of whom the nation insists upon having a fresh portrait every year. Nothing can be more gratifying than this proof of the affectionate regard which the people has for its instructors.

Literature is held in such honour in England, that there is a sum of near twelve hundred pounds per annum set apart to pension deserving persons following that profession. And a great compliment this is, too, to the professors, and a proof of their generally prosperous and flourishing condition. They are generally so rich and thrifty, that scarcely any money is wanted to help them.

If every word of this is true, how, I should like to know, am I to write about Literary Snobs?

Chapter Last

How it is that we have come to No. 52 of this present series of papers, my dear friends and brother Snobs, I hardly know—but for a whole mortal year have we been together, prattling, and abusing the human race; and were we to live for a hundred years more, I believe there is plenty of subject for conversation in the enormous theme of Snobs.

The national mind is awakened to the subject. Letters pour in every day, conveying marks of sympathy; directing the attention of the Snob of England to races of Snobs yet undescribed. "Where are your Theatrical Snobs; your Commercial Snobs; your Medical and Chirurgical Snobs; your Official Snobs; your Legal Snobs; your Artistical Snobs; your Musical Snobs; your Sporting Snobs?" write my esteemed correspondents: "Surely you are not going to miss the Cambridge Chancellor election, and omit showing up your Don Snobs who are coming, cap in hand, to a young Prince of six-and-twenty, and to implore him to be the chief of their renowned University?" writes a friend who seals with the signet of the Cam and Isis Club: "Pray, pray," cries another, "now the Operas are opening, give us a lecture about Omnibus Snobs." Indeed, I should like to write a chapter about the Snobbish Dons very much, and another about the Snobbish Dandies. Of my dear Theatrical Snobs I think with a pang; and I can hardly break away from some Snobbish artists, with whom I have long, long intended to have a palaver.

But what's the use of delaying? When they were done there would be fresh Snobs to portray. The labour is endless. No single man could complete it. Here are but fifty-two bricks—and a pyramid to build. It is best to stop. As JONES always quits the room as soon as he has said his good thing,—as CINCINNATUS and GENERAL WASHINGTON both retired into private life in the height of their popularity,—as PRINCE ALBERT, when he laid the first stone of the Exchange, left the bricklayers to complete that edifice, and went home to his royal dinner,—as the poet BUNN comes forward at the end of the season, and with feelings too tumultuous to describe, blesses his *kyind* friends over the footlights: so, friends, in the flush of conquest and the splendour of victory, amid the shouts and the plaudits of a people—triumphant yet modest—the Snob of England bids ye farewell.

But only for a season. Not for ever. No, no. There is one celebrated author whom I admire very much—who has been taking leave of the public any time these ten years in his prefaces, and always comes back again when everybody is glad to see him. How can he have the heart to be saying good-bye, so often? I believe that BUNN *is* affected when he blesses the people. Parting is always painful. Even the familiar bore is dear to you. I should be sorry to shake hands even with JAWKINS for the last time. I think a well-constituted convict, on coming home from transportation, ought to be rather sad when he takes leave of Van Dieman's Land. When the curtain goes down on the last night of a pantomime, poor old clown must be very dismal, depend on it. Ha! with what joy he rushes forward on the evening of the 26th of December next, and says— "How are you?—Here we are!" But I am growing too sentimental:—to return to the theme.

THE NATIONAL MIND IS AWAKENED TO THE SUBJECT OF SNOBS. The word Snob has taken a place in our honest English Vocabulary. We can't define it, perhaps. We can't say what it is, any more than we can define Wit, or Humour, or Humbug, but we *know* what it is. Some weeks since, happening to have the felicity to sit next to a young lady at a hospitable table, where poor old JAWKINS was holding forth in a very absurd pompous manner, I wrote upon the spotless damask "S——B," and called my neighbour's attention to the little remark.

That young lady smiled. She knew it at once. Her mind straightway filled up the two letters concealed by apostrophic reserve, and I read in her assenting eyes that she knew JAWKINS was a Snob. You seldom get them to make use of the word as yet, it is true; but it is inconceivable how pretty an expression their little smiling mouths assume when they speak it out. If any young lady doubts, just let her go up to her own room, look at herself steadily in the glass, and say

"Snob." If she tries this simple experiment, my life for it, she will smile, and own that the word becomes her mouth amazingly. A pretty little round word, all composed of soft letters, with a hiss at the beginning, just to make it piquant, as it were.

JAWKINS, meanwhile, went on blundering and bragging and boring, quite unconsciously. And so he will, no doubt, go on roaring and braying to the end of time, or at least so long as people will hear him. You cannot alter the nature of men and Snobs by any force of satire; as, by laying ever so many stripes on a donkey's back you can't turn him into a zebra.

But we can warn the neighbourhood that the person whom they and JAWKINS admire is an impostor. We can apply the Snob test to him, and try whether he is conceited and a quack, whether pompous and lacking humility—whether uncharitable and proud of his narrow soul. How does he treat a great man—how regard a small one? How does he comport himself in the presence of His Grace the Duke; and how in that of SMITH, the tradesman?

And it seems to me that all English society is cursed by this mammoniacal superstition; and that we are sneaking and bowing and cringing on the one hand, or bullying and scorning on the other, from the lowest to the highest. My wife speaks with great circumspection—"proper pride," she calls it—to our neighbour the tradesman's lady; and she, I mean MRS. SNOB,—ELIZA—would give one of her eyes to go to Court, as her cousin the Captain's wife did. She, again, is a good soul, but it costs her agonies to be obliged to confess that we live in Upper Thompson Street, Somer's Town. And though I believe in her heart MRS. WHISKERINGTON is fonder of us than of her cousins, the SMIGSMAGS, you should hear how she goes on prattling about LADY SMIGSMAG,—and "I said to SIR JOHN, my dear JOHN"; and about the SMIGSMAGS' house and parties in Hyde Park Terrace.

LADY SMIGSMAG, when she meets ELIZA,—who is a sort of a kind of a species of a connexion of the family, pokes out one finger, which my wife is at liberty to embrace in the most cordial manner she can devise. But, oh, you should see her ladyship's behavior on her first-chop dinner-party days, when LORD and LADY LONGEARS come!

I can bear it no longer—this diabolical invention of gentility which kills natural kindliness and honest friendship. Proper pride, indeed! Rank and precedence, forsooth! The table of ranks and degrees is a lie, and should be flung into the fire. Organise rank and precedence! that was well for the masters of ceremonies of former ages. Come forward, some great marshal, and organise EQUALITY in society, and your rod shall swallow up all the juggling old court gold-sticks. If this is not gospel truth—if the world does not tend to this—if hereditary-great-man worship is not a humbug and an idolatry—let us have the STUARTS back again, and crop the Free Press's ears in the pillory.

If ever our cousins the Smigsmags asked me to meet Lord Longears, I would like to take an opportunity after dinner and say, in the most good-natured way in the world:—Sir, Fortune makes you a present of a number of thousand pounds every year. The ineffable wisdom of our ancestors has placed you as a chief and hereditary legislator over me. Our admirable Constitution (the pride of Britons and envy of surrounding nations) obliges me to receive you as my senator, superior, and guardian. Your eldest son, Fitz-Heehaw, is sure of a place in Parliament; your younger sons the De Brays, will kindly condescend to be post-captains and lieutenant-colonels, and to represent us in foreign courts, or to take a good living when it falls convenient. These prizes our admirable Constitution (the pride and envy of, &c.) pronounces to be your due: without count of your dulness, your vices, your selfishness; or your entire incapacity and folly. Dull as you may be (and we have as good a right to assume that my lord is an ass, as the other proposition, that he is an enlight-ened patriot);—dull, I say, as you may be, no one will accuse you of such monstrous folly, as to suppose that you are indifferent to the good luck which you possess, or have any inclination to part with it. No—and patriots as we are, under happier circumstances, Smith and I, I have no doubt, were we dukes ourselves, would stand by our order.

We would submit good-naturedly to sit in a high place. We would acquiesce in that admirable Constitution (pride and envy of, &c.) which made us chiefs and the world our inferiors; we would not cavil particularly at that notion of hereditary superiority which brought so many simple people cringing to our knees. May be we would rally round the Corn-Laws; we would make a stand against the Reform Bill; we would die rather than repeal the acts against Catho-lics and Dissenters; we would, by our noble system of class-legislation, bring Ireland to its present admirable condition.

But Smith and I are not Earls as yet. We don't believe that it is for the interest of Smith's army that young De Bray should be a Colonel at five-and-twenty,—of Smith's diplomatic relations that Lord Longears should go Am-bassador to Constantinople,—of our politics, that Longears should put his hereditary foot into them—any more than we believe it is for the interest of science that His Royal Highness Dr. Prince Albert should be Chancellor of the University of Cambridge. Smith says, that, as a Chief of a University, he will have a Smith's prizeman.

When Dr. Prince Blucher was complimented with a degree, the old dragoon burst out laughing, and said—"Me a Doctor? They ought to make Gneisenau an apothecary"; but Gneisenau, though a better General, was not a Prince; it was the Prince that the Snobs worshipped, and invested with their tom-foolish diploma.

This booing and cringing Smith believes to be the act of Snobs; and he will do all in his might and main to be a Snob and to submit to Snobs no longer. To LONGEARS, he says, "I can't help seeing, LONGEARS, that I am as good as you. I can spell even better; I can think quite as rightly; I will not have you for my master, or black your shoes any more. Your footmen do it, but they are paid; and the fellow who comes to get a list of the company when you give a banquet or a dancing breakfast at Longueoreille House, gets money from the newspapers for performing that service. But for myself, thank you for nothing, LONGEARS, my boy, and I don't wish to pay you any more than I owe. I will take off my hat to WELLINGTON because he is WELLINGTON; but to you—who are you?"

I am sick of Court Circulars. I loathe *haut-ton* intelligence. I believe such words as Fashionable, Exclusive, Aristocratic, and the like, to be wicked unchristian epithets, that ought to be banished from honest vocabularies. A court system, that sends men of genius to the second-table, I hold to be a Snobbish system. A Society that sets up to be polite, and ignores Arts and Letters, I hold to be a Snobbish Society. You, who despise your neighbour, are a Snob; you, who forget your own friends, meanly to follow after those of a higher degree, are a Snob; you who are ashamed of your poverty, and blush for your calling, are a Snob; as are you who boast of your pedigree, or are proud of your wealth.

To laugh at such is *Mr. Punch's* business. May he laugh honestly, hit no foul blow, and tell the truth when at his very broadest grin—never forgetting that if Fun is good, Truth is still better, and Love best of all.

CHARLES DICKENS (1812–70)

Demoralisation and Total Abstinence (1849)

*L*ike Thackeray, Dickens was a journalist before becoming a novelist; his first
writings were reports on debates in Parliament. And he remained a journalist
even while he was being phenomenally successful as a novelist. Indeed, his novels
have been interpreted (or misinterpreted) as a superior form of journalism—tracts
for the times, exposing the iniquities and absurdities of society. When he wrote this
article on teetotalers for the Examiner, he was also writing David Copperfield, the
first part of which had appeared a few months earlier.

"There have been at work among us," a minister told his flock in 1853, "three
great social agencies: The London City Mission; the novels of Mr. Dickens; the
cholera."[1] Dickens's novels are usually characterized as social novels. And so they
are—with a difference; they are social novels cum morality plays. The class society of
Victorian England was a subtext of his novels, but the classes do not carry the
burden of the moral tale; it is individuals who do that. And the "good" individuals
do not correspond with the poor, nor the "bad" with the rich. Virtues and vices are
equally distributed among all classes.

Moreover, Dickens the novelist was not always Dickens the journalist or the
reformer. While his novels satirized such educational innovations as training colleges for teachers and "ragged schools" for the poor, he himself was a public and

---

Charles Dickens (1812–70), "Demoralisation and Total Abstinence," *Examiner*, October 27,
1849. Reprinted in *Dickens' Journalism*, ed. Michael Slater (London, 1996), II, 161–69.

1. G. M. Young, *Victorian England: Portrait of an Age* ([1936] New York, 1954), p. 89.

prominent advocate of both. Yet there was a common denominator that united both Dickenses, a moral imagination that was as compassionate as it was hard-headed, that appreciated the reality of social problems (drunkenness, in the case of this essay in the Examiner*) and the fallacies of the well-intentioned but narrow-minded policies (teetotalism) designed to correct them.*

I t is a characteristic of the age that it comprehends a large class of minds apparently unable to distinguish between use and abuse. Because war is costly, because the horrors inseparable from it are great, because its triumphs and successes are of very little worth when balanced against the immense price, moral and physical, at which they are purchased, a number of well-meaning men spring up who would disarm England. And this too, at a time when a deplorable reaction towards tyranny is visible throughout Europe, and when it is, of all times, most important for the hopes of the world that a free country, abhorrent of the detestable cruelties practised by absolute government, should be in a bold and strong position. We can imagine nothing more agreeable to Austria (unless it be the murdering of noble men) than the abandonment of all the barracks and arsenals of this kingdom to statues of Mr Elihu Burritt; but, precisely because Austria is not agreeable to us, we are not agreeable to this, and, as a choice of two evils, would infinitely prefer a fleet and an army to any amount of Mr Elihu Burritt—though we have no doubt he is a very honest man in his way.

So, because drunkenness is, for the most part, inseparably associated with crime and misery, a leap is made at the conclusion that there must be no drinking. Because Bill Brute, the robber in Newgate, and Mr Brallaghan of Killalloo, resident down the next court, make wild beasts of themselves under the influence of strong liquor, therefore Jones, the decent and industrious mechanic, going to Hampton Court for a summer day with his wife and family, is not to have his pint of beer and his glass of gin and water—a proposition which we make bold to say is simply ridiculous. So, because certain zealots take it into their hot heads that there is going to be a Post-office delivery of letters in London on a Sunday—which none but themselves have ever dreamed of—straightway there is to be an agitation for putting a stop to the delivery of any letters, anywhere, under any circumstances, on a Sunday. And so on, to the end of a long chapter.

All these wrong conclusions, from premises that are to a certain extent right, have a strong family likeness in the manner of their enforcement. The members of a Peace Society proclaim, as an original discovery, that war is a mighty evil. The members of a Tee-total Society proclaim, as an original discovery, that a drunken man or woman is a degraded object. Nobody has ever arrived at either of these advanced stages of enlightenment before; nobody ever can arrive at either of them without being a member of the Peace Society or the Tee-total

Society. The one thing wanting in this world is the one Society, whose claims chance at the moment to be thrust upon us. Thus, in reading the newspaper advertisements, we find that Morison's pills are the only cure for every disease to which human nature is liable, until we stumble on Professor Holloway, and find that his is the only nostrum for all the ills that flesh is heir to!

The same strong family likeness, among the misbegotten children of Cant, is to be observed in the illogical, irrational, unscrupulous, and wanton way, in which facts are perverted, sweeping assertions hazarded, and motives wrong-fully attributed, to support the one idea. Quack society, quack medicine, or quack Post-office opposition, it is all the same! Down goes poor truth, at the first charge, into the dust, and away ride the whole field, whooping, pell mell, over her!

Mr Beggs, who has just written an elaborate treatise on what he calls the "Extent and Causes of Juvenile Depravity," gives us two good instances of sweeping assertion. In 1839, when an official inquiry showed the number of known prostitutes in London to be 7,000, a voluntary association, multiplying them by nearly twelve, manfully stated them at 80,000! No assertion is more common in "Temperance Literature" than the assertion that 60,000 drunkards die annually in this kingdom. Now, the fact is, says Mr Beggs, that 10,000—one-sixth of this amount—is a high estimate, for which there is no warrant in any known data. The favourite temperance statement of the sixty thousand, "making deductions for children under fifteen, and aged persons above eighty, as well as for the smaller proportion of female than male inebriates, gives us *every fourth or fifth person dying a drunkard!*" Is it not almost time that we had a Temperance Society in strong statements as well as strong drinks?

But Mr Beggs, while he repudiates these exaggerated falsehoods, still pleads the total abstinence (miscalled, in a similar want of honesty, the temperance cause), and calls upon the women of England—not the drunken women, as one might suppose, but the women who do not get drunk—to "dash down the cup," and upon the men—again, not the drunken men, but the sober—to "banish the social glass," &c. &c., occasionally in an excited strain which is more like the Temperance Literature whose assertions he holds in such just estimation, than the patient pursuer of facts he generally shows himself to be. Premising that his elaborate treatise is, in a revised and improved form, an essay written by him in competition for a Hundred Pound prize recently offered for the best essay on Juvenile Depravity; that the adjudicators awarded it the second prize; and that without making any pretensions to novelty of reflection or suggestion on the momentous subject of which it treats, it contains a mass of important and well-arranged facts,—we propose to reason a little on this total abstinence question, and to investigate one or two main positions of its advocates, sustained by Mr Beggs.

Now, we will begin by expressing our opinion that Total Abstinence Societies beg the whole question, and that drunkenness, in this country, is already made disgraceful. It is regarded as a low, abandoned, miserable vice. While it is the vice of the poor and wretched, and the guilty, it is not the vice of the upper classes, or of the middle classes (whose improvement within the last hundred years is in no respect more remarkable than in this); and it is not, generally speaking, the vice of the great body of respectable mechanics, or of servants, or of small tradesmen. We hold that it is quite as often the consequence as the cause of the condition in which the poor and wretched are found; and that it prevails in the low depths of society, as an evil of vast extent, because those depths have been too long unfathomed and unsunned, and because, while all above them has been undergoing some improvement, their moral condition has got worse and worse, until it is as bad as bad can be. If every motherly, good woman in England were to dash down her cup, in compliance with the invocation of Mr Beggs (which we seem to have heard before), and if every well-conducted man were to banish his social glass and fly with enthusiasm to the pump, there would not be, we sincerely believe, one drunken man or woman the less, within the compass of the United Kingdom—why should there be? But, if the women of England could dash down the window tax, and the water monopoly, and the stifling walls and roofs that keep out air; and could dash open the doors of some new schools for poor people's children—emphatically poor people's children—where common sense and common duty should be taught in common terms; and if the men of England could banish the social filth, indecency, and degradation in which scores upon scores of thousands are forced to wear out life,—they might just leave their cups and their social glasses alone, and keep their whole little possession of crockery exactly in its present state.

We object, altogether, to the evidence of confirmed criminals in prisons, about the cup and the social glass. We have no doubt of their having been drunkards; we have no doubt of their having abused everything they should have used; but we believe that they lied, deceived, and violated the whole table of the law, through many causes. Mr Beggs supplies us with a return of the answers made by certain prisoners to the question, What did they assign as the first cause of their falling into error? One might reasonably suppose that some few people lapsed into crime by reason of a want of control over their passions, through the disregard of truth, from not holding theft in abhorrence, from indulgence in other sensual pleasures than drink, from cupidity, from greed of many kinds. Not at all. These are not the answers. Drink is the favourite, and there is a run upon the favourite. Now it is, or it may be, within the observation of every man, that these people constantly think there is an excuse for what they have done in drink. Nothing is more common in the police reports than for a prisoner to say he was drunk when he committed the offence with which he is charged; and for the assertion, on the magistrate's referring to the inspector who took the charge, turning out to be wholly untrue. Besides this, we will engage that ninety out of a hundred of all the prisoners in all the gaols in the United Kingdom would, without the least reference to fact, return exactly such an answer to such a question as they thought would be agreeable to the questioner; and that if a notion arose that the wearing of brass buttons led to crime, and they were questioned to elucidate that point, we should have such answers as, "I was happy till I wore brass buttons," "Brass buttons did it," "Buttons is the cause of my being here," all down long columns of a grave return.

One Mr Rotch—we had almost written Mr Botch, remembering his sheep-shearing, to which we referred some time ago—who is a magnate among prisoners, writes a pathetic letter to Mr Beggs, printed in the appendix to his volume, in which he says:

> So true is what you say (that while the more respectable of our countrymen alone have the power to change this drinking system, it is they who give respectability to it), that the moment my term of office as a visiting justice of Coldbath Fields expired, and I went out of the committee by rotation, a wicked crusade was immediately commenced against all the warders and sub-warders who had signed the temperance pledge. The governor insulted them; the subordinates designated them as "Rotch's Saints."

We notice this, not because the chief of these saints was discharged from his office for drunkenness (which we, however, know to be the fact), nor to comment on the honest use of the term drinking customs in the sense of drunken customs, and the calumnious accusation against the respectable portion of the community of countenancing them, but to point out the monstrous absurdity and impropriety of an indiscriminate administration of this pledge to common London thieves and vagabonds *in prison*—to such of them, in short, as chose to take it from the hands of Mr Rotch, in the palmy days of his superseded visitation. Any one in the least degree acquainted with the habits of these persons, knows that there is nothing the generality of them would not profess, when at that disadvantage, to curry favour with a man in power. In the monotony and restraint of their prison life, any opportunity of "doing" such a man, with a solemn face, would be esteemed, besides, as a joke of the first magnitude. The fun of taking the pledge where there was nothing but water to be got, with the prospect of breaking it the moment the prison gate should open on the gin-shops, can only have been equalled by their delicate enjoyment of the jest of being supposed to hold that solemn promise in the least regard, when lying was known to be the trade and business of their lives. Nevertheless we are uncharitable enough to begrudge them this hypocritical relaxation, on the ground of its having a most demoralising and pernicious tendency. We contend that a prison-yard is not fit pasturage for Mr Rotch's hobby, or Mr anybody else's; and we believe that the last state of those men was worse than the first.

Here is a case against strong drink from Mr Beggs' book. The subject is a girl:

> It appears that she had been indulgently and well brought up, that she had obtained at a very early age an excellent situation as nursery-maid in a family which had been known to her widowed mother in more prosperous days. All went on smoothly until, in one of her holidays, she fell in with some female companions and went with them to the tea-gardens. At this place she met with a gentleman who paid her polite and particular attention. The acquaintanceship was continued for some time. She was flattered by his addresses,—she was frequently invited to accompany him to amusements for which she had every inclination; but as she could not accept them on account of the rules of the family in which she lived, she began to feel her situation irksome. One evening she obtained leave of absence on some pretence until a later hour, and went with her admirer to a ball, from which she was hurried away, after having in a moment of excessive fatigue swallowed a small glass of wine-negus. She scarcely recollected what took place afterwards, but found herself in the morning away from her kind friends in a strange place, and at the mercy of him who had wronged her.

We do not quite understand what share the "small glass of wine-negus" is supposed to have had in this melancholy history. If it were drugged, we presume a cup of tea might have been drugged too. If the poor girl was stupified by the unassisted fumes of the negus (which we must beg to be excused for not believing), we suppose that a total abstinence from the negus on the part of Clapham and Stoke Newington would not have prevented the negus from being in those tea-gardens, or the poor girl from drinking it. If it be contended that, for the sake of all poor girls in the like peril, there must be no tea-gardens and no negus—that because they are *not* virtuous, there shall be no cakes and ale—then we cannot stop there. There must be no liberty, no holiday, no breathing of fresh air. There must be an immense procession of police-vans in connexion with the churches, on Sundays, carrying young people to and from the services closeted up from temptation. If those who do not misuse opportunities of innocent enjoyment, are to suffer for those who do, we must come to this complexion. We must put the whole world in mourning, and give up social life as a bad job.

The number of uneducated children in London, according to the first annual report of the Ragged School Union, considerably exceeds 100,000, of which number it has since been ascertained, by an examination from house to house, that 16,000 are to be found in Spitalfields and Bethnalgreen alone. Says Mr Beggs in one place, "the causes of juvenile immorality must be sought not only in the want of education, but in the drinking habits of the community." Says Mr Beggs in another place, "could we lose our familiarity with the scenes of misery drink produces, and after a temporary forgetfulness, awaken up to a sight of what one single gin-shop could disclose, would it not be banished from our tables and renounced by all good men?" Why should it be banished from our tables and renounced by all good men? What would be the use of its being banished from our tables, and renounced by all good men? Most of us know perfectly well what heartrending sights of misery and woe a single gin-shop can disclose, without being put under the influence of chloroform, and waking up again, for the purpose. But what *we* drink has no part in that; and the draining of all the rivers of the earth for our drink, would not quench a spark of that baleful fire. We abstain from bad language, from horrible oaths, from filthy and profane conversation, from fighting and kicking. Our abstinence is no example to the lowest orders. And why? Because their lives are lives of ignorance, indecency, squalor, filth, neglect, and desolate wretchedness. Every incident in every such life, every minute of every day of every year of every such life, is a provocation to drunkenness; and while such lives are led by scores of thousands of people in the capital of the world alone, drunkenness will flourish, though the sober people were to drink the sea dry.

"The causes of juvenile depravity must be sought, not only in the want of education, but in the drinking habits of the community." For "drinking" read "drunken," and for "community" read "lowest orders,"—to be plain and honest, for once, in this kind of statement,—and we assent to the proposition. But Mr Beggs knows (he states that he knows, over and over again, afterwards) that drunkenness is the inseparable companion of ignorance. Drunkenness, dirt, and ignorance, are the three Fates of the wretched. And are we to be told, being out of Bedlam, that the removal of the ignorance, and the removal of the dirt, would not remove the drunkenness, because the middle and the upper classes choose to set the example of moderation instead of abstinence? If the lowest classes were brought within the influence of any wholesome example at all, which they are not now, is there no example in that quality of moderation which Tee-Total Societies so sorely need?

"Among the institutions which are the glory and the pride of our time," says Mr Beggs, "we place Sabbath-schools." We are not quite so enthusiastic as Mr Beggs on this point, though we give great credit to that "noble band" of whom he speaks, the teachers in the Sunday-schools. But we consider that a system of education infinitely more judiciously administered, and taking a wider worldly range, than any which obtains in any Sunday-school, is necessary for these miserable people whom the Sunday-schools have hitherto addressed in vain; and we consider that for all young people it is very dangerous to make the Sunday (as it is the tendency of the existing schools to do) too restrictive and severe. Let us turn to Mr Beggs on Sunday-schools.

Mr T. B. Smithies, of York, a zealous Sabbath-school teacher, informs us, that he recently visited one of the prisons in York Castle, in which were fourteen convicts, principally youths under fourteen years of age. On conversing with them, he found *that thirteen of them had been Sunday-scholars,* and ten out of the thirteen acknowledged that drink had brought them there. A medical gentleman connected with a public institution had been curious enough to inquire into the moral condition of a number of unfortunate women who had been brought under his care. His inquiries were made in relation to their previous modes of life, education, cause of fall, &c. Out of thirty cases, where he felt he might rely upon the statements, he found that twenty-four were under twenty years of age, and eighteen had commenced a vicious course of life before they were seventeen; *fourteen had been educated in Sunday-schools,* the remainder had received no education of any kind. One had been a governess, and another a publican's daughter. A warm friend of Sunday-schools and the temperance cause states, that in a town in Lancashire no less than *four unfortunate females were seen together in the street, every one of whom had been a teacher in a Sabbath-school.* In a large proportion of the cases, drink or drinking establishments was the first cause of their fall. The Committee of the Rochdale Temperance Society commenced, a short time back, a most important inquiry in relation to Sabbath-school children. "A few months ago a member of the Committee visited one of the singing saloons in Rochdale, and on a Saturday evening, about eleven o'clock, he observed sixteen boys and girls seated at a table in front of the stage; several of the lads had long pipes each, with a glass or jug containing intoxicating liquor, and *no less than fourteen of the number were members of the Bible classes in different Sunday-schools.* There they sat, listening to the most obscene songs, witnessing scenes of the most immoral kind, and swallowing liquid fire." It is added, "*These sinks of iniquity are thronged with old Sunday scholars, especially on Sunday evenings,* and not infrequently until twelve o'clock." Still further, "*The appalling results of the drinking system are not wholly confined to the scholars; many a promising teacher has fallen a victim.*"

This is all owing to drink, of course, and particularly to the sober women who have not dashed down their cups, and the sober men who have not banished their social glasses. But, there are minds so constituted, perhaps, as to infer from these premises that there must be something a little amiss in the Sunday-schools themselves—unless they have a special dispensation from being known by their fruits, like all other institutions.

It is a good instance of the confusion of ideas which prevails among the declaimers about total abstinence, that the strongest piece of evidence in all this volume goes directly to the advantages of moderation, and has nothing in the world to do with total abstinence. In certain coal, copper, tin, and chemical works in Glamorganshire, employing, of men, women, and children, about 4,500, it appears that a most just and humane system of society has been established by the employers. "The sanitary condition of their dwellings is of the most favourable kind, with suitable accommodation for the wants of families." There are churches and chapels. There are schools. There are lectures on useful and entertaining subjects. There is singing in classes. There are innocent and healthful sports. Is there anything more? A little more.

The temptation of the public-house is as far as possible removed. THERE ARE ONLY TWO allowed upon the property of the Company, *which are also kept under strict regulations, and are never open after ten o'clock at night.* Mr Vigurs adds the remarkable testimony (in most striking contrast with the degraded sensuality of the people of the great works "on the hills" of Monmouthshire and Brecon), *that he does not remember to have seen, during his long residence, a drunken man wandering about, or that a case, arising out of drunkenness, was once brought before the magistrates.*

It does not appear that these good employers have done any damage to their own cups and social glasses. It does not appear that they have got upon platforms to deliver statements "cooked" like Mr Hudson's accounts, or sought to make a braggart reputation by administering pledges, to be broken like the same honourable gentleman's iron diadem. But they have bestirred themselves, like men of energy and sense—like good, practical, earnest, honest, faithful, resolute men—to raise their work-people to a condition of cleanliness, comfort, steady industry, instruction, relaxation, self-respect. And the condition of their work-people is in startling contrast with the degraded sensuality of other work-people similarly employed, and there is no drunkenness among them! And this it is that is needful to be done, on a great scale, for the moral redemption of the prostrate thousands in this kingdom. Drunkenness is rife among the very poor and wretched, as every other low and sensual vice is rife among them, because, for years, they have been left behind in the march of civilisation, and have been sinking deeper and deeper down into the mire, left in the track of the advancing forces. Where drunkenness obtains among workmen who receive good wages, as among the miners, and the iron-workers in the North, it is bred in similar causes. Their occupation is of an exhausting kind; a state of lassitude succeeds, demanding some relief, and having none; their ignorance is dense, their little towns and villages are miserable, and their only refuge is in that accursed vice, born as naturally of such a state of things as fire and smoke of lighted gunpowder. No such attempt as that made at the Glamorganshire works, has ever been discreetly made, and failed. The time is close at hand, when the Government, in imitation of such gallant individuals, must cope with the great evil and great danger of this country, or there is no hope left in us.

But, before such an effort can be made with any chance of success, a deep conviction of its necessity, and a full determination on the part of all classes of society to co-operate for such an end, must spread throughout the length and breadth of England. Now, we tell the total abstinence declaimers plainly, that the association of this great question with the emphatic, homely English phrase of humbug; with Jesuitical perversions of all fact, and truth, and fair deduction; with slanderous aspersions of the industrious and well-conducted parts of the community; with visitations of their own failure on the rational and reasonable home-enjoyments of honest men, who are capable of self-control; is fatal to that state of union and preparation. If they would rest their case on the fair ground of temperance for those who can be temperate, and total abstinence for those who cannot be temperate, and would be content to parade the good they have done (which we do not dispute) in the exceptional cases where persons having no excuse for such misconduct, have yielded to a depraved passion for strong liquor and fallen into a gulf of misery, we should regard them as a good example, and a public benefit. But, running a-muck like mad Malays, we look upon them as a bad example, and a public evil, only less intolerable than drunkenness itself.

For, the condition of the lowest classes in this country, and the ever-rising, ever-increasing generation of unhappy beings included under that denomination, is a question far too momentous to be trifled with, by the weakness or the unscrupulous devotion to one idea, of any order of men. "There is a poor blind Samson in this land," writes Mr Longfellow of slavery in America; but there is a poor blind Samson in *this* land, as dangerous as he. Like the strong man of old, he is led by a child—an ignorant child. Like him, he has his sinewy arms—one branded Pauperism, and the other Crime—already round the pillars whereupon the house standeth. Let us beware of him in time, before he makes his awful prayer to be avenged upon us for his blindness, and brings the edifice upon himself, and us—a heap of ruins!

Mid-Victorian England

GEORGE ELIOT (1819–80)

Evangelical Teaching: Dr. Cumming (1855)

*G*eorge Eliot, too, was a journalist before she was a novelist, and afterward as
well. Unlike most, she was a considerable intellectual as well. Whereas
Dickens's articles, even on serious subjects, were casual and personal, appropriate for
the weeklies in which they appeared, Eliot's were sober and analytic, review essays in
the Westminster Review *mode. Her first essay in that journal in 1851 (when she
was thirty-one), a review of a two-volume work on the religion of Greeks and
Hebrews, earned her the editorship of the journal (in fact if not quite in title). In the
following half-dozen years, she wrote other essays, including this on John Cumming
as well as four essays on Heinrich Heine, which virtually introduced him to
England—all this while translating Ludwig Feuerbach's* Essence of Christianity
from German and Spinoza's Ethics *from Latin. (She had earlier, at the age of
twenty-seven, translated David Strauss's* Life of Jesus.*)*

*The renowned novelist and formidable intellectual was a still more formidable
moralist. Lord Acton, himself no mean moralist, described Eliot as "a consummate
expert in the pathology of conscience," emblematic of "a generation distracted
between the intense need of believing and the difficulty of belief."*[1] *Three years after
publishing her critique of Cumming, a minister of the Scottish National Church in*

George Eliot (1819–80), "Evangelical Teaching: Dr. Cumming," *Westminster Review,*
October 1855. Reprinted in *Essays of George Eliot,* ed. Thomas Pinney (London, 1963),
pp. 158–89.

1. Acton, "George Eliot's Life" (*Nineteenth Century,* 1885), reprinted in *Historical Essays
and Studies,* ed. J. N. Figgis and R. V. Laurence (London, 1908), pp. 277, 303.

London who was a literal-minded interpreter of Scripture and a narrow-minded practitioner of his faith, Eliot published Scenes of Clerical Life. *That novel portrayed a quite different and far more sympathetic Evangelicalism, one that "brought into palpable existence and operation . . . that idea of duty, that recognition of something to be lived for beyond the mere satisfaction of self, which is to the moral life what the addition of a great central ganglion is to animal life."*[2]

G iven, a man with moderate intellect, a moral standard not higher than the average, some rhetorical affluence and great glibness of speech, what is the career in which, without the aid of birth or money, he may most easily attain power and reputation in English society? Where is that Goshen of mediocrity in which a smattering of science and learning will pass for profound instruction, where platitudes will be accepted as wisdom, bigoted narrowness as holy zeal, unctuous egoism as God-given piety? Let such a man become an evangelical preacher; he will then find it possible to reconcile small ability with great ambition, superficial knowledge with the prestige of erudition, a middling morale with a high reputation for sanctity. Let him shun practical extremes and be ultra only in what is purely theoretic: let him be stringent on predestination, but latitudinarian on fasting; unflinching in insisting on the Eternity of punishment, but diffident of curtailing the substantial comforts of Time; ardent and imaginative on the pre-millennial advent of Christ, but cold and cautious towards every other infringement of the *status quo.* Let him fish for souls not with the bait of inconvenient singularity, but with the dragnet of comfortable conformity. Let him be hard and literal in his interpretation only when he wants to hurl texts at the heads of unbelievers and adversaries, but when the letter of the Scriptures presses too closely on the genteel Christianity of the nineteenth century, let him use his spiritualizing alembic and disperse it into impalpable ether. Let him preach less of Christ than of Antichrist; let him be less definite in showing what sin is than in showing who is the Man of Sin, less expansive on the blessedness of faith than on the accursedness of infidelity. Above all, let him set up as an interpreter of prophecy, and rival Moore's Almanack in the prediction of political events, tickling the interest of hearers who are but moderately spiritual by showing how the Holy Spirit has dictated problems and charades for their benefit, and how, if they are ingenious enough to solve these, they may have their Christian graces nourished by learning precisely to whom they may point as the "horn that had eyes," "the lying prophet," and the "unclean spirits." In this way he will draw men to him by the strong cords of their passions, made reason-proof by being baptized with the name of piety. In this way he may gain a metropolitan pulpit; the avenues to his

2. Eliot, *Scenes of Clerical Life* ([1858] Phila., n.d.), p. 342.

church will be as crowded as the passages to the opera; he has but to print his prophetic sermons and bind them in lilac and gold, and they will adorn the drawing-room table of all evangelical ladies, who will regard as a sort of pious "light reading" the demonstration that the prophecy of the locusts whose sting is in their tail, is fulfilled in the fact of the Turkish commander's having taken a horse's tail for his standard, and that the French are the very frogs predicted in the Revelations.

Pleasant to the clerical flesh under such circumstances is the arrival of Sunday! Somewhat at a disadvantage during the week, in the presence of working-day interests and lay splendours, on Sunday the preacher becomes the cynosure of a thousand eyes, and predominates at once over the Amphitryon with whom he dines, and the most captious member of his church or vestry. He has an immense advantage over all other public speakers. The platform orator is subject to the criticism of hisses and groans. Counsel for the plaintiff expects the retort of counsel for the defendant. The honourable gentleman on one side of the House is liable to have his facts and figures shown up by his honourable friend on the opposite side. Even the scientific or literary lecturer, if he is dull or incompetent, may see the best part of his audience quietly slip out one by one. But the preacher is completely master of the situation: no one may hiss, no one may depart. Like the writer of imaginary conversations, he may put what imbecilities he pleases into the mouths of his antagonists, and swell with triumph when he has refuted them. He may riot in gratuitous assertions, confident that no man will contradict him; he may exercise perfect free-will in logic, and invent illustrative experience; he may give an evangelical edition of history with the inconvenient facts omitted:—all this he may do with impunity, certain that those of his hearers who are not sympathizing are not listening. For the Press has no band of critics who go the round of the churches and chapels, and are on the watch for a slip or defect in the preacher, to make a "feature" in their article: the clergy are, practically, the most irresponsible of all talkers. For this reason, at least, it is well that they do not always allow their discourses to be merely fugitive, but are often induced to fix them in that black and white in which they are open to the criticism of any man who has the courage and patience to treat them with thorough freedom of speech and pen.

It is because we think this criticism of clerical teaching desirable for the public good, that we devote some pages to Dr. Cumming. He is, as every one knows, a preacher of immense popularity, and of the numerous publications in which he perpetuates his pulpit labours, all circulate widely, and some, according to their title-page, have reached the sixteenth thousand. Now our opinion of these publications is the very opposite of that given by a newspaper eulogist: we do *not* "believe that the repeated issues of Dr. Cumming's thoughts are having a beneficial effect on society," but the reverse; and hence, little inclined as we are to dwell on his pages, we think it worth while to do so, for the sake of pointing out in them what we believe to be profoundly mistaken and pernicious. Of Dr. Cumming personally we know absolutely nothing: our acquaintance with him is confined to a perusal of his works, our judgment of him is founded solely on the manner in which he has written himself down on his pages. We know neither how he looks nor how he lives. We are ignorant whether, like St. Paul, he has a bodily presence that is weak and contemptible, or whether his person is as florid and as prone to amplification as his style. For aught we know, he may not only have the gift of prophecy, but may bestow the profits of all his works to feed the poor, and be ready to give his own body to be burned with as much alacrity as he infers the everlasting burning of Roman-catholics and Puseyites. Out of the pulpit he may be a model of justice, truthfulness, and the love that thinketh no evil; but we are obliged to judge of his charity by the spirit we find in his sermons, and shall only be glad to learn that his practice is, in many respects, an amiable *non sequitur* from his teaching.

Dr. Cumming's mind is evidently not of the pietistic order. There is not the slightest leaning towards mysticism in his Christianity—no indication of religious raptures, of delight in God, or spiritual communion with the Father. He is most at home in the forensic view of Justification, and dwells on salvation as a scheme rather than as an experience. He insists on good works as the sign of justifying faith, as labours to be achieved to the glory of God, but he rarely represents them as the spontaneous, necessary outflow of a soul filled with Divine love. He is at home in the external, the polemical, the historical, the circumstantial, and is only episodically devout and practical. The great majority of his published sermons are occupied with argument or philippic against Romanists and unbelievers, with "vindications" of the Bible, with the political interpretation of prophecy, or the criticism of public events; and the devout aspiration, or the spiritual and practical exhortation, is tacked to them as a sort of fringe in a hurried sentence or two at the end. He revels in the demonstration that the Pope is the Man of Sin; he is copious on the downfall of the Ottoman empire; he appears to glow with satisfaction in turning a story which tends to show how he abashed an "infidel"; it is a favourite exercise with him to form conjectures of the process by which the earth is to be burned up, and to picture Dr. Chalmers and Mr. Wilberforce being caught up to meet Christ in the air, while Romanists, Puseyites, and infidels are given over to gnashing of teeth. But of really spiritual joys and sorrows, of the life and death of Christ as a manifestation of love that constrains the soul, of sympathy with that yearning over the lost and erring which made Jesus weep over Jerusalem, and prompted the sublime prayer, "Father, forgive them," of the gentler fruits of the Spirit, and the peace of God which passeth understanding—of all this, we find little trace in Dr. Cumming's discourses.

His style is in perfect correspondence with this habit of mind. Though diffuse, as that of all preachers must be, it has rapidity of movement, perfect clearness, and some aptness of illustration. He has much of that literary talent which makes a good journalist—the power of beating out an idea over a large space, and of introducing far-fetched *à propos*. His writings have, indeed, no high merit: they have no originality or force of thought, no striking felicity of presentation, no depth of emotion. Throughout nine volumes we have alighted on no passage which impressed us as worth extracting, and placing among the "beauties" of evangelical writers, such as Robert Hall, Foster the Essayist, or Isaac Taylor. Everywhere there is commonplace cleverness, no-where a spark of rare thought, of lofty sentiment, or pathetic tenderness. We feel ourselves in company with a voluble retail talker, whose language is exuber-ant but not exact, and to whom we should never think of referring for precise information, or for well-digested thought and experience. His argument con-tinually slides into wholesale assertion and vague declamation, and in his love of ornament he frequently becomes tawdry. For example, he tells us (Apoc. Sketches, p. 265), that "Botany weaves around the cross her amaranthine garlands; and Newton comes from his starry home—Linnæus from his flowery resting-place—and Werner and Hutton from their subterranean graves at the voice of Chalmers, to acknowledge that all they learned and elicited in their respective provinces, has only served to show more clearly that Jesus of Naza-reth is enthroned on the riches of the universe";—and so prosaic an injunction to his hearers as that they should choose a residence within an easy distance of church, is magnificently draped by him as an exhortation to prefer a house "that basks in the sunshine of the countenance of God." Like all preachers of his class, he is more fertile in imaginative paraphrase than in close exposition, and in this way he gives us some remarkable fragments of what we may call the romance of Scripture, filling up the outline of the record with an elaborate colouring quite undreamed of by more literal minds. The serpent, he informs us, said to Eve, "Can it be so? Surely you are mistaken, that God hath said you shall die, a creature so fair, so lovely, so beautiful. It is impossible. *The laws of nature and physical science tell you that my interpretation is correct;* you shall not die. I can tell you by my own experience as an angel that you shall be as gods, knowing good and evil" (Apoc. Sketches, p. 294). Again, according to Dr. Cumming, Abel had so clear an idea of the Incarnation and Atonement, that when he offered his sacrifice "he must have said, 'I feel myself a guilty sinner, and that in myself I cannot meet thee alive; I lay on thine altar this victim, and I shed its blood as my testimony that mine should be shed; and I look for forgiveness and undeserved mercy through Him who is to bruise the serpent's head, and whose atonement this typifies.'" (Occas. Disc. vol. i, p. 23.) Indeed, his productions are essentially ephemeral; he is essentially a journalist, who writes sermons instead of leading articles, who, instead of venting diatribes against her Majesty's Ministers, directs his power of invective against Cardinal Wiseman and the Puseyites,—instead of declaiming on public spirit, perorates on the "glory of God." We fancy he is called, in the more refined evangelical circles, an "intellectual preacher"; by the plainer sort of Christians, a "flowery preacher"; and we are inclined to think that the more spiritually-minded class of believers, who look with greater anxiety for the kingdom of God within them than for the visible advent of Christ in 1864, will be likely to find Dr. Cumming's declamatory flights and historico-prophetical exercitations as little better than "cloutes o' cauld parritch."

Such is our general impression from his writings after an attentive perusal. There are some particular characteristics which we shall consider more closely, but in doing so we must be understood as altogether declining any doctrinal discussion. We have no intention to consider the grounds of Dr. Cumming's dogmatic system, to examine the principles of his prophetic exegesis, or to question his opinion concerning the little horn, the river Euphrates, or the seven vials. We identify ourselves with no one of the bodies whom he regards it as his special mission to attack: we give our adhesion neither to Romanism, Puseyism, nor to that anomalous combination of opinions which he introduces to us under the name of Infidelity. It is simply as spectators that we criticize Dr. Cumming's mode of warfare, and we concern ourselves less with what he holds to be Christian truth than with his manner of enforcing that truth, less with the doctrines he teaches than with the moral spirit and tendencies of his teaching.

One of the most striking characteristics of Dr. Cumming's writings is *unscrupulosity of statement.* His motto apparently is, *Christianitatem, quocunque modo, Christianitatem;* and the only system he includes under the term Christianity is Calvinistic Protestantism. Experience has so long shown that the human brain is a congenial nidus for inconsistent beliefs, that we do not pause to inquire how Dr. Cumming, who attributes the conversion of the unbelieving to the Divine Spirit, can think it necessary to cooperate with that Spirit by argumentative white lies. Nor do we for a moment impugn the genuineness of his zeal for Christianity, or the sincerity of his conviction that the doctrines he preaches are necessary to salvation; on the contrary, we regard the flagrant unveracity that we find on his pages as an indirect result of that conviction—as a result, namely, of the intellectual and moral distortion of view which is inevitably produced by assigning to dogmas, based on a very complex structure of evidence, the place and authority of first truths. A distinct appreciation of the value of evidence—in other words, the intellectual perception of truth—is more closely allied to truthfulness of statement, or the moral quality of veracity, than is generally admitted. There is not a more pernicious fallacy afloat in common parlance, than the wide distinction made between intellect and morality. Amiable impulses without intellect, man may have in common with dogs and horses; but morality, which is specifically human, is dependent on the regulation of feeling by intellect. All human beings who can be said to be in any degree moral have their impulses guided, not indeed always by their own intellect, but by the intellect of human beings who have gone before them, and created traditions and associations which have taken the rank of laws. Now that highest moral habit, the constant preference of truth both theoretically and practically, preeminently demands the cooperation of the intellect with the impulses; as is indicated by the fact that it is only found in anything like completeness in the highest class of minds. In accordance with this we think it is found that, in proportion as religious sects exalt feeling above intellect, and believe themselves to be guided by direct inspiration rather than by a spontaneous exertion of their faculties—that is, in proportion as they are removed from rationalism—their sense of truthfulness is misty and confused. No one can have talked to the more enthusiastic Methodists and listened to their stories of miracles without perceiving that they require no other passport to a statement than that it accords with their wishes and their general conception of God's dealings; nay, they regard as a symptom of sinful scepticism an inquiry into the evidence for a story which they think unquestionably tends to the glory of God, and in retailing such stories, new particulars, further tending to his glory, are "borne in" upon their minds. Now, Dr. Cumming, as we have said, is no enthusiastic pietist: within a certain circle—within the mill of evangelical orthodoxy, his intellect is perpetually at work; but that principle of sophistication which our friends the Methodists derive from the predominance of their pietistic feelings, is involved for him in the doctrine of verbal inspiration; what is for them a state of emotion submerging the intellect, is with him a formula imprisoning the intellect, depriving it of its proper function—the free search for truth—and making it the mere servant-of-all-work to a foregone conclusion. Minds fettered by this doctrine no longer inquire concerning a proposition whether it is attested by sufficient evidence, but whether it accords with Scripture; they do not search for facts, as such, but for facts that will bear out their doctrine. They become accustomed to reject the more direct evidence in favour of the less direct, and where adverse evidence reaches demonstration they must resort to devices and expedients in order to explain away contradiction. It is easy to see that this mental habit blunts not only the perception of truth, but the sense of truthfulness, and that the man whose faith drives him into fallacies, treads close upon the precipice of falsehood.

We have entered into this digression for the sake of mitigating the inference that is likely to be drawn from that characteristic of Dr. Cumming's works to which we have pointed. He is much in the same intellectual condition as that Professor of Padua, who, in order to disprove Galileo's discovery of Jupiter's satellites, urged that as there were only seven metals there could not be more than seven planets—a mental condition scarcely compatible with candour. And we may well suppose that if the Professor had held the belief in seven planets, and no more, to be a necessary condition of salvation, his mental vision would have been so dazed that even if he had consented to look through Galileo's telescope, his eyes would have reported in accordance with his inward alarms rather than with the external fact. So long as a belief in propositions is regarded as indispensable to salvation, the pursuit of truth *as such* is not possible, any more than it is possible for a man who is swimming for his life to make meteorological observations on the storm which threatens to over-whelm him. The sense of alarm and haste, the anxiety for personal safety, which Dr. Cumming insists upon as the proper religious attitude, unmans the nature, and allows no thorough, calm-thinking, no truly noble, disinterested feeling. Hence, we by no means suspect that the unscrupulosity of statement with which we charge Dr. Cumming, extends beyond the sphere of his theo-logical prejudices; we do not doubt that, religion apart, he appreciates and practises veracity.

A grave general accusation must be supported by details, and in adducing these, we purposely select the most obvious cases of misrepresentation—such as require no argument to expose them, but can be perceived at a glance. Among Dr. Cumming's numerous books, one of the most notable for unscrupulosity of statement is the "Manual of Christian Evidences," written, as he tells us in his Preface, not to give the deepest solutions of the difficulties in question, but to furnish Scripture-Readers, City Missionaries, and Sunday School Teachers, with a "ready reply" to sceptical arguments. This announcement that *readiness* was the chief quality sought for in the solutions here given, modifies our inference from the other qualities which those solutions present; and it is but fair to presume, that when the Christian disputant is not in a hurry, Dr. Cumming would recommend replies less ready and more veracious. Here is an example of what in another place he tells his readers is "change in their pocket. . . . a little ready argument which they can employ, and therewith answer a fool according to his folly." From the nature of this argumentative small coin, we are inclined to think Dr. Cumming understands answering a fool according to his folly to mean, giving him a foolish answer. We quote from the "Manual of Christian Evidences," p. 62.

Some of the gods which the heathen worshipped were among the great-est monsters that ever walked the earth. Mercury was a thief; and because he was an expert thief, he was enrolled among the gods. Bacchus was a mere sensualist and drunkard; and therefore he was enrolled among the gods. Venus was a dissipated and abandoned courtezan; and therefore she was enrolled among the goddesses. Mars was a savage, that gloried in battle and in blood; and therefore he was deified and enrolled among the gods.

Does Dr. Cumming believe the purport of these sentences? If so, this passage is worth handing down as his theory of the Greek myth—as a specimen of the astounding ignorance which was possible in a metropolitan preacher, A.D. 1854. And if he does not believe them. . . . The inference must then be, that he thinks delicate veracity about the ancient Greeks is not a Christian virtue, but only a "splendid sin" of the unregenerate. This inference is rendered the more probable by our finding, a little further on, that he is not more scrupulous about the moderns, if they come under his definition of "Infidels." But the passage we are about to quote in proof of this has a worse quality than its discrepancy with fact. Who that has a spark of generous feeling, that rejoices in the presence of good in a fellow-being, has not dwelt with pleasure on the thought that Lord Byron's unhappy career was ennobled and purified towards its close by a high and sympathetic purpose, by honest and energetic efforts for his fellow-men? Who has not read with deep emotion those last pathetic lines, beautiful as the afterglow of sunset, in which love and resignation are mingled with something of a melancholy heroism? Who has not lingered with compassion over the dying scene at Missolonghi—the sufferer's inability to make his farewell messages of love intelligible, and the last long hours of silent pain? Yet for the sake of furnishing his disciples with a "ready reply," Dr. Cumming can prevail on himself to inoculate them with a bad-spirited falsity like the following:

> We have one striking exhibition of *an infidel's brightest thoughts,* in some lines *written in his dying moments* by a man, gifted with great genius, capable of prodigious intellectual prowess, but of worthless principle, and yet more worthless practices—I mean the celebrated Lord Byron. He says—

> Though gay companions o'er the bowl
>   Dispel awhile the sense of ill
> Though pleasure fills the maddening soul,
>   The heart—*the heart* is lonely still.

> Ay, but to die, and go, alas!
>   Where all have gone and all must go;
> To be the *Nothing* that I was,
>   Ere born to life and living woe!

Count o'er the joys thine hours have seen,
  Count o'er thy days from anguish free,
And know, whatever thou hast been,
  'Tis *something better* not to be.

Nay, for myself, so dark my fate
  Through every turn of life hath been,
Man and the *world* so much *I hate*
  I care not when I quit the scene.

It is difficult to suppose that Dr. Cumming can have been so grossly imposed upon—that he can be so ill-informed as really to believe that these lines
were "written" by Lord Byron in his dying moments; but, allowing him the full
benefit of that possibility, how shall we explain his introduction of this feebly
rabid doggrel as "an infidel's brightest thoughts"?

In marshalling the evidences of Christianity, Dr. Cumming directs most of
his arguments against opinions that are either totally imaginary, or that belong
to the past rather than to the present, while he entirely fails to meet the
difficulties actually felt and urged by those who are unable to accept Revelation. There can hardly be a stronger proof of misconception as to the character
of free-thinking in the present day, than the recommendation of Leland's
"Short and Easy Method with the Deists"—a method which is unquestionably
short and easy for preachers disinclined to reconsider their stereotyped modes
of thinking and arguing, but which has quite ceased to realize those epithets in
the conversion of Deists. Yet Dr. Cumming not only recommends this book,
but takes the trouble himself to write a feebler version of its arguments. For
example, on the question of the genuineness and authenticity of the New
Testament writings, he says:—"If, therefore, at a period long subsequent to the
death of Christ, a number of men had appeared in the world, drawn up a book
which they christened by the name of Holy Scripture, and recorded these
things which appear in it as facts when they were only the fancies of their own
imagination, surely the *Jews* would have instantly reclaimed that no such
events transpired, that no such person as Jesus Christ appeared in their capital,
and that *their* crucifixion of Him, and their alleged evil treatment of his
apostles, were mere fictions." It is scarcely necessary to say that, in such argument as this, Dr. Cumming is beating the air. He is meeting a hypothesis
which no one holds, and totally missing the real question. The only type of
"infidel" whose existence Dr. Cumming recognises is that fossil personage who
"calls the Bible a lie and a forgery." He seems to be ignorant—or he chooses to
ignore the fact—that there is a large body of eminently instructed and earnest
men who regard the Hebrew and Christian Scriptures as a series of historical
documents, to be dealt with according to the rules of historical criticism, and

that an equally large number of men, who are not historical critics, find the dogmatic scheme built on the letter of the Scriptures opposed to their profoundest moral convictions. Dr. Cumming's infidel is a man who, because his life is vicious, tries to convince himself that there is no God, and that Christianity is an imposture, but who is all the while secretly conscious that he is opposing the truth, and cannot help "letting out" admissions "that the Bible is the Book of God." We are favoured with the following "Creed of the Infidel":

> I believe that there is no God, but that matter is God, and God is matter; and that it is no matter whether there is any God or not. I believe also that the world was not made, but that the world made itself, or that it had no beginning, and that it will last for ever. I believe that man is a beast; that the soul is the body, and that the body is the soul; and that after death there is neither body nor soul. I believe that there is no religion, that *natural religion is the only religion, and all religion unnatural.* I believe not in Moses; I believe in the first philosophers. I believe not in the evangelists; I believe in Chubb, Collins, Toland, Tindal, and Hobbes. I believe in Lord Bolingbroke, and I believe not in St. Paul. I believe not in revelation; *I believe in tradition; I believe in the Talmud: I believe in the Koran;* I believe not in the Bible. I believe in Socrates; I believe in Confucius; I believe in Mahomet; I believe not in Christ. And lastly, I *believe* in all unbelief.

The intellectual and moral monster whose creed is this complex web of contradictions, is, moreover, according to Dr. Cumming, a being who unites much simplicity and imbecility with his Satanic hardihood—much tenderness of conscience with his obdurate vice. Hear the "proof":

> I once met with an acute and enlightened infidel, with whom I reasoned day after day, and for hours together; I submitted to him the internal, the external, and the experimental evidences, but made no impression on his scorn and unbelief. At length I entertained a suspicion that there was something morally, rather than intellectually wrong, and that the bias was not in the intellect, but in the heart; one day therefore I said to him— "I must now state my conviction, and you may call me uncharitable, but duty compels me; you are living in some known and gross sin." *The man's countenance became pale; he bowed and left me.—Man. of Evidences,* p. 254.

Here we have the remarkable psychological phenomenon of an "acute and enlightened" man who, deliberately purposing to indulge in a favourite sin, and regarding the Gospel with scorn and unbelief, is, nevertheless, so much more scrupulous than the majority of Christians, that he cannot "embrace sin and the Gospel simultaneously"; who is so alarmed at the Gospel in which he does not believe, that he cannot be easy without trying to crush it; whose acuteness and enlightenment suggest to him, as a means of crushing the Gospel, to argue from day to day with Dr. Cumming; and who is withal so naïve that he is taken by surprise when Dr. Cumming, failing in argument, resorts to accusation, and so tender in conscience that, at the mention of his sin, he turns pale and leaves the spot. If there be any human mind in existence capable of holding Dr. Cumming's "Creed of the Infidel," of at the same time believing in tradition and "believing in all unbelief," it must be the mind of the infidel just described, for whose existence we have Dr. Cumming's *ex officio* word as a theologian; and to theologians we may apply what Sancho Panza says of the bachelors of Salamanca, that they never tell lies—except when it suits their purpose.

The total absence from Dr. Cumming's theological mind of any demarcation between fact and rhetoric is exhibited in another passage, where he adopts the dramatic form:

> Ask the peasant on the hills—*and I have asked amid the mountains of Braemar and Dee-side,*—"How do you know that this book is Divine, and that the religion you profess is true? You never read Paley?" "No, I never heard of him,"—"You have never read Butler?" "No, I have never heard of him."—"Nor Chalmers?" "No, I do not know him."—"You have never read any books on evidence?" "No, I have read no such books."—"Then, how do you know this book is true?" "Know it! Tell me that the Dee, the Clunie, and the Garrawalt, the streams at my feet, do not run; that the winds do not sigh amid the gorges of these blue hills; that the sun does not kindle the peaks of Loch-na-Gar; tell me my heart does not beat, and I will believe you; but do not tell me the Bible is not Divine. I have found its truth illuminating my footsteps; its consolations sustaining my heart. May my tongue cleave to my mouth's roof, and my right hand forget its cunning, if I ever deny what is my deepest inner experience, that this blessed book is the book of God."—*Church before the Flood,* p. 35.

Dr. Cumming is so slippery and lax in his mode of presentation, that we find it impossible to gather whether he means to assert, that this is what a peasant on the mountains of Braemar *did* say, or that it is what such a peasant *would* say: in the one case, the passage may be taken as a measure of his truthfulness; in the other, of his judgment.

His own faith, apparently, has not been altogether intuitive, like that of his rhetorical peasant, for he tells us (Apoc. Sketches, p. 405) that he has himself experienced what it is to have religious doubts. "I was tainted while at the University by this spirit of scepticism. I thought Christianity might not be true. The very possibility of its being true was the thought I felt I must meet and settle. Conscience could give me no peace till I had settled it. I read, and I have read from that day, for fourteen or fifteen years, till this, and now I am as convinced, upon the clearest evidence, that this book is the book of God as that I now address you." This experience, however, instead of impressing on him the fact that doubt may be the stamp of a truth-loving mind—that *sunt quibus non credidisse honor est, et fidei futuræ pignus*—seems to have produced precisely the contrary effect. It has not enabled him even to conceive the condition of a mind "perplext in faith but pure in deeds," craving light, yearning for a faith that will harmonize and cherish its highest powers and aspirations, but unable to find that faith in dogmatic Christianity. His own doubts apparently were of a different kind. Nowhere in his pages have we found a humble, candid, sympathetic attempt to meet the difficulties that may be felt by an ingenuous mind. Everywhere he supposes that the doubter is hardened, conceited, consciously shutting his eyes to the light—a fool who is to be answered according to his folly—that is, with ready replies made up of reckless assertions, of apocryphal anecdotes, and, where other resources fail, of vituperative imputations. As to the reading which he has prosecuted for fifteen years—*either* it has left him totally ignorant of the relation which his own religious creed bears to the criticism and philosophy of the nineteenth century, *or* he systematically blinks that criticism and that philosophy; and instead of honestly and seriously endeavouring to meet and solve what he knows to be the real difficulties, contents himself with setting up popinjays to shoot at, for the sake of confirming the ignorance and winning the cheap admiration of his evangelical hearers and readers. Like the Catholic preacher who, after throwing down his cap and apostrophizing it as Luther, turned to his audience and said, "You see this heretical fellow has not a word to say for himself," Dr. Cumming, having drawn his ugly portrait of the infidel, and put arguments of a convenient quality into his mouth, finds a "short and easy method" of confounding this "croaking frog."

In his treatment of infidels, we imagine he is guided by a mental process which may be expressed in the following syllogism: Whatever tends to the glory of God is true; it is for the glory of God that infidels should be as bad as possible; therefore, whatever tends to show that infidels are as bad as possible is true. All infidels, he tells us, have been men of "gross and licentious lives." Is there not some well-known unbeliever, David Hume, for example, of whom even Dr. Cumming's readers may have heard as an exception? No matter. Some one suspected that he was *not* an exception, and as that suspicion tends to the glory of God, it is one for a Christian to entertain. (See "Man. of Ev." p. 73.)— If we were unable to imagine this kind of self-sophistication, we should be obliged to suppose that, relying on the ignorance of his evangelical disciples, he fed them with direct and conscious falsehoods. "Voltaire," he informs them, "declares there is no God"; he was "an antitheist, that is, one who deliberately and avowedly opposed and hated God; who swore in his blasphemy that he would dethrone him"; and "advocated the very depths of the lowest sensuality." With regard to many statements of a similar kind, equally at variance with truth, in Dr. Cumming's volumes, we presume that he has been misled by hearsay or by the secondhand character of his acquaintance with free-thinking literature. An evangelical preacher is not obliged to be well-read. Here, however, is a case which the extremest supposition of educated ignorance will not reach. Even books of "evidences" quote from Voltaire the line—"Si Dieu n'existait pas, il faudrait l'inventer"; even persons fed on the mere whey and buttermilk of literature, must know that in philosophy Voltaire was nothing if not a theist—must know that he wrote not against God, but against Jehovah, the God of the Jews, whom he believed to be a false God—must know that to say Voltaire was an atheist on this ground is as absurd as to say that a Jacobite opposed hereditary monarchy, because he declared the Brunswick family had no title to the throne. That Dr. Cumming should repeat the vulgar fables about Voltaire's death, is merely what we might expect from the specimens we have seen of his illustrative stories. A man whose accounts of his own experience are apocryphal, is not likely to put borrowed narratives to any severe test.

The alliance between intellectual and moral perversion is strikingly typified by the way in which he alternates from the unveracious to the absurd, from misrepresentation to contradiction. Side by side with the adduction of "facts" such as those we have quoted, we find him arguing on one page that the Trinity was too grand a doctrine to have been conceived by man, and was *therefore* Divine; and on another page, that the Incarnation *had* been pre-conceived by man, and is *therefore* to be accepted as Divine. But we are less concerned with the fallacy of his "ready replies," than with their falsity; and even of this we can only afford space for a very few specimens. Here is one: "There is a *thousand times* more proof that the gospel of John was written by him than there is that the Αναβασις was written by Xenophon, or the Ars Poetica by Horace." If Dr. Cumming had chosen Plato's Epistles or Anacreon's Poems, instead of the Anabasis or the Ars Poetica, he would have reduced the extent of the falsehood, and would have furnished a ready reply which would have been equally effective with his Sunday-school teachers and their disputants. Hence we conclude this prodigality of misstatement, this exuberance of mendacity, is an effervescence of zeal *in majorem gloriam Dei.* Elsewhere he tells us that "the idea of the author of the 'Vestiges' is, that man is the development of a monkey, that the monkey is the embryo man, so that *if you keep a baboon long enough, it will develope itself into a man.*" How well Dr. Cumming has qualified himself to judge of the ideas in "that very unphilosophical book," as he pronounces it, may be inferred from the fact that he implies the author of the "Vestiges" to have *originated* the nebular hypothesis.

In the volume from which the last extract is taken, even the hardihood of assertion is surpassed by the suicidal character of the argument. It is called "The Church before the Flood," and is devoted chiefly to the adjustment of the question between the Bible and Geology. Keeping within the limits we have prescribed to ourselves, we do not enter into the matter of this discussion; we merely pause a little over the volume in order to point out Dr. Cumming's mode of treating the question. He first tells us that "the Bible has not a single scientific error in it"; that "*its slightest intimations of scientific principles or natural phenomena have in every instance been demonstrated to be exactly and strictly true,*" and he asks:

> How is it that Moses, with no greater education than the Hindoo or the ancient philosopher, has written his book, touching science at a thousand points, so accurately, that scientific research has discovered no flaws in it; and yet in those investigations which have taken place in more recent centuries, it has not been shown that he has committed one single error, or made one solitary assertion which can be proved by the maturest science, or by the most eagle-eyed philosopher, to be incorrect, scientifically or historically?

According to this, the relation of the Bible to Science should be one of the strong points of apologists for Revelation: the scientific accuracy of Moses should stand at the head of their evidences; and they might urge with some cogency, that since Aristotle, who devoted himself to science, and lived many ages after Moses, does little else than err ingeniously, this fact, that the Jewish Lawgiver, though touching science at a thousand points, has written nothing that has not been "demonstrated to be exactly and strictly true," is an irrefragable proof of his having derived his knowledge from a supernatural source. How does it happen, then, that Dr. Cumming forsakes this strong position? How is it that we find him, some pages further on, engaged in reconciling Genesis with the discoveries of science, by means of imaginative hypotheses and feats of "interpretation"? Surely, that which has been demonstrated to be exactly and strictly true does not require hypothesis and critical argument, in order to show that it may *possibly* agree with those very discoveries by means of which its exact and strict truth has been demonstrated. And why should Dr. Cumming suppose, as we shall presently find him supposing, that men of science hesitate to accept the Bible, because it appears to contradict their discoveries? By his own statement, that appearance of contradiction does not exist; on the contrary, it has been demonstrated that the Bible precisely agrees with their discoveries. Perhaps, however, in saying of the Bible that its "slightest intimations of scientific principles or natural phenomena have in every instance been demonstrated to be exactly and strictly true," Dr. Cumming merely means to imply that theologians have found out a way of explaining the biblical text so that it no longer, in their opinion, appears to be in contradiction with the discoveries of science. One of two things, therefore: either, he uses language without the slightest appreciation of its real meaning; or, the assertions he makes on one page are directly contradicted by the arguments he urges on another.

Dr. Cumming's principles—or, we should rather say, confused notions—of biblical interpretation, as exhibited in this volume, are particularly significant of his mental calibre. He says ("Church before the Flood," p. 93): "Men of science, who are full of scientific investigation and enamoured of scientific discovery, will hesitate before they accept a book which, they think, contradicts the plainest and the most unequivocal disclosures they have made in the bowels of the earth, or among the stars of the sky. To all these we answer, as we have already indicated, there is not the least dissonance between God's written book and the most mature discoveries of geological science. One thing, however, there may be; *there may be a contradiction between the discoveries of geology and our preconceived interpretations of the Bible.* But this is not because the Bible is wrong, but because our interpretation is wrong." (The italics in all cases are our own.)

Elsewhere he says: "It seems to me plainly evident that the record of Genesis, when read fairly, and not in the light of our prejudices,—*and mind you, the essence of Popery is to read the Bible in the light of our opinions, instead of viewing our opinions in the light of the Bible, in its plain and obvious sense,*—falls in perfectly with the assertion of geologists."

On comparing these two passages, we gather that when Dr. Cumming, under stress of geological discovery, assigns to the biblical text a meaning entirely different from that which, on his own showing, was universally ascribed to it for more than three thousand years, he regards himself as "viewing his opinions in the light of the Bible in its plain and obvious sense"! Now he is reduced to one of two alternatives: either, he must hold that the "plain and obvious meaning" of the whole Bible differs from age to age, so that the criterion of its meaning lies in the sum of knowledge possessed by each successive age—the Bible being an elastic garment for the growing thought of mankind; or, he must hold that some portions are amenable to this criterion, and others not so. In the former case, he accepts the principle of interpretation adopted by the early German rationalists; in the latter case, he has to show a further criterion by which we can judge what parts of the Bible are elastic and what rigid. If he says that the interpretation of the text is rigid wherever it treats of doctrines necessary to salvation, we answer, that for doctrines to be necessary to salvation they must first be true; and in order to be true, according to his own principle, they must be founded on a correct interpretation of the biblical text. Thus he makes the necessity of doctrines to salvation the criterion of infallible interpretation, and infallible interpretation the criterion of doctrines being necessary to salvation. He is whirled round in a circle, having, by admitting the principle of novelty in interpretation, completely deprived himself of a basis. That he should seize the very moment in which he is most palpably betraying that he has no test of biblical truth beyond his own opinion, as an appropriate occasion for flinging the rather novel reproach against Popery that its essence is to "read the Bible in the light of our opinions," would be an almost pathetic self-exposure, if it were not disgusting. Imbecility that is not even meek, ceases to be pitiable and becomes simply odious.

Parenthetic lashes of this kind against Popery are very frequent with Dr. Cumming, and occur even in his more devout passages, where their introduction must surely disturb the spiritual exercises of his hearers. Indeed, Roman-catholics fare worse with him even than infidels. Infidels are the small vermin—the mice to be bagged *en passant*. The main object of his chace—the rats which are to be nailed up as trophies—are the Roman-catholics. Romanism is the master-piece of Satan; but re-assure yourselves! Dr. Cumming has been created. Antichrist is enthroned in the Vatican; but he is stoutly withstood by the Boanerges of Crowncourt. The personality of Satan, as might be expected, is a very prominent tenet in Dr. Cumming's discourses; those who doubt it are, he thinks, "generally specimens of the victims of Satan as a triumphant seducer"; and it is through the medium of this doctrine that he habitually contemplates Roman-catholics. They are the puppets of which the devil holds the strings. It is only exceptionally that he speaks of them as fellow-men, acted on by the same desires, fears, and hopes as himself; his *rule* is to hold them up to his hearers as foredoomed instruments of Satan, and vessels of wrath. If he is obliged to admit that they are "no shams," that they are "thoroughly in earnest"—that is because they are inspired by hell, because they are under an "infra-natural" influence. If their missionaries are found wherever Protestant missionaries go, this zeal in propagating their faith is not in them a consistent virtue, as it is in Protestants, but a "melancholy fact," affording additional evidence that they are instigated and assisted by the devil. And Dr. Cumming is inclined to think that they work miracles, because that is no more than might be expected from the known ability of Satan who inspires them. He admits, indeed, that "there is a fragment of the Church of Christ in the very bosom of that awful apostasy," and that there are members of the Church of Rome in glory; but this admission is rare and episodical—is a declaration, *pro forma,* about as influential on the general disposition and habits as an aristocrat's profession of democracy.

This leads us to mention another conspicuous characteristic of Dr. Cumming's teaching—the *absence of genuine charity.* It is true that he makes large profession of tolerance and liberality within a certain circle; he exhorts Christians to unity; he would have Churchmen fraternize with Dissenters, and exhorts these two branches of God's family to defer the settlement of their differences till the millennium. But the love thus taught is the love of the *clan,* which is the correlative of antagonism to the rest of mankind. It is not sympathy and helpfulness towards men as men, but towards men as Christians, and as Christians in the sense of a small minority. Dr. Cumming's religion may demand a tribute of love, but it gives a charter to hatred; it may enjoin charity, but it fosters all uncharitableness. If I believe that God tells me to love my enemies, but at the same time hates His own enemies and requires me to have one will with Him, which has the larger scope, love or hatred? And we refer to those pages of Dr. Cumming's in which he opposes Roman-catholics, Puseyites, and infidels—pages which form the larger proportion of what he has published—for proof that the idea of God which both the logic and spirit of his discourses keep present to his hearers, is that of a God who hates his enemies, a God who teaches love by fierce denunciations of wrath—a God who encourages obedience to his precepts by elaborately revealing to us that his own government is in precise opposition to those precepts. We know the usual evasions on this subject. We know Dr. Cumming would say that even Roman-catholics are to be loved and succoured as men; that he would help even that "unclean spirit," Cardinal Wiseman, out of a ditch. But who that is in the slightest degree acquainted with the action of the human mind, will believe that any genuine and large charity can grow out of an exercise of love which is always to have an *arrière-pensée* of hatred? Of what quality would be the conjugal love of a husband who loved his spouse as a wife, but hated her as a woman? It is reserved for the regenerate mind, according to Dr. Cumming's conception of it, to be "wise, amazed, temperate and furious, loyal and neutral, in a moment." Precepts of charity uttered with faint breath at the end of a sermon are perfectly futile, when all the force of the lungs has been spent in keeping the hearer's mind fixed on the conception of his fellow-men, not as fellow-sinners and fellow-sufferers, but as agents of hell, as automata through whom Satan plays his game upon earth,—not on objects which call forth their reverence, their love, their hope of good even in the most strayed and perverted, but on a minute identification of human things with such symbols as the scarlet whore, the beast out of the abyss, scorpions whose sting is in their tails, men who have the mark of the beast, and unclean spirits like frogs. You might as well attempt to educate a child's sense of beauty by hanging its nursery with the horrible and grotesque pictures in which the early painters represented the Last Judgment, as expect Christian graces to flourish on that prophetic interpretation which Dr. Cumming offers as the principal nutriment of his flock. Quite apart from the critical basis of that interpretation, quite apart from the degree of truth there may be in Dr. Cumming's prognostications—questions into which we do not choose to enter—his use of prophecy must be *a priori* condemned in the judgment of right-minded persons, by its results as testified in the net moral effect of his sermons. The best minds that accept Christianity as a divinely inspired system, believe that the great end of the Gospel is not merely the saving but the educating of men's souls, the creating within them of holy dispositions, the subduing of egoistical pretensions, and the perpetual enhancing of the desire that the will of God—a will synonymous with goodness and truth—may be done on earth. But what relation to all this has a system of interpretation which keeps the mind of the Christian in the position of a spectator at a gladiatorial show, of which Satan is the wild beast in the shape of the great red dragon, and two-thirds of mankind the victims—the whole provided and got up by God for the edification of the saints? The demonstration that the Second Advent is at hand, if true, can have no really holy, spiritual effect; the highest state of mind inculcated by the Gospel is resignation to the disposal of God's providence—"Whether we live, we live unto the Lord; whether we die, we die unto the Lord"—not an eagerness to see a temporal manifestation which shall confound the enemies of God and give exaltation to the saints; it is to dwell in Christ by spiritual communion with his nature, not to fix the date when He shall appear in the sky. Dr. Cumming's delight in shadowing forth the downfall of the Man of Sin, in prognosticating the battle of Gog and Magog, and in advertizing the pre-millennial Advent, is simply the transportation of political passions on to a so-called religious platform; it is the anticipation of the triumph of "our party," accomplished by our principal men being "sent for" into the clouds. Let us be understood to speak in all seriousness. If we were in search of amusement, we should not seek for it by examining Dr. Cumming's works in order to ridicule them. We are simply discharging a disagreeable duty in delivering our opinion that, judged by the highest standard even of orthodox Christianity, they are little calculated to produce:

> A closer walk with God,
> A calm and heavenly frame; [William Cowper]

but are more likely to nourish egoistic complacency and pretension, a hard and condemnatory spirit towards one's fellow-men, and a busy occupation with the minutiæ of events, instead of a reverent contemplation of great facts and a wise application of great principles. It would be idle to consider Dr. Cumming's theory of prophecy in any other light,—as a philosophy of history or a specimen of biblical interpretation; it bears about the same relation to the extension of genuine knowledge as the astrological "house" in the heavens bears to the true structure and relations of the universe.

The slight degree in which Dr. Cumming's faith is imbued with truly human sympathies, is exhibited in the way he treats the doctrine of Eternal Punishment. *Here* a little of that readiness to strain the letter of the Scriptures which he so often manifests when his object is to prove a point against Romanism, would have been an amiable frailty if it had been applied on the side of mercy. When he is bent on proving that the prophecy concerning the Man of Sin, in the Second Epistle to the Thessalonians, refers to the Pope, he can extort from the innocent word καθισαι the meaning *cathedrize,* though why we are to translate "He as God cathedrizes in the temple of God," any more than we are to translate "cathedrize here, while I go and pray yonder," it is for Dr. Cumming to show more clearly than he has yet done. But when rigorous literality will favour the conclusion that the greater proportion of the human race will be eternally miserable—*then* he is rigorously literal.

He says: "The Greek words, εἰς τους αἰῶνας των αἰῶνων here translated 'everlasting,' signify literally 'unto the ages of ages'; αἰεὶ ὢν, 'always being,' that is, everlasting, ceaseless existence. Plato uses the word in this sense when he says, 'The gods that live for ever.' *But I must also admit,* that this word is used several times in a limited extent,—as for instance, 'The everlasting hills.' Of course, this does not mean that there never will be a time when the hills will cease to stand; the expression here is evidently figurative, but it implies eternity. The hills shall remain as long as the earth lasts, and no hand has power to remove them but that Eternal One which first called them into being; *so the state of the soul* remains the same after death as long as the soul exists, and no one has power to alter it. The same word is often applied to denote the existence of God—'the Eternal God.' Can we limit the word when applied to Him? Because occasionally used in a limited sense, we must not infer it is always so. 'Everlasting' plainly means in Scripture 'without end'; it is only to be explained figuratively when it is evident it cannot be interpreted in any other way."

We do not discuss whether Dr. Cumming's interpretation accords with the meaning of the New Testament writers: we simply point to the fact that the text becomes elastic for him when he wants freer play for his prejudices, while he makes it an adamantine barrier against the admission that mercy will ultimately triumph,—that God, *i.e.,* Love, will be all in all. He assures us that he does not "delight to dwell on the misery of the lost": and we believe him. That misery does not seem to be a question of feeling with him, either one way or the other. He does not merely resign himself to the awful mystery of eternal punishment; he contends for it. Do we object, he asks, to everlasting happiness? then why object to everlasting misery?—reasoning which is perhaps felt to be cogent by theologians who anticipate the everlasting happiness for themselves, and the everlasting misery for their neighbours.

The compassion of some Christians has been glad to take refuge in the opinion, that the Bible allows the supposition of annihilation for the impenitent: but the rigid sequence of Dr. Cumming's reasoning will not admit of this idea. He sees that flax is made into linen, and linen into paper; that paper, when burnt, partly ascends as smoke and then again descends in rain, or in dust and carbon. "Not one particle of the original flax is lost, although there may be not one particle that has not undergone an entire change: annihilation is not, but change of form is. *It will be thus with our bodies at the resurrection.* The death of the body means not annihilation. *Not one feature of the face* will be annihilated." Having established the perpetuity of the body by this close and clear analogy, namely, that *as* there is a total change in the particles of flax in consequence of which they no longer appear as flax, *so* there will *not* be a total change in the particles of the human body, but they will re-appear as the human body, he does not seem to consider that the perpetuity of the body involves the perpetuity of the soul, but requires separate evidence for this, and finds such evidence by begging the very question at issue; namely, by asserting that the text of the Scriptures implies "the perpetuity of the punishment of the lost, and the consciousness of the punishment which they endure." Yet it is drivelling like this which is listened to and lauded as eloquence by hundreds, and which a Doctor of Divinity can believe that he has his "reward as a saint" for preaching and publishing!

One more characteristic of Dr. Cumming's writings, and we have done. This is the *perverted moral judgment* that everywhere reigns in them. Not that this perversion is peculiar to Dr. Cumming: it belongs to the dogmatic system which he shares with all evangelical believers. But the abstract tendencies of systems are represented in very different degrees, according to the different characters of those who embrace them; just as the same food tells differently on different constitutions: and there are certain qualities in Dr. Cumming that cause the perversion of which we speak to exhibit itself with peculiar prominence in his teaching. A single extract will enable us to explain what we mean:

> The "thoughts" are evil. If it were possible for human eye to discern and to detect the thoughts that flutter round the heart of an unregenerate man—to mark their hue and their multitude, it would be found that they are indeed "evil." We speak not of the thief, and the murderer, and the adulterer, and such like, whose crimes draw down the cognizance of earthly tribunals, and whose unenviable character it is to take the lead in the paths of sin; but we refer to the men who are marked out by their practice of many of the seemliest moralities of life—by the exercise of the kindliest affections, and the interchange of the sweetest reciprocities—and of these men, if unrenewed and unchanged, we pronounce that their

thoughts are evil. To ascertain this, we must refer to the object around which our thoughts ought continually to circulate. The Scriptures assert that this object is *the glory of God;* that for this we ought to think, to act, and to speak; and that in thus thinking, acting, and speaking, there is involved the purest and most endearing bliss. Now it will be found true of the most amiable men, that with all their good society and kindliness of heart, and all their strict and unbending integrity, they never or rarely think of the glory of God. The question never occurs to them—Will this redound to the glory of God? Will this make his name more known, his being more loved, his praise more sung? And just inasmuch as their every thought comes short of this lofty aim, in so much does it come short of good, and entitle itself to the character of evil. If the glory of God is not the absorbing and the influential aim of their thoughts, then they are evil; but God's glory never enters into their minds. They are amiable, because it chances to be one of the constitutional tendencies of their individual character, left uneffaced by the Fall; and *they are just and upright, because they have perhaps no occasion to be otherwise, or find it subservient to their interests to maintain such a character.*—(Occ. Disc. vol. i. p. 8). . . . Again we read (Ibid. p. 236), There are traits in the Christian character which the mere wordly man cannot understand. He can understand the outward morality, but he cannot understand the inner spring of it; he can understand Dorcas' liberality to the poor, but he cannot penetrate the ground of Dorcas' liberality. *Some men give to the poor because they are ostentatious, or because they think the poor will ultimately avenge their neglect; but the Christian gives to the poor, not only because he has sensibilities like other men,* but because inasmuch as ye did it to the least of these my brethren ye did it unto me.

Before entering on the more general question involved in these quotations, we must point to the clauses we have marked with italics, where Dr. Cumming appears to express sentiments which, we are happy to think, are not shared by the majority of his brethren in the faith. Dr. Cumming, it seems, is unable to conceive that the natural man can have any other motive for being just and upright than that it is useless to be otherwise, or that a character for honesty is profitable; according to his experience, between the feelings of ostentation and selfish alarm and the feeling of love to Christ, there lie no sensibilities which can lead a man to relieve want. Granting, as we should prefer to think, that it is Dr. Cumming's exposition of his sentiments which is deficient rather than his sentiments themselves, still, the fact that the deficiency lies precisely here, and that he can overlook it not only in the haste of oral delivery but in the examination of proof-sheets, is strongly significant of his mental bias—of the faint degree in which he sympathizes with the disinterested elements of human feeling, and of the fact, which we are about to dwell upon, that those feelings are totally absent from his religious theory. Now, Dr. Cumming invariably assumes that, in fulminating against those who differ from him, he is standing on a moral elevation to which they are compelled reluctantly to look up; that his theory of motives and conduct is in its loftiness and purity a perpetual rebuke to their low and vicious desires and practice. It is time he should be told that the reverse is the fact; that there are men who do not merely cast a superficial glance at his doctrine, and fail to see its beauty or justice, but who, after a close consideration of that doctrine, pronounce it to be subversive of true moral development, and therefore positively noxious. Dr. Cumming is fond of showing-up the teaching of Romanism, and accusing it of undermining true morality: it is time he should be told that there is a large body, both of thinkers and practical men, who hold precisely the same opinion of his own teaching—with this difference, that they do not regard it as the inspiration of Satan, but as the natural crop of a human mind where the soil is chiefly made up of egoistic passions and dogmatic beliefs.

Dr. Cumming's theory, as we have seen, is that actions are good or evil according as they are prompted or not prompted by an exclusive reference to the "glory of God." God, then, in Dr. Cumming's conception, is a being who has no pleasure in the exercise of love and truthfulness and justice, considered as effecting the well-being of his creatures; He has satisfaction in us only in so far as we exhaust our motives and dispositions of all relation to our fellow-beings, and replace sympathy with men by anxiety for the "glory of God." The deed of Grace Darling, when she took a boat in the storm to rescue drowning men and women, was not good if it was only compassion that nerved her arm and impelled her to brave death for the chance of saving others; it was only good if she asked herself—Will this redound to the glory of God? The man who endures tortures rather than betray a trust, the man who spends years in toil in order to discharge an obligation from which the law declares him free, must be animated not by the spirit of fidelity to his fellow-man, but by a desire to make "the name of God more known." The sweet charities of domestic life—the ready hand and the soothing word in sickness, the forebearance towards frailties, the prompt helpfulness in all efforts and sympathy in all joys, are simply evil if they result from a "constitutional tendency," or from dispositions disciplined by the experience of suffering and the perception of moral loveliness. A wife is not to devote herself to her husband out of love to him and a sense of the duties implied by a close relation—she is to be a faithful wife for the glory of God; if she feels her natural affections welling up too strongly, she is to repress them; it will not do to act from natural affection—she must think of the glory of God. A man is to guide his affairs with energy and discretion, not from an honest desire to fulfil his responsibilities as a member of society and a father, but—that "God's praise may be sung." Dr. Cumming's Christian pays his debts for the glory of God; were it not for the coercion of that supreme motive, it would be evil to pay them. A man is not to be just from a feeling of justice; he is not to help his fellow-men out of good-will to his fellow-men; he is not to be a tender husband and father out of affection: all these natural muscles and fibres are to be torn away and replaced by a patent steel-spring—anxiety for the "glory of God."

Happily, the constitution of human nature forbids the complete prevalence of such a theory. Fatally powerful as religious systems have been, human nature is stronger and wider than religious systems, and though dogmas may hamper, they cannot absolutely repress its growth: build walls round the living tree as you will, the bricks and mortar have by and bye to give way before the slow and sure operation of the sap. But next to that hatred of the enemies of God which is the principle of persecution, there perhaps has been no perversion more obstructive of true moral development than this substitution of a reference to the glory of God for the direct promptings of the sympathetic feelings. Benevolence and justice are strong only in proportion as they are directly and inevitably called into activity by their proper objects: pity is strong only because we are strongly impressed by suffering; and only in proportion as it is compassion that speaks through the eyes when we soothe, and moves the arm when we succour, is a deed strictly benevolent. If the soothing or the succour be given because another being wishes or approves it, the deed ceases to be one of benevolence, and becomes one of deference, of obedience, of self-interest, or vanity. Accessory motives may aid in producing an *action*, but they pre-suppose the weakness of the direct motive; and conversely, when the direct motive is strong, the action of accessory motives will be excluded. If then, as Dr. Cumming inculcates, the glory of God is to be "the absorbing and the influential aim" in our thoughts and actions, this must tend to neutralize the human sympathies; the stream of feeling will be diverted from its natural current in order to feed an artificial canal. The idea of God is really moral in its influence—it really cherishes all that is best and loveliest in man—only when God is contemplated as sympathizing with the pure elements of human feeling, as possessing infinitely all those attributes which we recognize to be moral in humanity. In this light, the idea of God and the sense of His presence intensify all noble feeling, and encourage all noble effort, on the same principle that human sympathy is found a source of strength: the brave man feels braver when he knows that another stout heart is beating time with his; the devoted woman who is wearing out her years in patient effort to alleviate suffering or save vice from the last stages of degradation, finds aid in the pressure of a friendly hand which tells her that there is one who understands her deeds, and in her place would do the like. The idea of a God who not only sympathizes with all we feel and endure for our fellow-men, but who will pour new life into our too languid love, and give firmness to our vacillating purpose, is an extension and multiplication of the effects produced by human sympathy; and it has been intensified for the better spirits who have been under the influence of orthodox Christianity, by the contemplation of Jesus as "God manifest in the flesh." But Dr. Cumming's God is the very opposite of all this: he is a God who instead of sharing and aiding our human sympathies, is directly in collision with them; who instead of strengthening the bond between man and man, by encouraging the sense that they are both alike the objects of His love and care, thrusts himself between them and forbids them to feel for each other except as they have relation to Him. He is a God, who, instead of adding his solar force to swell the tide of those impulses that tend to give humanity a common life in which the good of one is the good of all, commands us to check those impulses, lest they should prevent us from thinking of His glory. It is in vain for Dr. Cumming to say that we are to love man for God's sake: with the conception of God which his teaching presents, the love of man for God's sake involves, as his writings abundantly show, a strong principle of hatred. We can only love one being for the sake of another when there is an habitual delight in associating the idea of those two beings—that is, when the object of our indirect love is a source of joy and honour to the object of our direct love: but, according to Dr. Cumming's theory, the majority of mankind—the majority of his neighbours are in precisely the opposite relation to God. His soul has no pleasure in them, they belong more to Satan than to Him, and if they contribute to His glory, it is against their will. Dr. Cumming then can only love *some* men for God's sake; the rest he must in consistency *hate* for God's sake.

There must be many, even in the circle of Dr. Cumming's admirers, who would be revolted by the doctrine we have just exposed, if their natural good sense and healthy feeling were not early stifled by dogmatic beliefs, and their reverence misled by pious phrases. But as it is, many a rational question, many a generous instinct, is repelled as the suggestion of a supernatural enemy, or as the ebullition of human pride and corruption. This state of inward contradiction can be put an end to only by the conviction that the free and diligent exertion of the intellect, instead of being a sin, is a part of their responsibility— that Right and Reason are synonymous. The fundamental faith for man is faith in the result of a brave, honest, and steady use of all his faculties:

> Let knowledge grow from more to more
> But more of reverence in us dwell;
> That mind and soul according well
> May make one music as before,
> But vaster. [Tennyson, *In Memoriam*]

Before taking leave of Dr. Cumming, let us express a hope that we have in no case exaggerated the unfavourable character of the inferences to be drawn from his pages. His creed often obliges him to hope the worst of men, and to exert himself in proving that the worst is true; but thus far we are happier than he. We have no theory which requires us to attribute unworthy motives to Dr. Cumming, no opinions, religious or irreligious, which can make it a gratification to us to detect him in delinquencies. On the contrary, the better we are able to think of him as a man, while we are obliged to disapprove him as a theologian, the stronger will be the evidence for our conviction, that the tendency towards good in human nature has a force which no creed can utterly counteract, and which ensures the ultimate triumph of that tendency over all dogmatic perversions.

WALTER BAGEHOT (1826–77)

"Dull Government," "Average Government," and "Thinking Government" (1856)

*T*he most astute historian of Victorian England, G. M. Young, entitled his essay on Bagehot *"The Greatest Victorian"*—*"a man who was in and of his age, and who could have been of no other: a man with sympathy to share, and genius to judge, its sentiments and movements:* . . . *whose influence, passing from one fit mind to another, could transmit, and can still impart, the most precious element in Victorian civilization, its robust and masculine sanity."*[1] *Bagehot's essays preaching the virtues of "dullness" and the pitfalls of "thought," in prose that is eminently thoughtful and anything but dull, may be offered in evidence of that encomium.*

In earlier essays on the 1851 coup d'état that overthrew the Second Republic, Bagehot had made the famous (or infamous) pronouncement that "the most essential quality for a free people, whose liberty is to be progressive, permanent, and on a large scale, . . . *is much stupidity.* . . . *Nations, just as individuals, may be too clever to be practical, and not dull enough to be free."*[2] *The genius of the English, he insisted, was to be both dull and free. Later, in* The English Constitution *(1865),*

Walter Bagehot (1826–77), "Dull Government," "Average Government," "Thinking Government," *Saturday Review,* February 16 to April 19, 1856. Reprinted in *Collected Works of Walter Bagehot,* ed. Norman St-John-Stevas (London, 1974), VI, 81–98.

1. G. M. Young, *Victorian Essays,* ed. W. D. Hancock (Oxford, 1962), p. 126.
2. "Letters on the French Coup D'Etat of 1851," *Inquirer,* January 20, 1852, in *Collected Works,* IV, 50–53.

he qualified this dictum. It is "the dull traditional habit of mankind that guides most men's actions," he declared, but he then went on to favor the parliamentary rather than presidential system of government because Parliament had the useful function of serving as "the great scene of debate, the great engine of popular instruction and political controversy."[3] In his final major work, Physics and Politics *(1872), he went so far as to praise "government by discussion" as the unique feature of the modern age, discussion having the virtue of promoting an "animated moderation," a "vigorous moderateness in mind and body."[4]*

Dull Government

P arliament is a great thing, but it is not a cheerful thing. Just reflect on the existence of "Mr. SPEAKER." First, a small man speaks to him—then a shrill man speaks to him—then a man who cannot speak *will* speak to him. He leads a life of "passing tolls," joint-stock companies, and members out of order. Life is short, but the forms of the House are long. Mr. Ewart complains that a multitude of members, including the Prime Minister himself, actually go to sleep. The very morning paper feels the weight of this leaden *régime*. Even in the dullest society you hear complaints of the dullness of Parliament—of the representative tedium of the nation.

That an Englishman should grumble is quite right, but that he should grumble at gravity is hardly right. He is rarely a lively being himself, and he should have a sympathy with those of his kind. And he should further be reminded that his criticism is out of place—that dullness in matters of government is a good sign, and not a bad one—that, in particular, dullness in parliamentary government is a test of its excellence, an indication of its success. The truth is, all the best business is a little dull. If you go into a merchant's counting-house, you see steel pens, vouchers, files, books of depressing magnitude, desks of awful elevation, staid spiders, and sober clerks moving among the implements of tedium. No doubt, to the parties engaged, much of this is very attractive. "What," it has been well said, "are technicalities to those without, are realities to those within." To every line in those volumes, to every paper on those damp files, there has gone doubt, decision, action—the work of a considerate brain, the touch of a patient hand. Yet even to those engaged, it is commonly the least interesting business which is the best. The more the doubt, the greater the liability to error—the longer the consideration, generally the worse the result—the more the pain of decision, the greater the likelihood of failure. In Westmin-

3. *The English Constitution* (1867), in *Collected Works*, V, 209, 216. (The essay "The Cabinet" first appeared in the *Fortnightly Review*, May 15, 1865.)
4. *Physics and Politics* (1872), in *Collected Works*, VII, 124, 131–32. (The essay "The Age of Discussion" appeared in the *Fortnightly Review*, Jan. 1, 1872.)

ster Hall, they have a legend of a litigant who stopped his case because the lawyers said it was "interesting." "Ah," he remarked afterwards, "they were going up to the 'Lords' with it, and I should never have seen my money." To parties concerned in law, the best case is a plain case. To parties concerned in trade, the best transaction is a plain transaction—the sure result of familiar knowledge; in political matters, the best sign that things are going well is that there should be nothing difficult—nothing requiring deep contention of mind—no anxious doubt, no sharp resolution, no lofty and patriotic execution. The opportunity for these qualities is the danger of the commonwealth. You cannot have a Chatham in time of peace—you cannot storm a Redan in Somersetshire. There is no room for glorious daring in periods of placid happiness.

And if this be the usual rule, certainly there is nothing in the nature of parliamentary government to exempt it from its operation. If business is dull, business wrangling is no better. It is dull for an absolute minister to have to decide on passing tolls, but it is still duller to hear a debate on them—to have to listen to the two extremes and the *via media.* One honourable member considers that the existing ninepence ought to be maintained; another thinks it ought to be abolished; and a third—the independent thinker—has statistics of his own, and suggests that fourpence-halfpenny would "attain the maximum of revenue with the minimum of inconvenience"—only he could wish there were a decimal coinage to "facilitate the calculations of practical pilots." Of course this is not the highest specimen of parliamentary speaking. Doubtless, on great questions, when the public mind is divided, when the national spirit is roused, when powerful interests are opposed, when large principles are working their way, when deep difficulties press for a decision, there is an opportunity for noble eloquence. But these very circumstances are the signs, perhaps of calamity, certainly of political difficulty and national doubt. The national spirit is not roused in happy times—powerful interests are not divided in years of peace—the path of great principles is marked through history by trouble, anxiety, and conflict. An orator requires a topic. "Thoughts that breathe and words that burn" will not suit the "liability of joint-stock companies"—you cannot shed tears over a "toll." Where can there be a better proof of national welfare than that Disraeli cannot be sarcastic, and that Lord Derby fails in a diatribe? Happy is the country which is at peace within its borders—yet stupid is the country when the opposition is without a cry.

Moreover, when parliamentary business is a bore, it is a bore which cannot be overlooked. There is much torpor secreted in the *bureaux* of an absolute government, but no one hears of it—no one knows of its existence. In England it is different. With pains and labour—by the efforts of attorneys—by the votes of freeholders—you collect more than six hundred gentlemen; and the question is, what are they to do? As they come together at a specific time, it would seem that they do so for a specific purpose—but what it is they do not know. It is the business of the Prime Minister to discover it for them. It is extremely hard on an effervescent First Lord to have to set people down to mere business—to bore them with slow reforms—to explain details they cannot care for—to abolish abuses they never heard of—to consume the hours of the night among the perplexing details of an official morning. But such is the Constitution. The Parliament is assembled—some work must be found for it—and this is all that there is. The details which an autocratic government most studiously conceals are exposed in open day—the national sums are done in public—finance is made the most of. If the war had not intervened, who knows that by this time Parliament would not be commonly considered "The Debating Board of Trade"? Intelligent foreigners can hardly be brought to understand this. It puzzles them to imagine how any good or smooth result can be educed from so much jangling, talking, and arguing. M. de Montalembert has described amazement as among his predominant sensations in England. He felt, he says, as if he were in a manufactory—where wheels rolled, and hammers sounded, and engines crunched—where all was certainly noise, and where all seemed to be confusion—but from which, nevertheless, by a miracle of industrial art, some beautiful fabric issued, soft, complete, and perfect. Perhaps this simile is too flattering to the neatness of our legislation, but it happily expresses the depressing noise and tedious din by which its results are really arrived at.

As are the occupations, so are the men. Different kinds of government cause an endless variety in the qualities of statesmen. Not a little of the interest of political history consists in the singular degree in which it shows the mutability and flexibility of human nature. After various changes, we are now arrived at the business statesman—or rather, the business speaker. The details which have to be alluded to, the tedious reforms which have to be effected, the long figures which have to be explained, the slow arguments which require a reply—the heaviness of subjects, in a word—have caused a corresponding weight in our oratory. Our great speeches are speeches of exposition—our eloquence is an eloquence of detail. No one can read or hear the speeches of our ablest and most enlightened statesmen without being struck with the contrast which they exhibit—we do not say to the orations of antiquity (which were delivered under circumstances too different to allow of a comparison), but to the great parliamentary displays of the last age—of Pitt, or Fox, or Canning. Differing from each other as the latter do in most of their characteristics, they all fall exactly within Sir James Mackintosh's definition of parliamentary oratory—"animated and continuous after-dinner conversation." They all have a gentlemanly effervescence and lively agreeability. They are suitable to times when the questions discussed were few, simple, and large—when detail was not—when the first requisite was a pleasant statement of obvious considerations. We

are troubled—at least our orators are troubled—with more complex and difficult topics. The patient exposition, the elaborate minuteness, the exhaustive
disquisition, of modern parliamentary eloquence, would formerly have been
out of place—they are now necessary on complicated subjects, which require
the exercise of a laborious intellect, and a discriminating understanding. We
have not gained in liveliness by the change, and those who remember the great
speakers of the last age are the loudest in complaining of our tedium. The old
style still lingers on the lips of Lord Palmerston; but it is daily yielding to a
more earnest and practical, to a sober *before*-dinner style.

It is of no light importance that these considerations should be recognised,
and their value carefully weighed. It has been the bane of many countries
which have tried to obtain freedom, but failed in the attempt, that they have
regarded popular government rather as a means of intellectual excitement than
as an implement of political work. The preliminary discussion was more interesting than the consequent action. They found it pleasanter to refine arguments than to effect results—more glorious to expand the mind with general
ratiocination than to contract it to actual business. They wished, in a word, to
have a popular government, without, at the same time, having a dull government. The English people have never yet forgotten what some nations have
scarcely ever remembered—that politics are a kind of business—that they bear
the characteristics, and obey the laws, inevitably incident to that kind of
human action. Steady labour and dull material—wrinkles on the forehead and
figures on the tongue—these are the English admiration. We may prize more
splendid qualities on uncommon occasions, but these are for daily wear. You
cannot have an æra *per annum*—if every year had something memorable for
posterity, how would posterity ever remember it? Dullness is our line, as cleverness is that of the French. Woe to the English people if they ever forget that, all
through their history, heavy topics and tedious talents have awakened the
admiration and engrossed the time of their Parliament and their country.

Average Government

Many persons are for ever demanding a great statesman. They should be
asked, however, what they want him for? People should consider the use of
people. It may be well to think what manner of man a commanding statesman
really is. The description of such a personage divides itself into two parts—his
disposition and his intellect. What the disposition of a first-rate practical man
naturally is, the reading world has just had unusual opportunities of learning.
Both ancient and modern times have contributed to its illustration. Mr. Grote
has given us a description of Alexander the Great; and Napoleon, in his letters
to his brother, has left the picture of himself. Different as were the circum-

stances and intellect of the two heroes, one might fancy that, in both cases, it was the same overbearing character. "What is the world that it should strive to contend against *me?*" was the motto of both—in both we see the naturalness of the alliance between imperial talents and imperious mind. Men who can govern wish to govern—men who can rule will rule. A sense of power animates the powerful. Those who have passed their lives in overcoming enormous obstacles—to whom "difficulty is a helper," and whom no adversary can rival— cannot avoid feeling their strength. It is proved to them by the whole experience of their lives. An intense self-reliance is natural to men who can prove an overbearing ability by tangible results—who are successful in verifiable action.

It may further be asked, what we can do with the imperial disposition in this country? There are persons who are quite aware. By one of those curious fatalities which give an interest to intellectual history, the University of Oxford has for some years been fertile in novelty and paradox. Such are the designs of men. The English people wished a centre of tradition for their ancestral belief—they built quiet cloisters, they devised dull tutors, they endowed mouldering colleges. They wanted a place where nothing new would ever be discovered, and where only what was old would thrive. The result is a reaction against the past—a marked opposition to English ideas. It is not within our province to speak of the theological speculations of the past twenty years; but it is very material to our present purpose to point out that the last exposed heresy is a hatred of the English Constitution. The aged Politics of Aristotle have been introduced into the discussion. A Mr. Congreve has published an edition of them in which he tells us plainly that our constitutional system is "effete"—that "our governing classes are incompetent"—that our hope is a despotism popular with the lower classes, or, as he phrases it, "a monocratic dictatorial power supported by the adhesion of the proletariat." The accomplished gentleman is possessed with the idea; and in another work, in some lectures at Edinburgh, he bursts forth in the midst of the most arid history, with an aspiration for the rule of the great Protector. We do not know if any gentleman from the banks of the Isis contemplates commencing the career of a Cromwell, but surely, if not, the obvious plan is to apply to Napoleon the Third. He is a shrewd man—he has the talents for empire—and doubtless he would *contract* to govern England. His taste is lavish, and he might be a little dear; but what is gold to mind? *He* would not reign without governing and under his vigorous rule, admirable lecturers might perhaps, be delicately compressed.

But, passing from these original speculations, what place is there just now for the dictatorial disposition, under the English Constitution? Surely it would be difficult to find. The English idea is a committee—we are born with a belief in a green cloth, clean pens, and twelve men with grey hair. In topics of belief the ultimate standard is a jury. "A jury," as a living judge once said, "would decide this, but how they would decide it, I cannot think." As a jury will discover everything, a board will determine anything, "We speak," observed Lord Brougham, "of the *wisdom* of Parliament." The whole fabric of English society is based upon discussion—all our affairs are decided, after the giving of reasons, by the compromise of opinions. What has the overweening dictator to do here? He is too clever to give reasons, too proud to compromise his judgment. He is himself alone. A dictator will not save us—we require discussion, explanation, controversy. Of course, at particular crises, all this must be abandoned. At perilous epochs, we need practically uncontrolled power; and even an irritable distrust is best allayed by a fresh confidence in a firm and lofty mind. If, on the 1st of February last year, there had been a Chatham in the country, Chatham would have been Prime Minister; but he would not have been so long. We get tired of being commanded. Long before January, 1857, he would have become an "impracticable man"—an opposition orator.

The intellect of the enormous statesman is just as unfit for our circumstances as his disposition. His characteristic is far-seeing originality. In the recesses of his closet, by the mere force of his own understanding, he evolves a set of measures and a course of policy, years before his age, such as the people about him cannot comprehend, such as only posterity will really appreciate. Of what use is this in the House of Commons? That assembly is alive; and though posterity is going to be born, in the meantime there are the contemporaries of the great statesman, sitting in tedium, discussing the affairs of the nation. The condition of a free government is that you must persuade the present generation; and the *gouvernement des avocats,* as the Emperor Nicholas called it, has this for its principle—that you must persuade the average man. You do not address the select intellects of the age, or the more experienced intellect of the next age—but the actual rural individual—the dreary ordinary being. "It is all very well," said an able Whig, "for *The Times* to talk of the intelligence of public opinion—that only means that the public buy *The Times;* public opinion, sir, is the opinion of the bald-headed man at the end of the omnibus."— "Do not tell me of Mr. Pitt," said a surviving Tory—"Mr. Pitt would have found it a very different thing in these days. Mr. Pitt, sir, would have had to persuade Joseph Hume." In truth, one of the dispensations of nature is the opacity of the average man. Nature has provided against the restlessness of genius by the obstinacy of stupidity. The man of genius is an age or two in advance. By incessant industry, subtle argument, or a penetrating eloquence, he impresses his new ideas, first, on the highest minds—next, on the next highest—and it is only after his death that they descend to the inferior *strata,* and become the property of the world. This exactly disqualifies him from agreeing with those about him, from forming a party on a basis of common sympathy, from carrying out what the people wish—from administering, as a statesman must, the creed of his time.

These reflections explain a peculiarity of English history. We have almost always been governed by what Mr. Disraeli has termed "Arch-Mediocrities." From the days of Lord Burghley down to those of Lord Liverpool, we have been governed, for the longest periods and with the greatest ease, by men who were essentially common men—men who never said anything which any one in an omnibus could not understand—men who were never visited by the far-reaching thoughts or exciting aspirations of ardent genius, but who possessed the usual faculties of mankind in an unusual degree—men who were clear upon common points, who knew what people were just going to know, and who could embody in a bill exactly what the commonalty thought should be embodied in a bill. Of course, there may be, now and then, exceptions; for in this complicated world, unlimited principles abound in error. A great man who for years has advocated a great truth may at times be at last rewarded by carrying it out; and the punishment of calamity may teach the multitude what, a short time before, it required a great sagacity to foresee. But these events are, in their nature, exceptions. Regular business forms the regular statesman—quiet habits, sober thoughts, common aims are his obvious characteristics. He is what other men would wish to be. "Be *as* other men," is the precept, "and you will be above other men—be *ordinary,* and you will be great."

Certainly there is nothing at the present moment which emancipates us from the habitual condition of free government. There are no special questions just now which call for the intervention of a man of genius. Our current domestic questions are a heap of specialties. "Passing tolls," "registration of companies," "county constabulary," "chancery reform"—these are the occupations of our life. Fancy Lord Chatham discussing a toll-bill. What a gulph from Bonaparte to a policeman—from Alexander to a master in chancery! The details of the interior, "the streets and fountains which we are repairing, and the battlements which we are whitening"—to borrow from the historian of Greece the phrase of the Olynthiacs—cannot afford scope either for the excitable temperament or for the deep discernment of original genius.

In foreign politics, it is different, and yet the same. We are pretty well agreed about principles—the difficulties are difficulties of fact. We know that we ought to rejoice at freedom, that we should show sympathy with it where it is likely to be stable, and that we should not allow it, even when unstable, to be trodden out by neighbouring despots; but, as the one-armed captain remarked, "The bearings of them observations lies in the application on 'em." We wish to know in what particular states is real freedom—where it is likely to be stable—what risk this republic runs from that despot; and these matters of fact are scarcely fit for the man of genius, as we abstractedly conceive him. At least, if we want a genius in foreign policy, it is a genius of investigation—if in domestic, it is a genius of detail.

Thinking Government

What mankind really wish to economise is thought. Admirable speculators publish beautiful eulogiums on the employment of the faculties, and the universal creed is, that the exertion of the reason is the highest and truest of human enjoyments; yet if a steady observer really looks at actual life, he will see that men never think if they can help it—that they require to be goaded towards it—that they invent devices to avoid it—that, however greedy of enjoyment in other ways, they decline, if possible, to enjoy themselves in this.

One of these devices is, activity. People rush to and fro. They are never still. They go to eight committees in a day, taking care to be pretty late at each—they look at their watches the moment they get there—they spurt out rapid errors. If you suggest a little reflection before doing anything, they say, "Don't bother about that *now*"; and when all has gone wrong, they have the ready plea, "I was so occupied, I could not give *it* a thought." In their own circles, such men are always considered wonderful men of business. It is natural their wives and families should believe in them; for they spend so much toil and trouble, they make everybody so uncomfortable, in order to boil a pea, that those who know no better of course suppose that the pea is boiled. Nevertheless it is not—this impetuous activity is content with the boiling apparatus, and does not regard the useful result. It is among our middle classes, who are often held up as the sole models of men of action, that this kind of error is most rife. Place an active, uneducated man in miscellaneous affairs, and it is nearly certain that he will commit this mistake. He will begin to *do* something—he will state that he is a "practical man"—it will never strike him that there is an essential preliminary to wise exertion. His mind has not been trained to observe the varied relations of complicated phenomena, or to unravel the knotty thread of tangled topics; and so he will be apt to work ten hours a day at what it is scarcely necessary to do at all. He will leave undone the one little, essential, difficult matter—the point of *judgment*—on which alone it was necessary to act or to decide. We do not say that the middle classes manage their own affairs on this principle, though there is a great deal more of it, even in them, than a charitable philosopher would be ready to suspect. Still they have habit, and bringing up, and arithmetic to control them. The ledger guides the mind—the sense of responsibility, of actual definite money-loss, represses undue activity, and compels men to a certain discretion. But if such persons—and they are exactly those whom a government, if compelled to select, would, from their conspicuousness, choose as the representative men of the middle classes—were placed among great national affairs, and not paid a percentage on those affairs, but an inevitable salary from the indestructible taxation, they would act as *very* busy members of Parliament now act. They would run quickly from committee to committee, and make a tour of great questions.

In our administrative departments, happily, this state of things does not prevail. A certain aristocratic *laissez-aller* rather pervades them. In a public office, it would be indecorous to rush like a mighty wind. Yet it would be a great error to imagine that, in so large a department of human life, no expedient to economise thought and to dispense, *pro tanto*, with the pain of reflection, had been discovered and adopted. That resource is what are called business habits. There is such a thing as the pomp of order. In every public office there is a grave official personage, who is always neat, whose papers are always filed, whose handwriting is always regular, who is considered a monster of experience, who can minute any proceeding, and docket any document. There is no finer or more saving investment of exertion than the formation of such habits. Under their safeguard, you may omit anything, and commit every blunder. The English people never expect any one to be original. If it can be said, "The gentleman whose conduct is so harshly impugned is a man of long experience, who is not wont to act hastily—who is remarkable for official precision—in whom many Secretaries of State have placed much reliance," that will do; and it will not be too anxiously inquired what such a man has done. The immense probability is that he has done nothing. He is well aware that, so long as he can say anything is "under consideration," he is safe—and so long as he is safe, he is happy. His education, too, has not fitted him for much exertion. He entered the office young—he copied letters for five years—he made an index of papers for nine months—he made analyses of documents for five years more. When he commenced at last to transact business, it was of a strictly formal character; and he was upwards of twenty years in the public service before he ever decided on anything of essential importance. No wonder that he is unwilling to decide anything—that he refers everything—that he corresponds in his best handwriting with another public office—that, when you want him, you find him entering a minute, "That after mature deliberation, my Lords have postponed the consideration of what has taken place." In actual life, it is really very difficult not to over-estimate the usefulness of such a man. His appearance is so regular—his habits so precise—he has such a command of the instruments of utility—that it is difficult to imagine he does nothing. Only after considerable observation can it be learnt that it is this very command over the forms of action which enables him safely to neglect its essence—that it is his very familiarity with the rules of experience that enables him to apply them mechanically to instances to which they have only an outward reference and no real applicability. It is odd how some of the most gifted of our administrative reformers mistake the true point. The honourable member for Tynemouth, for example, who is a man of business, brought a great charge against the Admiralty that they did not keep the accounts duly and precisely. Of course Sir James Graham had no difficulty in showing that the figures were excellently summed, that the ledger was for ever posted, that all the entries were made most legibly and with extreme care. The more plausible charge would have been precisely the contrary; for it is the tendency of official men to regard what goes on within the office as always more important than what takes place without it. The more probable assumption would have been, that the entries were most correct, but that the transactions were wrong—that the book-keeping was admirable, but the affairs recorded feeble and insufficient. Arithmetic is, indeed, one of the established devices of the pseudo-official mind. When he is much pressed, he commonly adds up something. The mechanical nature of the operation rather suits him—he does it quite right—and his notion of figures rather resembles that of a celebrated actuary, whose wife observed, "Isn't it very odd that the Government could send out things three thousand miles, and *that* Filder could not get them up six," and who replied, "My dear, how you talk, consider the figures, it was only an error of one-fifth per cent." Very many sums are commonly done, and publicly quoted, which have no more real relation to the subject-matter than that of this gifted gentleman.

Our Constitution presents us with yet another contrast to that simple and patient reflection which would naturally seem to be the habit of mind fitted for the judicious conduct of political affairs. All politicians are required to have all opinions. A voting acquaintance with all topics is required from every member of Parliament. From those in high place much more is exacted—they are required to have a ready, producible, defensible view of all great questions. Mr. Macaulay, who has been placed in a position to observe, tells us that, in his judgment, the effects of this are the most serious set-off to the advantages of free government. The habit of debating, and the necessity of making a speech, compel the finest intellects in the country to put forward daily arguments such as no man of sense would think of putting into a scientific treatise. He might have gone further, and said that the habit of always advancing a view commonly destroys the capacity for holding a view. The laxity of principle imputed to old politicians is, by the time they are old, as much intellectual as moral. They have argued on all sides of everything, till they can believe on no side of anything. A characteristic of the same sort has been observed in journalism. One of our most celebrated contemporaries was asked his opinion on ten great subjects in succession, and on its appearing that he had no opinion, he said, apologetically, "You see, ma'am, I have written for *The Times.*"

We are well aware that something of this kind is inevitable. We do not expect from a professional politician the elaborate consideration of a closet philosopher—their ends are different, and their responsibilities are different. We do not wish to abolish official form, and to abandon the most delicate of practical matters to the sudden rush of the uncultivated mind. We admit—if need were, we would maintain—that there are many settled habits—that there is a certain exterior show and seeming—the possession of which is, in this world, a necessary preliminary to important employment. People will not trust you to act well unless you seem to be a person who would act well. Nor do we forget that business is an affair of body as well as of mind. In our objection to a precipitate and unthinking strength, we have no desire to reduce the public service to a sole dependence on feeble thought—on pale and inexecutive ability. We would only stipulate that, previously to all action, in the midst of the correct forms, and without respect to the exigencies of debate, our public men should find room for some painful thought—should give themselves at least a reasonable time for patient and anxious reflection.

JOHN STUART MILL (1806–73)

A Few Words on Non-Intervention (1859)

*T*he immediate occasion of this essay was Palmerston's opposition to the construction of the Suez Canal by the French, on the grounds that such a project
was inimical to England's economic and national interests. In his Autobiography,
Mill explained that he was prompted to write this essay by a desire to vindicate
England from "the imputations commonly brought against her on the Continent, of
a peculiar selfishness in matters of foreign policy," imputations given color by the
"low tone" of such statesmen as Palmerston who spoke of English policy "as concerned
only with English interests." At the same time he wanted to take the opportunity to
reflect upon a subject that had long concerned him: "the true principles of international morality, and the legitimate modifications made in it by difference of times
and circumstances."[1]

Mill's initial purpose was reflected in the stirring opening pages of the essay,
portraying England as a great nation, the least aggressive and the least selfish of all
nations, the least guilty of the obloquy that was being visited upon it. The main
thrust of the paper, however, was the issue of intervention. When was it right, not
merely prudent, for a great nation like England to intervene in the affairs of another
nation, whether in the event of a civil war or a war against an occupying and
despotic power? When, in short, was it right "to go to war for an idea"? Here Mill

John Stuart Mill (1806–73), "A Few Words on Non-Intervention," *Fraser's Magazine*,
December 1859. Reprinted in Mill, *Essays on Politics and Culture*, ed. Gertrude Himmelfarb
(New York, 1962), pp. 396–413.
1. *Autobiography* (New York, 1924), p. 183.

was responding to the wars of national liberation on the Continent, the "noble struggle," for example, of Hungary in 1849 to liberate itself from Austria, which was thwarted when Russia came to the help of Austria while England and France remained neutral. (It is curious that Mill did not mention the Italian war of liberation, which concluded only months before he wrote this essay.) A century and a half later, the terms in which Mill framed this issue are uncannily familiar.

There is a country in Europe, equal to the greatest in extent of dominion, far exceeding any other in wealth, and in the power that wealth bestows, the declared principle of whose foreign policy is, to let other nations alone. No country apprehends or affects to apprehend from it any aggressive designs. Power, from of old, is wont to encroach upon the weak, and to quarrel for ascendancy with those who are as strong as itself. Not so this nation. It will hold its own, it will not submit to encroachment, but if other nations do not meddle with it, it will not meddle with them. Any attempt it makes to exert influence over them, even by persuasion, is rather in the service of others, than of itself; to mediate in the quarrels which break out between foreign States, to arrest obstinate civil wars, to reconcile belligerents, to intercede for mild treatment of the vanquished, or finally, to procure the abandonment of some national crime and scandal to humanity, such as the slave-trade. Not only does this nation desire no benefit to itself at the expense of others, it desires none in which all others do not as freely participate. It makes no treaties stipulating for separate commercial advantages. If the aggressions of barbarians force it to a successful war, and its victorious arms put it in a position to command liberty of trade, whatever it demands for itself it demands for all mankind. The cost of the war is its own; the fruits it shares in fraternal equality with the whole human race. Its own ports and commerce are free as the air and the sky: all its neighbours have full liberty to resort to it, paying either no duties, or, if any, generally a mere equivalent for what is paid by its own citizens; nor does it concern itself though they, on their part, keep all to themselves, and persist in the most jealous and narrow-minded exclusion of its merchants and goods.

A nation adopting this policy is a novelty in the world; so much so, it would appear, that many are unable to believe it when they see it. By one of the practical paradoxes which often meet us in human affairs, it is this nation which finds itself, in respect of its foreign policy, held up to obloquy as the type of egoism and selfishness; as a nation which thinks of nothing but of outwitting and out-generalling its neighbours. An enemy, or a self-fancied rival who had been distanced in the race, might be conceived to give vent to such an accusation in a moment of ill-temper. But that it should be accepted by lookers-on, and should pass into a popular doctrine, is enough to surprise even those who have best sounded the depths of human prejudice. Such, however, is the estimate of the foreign policy of England most widely current on the Continent. Let us not flatter ourselves that it is merely the dishonest pretence of enemies, or of those who have their own purposes to serve by exciting odium against us, a class including all the Protectionist writers, and the mouthpieces of all the despots and of the Papacy. The more blameless and laudable our policy might be, the more certainly we might count on its being misrepresented and failed at by these worthies. Unfortunately the belief is not confined to those whom they can influence, but is held with all the tenacity of a prejudice, by innumerable persons free from interested bias. So strong a hold has it on their minds, that when an Englishman attempts to remove it, all their habitual politeness does not enable them to disguise their utter unbelief in his disclaimer. They are firmly persuaded that no word is said, nor act done, by English statesmen in reference to foreign affairs, which has not for its motive principle some peculiarly English interest. Any profession of the contrary appears to them too ludicrously transparent an attempt to impose upon them. Those most friendly to us think they make a great concession in admitting that the fault may possibly be less with the English people, than with the English Government and aristocracy. We do not even receive credit from them for following our own interest with a straightforward recognition of honesty as the best policy. They believe that we have always other objects than those we avow; and the most far-fetched and unplausible suggestion of a selfish purpose appears to them better entitled to credence than anything so utterly incredible as our disinterestedness. Thus, to give one instance among many, when we taxed ourselves twenty millions (a prodigious sum in their estimation) to get rid of negro slavery, and, for the same object, perilled, as everybody thought, destroyed as many thought, the very existence of our West Indian colonies, it was, and still is, believed, that our fine professions were but to delude the world, and that by this self-sacrificing behaviour we were endeavouring to gain some hidden object, which could neither be conceived nor described, in the way of pulling down other nations. The fox who had lost his tail had an intelligible interest in persuading his neighbours to rid themselves of theirs; but we, it is thought by *our* neighbours, cut off our own magnificent brush, the largest and finest of all, in hopes of reaping some inexplicable advantage from inducing others to do the same.

It is foolish attempting to despise all this—persuading ourselves that it is not our fault, and that those who disbelieve *us* would not believe though one should rise from the dead. Nations, like individuals, ought to suspect some fault in themselves when they find they are generally worse thought of than they think they deserve; and they may well know that they are somehow in fault when almost everybody but themselves thinks them crafty and hypocritical. It is not solely because England has been more successful than other nations in gaining what they are all aiming at, that they think she must be following after it with a more ceaseless and a more undivided chase. This indeed is a powerful predisposing cause, inclining and preparing them for the belief. It is a natural supposition that those who win the prize have striven for it; that superior success must be the fruit of more unremitting endeavour; and where there is an obvious abstinence from the ordinary arts employed for distancing competitors, and they are distanced nevertheless, people are fond of believing that the means employed must have been arts still more subtle and profound. This preconception makes them look out in all quarters for indications to prop up the selfish explanation of our conduct. If our ordinary course of action does not favour this interpretation, they watch for exceptions to our ordinary course, and regard these as the real index to the purposes within. They moreover accept literally all the habitual expressions by which we represent ourselves as worse than we are; expressions often heard from English statesmen, next to never from those of any other country—partly because Englishmen, beyond all the rest of the human race, are so shy of professing virtues that they will even profess vices instead; and partly because almost all English statesmen, while careless to a degree which no foreigner can credit, respecting the impression they produce on foreigners, commit the obtuse blunder of supposing that low objects are the only ones to which the minds of their non-aristocratic fellow-countrymen are amenable, and that it is always expedient, if not necessary, to place those objects in the foremost rank.

All, therefore, who either speak or act in the name of England, are bound by the strongest obligations, both of prudence and of duty, to avoid giving either of these handles for misconstruction: to put a severe restraint upon the mania of professing to act from meaner motives than those by which we are really actuated, and to beware of perversely or capriciously singling out some particular instance in which to act on a worse principle than that by which we are ordinarily guided. Both these salutary cautions our practical statesmen are, at the present time, flagrantly disregarding.

We are now in one of those critical moments, which do not occur once in a generation, when the whole turn of European events, and the course of European history for a long time to come, may depend on the conduct and on the estimation of England. At such a moment, it is difficult to say whether by their sins of speech or of action our statesmen are most effectually playing into the hands of our enemies, and giving most colour of justice to injurious misconception of our character and policy as a people.

To take the sins of speech first: What is the sort of language held in every oration which, during the present European crisis, any English minister, or almost any considerable public man, addresses to parliament or to his constituents? The eternal repetition of this shabby *refrain*—"We did not interfere, because no English interest was involved"; "We ought not to interfere where no English interest is concerned." England is thus exhibited as a country whose most distinguished men are not ashamed to profess, as politicians, a rule of action which no one, not utterly base, could endure to be accused of as the maxim by which he guides his private life; not to move a finger for others unless he sees his private advantage in it. There is much to be said for the doctrine that a nation should be willing to assist its neighbours in throwing off oppression and gaining free institutions. Much also may be said by those who maintain that one nation is incompetent to judge and act for another, and that each should be left to help itself, and seek advantage or submit to disadvantage as it can and will. But of all attitudes which a nation can take up on the subject of intervention, the meanest and worst is to profess that it interferes only when it can serve its own objects by it. Every other nation is entitled to say, "It seems, then, that non-interference is not a matter of principle with you. When you abstain from interference, it is not because you think it wrong. You have no objection to interfere, only it must not be for the sake of those you interfere with; they must not suppose that you have any regard for their good. The good of others is not one of the things you care for; but you are willing to meddle, if by meddling you can gain anything for yourselves." Such is the obvious interpretation of the language used.

There is scarcely any necessity to say, writing to Englishmen, that this is not what our rulers and politicians really mean. Their language is not a correct exponent of their thoughts. They mean a part only of what they seem to say. They do mean to disclaim interference for the sake of doing good to foreign nations. They are quite sincere and in earnest in repudiating this. But the other half of what their words express, a willingness to meddle if by doing so they can promote any interest of England, they do not mean. The thought they have in their minds, is not the interest of England, but her security. What they would say, is, that they are ready to act when England's safety is threatened, or any of her interests hostilely or unfairly endangered. This is no more than what all nations, sufficiently powerful for their own protection, do, and no one questions their right to do. It is the common right of self-defence. But if we mean this, why, in Heaven's name, do we take every possible opportunity of saying, instead of this, something exceedingly different? Not self-defence, but aggrandizement, is the sense which foreign listeners put upon our words. Not simply to protect what we have, and that merely against unfair arts, not against fair rivalry; but to add to it more and more without limit, is the purpose for which foreigners think we claim the liberty of intermeddling with them and their affairs. If our actions make it impossible for the most prejudiced observer to believe that we aim at or would accept any sort of mercantile monopolies, this has no effect on their minds but to make them think that we have chosen a more cunning way to the same end. It is a generally accredited opinion among Continental politicians, especially those who think themselves particularly knowing, that the very existence of England depends upon the incessant acquisition of new markets for our manufactures; that the chase after these is an affair of life and death to us; and that we are at all times ready to trample on every obligation of public or international morality, when the alternative would be, pausing for a moment in that race. It would be superfluous to point out what profound ignorance and misconception of all the laws of national wealth, and all the facts of England's commercial condition, this opinion presupposes: but such ignorance and misconception are unhappily very general on the Continent; they are but slowly, if perceptibly, giving way before the advance of reason; and for generations, perhaps, to come, we shall be judged under their influence. Is it requiring too much from our practical politicians to wish that they would sometimes bear these things in mind? Does it answer any good purpose to express ourselves as if we did not scruple to profess that which we not merely scruple to do, but the bare idea of doing which never crosses our minds? Why should we abnegate the character we might with truth lay claim to, of being incomparably the most conscientious of all nations in our national acts? Of all countries which are sufficiently powerful to be capable of being dangerous to their neighbours, we are perhaps the only one whom mere scruples of conscience would suffice to deter from it. We are the only people among whom, by no class whatever of society, is the interest or glory of the nation considered to be any sufficient excuse for an unjust act; the only one which regards with jealousy and suspicion, and a proneness to hostile criticism, precisely those acts of its Government which in other countries are sure to be hailed with applause, those by which territory has been acquired, or political influence extended. Being in reality better than other nations, in at least the negative part of international morality, let us cease, by the language we use, to give ourselves out as worse.

But if we ought to be careful of our language, a thousand times more obligatory is it upon us to be careful of our deeds, and not suffer ourselves to be betrayed by any of our leading men into a line of conduct on some isolated point, utterly opposed to our habitual principles of action—conduct such that if it were a fair specimen of us, it would verify the calumnies of our worst enemies, and justify them in representing not only that we have no regard for the good of other nations, but that we actually think their good and our own incompatible, and will go all lengths to prevent others from realizing even an advantage in which we ourselves are to share. This pernicious, and, one can scarcely help calling it, almost insane blunder, we seem to be committing on the subject of the Suez Canal.

It is the universal belief in France that English influence at Constantinople,

strenuously exerted to defeat this project, is the real and only invincible obstacle to its being carried into effect. And unhappily the public declarations of our
present Prime Minister not only bear out this persuasion, but warrant the
assertion that we oppose the work because, in the opinion of our Government,
it would be injurious to the interest of England. If such be the course we are
pursuing, and such the motive of it, and if nations have duties, even negative
ones, towards the weal of the human race, it is hard to say whether the folly or
the immorality of our conduct is the most painfully conspicuous.

Here is a project, the practicability of which is indeed a matter in dispute,
but of which no one has attempted to deny that, supposing it realized, it would
give a facility to commerce, and consequently a stimulus to production, an
encouragement to intercourse, and therefore to civilization, which would entitle it to a high rank among the great industrial improvements of modern times.
The contriving of new means of abridging labour and economizing outlay in
the operations of industry, is the object to which the larger half of all the
inventive ingenuity of mankind is at present given up; and this scheme, if
realized, will save, on one of the great highways of the world's traffic, the
circumnavigation of a continent. An easy access of commerce is the main
source of that material civilization, which, in the more backward regions of the
earth, is the necessary condition and indispensable machinery of the moral;
and this scheme reduces practically by one half, the distance, commercially
speaking, between the self-improving nations of the world and the most important and valuable of the unimproving. The Atlantic Telegraph is esteemed
an enterprise of world-wide importance because it abridges the transit of mercantile intelligence merely. What the Suez Canal would shorten is the transport
of the goods themselves, and this to such an extent as probably to augment it
manifold.

Let us suppose, then—for in the present day the hypothesis is too un-
English to be spoken of as anything more than a supposition—let us suppose
that the English nation saw in this great benefit to the civilized and uncivilized
world a danger or damage to some peculiar interest of England. Suppose, for
example, that it feared, by shortening the road, to facilitate the access of foreign
navies to its Oriental possessions. The supposition imputes no ordinary degree
of cowardice and imbecility to the national mind; otherwise it could not but
reflect that the same thing which would facilitate the arrival of an enemy,
would facilitate also that of succour; that we have had French fleets in the
Eastern seas before now, and have fought naval battles with them there, nearly
a century ago; that if we ever became unable to defend India against them, we
should assuredly have them there without the aid of any canal; and that our
power of resisting an enemy does not depend upon putting a little more or less
of obstacle in the way of his coming, but upon the amount of force which we

are able to oppose to him when come. Let us assume, however, that the success of the project would do more harm to England in some separate capacity, than the good which, as the chief commercial nation, she would reap from the great increase of commercial intercourse. Let us grant this: and I now ask, what then? Is there any morality, Christian or secular, which bears out a nation in keeping all the rest of mankind out of some great advantage, because the consequences of their obtaining it may be to itself, in some imaginable contingency, a cause of inconvenience? Is a nation at liberty to adopt as a practical maxim, that what is good for the human race is bad for itself, and to withstand it accordingly? What is this but to declare that its interest and that of mankind are incompatible—that, thus far at least, it is the enemy of the human race? And what ground has it of complaint if, in return, the human race determine to be *its* enemies? So wicked a principle, avowed and acted on by a nation, would entitle the rest of the world to unite in a league against it, and never to make peace until they had, if not reduced it to insignificance, at least sufficiently broken its power to disable it from ever again placing its own self-interest before the general prosperity of mankind.

There is no such base feeling in the British people. They are accustomed to see their advantage in forwarding, not in keeping back, the growth in wealth and civilization of the world. The opposition of the Suez Canal has never been a national opposition. With their usual indifference to foreign affairs, the public in general have not thought about it, but have left it, as (unless when particularly excited) they leave all the management of their foreign policy, to those who, from causes and reasons connected only with internal politics, happen for the time to be in office. Whatever has been done in the name of England in the Suez affair has been the act of individuals; mainly, it is probable, of one individual; scarcely any of his countrymen either prompting or sharing his purpose, and most of those who have paid any attention to the subject (unfortunately a very small number) being, to all appearance, opposed to him.

But (it is said) the scheme cannot be executed. If so, why concern ourselves about it? If the project can come to nothing, why profess gratuitous immorality and incur gratuitous odium to prevent it from being tried? Whether it will succeed or fail is a consideration totally irrelevant; except thus far, that if it is sure to fail, there is in our resistance to it the same immorality, and an additional amount of folly; since, on that supposition, we are parading to the world a belief that our interest is inconsistent with its good, while if the failure of the project would really be any benefit to us, we are certain of obtaining that benefit by merely holding our peace.

As a matter of private opinion, the present writer, so far as he has looked into the evidence, inclines to agree with those who think that the scheme cannot be executed, at least by the means and with the funds proposed. But this is a consideration for the shareholders. The British Government does not deem it any part of its business to prevent individuals, even British citizens, from wasting their own money in unsuccessful speculations, though holding out no prospect of great public usefulness in the event of success. And if, though at the cost of their own property, they acted as pioneers to others, and the scheme, though a losing one to those who first undertook it, should, in the same or in other hands, realize the full expected amount of ultimate benefit to the world at large, it would not be the first nor the hundredth time that an unprofitable enterprise has had this for its final result.

There seems to be no little need that the whole doctrine of non-interference with foreign nations should be reconsidered, if it can be said to have as yet been considered as a really moral question at all. We have heard something lately about being willing to go to war for an idea. To go to war for an idea, if the war is aggressive, not defensive, is as criminal as to go to war for territory or revenue; for it is as little justifiable to force our ideas on other people, as to compel them to submit to our will in any other respect. But there assuredly are cases in which it is allowable to go to war, without having been ourselves attacked, or threatened with attack; and it is very important that nations should make up their minds in time, as to what these cases are. There are few questions which more require to be taken in hand by ethical and political philosophers, with a view to establish some rule or criterion whereby the justifiableness of intervening in the affairs of other countries, and (what is sometimes fully as questionable) the justifiableness of refraining from intervention, may be brought to a definite and rational test. Whoever attempts this, will be led to recognise more than one fundamental distinction, not yet by any means familiar to the public mind, and in general quite lost sight of by those who write in strains of indignant morality on the subject. There is a great difference (for example) between the case in which the nations concerned are of the same, or something like the same, degree of civilization, and that in which one of the parties to the situation is of a high, and the other of a very low, grade of social improvement. To suppose that the same international customs, and the same rules of international morality, can obtain between one civilized nation and another, and between civilized nations and barbarians, is a grave error, and one which no statesman can fall into, however it may be with those who, from a safe and unresponsible position, criticise statesmen. Among many reasons why the same rules cannot be applicable to situations so different, the two following are among the most important. In the first place, the rules of ordinary international morality imply reciprocity. But barbarians will not reciprocate. They cannot be depended on for observing any rules. Their minds are not capable of so great an effort, nor their will sufficiently under the influence of distant motives. In the next place, nations which are still barbarous have not got beyond the period during which it is likely to be for their benefit that they should be conquered and held in subjection by foreigners. Independence and nationality, so essential to the due growth and development of a people further advanced in improvement, are generally impediments to theirs. The sacred duties which civilized nations owe to the independence and nationality of each other, are not binding towards those to whom nationality and independence are either a certain evil, or at best a questionable good. The Romans were not the most clean-handed of conquerers, yet would it have been better for Gaul and Spain, Numidia and Dacia, never to have formed part of the Roman Empire? To characterize any conduct whatever towards a barbarous people as a violation of the law of nations, only shows that he who so speaks has never considered the subject. A violation of great principles of morality it may easily be; but barbarians have no rights as a *nation,* except a right to such treatment as may, at the earliest possible period, fit them for becoming one. The only moral laws for the relation between a civilized and a barbarous government, are the universal rules of morality between man and man.

The criticisms, therefore, which are so often made upon the conduct of the French in Algeria, or of the English in India, proceed, it would seem, mostly on a wrong principle. The true standard by which to judge their proceedings never having been laid down, they escape such comment and censure as might really have an improving effect, while they are tried by a standard which can have no influence on those practically engaged in such transactions, knowing as they do that it cannot, and if it could, ought not to be observed, because no human being would be the better, and many much the worse, for its observance. A civilized government cannot help having barbarous neighbours: when it has, it cannot always content itself with a defensive position, one of mere resistance to aggression. After a longer or shorter interval of forbearance, it either finds itself obliged to conquer them, or to assert so much authority over them, and so break their spirit, that they gradually sink into a state of dependence upon itself: and when that time arrives, they are indeed no longer formidable to it, but it has had so much to do with setting up and pulling down their governments, and they have grown so accustomed to lean on it, that it has become morally responsible for all evil it allows them to do. This is the history of the relations of the British Government with the native States of India. It never was secure in its own Indian possessions until it had reduced the military power of those States to a nullity. But a despotic government only exists by its military power. When we had taken away theirs, we were forced, by the necessity of the case, to offer them ours instead of it. To enable them to dispense with large armies of their own, we bound ourselves to place at their disposal, and they bound themselves to receive, such an amount of military force as made us in fact masters of the country. We engaged that this force should fulfil the purposes of a force, by defending the prince against all foreign and internal enemies. But being thus assured of the protection of a civilized power, and freed from the fear of internal rebellion or foreign conquest, the only checks which either restrain the passions or keep any vigour in the character of an Asiatic despot, the native Governments either became so oppressive and extortionate as to desolate the country, or fell into such a state of nerveless imbecility, that every one, subject to their will, who had not the means of defending himself by his own armed followers, was the prey of anybody who had a band of ruffians in his pay. The British Government felt this deplorable state of things to be its own work; being the direct consequence of the position in which, for its own security, it had placed itself towards the native governments. Had it permitted this to go on indefinitely, it would have deserved to be accounted among the worst political malefactors. In some cases (unhappily not in all) it had endeavoured to take precaution against these mischiefs by a special article in the treaty, binding the prince to reform his administration, and in future to govern in conformity to the advice of the British Government. Among the treaties in which a provision of this sort had been inserted, was that with Oude. For fifty years and more did the British Government allow this engagement to be treated with entire disregard; not without frequent remonstrances, and occasionally threats, but without ever carrying into effect what it threatened. During this period of half a century, England was morally accountable for a mixture of tyranny and anarchy, the picture of which, by men who knew it well, is appalling to all who read it. The act by which the Government of British India at last set aside treaties which had been so pertinaciouly violated, and assumed the power of fulfilling the obligation it had so long before incurred, of giving to the people of Oude a tolerable government, far from being the political crime it is so often ignorantly called, was a criminally tardy discharge of an imperative duty. And the fact, that nothing which had been done in all this century by the East India Company's Government made it so unpopular in England, is one of the most striking instances of what was noticed in a former part of this article— the predisposition of English public opinion to look unfavourably upon every act by which territory or revenue are acquired from foreign States, and to take part with any government, however unworthy, which can make out the merest semblance of a case of injustice against our own country.

But among civilized peoples, members of an equal community of nations, like Christian Europe, the question assumes another aspect, and must be decided on totally different principles. It would be an affront to the reader to discuss the immorality of wars of conquest, or of conquest even as the consequence of lawful war; the annexation of any civilized people to the dominion of another, unless by their own spontaneous election. Up to this point, there is no

difference of opinion among honest people; nor on the wickedness of commencing an aggressive war for any interest of our own, except when necessary
to avert from ourselves an obviously impending wrong. The disputed question
is that of interfering in the regulation of another country's internal concerns;
the question whether a nation is justified in taking part, on either side, in the
civil wars or party contests of another; and chiefly, whether it may justifiably
aid the people of another country in struggling for liberty; or may impose on a
country any particular government or institutions, either as being best for the
country itself, or as necessary for the security of its neighbours.

Of these cases, that of a people in arms for liberty is the only one of any
nicety, or which, theoretically at least, is likely to present conflicting moral
considerations. The other cases which have been mentioned hardly admit of
discussion. Assistance to the government of a country in keeping down the
people, unhappily by far the most frequent case of foreign intervention, no one
writing in a free country needs take the trouble of stigmatizing. A government
which needs foreign support to enforce obedience from its own citizens, is one
which ought not to exist; and the assistance given to it by foreigners is hardly
ever anything but the sympathy of one despotism with another. A case requiring consideration is that of a protracted civil war, in which the contending
parties are so equally balanced that there is no probability of a speedy issue; or
if there is, the victorious side cannot hope to keep down the vanquished but by
severities repugnant to humanity, and injurious to the permanent welfare of
the country. In this exceptional case it seems now to be an admitted doctrine,
that the neighbouring nations, or one powerful neighbour with the acquies-
cence of the rest, are warranted in demanding that the contest shall cease, and a
reconciliation take place on equitable terms of compromise. Intervention of
this description has been repeatedly practised during the present generation,
with such general approval, that its legitimacy may be considered to have
passed into a maxim of what is called international law. The interference of the
European Powers between Greece and Turkey, and between Turkey and Egypt,
were cases in point. That between Holland and Belgium was still more so. The
intervention of England in Portugal, a few years ago, which is probably less
remembered than the others, because it took effect without the employment of
actual force, belongs to the same category. At the time, this interposition had
the appearance of a bad and dishonest backing of the government against the
people, being so timed as to hit the exact moment when the popular party had
obtained a marked advantage, and seemed on the eve of overthrowing the
government, or reducing it to terms. But if ever a political act which looked ill
in the commencement could be justified by the event, this was; for, as the fact
turned out, instead of giving ascendancy to a party, it proved a really healing
measure; and the chiefs of the so-called rebellion were, within a few years, the

honoured and successful ministers of the throne against which they had so lately fought.

With respect to the question, whether one country is justified in helping the people of another in a struggle against their government for free institutions, the answer will be different, according as the yoke which the people are attempting to throw off is that of a purely native government, or of foreigners; considering as one of foreigners, every government which maintains itself by foreign support. When the contest is only with native rulers, and with such native strength as those rulers can enlist in their defence, the answer I should give to the question of the legitimacy of intervention is, as a general rule, No. The reason is, that there can seldom be anything approaching to assurance that intervention, even if successful, would be for the good of the people themselves. The only test possessing any real value, of a people's having become fit for popular institutions, is that they, or a sufficient portion of them to prevail in the contest, are willing to brave labour and danger for their liberation. I know all that may be said. I know it may be urged that the virtues of freemen cannot be learnt in the school of slavery, and that if a people are not fit for freedom, to have any chance of becoming so they must first be free. And this would be conclusive, if the intervention recommended would really give them freedom. But the evil is, that if they have not sufficient love of liberty to be able to wrest it from merely domestic oppressors, the liberty which is bestowed on them by other hands than their own, will have nothing real, nothing permanent. No people ever was and remained free, but because it was determined to be so; because neither its rulers nor any other party in the nation could compel it to be otherwise. If a people—especially one whose freedom has not yet become prescriptive—does not value it sufficiently to fight for it, and maintain it against any force which can be mustered *within* the country, even by those who have the command of the public revenue, it is only a question in how few years or months that people will be enslaved. Either the government which it has given to itself, or some military leader or knot of conspirators who contrive to subvert the government, will speedily put an end to all popular institutions: unless indeed it suits their convenience better to leave them standing, and be content with reducing them to mere forms; for, unless the spirit of liberty is strong in a people, those who have the executive in their hands easily work any institutions to the purposes of despotism. There is no sure guarantee against this deplorable issue, even in a country which has achieved its own freedom; as may be seen in the present day by striking examples both in the Old and New Worlds: but when freedom has been achieved *for* them, they have little prospect indeed of escaping this fate. When a people has had the misfortune to be ruled by a government under which the feelings and the virtues needful for maintaining freedom could not develope themselves, it is during an arduous struggle to become free by their own efforts that these feelings and virtues have the best chance of springing up. Men become attached to that which they have long fought for and made sacrifices for; they learned to appreciate that on which their thoughts have been much engaged; and a contest in which many have been called on to devote themselves for their country, is a school in which they learn to value their country's interest above their own.

It can seldom, therefore—I will not go so far as to say never—be either judicious or right, in a country which has a free government, to assist, otherwise than by the moral support of its opinion, the endeavours of another to extort the same blessing from its native rulers. We must except, of course, any case in which such assistance is a measure of legitimate self-defence. If (a contingency by no means unlikely to occur) this country, on account of its freedom, which is a standing reproach to despotism everywhere, and an encouragement to throw it off, should find itself menaced with attack by a coalition of Continental despots, it ought to consider the popular party in every nation of the Continent as its natural ally: the Liberals should be to it, what the Protestants of Europe were to the Government of Queen Elizabeth. So, again, when a nation, in her own defence, has gone to war with a despot, and has had the rare good fortune not only to succeed in her resistance, but to hold the conditions of peace in her own hands, she is entitled to say that she will make no treaty, unless with some other ruler than the one whose existence as such may be a perpetual menace to her safety and freedom. These exceptions do but set in a clearer light the reasons of the rule; because they do not depend on any failure of those reasons, but on considerations paramount to them, and coming under a different principle.

But the case of a people struggling against a foreign yoke, or against a native tyranny upheld by foreign arms, illustrates the reasons for non-intervention in an opposite way; for in this case the reasons themselves do not exist. A people the most attached to freedom, the most capable of defending and of making a good use of free institutions, may be unable to contend successfully for them against the military strength of another nation much more powerful. To assist a people thus kept down, is not to disturb the balance of forces on which the permanent maintenance of freedom in a country depends, but to redress that balance when it is already unfairly and violently disturbed. The doctrine of non-intervention, to be a legitimate principle of morality, must be accepted by all governments. The despots must consent to be bound by it as well as the free States. Unless they do, the profession of it by free countries comes but to this miserable issue, that the wrong side may help the wrong, but the right must not help the right. Intervention to enforce non-intervention is always rightful, always moral, if not always prudent. Though it be a mistake to *give* freedom to a people who do not value the boon, it cannot but be right to insist that if they do value it, they shall not be hindered from the pursuit of it by foreign coercion. It might not have been right for England (even apart from the question of prudence) to have taken part with Hungary in its noble struggle against Austria; although the Austrian Government in Hungary was in some sense a foreign yoke. But when, the Hungarians having shown themselves likely to prevail in this struggle, the Russian despot interposed, and joining his force to that of Austria, delivered back the Hungarians, bound hand and foot, to their exasperated oppressors, it would have been an honourable and virtuous act on the part of England to have declared that this should not be, and that if Russia gave assistance to the wrong side, England would aid the right. It might not have been consistent with the regard which every nation is bound to pay to its own safety, for England to have taken up this position single-handed. But England and France together could have done it; and if they had, the Russian armed intervention would never have taken place, or would have been disastrous to Russia alone: while all that those Powers gained by not doing it, was that they had to fight Russia five years afterwards, under more difficult circumstances, and without Hungary for an ally. The first nation which, being powerful enough to make its voice effectual, has the spirit and courage to say that not a gun shall be fired in Europe by the soldiers of one Power against the revolted subjects of another, will be the idol of the friends of freedom throughout Europe. That declaration alone will ensure the almost immediate emancipation of every people which desires liberty sufficiently to be capable of maintaining it: and the nation which gives the word will soon find itself at the head of an alliance of free peoples, so strong as to defy the efforts of any number of confederated despots to bring it down. The prize is too glorious not to be snatched sooner or later by some free country; and the time may not be distant when England, if she does not take this heroic part because of its heroism, will be compelled to take it from consideration for her own safety.

JOHN RUSKIN (1819–1900)

The Roots of Honour (1860)

*T*he year 1860 is often said to be the demarcating line in Ruskin's life, the year when the critic of art (Modern Painters had just been completed) was transmuted into the critic of society (with the appearance of the first chapters of Unto This Last). But the critic of society was there all along. Almost a decade earlier, while everyone else was hailing the Crystal Palace as the inauguration of a new era, testifying to England's renewed will and vitality, Ruskin denounced it as a monstrosity, inhuman and unnatural, all that iron and glass an affront to the mind and the senses. Two years later, in the unlikely setting of the Stones of Venice, in a chapter praising Gothic architecture, he decried the division of labor, that "great civilized invention" of modern times, as dehumanizing and degrading, reducing the worker to the maker of "the point of a pin or the head of a nail."[1]

Ruskin did not mention Adam Smith by name, but his allusions to pin- and nail-making clearly echo the famous opening pages of Wealth of Nations. In an equally famous passage toward the end of the book, Smith, even more eloquently than Ruskin, deplored the effects of the division of labor, which rendered a man "as stupid and ignorant as it is possible for a human creature to become." This would be the condition of "the great body of the people," Smith concluded, "unless government

John Ruskin (1819–1900), "The Roots of Honour," *Cornhill Magazine*, August 1860. Reprinted in *Unto This Last*, ed. Clive Wilmer ([1862] London, 1985), pp. 167–79.
1. John Ruskin, *The Stones of Venice* ([1853] London, 1905), II, 162.

takes some pains to prevent it."[2] *Had Ruskin read the whole of the book, he might not have damned Smith, on the centenary of the publication of the* Wealth of Nations, *as that "half-bred and half-witted Scotchman" who deliberately perpetrated the blasphemy "Thou shalt hate the Lord thy God, damn His laws, and covet thy neighbour's goods."*[3]

Ruskin's essays, published in 1860–62 and reprinted under the title Unto This Last, *were a vigorous and sustained attack on political economy. After the fourth of the essays, Thackeray, then editor of the* Cornhill, *responding to critics who were shocked by the assault upon the received wisdom about society and political economy, called a halt to the series. Ruskin always maintained that* Unto This Last *was his best book, in spite of the fact that it sold poorly. Today it is said to be one of the favorite books of Gandhi and Martin Luther King. One wonders whether those admirers would be entirely comfortable with Ruskin's description of himself: "Of course I am a Socialist—of the most stern sort—but I am also a Tory of the sternest sort," and, he added, "a violent Illiberal."*[4]

A mong the delusions which at different periods have possessed themselves of the minds of large masses of the human race, perhaps the most curious—certainly the least creditable—is the modern *soi-disant* science of political economy, based on the idea that an advantageous code of social action may be determined irrespectively of the influence of social affection.

Of course, as in the instances of alchemy, astrology, witchcraft, and other such popular creeds, political economy has a plausible idea at the root of it. "The social affections," says the economist, "are accidental and disturbing elements in human nature; but avarice and the desire of progress are constant elements. Let us eliminate the inconstants, and, considering the human being merely as a covetous machine, examine by what laws of labour, purchase, and sale, the greatest accumulative result in wealth is obtainable. Those laws once determined, it will be for each individual afterwards to introduce as much of the disturbing affectionate element as he chooses, and to determine for himself the result on the new conditions supposed."

This would be a perfectly logical and successful method of analysis, if the accidentals afterwards to be introduced were of the same nature as the powers first examined. Supposing a body in motion to be influenced by constant and inconstant forces, it is usually the simplest way of examining its course to trace

---

2. Adam Smith, *An Inquiry into the Nature and Causes of the Wealth of Nations* ([1776] New York, 1937), p. 735.
3. John Ruskin, *Fors Clavigera: Letters to the Workmen and Labourers of Great Britain* (1876), in *Works,* ed. E. T. Cook and Alexander Wedderburn (London, 1907), XXVIII, 516, 764.
4. Peter Quennell, *John Ruskin: The Portrait of a Prophet* (London, 1949), p. 163.

it first under the persistent conditions, and afterwards introduce the causes of variation. But the disturbing elements in the social problem are not of the same nature as the constant ones: they alter the essence of the creature under examination the moment they are added; they operate, not mathematically, but chemically, introducing conditions which render all our previous knowledge unavailable. We made learned experiments upon pure nitrogen, and have convinced ourselves that it is a very manageable gas: but, behold! the thing which we have practically to deal with is its chloride; and this, the moment we touch it on our established principles, sends us and our apparatus through the ceiling.

Observe, I neither impugn nor doubt the conclusion of the science if its terms are accepted. I am simply uninterested in them, as I should be in those of a science of gymnastics which assumed that men had no skeletons. It might be shown, on that supposition, that it would be advantageous to roll the students up into pellets, flatten them into cakes, or stretch them into cables; and that when these results were effected, the re-insertion of the skeleton would be attended with various inconveniences to their constitution. The reasoning might be admirable, the conclusions true, and the science deficient only in applicability. Modern political economy stands on a precisely similar basis. Assuming, not that the human being has no skeleton, but that it is all skeleton, it founds an ossifiant theory of progress on this negation of a soul; and having shown the utmost that may be made of bones, and constructed a number of interesting geometrical figures with death's-head and humeri, successfully proves the inconvenience of the reappearance of a soul among these corpuscular structures. I do not deny the truth of this theory: I simply deny its applicability to the present phase of the world.

This inapplicability has been curiously manifested during the embarrassment caused by the late strikes of our workmen. Here occurs one of the simplest cases, in a pertinent and positive form, of the first vital problem which political economy has to deal with (the relation between employer and employed); and, at a severe crisis, when lives in multitudes and wealth in masses are at stake, the political economists are helpless—practically mute: no demonstrable solution of the difficulty can be given by them, such as may convince or calm the opposing parties. Obstinately the masters take one view of the matter; obstinately the operatives another; and no political science can set them at one.

It would be strange if it could, it being not by "science" of any kind that men were ever intended to be set at one. Disputant after disputant vainly strives to show that the interests of the masters are, or are not, antagonistic to those of the men: none of the pleaders ever seeming to remember that it does not absolutely or always follow that the persons must be antagonistic because their interests are. If there is only a crust of bread in the house, and mother and children are starving, their interests are not the same. If the mother eats it, the children want it; if the children eat it, the mother must go hungry to her work. Yet it does not necessarily follow that there will be "antagonism" between them, that they will fight for the crust, and that the mother, being strongest, will get it, and eat it. Neither, in any other case, whatever the relations of the persons may be, can it be assumed for certain that, because their interests are diverse, they must necessarily regard each other with hostility, and use violence or cunning to obtain the advantage.

Even if this were so, and it were as just as it is convenient to consider men as actuated by no other moral influences than those which affect rats or swine, the logical conditions of the question are still indeterminable. It can never be shown generally either that the interests of master and labourer are alike, or that they are opposed; for, according to circumstances, they may be either. It is, indeed, always the interest of both that the work should be rightly done, and a just price obtained for it; but, in the division of profits, the gain of the one may or may not be the loss of the other. It is not the master's interest to pay wages so low as to leave the men sickly and depressed, nor the workman's interest to be paid high wages if the smallness of the master's profit hinders him from enlarging his business, or conducting it in a safe and liberal way. A stoker ought not to desire high pay if the company is too poor to keep the engine-wheels in repair.

And the varieties of circumstance which influence these reciprocal interests are so endless, that all endeavour to deduce rules of action from balance of expediency is in vain. And it is meant to be in vain. For no human actions ever were intended by the Maker of men to be guided by balances of expediency, but by balances of justice. He has therefore rendered all endeavours to determine expediency futile for evermore. No man ever knew, or can know, what will be the ultimate result to himself, or to others, of any given line of conduct. But every man may know, and most of us do know, what is a just and unjust act. And all of us may know also, that the consequences of justice will be ultimately the best possible, both to others and ourselves, though we can neither say what *is* best, or how it is likely to come to pass.

I have said balances of justice, meaning, in the term justice, to include affection,—such affection as one man *owes* to another. All right relations between master and operative, and all their best interests, ultimately depend on these.

We shall find the best and simplest illustration of the relations of master and operative in the position of domestic servants.

We will suppose that the master of a household desires only to get as much work out of his servants as he can, at the rate of wages he gives. He never allows them to be idle; feeds them as poorly and lodges them as ill as they will endure, and in all things pushes his requirements to the exact point beyond which he cannot go without forcing the servant to leave him. In doing this, there is no violation on his part of what is commonly called "justice." He agrees with the domestic for his whole time and service, and takes them;—the limits of hardship in treatment being fixed by the practice of other masters in his neighbourhood; that is to say, by the current rate of wages for domestic labour. If the servant can get a better place, he is free to take one, and the master can only tell what is the real market value of his labour, by requiring as much as he will give.

This is the politico-economical view of the case, according to the doctors of that science; who assert that by this procedure the greatest average of work will be obtained from the servant, and therefore the greatest benefit to the community, and through the community, by reversion, to the servant himself.

That, however, is not so. It would be so if the servant were an engine of which the motive power was steam, magnetism, gravitation, or any other agent of calculable force. But he being, on the contrary, an engine whose motive power is a Soul, the force of this very peculiar agent, as an unknown quantity, enters into all the political economist's equations, without his knowledge, and falsifies every one of their results. The largest quantity of work will not be done by this curious engine for pay, or under pressure, or by help of any kind of fuel which may be supplied by the chaldron. It will be done only when the motive force, that is to say, the will or spirit of the creature, is brought to its greatest strength by its own proper fuel: namely, by the affections.

It may indeed happen, and does happen often, that if the master is a man of sense and energy, a large quantity of material work may be done under mechanical pressure, enforced by strong will and guided by wise method; also it may happen, and does happen often, that if the master is indolent and weak (however good-natured), a very small quantity of work, and that bad, may be produced by the servant's undirected strength, and contemptuous gratitude. But the universal law of the matter is that, assuming any given quantity of energy and sense in master and servant, the greatest material result obtainable by them will be, not through antagonism to each other, but through affection for each other; and that, if the master, instead of endeavouring to get as much work as possible from the servant, seeks rather to render his appointed and necessary work beneficial to him, and to forward his interests in all just and wholesome ways, the real amount of work ultimately done, or of good rendered, by the person so cared for, will indeed be the greatest possible.

Observe, I say, "of good rendered," for a servant's work is not necessarily or always the best thing he can give his master. But good of all kinds, whether in material service, in protective watchfulness of his master's interest and credit, or in joyful readiness to seize unexpected and irregular occasions of help.

Nor is this one whit less generally true because indulgence will be frequently abused, and kindness met with ingratitude. For the servant who, gently treated, is ungrateful, treated ungently, will be revengeful; and the man who is dishonest to a liberal master will be injurious to an unjust one.

In any case, and with any person, this unselfish treatment will produce the most effective return. Observe, I am here considering the affections wholly as a motive power; not at all as things in themselves desirable or noble, or in any other way abstractedly good. I look at them simply as an anomalous force, rendering every one of the ordinary political economist's calculations nugatory; while, even if he desired to introduce this new element into his estimates, he has no power of dealing with it; for the affections only become a true motive power when they ignore every other motive and condition of political economy. Treat the servant kindly, with the idea of turning his gratitude to account, and you will get, as you deserve, no gratitude, nor any value for your kindness; but treat him kindly without any economical purpose, and all economical purposes will be answered; in this, as in all other matters, whosoever will save his life shall lose it, whoso loses it shall find it.

[. . .]

The next clearest and simplest example of relation between master and operative is that which exists between the commander of a regiment and his men.

Supposing the officer only desires to apply the rules of discipline so as, with least trouble to himself, to make the regiment most effective, he will not be able, by any rules or administration of rules, on this selfish principle, to develop the full strength of his subordinates. If a man of sense and firmness, he may, as in the former instance, produce a better result than would be obtained by the irregular kindness of a weak officer; but let the sense and firmness be the same in both cases, and assuredly the officer who has the most direct personal relations with his men, the most care for their interests, and the most value for their lives, will develop their effective strength, through their affection for his own person, and trust in his character, to a degree wholly unattainable by other means. This law applies still more stringently as the numbers concerned are larger: a charge may often be successful, though the men dislike their officers; a battle has rarely been won, unless they loved their general.

Passing from these simple examples to the more complicated relations existing between a manufacturer and his workmen, we are met first by certain curious difficulties, resulting, apparently, from a harder and colder state of moral elements. It is easy to imagine an enthusiastic affection existing among soldiers for the colonel. Not so easy to imagine an enthusiastic affection among cotton-spinners for the proprietor of the mill. A body of men associated for purposes of robbery (as a Highland clan in ancient times) shall be animated by perfect affection, and every member of it be ready to lay down his life for the life of his chief. But a band of men associated for purposes of legal production and accumulation is usually animated, it appears, by no such emotions, and none of them are in any wise willing to give his life for the life of his chief. Not only are we met by this apparent anomaly, in moral matters, but by others connected with it, in administration of system. For a servant or a soldier is engaged at a definite rate of wages, for a definite period; but a workman at a rate of wages variable according to the demand for labour, and with the risk of being at any time thrown out of his situation by chances of trade. Now, as, under these contingencies, no action of the affections can take place, but only an explosive action of *dis*affections, two points offer themselves for consideration in the matter.

The first—How far the rate of wages may be so regulated as not to vary with the demand for labour.

The second—How far it is possible that bodies of workmen may be engaged and maintained at such fixed rate of wages (whatever the state of trade may be), without enlarging or diminishing their number, so as to give them permanent interest in the establishment with which they are connected, like that of the domestic servants in an old family, or an *esprit de corps,* like that of the soldiers in a crack regiment.

The first question is, I say, how far it may be possible to fix the rate of wages, irrespectively of the demand for labour.

Perhaps one of the most curious facts in the history of human error is the denial by the common political economist of the possibility of thus regulating wages; while, for all the important, and much of the unimportant, labour, on the earth, wages are already so regulated.

We do not sell our prime-ministership by Dutch auction; nor, on the decease of a bishop, whatever may be the general advantages of simony, do we (yet) offer his diocese to the clergyman who will take the episcopacy at the lowest contract. We (with exquisite sagacity of political economy!) do indeed sell commissions; but not openly, generalships: sick, we do not inquire for a physician who takes less than a guinea; litigious, we never think of reducing six-and-eightpence to four-and-sixpence; caught in a shower, we do not canvass the cabmen, to find one who values his driving at less than sixpence a mile.

It is true that in all these cases there is, and in every conceivable case there must be, ultimate reference to the presumed difficulty of the work, or number of candidates for the office. If it were thought that the labour necessary to make a good physician would be gone through by a sufficient number of students with the prospect of only half-guinea fees, public consent would soon withdraw the unnecessary half-guinea. In this ultimate sense, the price of labour is indeed always regulated by the demand for it; but, so far as the practical and immediate administration of the matter is regarded, the best labour always has been, and is, as *all* labour ought to be, paid by an invariable standard.

"What!" the reader perhaps answers amazedly: "pay good and bad workmen alike?"

Certainly. The difference between one prelate's sermons and his successor's—or between one physician's opinion and another's,—is far greater, as respects the qualities of mind involved, and far more important in result to you personally, than the difference between good and bad laying of bricks (though that is greater than most people suppose). Yet you pay with equal fee, contentedly, the good and bad workmen upon your soul, and the good and bad workmen upon your body; much more may you pay, contentedly, with equal fees, the good and bad workmen upon your house.

"Nay, but I choose my physician, and my clergyman, thus indicating my sense of the quality of their work." By all means, also, choose your bricklayer; that is the proper reward of the good workman, to be "chosen." The natural and right system respecting all labour is, that it should be paid at a fixed rate, but the good workman employed, and the bad workman unemployed. The false, unnatural, and destructive system is when the bad workman is allowed to offer his work at half-price, and either take the place of the good, or force him by his competition to work for an inadequate sum.

This equality of wages, then, being the first object towards which we have to discover the directest available road, the second is, as above stated, that of maintaining constant numbers of workmen in employment, whatever may be the accidental demand for the article they produce.

I believe the sudden and extensive inequalities of demand, which necessarily arise in the mercantile operations of an active nation, constitute the only essential difficulty which has to be overcome in a just organization of labour. The subject opens into too many branches to admit of being investigated in a paper of this kind; but the following general facts bearing on it may be noted.

The wages which enable any workman to live are necessarily higher, if his work is liable to intermission, than if it is assured and continuous; and however severe the struggle for work may become, the general law will always hold, that men must get more daily pay if, on the average, they can only calculate on work three days a week than they would require if they were sure of work six days a week. Supposing that a man cannot live on less than a shilling a day, his seven shillings he must get, either for three days' violent work, or six days' deliberate work. The tendency of all modern mercantile operations is to throw both wages and trade into the form of a lottery, and to make the workman's pay depend on intermittent exertion, and the principal's profit on dexterously used chance.

In what partial degree, I repeat, this may be necessary in consequence of the activities of modern trade, I do not here investigate; contenting myself with the fact that in its fatallest aspects it is assuredly unnecessary, and results merely from love of gambling on the part of the masters, and from ignorance and sensuality in the men. The masters cannot bear to let any opportunity of gain escape them, and frantically rush at every gap and breach in the walls of Fortune, raging to be rich, and affronting, with impatient covetousness, every risk of ruin, while the men prefer three days of violent labour, and three days of drunkenness, to six days of moderate work and wise rest. There is no way in which a principal, who really desires to help his workmen, may do it more effectually than by checking these disorderly habits both in himself and them; keeping his own business operations on a scale which will enable him to pursue them securely, not yielding to temptations of precarious gain; and at the same time, leading his workmen into regular habits of labour and life, either by inducing them rather to take low wages, in the form of a fixed salary, than high wages, subject to the chance of their being thrown out of work; or, if this be impossible, by discouraging the system of violent exertion for nominally high day wages, and leading the men to take lower pay for more regular labour.

In effecting any radical changes of this kind, doubtless there would be great inconvenience and loss incurred by all the originators of the movement. That which can be done with perfect convenience and without loss, is not always the thing that most needs to be done, or which we are most imperatively required to do.

I have already alluded to the difference hitherto existing between regiments of men associated for purposes of violence, and for purposes of manufacture; in that the former appear capable of self-sacrifice—the latter, not; which singular fact is the real reason of the general lowness of estimate in which the profession of commerce is held, as compared with that of arms. Philosophically, it does not, at first sight, appear reasonable (many writers have endeavoured to prove it unreasonable) that a peaceable and rational person, whose trade is buying and selling, should be held in less honour than an unpeaceable and often irrational person, whose trade is slaying. Nevertheless, the consent of mankind has always, in spite of the philosophers, given precedence to the soldier.

And this is right.

For the soldier's trade, verily and essentially, is not slaying, but being slain. This, without well knowing its own meaning, the world honours it for. A bravo's trade is slaying; but the world has never respected bravos more than merchants: the reason it honours the soldier is, because he holds his life at the service of the State. Reckless he may be—fond of pleasure or of adventure—all kinds of bye-motives and mean impulses may have determined the choice of his profession, and may affect (to all appearance exclusively) his daily conduct in it; but our estimate of him is based on this ultimate fact—of which we are well assured—that put him in a fortress breach, with all the pleasures of the world behind him, and only death and his duty in front of him, he will keep his face to the front; and he knows that his choice may be put to him at any moment—and has beforehand taken his part—virtually takes such part continually—does, in reality, die daily.

Not less is the respect we pay to the lawyer and physician, founded ultimately on their self-sacrifice. Whatever the learning or acuteness of a great lawyer, our chief respect for him depends on our belief that, set in a judge's seat, he will strive to judge justly, come of it what may. Could we suppose that he would take bribes, and use his acuteness and legal knowledge to give plausibility to iniquitous decisions, no degree of intellect would win for him our respect. Nothing will win it, short of our tacit conviction, that in all important acts of his life justice is first with him; his own interest, second.

In the case of a physician, the ground of the honour we render him is clearer still. Whatever his science, we would shrink from him in horror if we found him regarding his patients merely as subjects to experiment upon; much more, if we found that, receiving bribes from persons interested in their deaths, he was using his best skill to give poison in the mask of medicine.

Finally, the principle holds with utmost clearness as it respects clergymen. No goodness of disposition will excuse want of science in a physician, or of shrewdness in an advocate; but a clergyman, even though his power of intellect be small, is respected on the presumed ground of his unselfishness and serviceableness.

Now, there can be no question but that the tact, foresight, decision, and other mental powers, required for the successful management of a large mercantile concern, if not such as could be compared with those of a great lawyer, general, or divine, would at least match the general conditions of mind required in the subordinate officers of a ship, or of a regiment, or in the curate of a country parish. If, therefore, all the efficient members of the so-called liberal professions are still, somehow, in public estimate of honour, preferred before the head of a commercial firm, the reason must lie deeper than in the measurement of their several powers of mind.

And the essential reason for such preference will be found to lie in the fact that the merchant is presumed to act always selfishly. His work may be very necessary to the community; but the motive of it is understood to be wholly personal. The merchant's first object in all his dealings must be (the public believe) to get as much for himself, and leave as little to his neighbour (or customer) as possible. Enforcing this upon him, by political statute, as the necessary principle of his action; recommending it to him on all occasions, and themselves reciprocally adopting it, proclaiming vociferously, for law of the universe, that a buyer's function is to cheapen, and a seller's to cheat,—the public, nevertheless, involuntarily condemn the man of commerce for his compliance with their own statement, and stamp him for ever as belonging to an inferior grade of human personality.

This they will find, eventually, they must give up doing. They must not cease to condemn selfishness; but they will have to discover a kind of commerce which is not exclusively selfish. Or, rather, they will have to discover that there never was, or can be, any other kind of commerce; that this which they have called commerce was not commerce at all, but cozening; and that a true merchant differs as much from a merchant according to laws of modern political economy, as the hero of the *Excursion* from Autolycus. They will find that commerce is an occupation which gentlemen will every day see more need to engage in, rather than in the businesses of talking to men, or slaying them; that, in true commerce, as in true preaching, or true fighting, it is necessary to admit the idea of occasional voluntary loss;—that sixpences have to be lost, as well as lives, under a sense of duty; that the market may have its martyrdoms as well as the pulpit; and trade its heroisms as well as war.

May have—in the final issue, must have—and only has not had yet, because men of heroic temper have always been misguided in their youth into other fields; not recognizing what is in our days, perhaps, the most important of all fields; so that, while many a zealous person loses his life in trying to teach the form of a gospel, very few will lose a hundred pounds in showing the practice of one.

The fact is, that people never have had clearly explained to them the true functions of a merchant with respect to other people. I should like the reader to be very clear about this.

Five great intellectual professions, relating to daily necessities of life, have hitherto existed—three exist necessarily, in every civilized nation:

The Soldier's profession is to *defend* it.

The Pastor's to *teach* it.

The Physician's to *keep it in health*.

The Lawyer's to *enforce justice* in it.

The Merchant's to *provide* for it.

And the duty of all these men is, on due occasion, to *die* for it.

"On due occasion," namely:—

The Soldier, rather than leave his post in battle.

The Physician, rather than leave his post in plague.

The Pastor, rather than teach Falsehood.

The Lawyer, rather than countenance Injustice.

The Merchant—what is *his* "due occasion" of death?

It is the main question for the merchant, as for all of us. For, truly, the man who does not know when to die, does not know how to live.

Observe, the merchant's function (or manufacturer's, for in the broad sense in which it is here used the word must be understood to include both) is to provide for the nation. It is no more his function to get profit for himself out of that provision than it is a clergyman's function to get his stipend. This stipend is a due and necessary adjunct, but not the object of his life, if he be a true clergyman, any more than his fee (or honorarium) is the object of life to a true physician. Neither is his fee the object of life to a true merchant. All three, if true men, have a work to be done irrespective of fee—to be done even at any cost, or for quite the contrary of fee; the pastor's function being to teach, the physician's to heal, and the merchant's, as I have said, to provide. That is to say, he has to understand to their very root the qualities of the thing he deals in, and the means of obtaining or producing it; and he has to apply all his sagacity and energy to the producing or obtaining it in perfect state, and distributing it at the cheapest possible price where it is most needed.

And because the production or obtaining of any commodity involves neces-sarily the agency of many lives and hands, the merchant becomes in the course of his business the master and governor of large masses of men in a more direct, though less confessed way, than a military officer or pastor; so that on him falls, in great part, the responsibility for the kind of life they lead: and it becomes his duty, not only to be always considering how to produce what he sells, in the purest and cheapest forms, but how to make the various employments involved in the production, or transference of it, most beneficial to the men employed.

And as into these two functions, requiring for their right exercise the highest intelligence, as well as patience, kindness, and tact, the merchant is bound to put all his energy, so for their just discharge he is bound, as soldier or physician is bound, to give up, if need be, his life, in such way as it may be demanded of him. Two main points he has in his providing function to maintain: first, his engagements (faithfulness to engagements being the real root of all possibili-ties, in commerce); and, secondly, the perfectness and purity of the thing provided; so that, rather than fail in any engagement, or consent to any deteri-oration, adulteration, or unjust and exorbitant price of that which he provides, he is bound to meet fearlessly any form of distress, poverty, or labour, which may, through maintenance of these points, come upon him.

Again: in his office as governor of the men employed by him, the merchant or manufacturer is invested with a distinctly paternal authority and respon-sibility. In most cases, a youth entering a commercial establishment is with-drawn altogether from home influence; his master must become his father, else he has, for practical and constant help, no father at hand: in all cases the master's authority, together with the general tone and atmosphere of his busi-ness, and the character of the men with whom the youth is compelled in the course of it to associate, have more immediate and pressing weight than the home influence, and will usually neutralize it either for good or evil; so that the only means which the master has of doing justice to the men employed by him is to ask himself sternly whether he is dealing with such subordinate as he would with his own son, if compelled by circumstances to take such a position.

Supposing the captain of a frigate saw it right, or were by any chance obliged, to place his own son in the position of a common sailor: as he would then treat his son, he is bound always to treat every one of the men under him. So, also, supposing the master of a manufactory saw it right, or were by any chance obliged, to place his own son in the position of an ordinary workman; as he would then treat his son, he is bound always to treat every one of his men. This is the only effective, true, or practical RULE which can be given on this point of political economy.

And as the captain of a ship is bound to be the last man to leave his ship in case of wreck, and to share his last crust with the sailors in case of famine, so the manufacturer, in any commercial crisis or distress, is bound to take the suffering of it with his men, and even to take more of it for himself than he allows his men to feel; as a father would in a famine, shipwreck, or battle, sacrifice himself for his son.

All which sounds very strange: the only real strangeness in the matter being, nevertheless, that it should so sound. For all this is true, and that not partially nor theoretically, but everlastingly and practically: all other doctrine than this respecting matters political being false in premises, absurd in deduction, and impossible in practice, consistently with any progressive state of national life; all the life which we now possess as a nation showing itself in the resolute denial and scorn, by a few strong minds and faithful hearts, of the economic principles taught to our multitudes, which principles, so far as accepted, lead straight to national destruction. Respecting the modes and forms of destruction to which they lead, and, on the other hand, respecting the farther practical working of true polity, I hope to reason farther in a following paper.

JOHN HENRY NEWMAN (1801–90)

General Answer to Mr. Kingsley (1864)

*I*n 1875, in a letter commenting on Charles Kingsley's death, Newman defended himself against the charge that he had been overly harsh in his Apologia in responding to Kingsley's accusation of untruthfulness. He was not angry, he insisted; indeed, so far from feeling any resentment against Kingsley, he was grateful to him for being "accidentally the instrument" given by God to vindicate his character and conduct.[1]

Composed in great haste (one eighty-page part was written in a twenty-two-hour stretch of time) in response to a single mean-spirited paragraph in a magazine, and appearing modestly in the form of weekly pamphlets, the Apologia was a personal triumph for Newman. It received enthusiastic reviews from such respectable (and nonreligious) journals as the Times, the Saturday Review, and the Spectator. Other readers, to be sure, as Newman acknowledged, were displeased by the tone of the book, finding it egotistical (the word was frequently used), self-serving, and unchristian. As late as 1933, the Anglican bishop Edmund Knox characterized it as "the work of one of the most self-centered of men . . . written in a passion of self-admiration," although even he conceded that it ranked "among the

John Henry Newman (1801–90), "General Answer to Mr. Kingsley," pamphlet, May 26, 1864. Reprinted in *Apologia Pro Vita Sua* (London, 1864), pp. 373–430. (In later editions this chapter was entitled "Position of My Mind Since 1845.")
1. Wilfrid Ward, *The Life of John Henry Cardinal Newman* (London, 1912), II, 45–46 (letter to William Cope, February 13, 1875).

greatest of the world's autobiographies."[2] *Today it is generally acknowledged to be a historic document comparable to such other great "self-centered" apologias as those by Saint Augustine and Jean-Jacques Rousseau.*

From the time that I became a Catholic, of course I have no further history of my religious opinions to narrate. In saying this, I do not mean to say that my mind has been idle, or that I have given up thinking on theological subjects; but that I have had no changes to record, and have had no anxiety of heart whatever. I have been in perfect peace and contentment. I never have had one doubt. I was not conscious to myself, on my conversion, of any difference of thought or of temper from what I had before. I was not conscious of firmer faith in the fundamental truths of revelation, or of more self-command; I had not more fervour; but it was like coming into port after a rough sea; and my happiness on that score remains to this day without interruption.

Nor had I any trouble about receiving those additional articles, which are not found in the Anglican Creed. Some of them I believed already, but not any one of them was a trial to me. I made a profession of them upon my reception with the greatest ease, and I have the same ease in believing them now. I am far of course from denying that every article of the Christian Creed, whether as held by Catholics or by Protestants, is beset with intellectual difficulties; and it is simple fact, that, for myself, I cannot answer those difficulties. Many persons are very sensitive of the difficulties of religion; I am as sensitive as any one; but I have never been able to see a connexion between apprehending those difficulties, however keenly, and multiplying them to any extent, and doubting the doctrines to which they are attached. Ten thousand difficulties do not make one doubt, as I understand the subject; difficulty and doubt are incommensurate. There of course may be difficulties in the evidence; but I am speaking of difficulties intrinsic to the doctrines, or to their compatibility with each other. A man may be annoyed that he cannot work out a mathematical problem, of which the answer is or is not given to him, without doubting that it admits of an answer, or that a particular answer is the true one. Of all points of faith, the being of a God is, to my own apprehension, encompassed with most difficulty, and borne in upon our minds with most power.

People say that the doctrine of Transubstantiation is difficult to believe; I did not believe the doctrine till I was a Catholic. I had no difficulty in believing it as soon as I believed that the Catholic Roman Church was the oracle of God, and that she had declared this doctrine to be part of the original revelation. It is difficult, impossible to imagine, I grant—but how is it difficult to believe? Yet

---

2. Charles Frederick Harrold, *John Henry Newman: An Expository and Critical Study of His Mind, Thought and Art* (London, 1945), p. 313.

Macaulay thought it so difficult to believe, that he had need of a believer in it of talents as eminent as Sir Thomas More, before he could bring himself to conceive that the Catholics of an enlightened age could resist "the overwhelming force of the argument against it." "Sir Thomas More," he says, "is one of the choice specimens of wisdom and virtue; and the doctrine of transubstantiation is a kind of proof charge. A faith which stands that test, will stand any test." But for myself, I cannot indeed prove it, I cannot tell *how* it is; but I say, "Why should not it be? What's to hinder it? What do I know of substance or matter? just as much as the greatest philosophers, and that is nothing at all";— so much is this the case, that there is a rising school of philosophy now, which considers phenomena to constitute the whole of our knowledge in physics. The Catholic doctrine leaves phenomena alone. It does not say that the phenomena go; on the contrary, it says that they remain: nor does it say that the same phenomena are in several places at once. It deals with what no one on earth knows any thing about, the material substances themselves. And, in like manner, of that majestic Article of the Anglican as well as of the Catholic Creed,—the doctrine of the Trinity in Unity. What do I know of the Essence of the Divine Being? I know that my abstract idea of three is simply incompatible with my idea of one; but when I come to the question of concrete fact, I have no means of proving that there is not a sense in which one and three can equally be predicated of the Incommunicable God.

But I am going to take upon myself the responsibility of more than the mere Creed of the Church; as the parties accusing me are determined I shall do. They say, that now, in that I am a Catholic, though I may not have offences of my own against honesty to answer for, yet, at least, I am answerable for the offences of others, of my co-religionists, of my brother priests, of the Church herself. I am quite willing to accept the responsibility; and, as I have been able, as I trust, by means of a few words, to dissipate, in the minds of all those who do not begin with disbelieving me, the suspicion with which so many Protestants start, in forming their judgment of Catholics, viz. that our Creed is actually set up in inevitable superstition and hypocrisy, as the original sin of Catholicism; so now I will go on, as before, identifying myself with the Church and vindicating it,— not of course denying the enormous mass of sin and ignorance which exists of necessity in that world-wide multiform Communion,—but going to the proof of this one point, that its system is in no sense dishonest, and that therefore the upholders and teachers of that system, as such, have a claim to be acquitted in their own persons of that odious imputation.

Starting then with the being of a God, (which, as I have said, is as certain to me as the certainty of my own existence, though when I try to put the grounds of that certainty into logical shape I find a difficulty in doing so in mood and figure to my satisfaction,) I look out of myself into the world of men, and there I see a sight which fills me with unspeakable distress. The world seems simply to give the lie to that great truth, of which my whole being is so full; and the effect upon me is, in consequence, as a matter of necessity, as confusing as if it denied that I am in existence myself. If I looked into a mirror, and did not see my face, I should have the sort of feeling which actually comes upon me, when I look into this living busy world, and see no reflexion of its Creator. This is, to me, one of the great difficulties of this absolute primary truth, to which I referred just now. Were it not for this voice, speaking so clearly in my conscience and my heart, I should be an atheist, or a pantheist, or a polytheist when I looked into the world. I am speaking for myself only; and I am far from denying the real force of the arguments in proof of a God, drawn from the general facts of human society, but these do not warm me or enlighten me; they do not take away the winter of my desolation, or make the buds unfold and the leaves grow within me, and my moral being rejoice. The sight of the world is nothing else than the prophet's scroll, full of "lamentations, and mourning, and woe."

To consider the world in its length and breadth, its various history, the many races of man, their starts, their fortunes, their mutual alienation, their conflicts; and then their ways, habits, governments, forms of worship; their enterprises, their aimless courses, their random achievements and acquirements, the impotent conclusion of long-standing facts, the tokens so faint and broken, of a superintending design, the blind evolution of what turn out to be great powers or truths, the progress of things, as if from unreasoning elements, not towards final causes, the greatness and littleness of man, his far-reaching aims, his short duration, the curtain hung over his futurity, the disappointments of life, the defeat of good, the success of evil, physical pain, mental anguish, the prevalence and intensity of sin, the pervading idolatries, the corruptions, the dreary hopeless irreligion, that condition of the whole race, so fearfully yet exactly described in the Apostle's words, "having no hope and without God in the world,"—all this is a vision to dizzy and appal; and inflicts upon the mind the sense of a profound mystery, which is absolutely beyond human solution.

What shall be said to this heart-piercing, reason-bewildering fact? I can only answer, that either there is no Creator, or this living society of men is in a true sense discarded from His presence. Did I see a boy of good make and mind, with the tokens on him of a refined nature, cast upon the world without provision, unable to say whence he came, his birth-place or his family connexions, I should conclude that there was some mystery connected with his history, and that he was one, of whom, from one cause or other, his parents were ashamed. Thus only should I be able to account for the contrast between the promise and condition of his being. And so I argue about the world;—*if* there be a God, *since* there is a God, the human race is implicated in some terrible aboriginal calamity. It is out of joint with the purposes of its Creator. This is a fact, a fact as true as the fact of its existence; and thus the doctrine of what is theologically called original sin becomes to me almost as certain as that the world exists, and as the existence of God.

And now, supposing it were the blessed and loving will of the Creator to interfere in this anarchical condition of things, what are we to suppose would be the methods which might be necessarily or naturally involved in His object of mercy? Since the world is in so abnormal a state, surely it would be no surprise to me, if the interposition were of necessity equally extraordinary—or what is called miraculous. But that subject does not directly come into the scope of my present remarks. Miracles as evidence, involve an argument; and of course I am thinking of some means which does not immediately run into argument. I am rather asking what must be the face-to-face antagonist, by which to withstand and baffle the fierce energy of passion and the all-corroding, all-dissolving scepticism of the intellect in religious inquiries? I have no intention at all to deny, that truth is the real object of our reason, and that, if it does not attain to truth, either the premiss or the process is in fault; but I am not speaking of right reason, but of reason as it acts in fact and concretely in fallen man. I know that even the unaided reason, when correctly exercised, leads to a belief in God, in the immortality of the soul, and in a future retribution; but I am considering it actually and historically; and in this point of view, I do not think I am wrong in saying that its tendency is towards a simple unbelief in matters of religion. No truth, however sacred, can stand against it, in the long run; and hence it is that in the pagan world, when our Lord came, the last traces of the religious knowledge of former times were all but disappearing from those portions of the world in which the intellect had been active and had had a career.

And in these latter days, in like manner, outside the Catholic Church things are tending, with far greater rapidity than in that old time from the circumstance of the age, to atheism in one shape or other. What a scene, what a prospect, does the whole of Europe present at this day! and not only Europe, but every government and every civilization through the world, which is under the influence of the European mind! Especially, for it most concerns us, how sorrowful, in the view of religion, even taken in its most elementary, most attenuated form, is the spectacle presented to us by the educated intellect of England, France, and Germany! Lovers of their country and of their race, religious men, external to the Catholic Church, have attempted various expedients to arrest fierce wilful human nature in its onward course, and to bring it into subjection. The necessity of some form of religion for the interests of humanity, has been generally acknowledged: but where was the concrete representative of things invisible, which would have the force and the toughness necessary to be a breakwater against the deluge? Three centuries ago the establishment of religion, material, legal, and social, was generally adopted as the best expedient for the purpose, in those countries which separated from the Catholic Church; and for a long time it was successful; but now the crevices of those establishments are admitting the enemy. Thirty years ago, education was relied upon: ten years ago there was a hope that wars would cease for ever, under the influence of commercial enterprise and the reign of the useful and fine arts; but will any one venture to say that there is any thing any where on this earth, which will afford a fulcrum for us, whereby to keep the earth from moving onwards?

The judgment, which experience passes on establishments or education, as a means of maintaining religious truth in this anarchical world, must be extended even to Scripture, though Scripture be divine. Experience proves surely that the Bible does not answer a purpose, for which it was never intended. It may be accidentally the means of the conversion of individuals; but a book, after all, cannot make a stand against the wild living intellect of man, and in this day it begins to testify, as regards its own structure and contents, to the power of that universal solvent, which is so successfully acting upon religious establishments.

Supposing then it to be the Will of the Creator to interfere in human affairs, and to make provisions for retaining in the world a knowledge of Himself, so definite and distinct as to be proof against the energy of human scepticism, in such a case,—I am far from saying that there was no other way,—but there is nothing to surprise the mind, if He should think fit to introduce a power into the world, invested with the prerogative of infallibility in religious matters. Such a provision would be a direct, immediate, active, and prompt means of withstanding the difficulty; it would be an instrument suited to the need; and, when I find that this is the very claim of the Catholic Church, not only do I feel no difficulty in admitting the idea, but there is a fitness in it, which recommends it to my mind. And thus I am brought to speak of the Church's infallibility, as a provision, adapted by the mercy of the Creator, to preserve religion in the world, and to restrain that freedom of thought, which of course in itself is one of the greatest of our natural gifts, and to rescue it from its own suicidal excesses. And let it be observed that, neither here nor in what follows, shall I have occasion to speak directly of the revealed body of truths, but only as they bear upon the defence of natural religion. I say, that a power, possessed of infallibility in religious teaching, is happily adapted to be a working instrument, in the course of human affairs, for smiting hard and throwing back the immense energy of the aggressive intellect:—and in saying this, as in the other things that I have to say, it must still be recollected that I am all along bearing in mind my main purpose, which is a defence of myself.

I am defending myself here from a plausible charge brought against Catholics, as will be seen better as I proceed. The charge is this:—that I, as a Catholic, not only make profession to hold doctrines which I cannot possibly believe in my heart, but that I also believe in the existence of a power on earth, which at its own will imposes upon men any new set of *credenda,* when it pleases, by a claim to infallibility; in consequence, that my own thoughts are not my own property; that I cannot tell that to-morrow I may not have to give up what I hold to-day, and that the necessary effect of such a condition of mind must be a degrading bondage, or a bitter inward rebellion relieving itself in secret infidelity, or the necessity of ignoring the whole subject of religion in a sort of disgust, and of mechanically saying every thing that the Church says, and leaving to others the defence of it. As then I have above spoken of the relation of my mind towards the Catholic Creed, so now I shall speak of the attitude which it takes up in the view of the Church's infallibility.

And first, the initial doctrine of the infallible teacher must be an emphatic protest against the existing state of mankind. Man had rebelled against his Maker. It was this that caused the divine interposition: and the first act of the divinely accredited messenger must be to proclaim it. The Church must denounce rebellion as of all possible evils the greatest. She must have no terms with it; if she would be true to her Master, she must ban and anathematize it. This is the meaning of a statement, which has furnished matter for one of those special accusations to which I am at present replying: I have, however, no fault at all to confess in regard to it; I have nothing to withdraw, and in consequence I here deliberately repeat it. I said, "The Catholic Church holds it better for the sun and moon to drop from heaven, for the earth to fail, and for all the many millions on it to die of starvation in extremest agony, as far as temporal affliction goes, than that one soul, I will not say, should be lost, but should commit one single venial sin, should tell one wilful untruth, or should steal one poor farthing without excuse." I think the principle here enunciated to be the mere preamble in the formal credentials of the Catholic Church, as an Act of Parliament might begin with a "*Whereas.*" It is because of the intensity of the evil which has possession of mankind, that a suitable antagonist has been provided against it; and the initial act of that divinely-commissioned power is of course to deliver her challenge and to defy the enemy. Such a preamble then gives a meaning to her position in the world, and an interpretation to her whole course of teaching and action.

In like manner she has ever put forth, with most energetic distinctness, those other great elementary truths, which either are an explanation of her mission or give a character to her work. She does not teach that human nature is irreclaimable, else wherefore should she be sent? not that it is to be shattered and reversed, but to be extricated, purified, and restored; not that it is a mere mass of evil, but that it has the promise of great things, and even now has a virtue and a praise proper to itself. But in the next place she knows and she preaches that such a restoration, as she aims at effecting in it, must be brought about, not simply through any outward provision of preaching and teaching, even though it be her own, but from a certain inward spiritual power or grace imparted directly from above, and which is in her keeping. She has it in charge to rescue human nature from its misery, but not simply by raising it upon its own level, but by lifting it up to a higher level than its own. She recognizes in it real moral excellence though degraded, but she cannot set it free from earth except by exalting it towards heaven. It was for this end that a renovating grace was put into her hands, and therefore from the nature of the gift, as well as from the reasonableness of the case, she goes on, as a further point, to insist, that all true conversion must begin with the first springs of thought, and to teach that each individual man must be in his own person one whole and perfect temple of God, while he is also one of the living stones which build up a visible religious community. And thus the distinctions between nature and grace, and between outward and inward religion, become two further articles in what I have called the preamble of her divine commission.

Such truths as these she vigorously reiterates, and pertinaciously inflicts upon mankind; as to such she observes no half-measures, no economical reserve, no delicacy or prudence. "Ye must be born again," is the simple, direct form of words which she uses after her Divine Master; "your whole nature must be re-born, your passions, and your affections, and your aims, and your conscience, and your will, must all be bathed in a new element, and reconsecrated to your Maker, and, the last not the least, your intellect." It was for repeating these points of her teaching in my own way, that certain passages of one of my Volumes have been brought into the general accusation which has been made against my religious opinions. The writer has said that I was demented if I believed, and unprincipled if I did not believe, in my statement that a lazy, ragged, filthy, story-telling beggar-woman, if chaste, sober, cheerful, and religious, had a prospect of heaven, which was absolutely closed to an accomplished statesman, or lawyer, or noble, be he ever so just, upright, generous, honourable, and conscientious, unless he had also some portion of the divine Christian grace; yet I should have thought myself defended from criticism by the words which our Lord used to the chief priests, "The publicans and harlots go into the kingdom of God before you." And I was subjected again to the same alternative of imputations, for having ventured to say that consent to an unchaste wish was indefinitely more heinous than any lie viewed apart from its causes, its motives, and its consequences: though a lie, viewed under the limitation of these conditions, is a random utterance, an almost outward act, not directly from the heart, however disgraceful it may be, whereas we have the express words of our Lord to the doctrine that "whoso looketh on a woman to lust after her, hath committed adultery with her already in his heart." On the strength of these texts I have surely as much right to believe in these doctrines as to believe in the doctrine of original sin, or that there is a supernatural revelation, or that a Divine Person suffered, or that punishment is eternal.

Passing now from what I have called the preamble of that grant of power, with which the Church is invested, to that power itself, Infallibility, I make two brief remarks: on the one hand, I am not here determining any thing about the essential seat of that power, because that is a question doctrinal, not historical and practical; nor, on the other hand, am I extending the direct subject-matter, over which that power has jurisdiction, beyond religious opinion:—and now as to the power itself.

This power, viewed in its fulness, is as tremendous as the giant evil which has called for it. It claims, when brought into exercise in the legitimate manner, for otherwise of course it is but dormant, to have for itself a sure guidance into the very meaning of every portion of the Divine Message in detail, which was committed by our Lord to His Apostles. It claims to know its own limits, and to decide what it can determine absolutely and what it cannot. It claims, moreover, to have a hold upon statements not directly religious, so far as this, to determine whether they indirectly relate to religion, and, according to its own definitive judgment, to pronounce whether or not, in a particular case, they are consistent with revealed truth. It claims to decide magisterially, whether infallibly or not, that such and such statements are or are not prejudicial to the Apostolic *depositum* of faith, in their spirit or in their consequences, and to allow them, or condemn and forbid them, accordingly. It claims to impose silence at will on any matters, or controversies, of doctrine, which on its own *ipse dixit,* it pronounces to be dangerous, or inexpedient, or inopportune. It claims that whatever may be the judgment of Catholics upon such acts, these acts should be received by them with those outward marks of reverence, submission, and loyalty, which Englishmen, for instance, pay to the presence of their sovereign, without public criticism on them, as being in their matter inexpedient, or in their manner violent or harsh. And lastly, it claims to have the right of inflicting spiritual punishment, of cutting off from the ordinary channels of the divine life, and of simply excommunicating, those who refuse to submit themselves to its formal declarations. Such is the infallibility lodged in the Catholic Church, viewed in the concrete, as clothed and surrounded by the appendages of its high sovereignty: it is, to repeat what I said above, a supereminent prodigious power sent upon earth to encounter and master a giant evil.

And now, having thus described it, I profess my own absolute submission to its claim. I believe the whole revealed dogma as taught by the Apostles, as committed by the Apostles to the Church, and as declared by the Church to me. I receive it, as it is infallibly interpreted by the authority to whom it is thus committed, and (implicitly) as it shall be, in like manner, further interpreted by that same authority till the end of time. I submit, moreover, to the universally received traditions of the Church, in which lies the matter of those new dogmatic definitions which are from time to time made, and which in all times are the clothing and the illustration of the Catholic dogma as already defined. And I submit myself to those other decisions of the Holy See, theological or not, through the organs which it has itself appointed, which, waiving the question of their infallibility, on the lowest ground come to me with a claim to be accepted and obeyed. Also, I consider that, gradually and in the course of ages, Catholic inquiry has taken certain definite shapes, and has thrown itself into the form of a science, with a method and a phraseology of its own, under the intellectual handling of great minds, such as St. Athanasius, St. Augustine, and St. Thomas; and I feel no temptation at all to break in pieces the great legacy of thought thus committed to us for these latter days.

All this being considered to be a profession *ex animo,* as on my own part, so also on the part of the Catholic body, as far as I know it, it will at first sight be said that the restless intellect of our common humanity is utterly weighed down to the repression of all independent effort and action whatever, so that, if this is to be the mode of bringing it into order, it is brought into order only to be destroyed. But this is far from the result, far from what I conceive to be the intention of that high Providence who has provided a great remedy for a great evil,—far from borne out by the history of the conflict between Infallibility and Reason in the past, and the prospect of it in the future. The energy of the human intellect "does from opposition grow"; it thrives and is joyous, with a tough elastic strength, under the terrible blows of the divinely-fashioned weapon, and is never so much itself as when it has lately been overthrown. It is the custom with Protestant writers to consider that, whereas there are two great principles in action in the history of religion, Authority and Private Judgment, they have all the Private Judgment to themselves, and we have the full inheritance and the superincumbent oppression of Authority. But this is not so; it is the vast Catholic body itself, and it only, which affords an arena for both combatants in that awful, never-dying duel. It is necessary for the very life of religion, viewed in its large operations and its history, that the warfare should be incessantly carried on. Every exercise of Infallibility is brought out into act by an intense and varied operation of the Reason, from within and without, and provokes again a re-action of Reason against it; and, as in a civil polity the State exists and endures by means of the rivalry and collision, the encroachments and defeats of its constituent parts, so in like manner Catholic Christendom is no simple exhibition of religious absolutism, but it presents a continuous picture of Authority and Private Judgment alternately advancing and retreating as the ebb and flow of the tide;—it is a vast assemblage of human beings with wilful intellects and wild passions, brought together into one by the beauty and the majesty of a Superhuman Power—into what may be called a large reformatory or training-school, not to be sent to bed, not to be buried alive, but for the melting, refining, and moulding, as in some moral factory, by an incessant noisy process, (if I may proceed to another metaphor,) of the raw material of human nature, so excellent, so dangerous, so capable of divine purposes.

St. Paul says in one place that his Apostolical power is given him to edification, and not to destruction. There can be no better account of the Infallibility of the Church. It is a supply for a need, and it does not go beyond that need. Its object is, and its effect also, not to enfeeble the freedom or vigour of human thought in religious speculation, but to resist and control its extravagance. What have been its great works? All of them in the distinct province of theology:—to put down Arianism, Eutychianism, Pelagianism, Manichæism, Lutheranism, Jansenism. Such is the broad result of its action in the past;—and now as to the securities which are given us that so it ever will act in time to come.

First, Infallibility cannot act outside of a definite circle of thought, and it must in all its decisions, or *definitions,* as they are called, profess to be keeping within it. The great truths of the moral law, of natural religion, and of Apostolical faith, are both its boundary and its foundation. It must not go beyond them, and it must ever appeal to them. Both its subject-matter, and its articles in that subject-matter, are fixed. Thus, in illustration, it does not extend to statements, however sound and evident, which are mere logical conclusions from the Articles of the Apostolic *Depositum;* again, it can pronounce nothing about the persons of heretics, whose works fall within its legitimate province. It must ever profess to be guided by Scripture and by tradition. It must refer to the particular Apostolic truth which it is enforcing, or (what is called) *defining.* Nothing, then, can be presented to me, in time to come, as part of the faith, but what I ought already to have received, and have not actually received, (if not) merely because it has not been told me. Nothing can be imposed upon me different in kind from what I hold already,—much less contrary to it. The new truth which is promulgated, if it is to be called new, must be at least homogeneous, cognate, implicit, viewed relatively to the old truth. It must be what I may even have guessed, or wished, to be included in the Apostolic revelation;

and at least it will be of such a character, that my thoughts readily concur in it or coalesce with it, as soon as I hear it. Perhaps I and others actually have always believed it, and the only question which is now decided in my behalf, is that I am henceforth to believe that I have only been holding what the Apostles held before me.

Let me take the doctrine which Protestants consider our greatest difficulty, that of the Immaculate Conception. Here I entreat the reader to recollect my main drift, which is this. I have no difficulty in receiving it: if *I* have no difficulty, why may not another have no difficulty also? why may not a hundred? a thousand? Now I am sure that Catholics in general have not any intellectual difficulty at all on the subject of the Immaculate Conception; and that there is no reason why they should. Priests have no difficulty. You tell me that they *ought* to have a difficulty;—but they have not. Be large-minded enough to believe, that men may reason and feel very differently from yourselves; how is it that men fall, when left to themselves, into such various forms of religion, except that there are various types of mind among them, very distinct from each other? From my testimony then about myself, if you believe it, judge of others also who are Catholics: we do not find the difficulties which you do in the doctrines which we hold; we have no intellectual difficulty in that in particular, which you call a novelty of this day. We priests need not be hypocrites, though we be called upon to believe in the Immaculate Conception. To that large class of minds, who believe in Christianity, after our manner,—in the particular temper, spirit, and light, (whatever word is used,) in which Catholics believe it,—there is no burden at all in holding that the Blessed Virgin was conceived without original sin; indeed, it is a simple fact to say, that Catholics have not come to believe it because it is defined, but it was defined because they believed it.

[. . .]

I am not going to criticize here that vast body of men, in the mass, who at this time would profess to be liberals in religion; and who look towards the discoveries of the age, certain or in progress, as their informants, direct or indirect, as to what they shall think about the unseen and the future. The Liberalism which gives a colour to society now, is very different from that character of thought which bore the name thirty or forty years ago. It is scarcely now a party; it is the educated lay world. When I was young, I knew the word first as giving name to a periodical, set up by Lord Byron and others. Now, as then, I have no sympathy with the philosophy of Byron. Afterwards, Liberalism was the badge of a theological school, of a dry and repulsive character, not very dangerous in itself, though dangerous as opening the door to evils which it did not itself either anticipate or comprehend. Now it is nothing else than that deep, plausible scepticism, of which I spoke above, as being the development of human reason, as practically exercised by the natural man.

The Liberal religionists of this day are a very mixed body, and therefore I am not intending to speak against them. There may be, and doubtless is, in the hearts of some or many of them a real antipathy or anger against revealed truth, which it is distressing to think of. Again; in many men of science or literature there may be an animosity arising from almost a personal feeling; it being a matter of party, a point of honour, the excitement of a game, or a consequence of soreness or annoyance occasioned by the acrimony or narrowness of apologists for religion, to prove that Christianity or that Scripture is untrustworthy. Many scientific and literary men, on the other hand, go on, I am confident, in a straightforward impartial way, in their own province and on their own line of thought, without any disturbance from religious opinion in themselves, or any wish at all to give pain to others by the result of their investigations. It would ill become me, as if I were afraid of truth of any kind, to blame those who pursue secular facts, by means of the reason which God has given them, to their logical conclusions: or to be angry with science because religion is bound to take cognizance of its teaching. But putting these particular classes of men aside, as having no special call on the sympathy of the Catholic, of course he does most deeply enter into the feelings of a fourth and large class of men, in the educated portions of society, of religious and sincere minds, who are simply perplexed,— frightened or rendered desperate, as the case may be,—by the utter confusion into which late discoveries or speculations have thrown their most elementary ideas of religion. Who does not feel for such men? who can have one unkind thought of them? I take up St. Augustine's beautiful words, "Illi in vos sæviant," &c. Let them be fierce with you who have no experience of the difficulty with which error is discriminated from truth, and the way of life is found amid the illusions of the world. How many Catholics have in their thoughts followed such men, many of them so good, so true, so noble! how often has the wish risen in their hearts that some one from among themselves should come forward as the champion of revealed truth against its opponents! Various persons, Catholic and Protestant, have asked me to do so myself; but I had several strong difficulties in the way. One of the greatest is this, that at the moment it is so difficult to say precisely what it is that is to be encountered and overthrown. I am far from denying that scientific knowledge is really growing, but it is by fits and starts; hypotheses rise and fall; it is difficult to anticipate which will keep their ground, and what the state of knowledge in relation to them will be from year to year. In this condition of things, it has seemed to me to be very undignified for a Catholic to commit himself to the work of chasing what might turn out to be phantoms, and in behalf of some special objections, to be ingenious in devising a theory, which, before it was completed, might have to give place to some theory newer still, from the fact that those former objections had already come to nought under the uprising of others. It seemed to be a time of all others, in which Christians had a call to be patient, in which they had no other way of helping those who were alarmed, than that of exhorting them to have a little faith and fortitude, and to "beware," as the poet says, "of dangerous steps." This seemed so clear to me, the more I thought, as to make me surmise, that, if I attempted what had so little promise in it, I should find that the highest Catholic authority was against the attempt, and that I should have spent my time and my thought, in doing what either it would be imprudent to bring before the public at all, or what, did I do so, would only complicate matters further which were already complicated more than enough. And I interpret recent acts of that authority as fulfilling my expectation; I interpret them as tying the hands of a controversialist, such as I should be, and teaching us that true wisdom, which Moses inculcated on his people, when the Egyptians were pursuing them, "Fear ye not, stand still; the Lord shall fight for you, and ye shall hold your peace." And so far from finding a difficulty in obeying in this case, I have cause to be thankful and to rejoice to have so clear a direction in a matter of difficulty.

[. . .]

There are of course intellectual habits which theology does not tend to form, as for instance the experimental, and again the philosophical; but that is because it *is* theology, not because of the gift of infallibility. But, as far as this goes, I think it could be shown that physical science on the other hand, or mathematical, affords but an imperfect training for the intellect. I do not see then how any objection about the narrowness of theology comes into our question, which simply is, whether the belief in an Infallible authority destroys the independence of the mind; and I consider that the whole history of the Church, and especially the history of the theological schools, gives a negative to the accusation. There never was a time when the intellect of the educated class was more active, or rather more restless, than in the middle ages. And then again all through Church history from the first, how slow is authority in interfering! Perhaps a local teacher, or a doctor in some local school, hazards a proposition, and a controversy ensues. It smoulders or burns in one place, no one interposing; Rome simply lets it alone. Then it comes before a Bishop; or some priest, or some professor in some other seat of learning takes it up; and then there is a second stage of it. Then it comes before a University, and it may be condemned by the theological faculty. So the controversy proceeds year after year, and Rome is still silent. An appeal perhaps is next made to a seat of authority inferior to Rome; and then at last after a long while it comes before the supreme power. Meanwhile, the question has been ventilated and turned over and over again, and viewed on every side of it, and authority is called upon to pronounce a decision, which has already been arrived at by reason. But even then, perhaps the supreme authority hesitates to do so, and nothing is determined on the point for years; or so generally and vaguely, that the whole controversy has to be gone through again, before it is ultimately determined. It is manifest how a mode of proceeding, such as this, tends not only to the liberty, but to the courage, of the individual theologian or controversialist. Many a man has ideas, which he hopes are true, and useful for his day, but he wishes to have them discussed. He is willing or rather would be thankful to give them up, if they can be proved to be erroneous or dangerous, and by means of controversy he obtains his end. He is answered, and he yields; or he finds that he is considered safe. He would not dare to do this, if he knew an authority, which was supreme and final, was watching every word he said, and made signs of assent or dissent to each sentence, as he uttered it. Then indeed he would be fighting, as the Persian soldiers, under the lash, and the freedom of his intellect might truly be said to be beaten out of him. But this has not been so:—I do not mean to say that, when controversies run high, in schools or even in small portions of the Church, an interposition may not rightly take place; and again, questions may be of that urgent nature, that an appeal must, as a matter of duty, be made at once to the highest authority in the Church; but, if we look into the history of controversy, we shall find, I think, the general run of things to be such as I have represented it. Zosimus treated Pelagius and Cœlestius with extreme forbearance; St. Gregory VII. was equally indulgent with Berengarius; by reason of the very power of the Popes they have commonly been slow and moderate in their use of it.

And here again is a further shelter for the individual reason:—the multitude of nations who are in the fold of the Church will be found to have acted for its protection, against any narrowness, if so, in the various authorities at Rome, with whom lies the practical decision of controverted questions. How have the Greek traditions been respected and provided for in the later Ecumenical Councils, in spite of the countries that held them being in a state of schism! There are important points of doctrine which have been (humanly speaking) exempted from the infallible sentence, by the tenderness with which its instruments, in framing it, have treated the opinions of particular places. Then, again, such national influences have a providential effect in moderating the bias which the local influences of Italy may exert upon the See of St. Peter. It stands to reason that, as the Gallican Church has in it an element of France, so Rome must have an element of Italy; and it is no prejudice to the zeal and devotion with which we submit ourselves to the Holy See to admit this plainly. It seems to me, as I have been saying, that Catholicity is not only one of the notes of the Church, but, according to the divine purposes, one of its securities.

I think it would be a very serious evil, which Divine Mercy avert! that the Church should be contracted in Europe within the range of particular nationalities. It is a great idea to introduce Latin civilization into America, and to improve the Catholics there by the energy of French Religion; but I trust that all European races will have ever a place in the Church, and assuredly I think that the loss of the English, not to say the German element, in its composition has been a most serious evil. And certainly, if there is one consideration more than another which should make us English grateful to Pius the Ninth, it is that, by giving us a Church of our own, he has prepared the way for our own habits of mind, our own manner of reasoning, our own tastes, and our own virtues, finding a place and thereby a sanctification, in the Catholic Church.

There is only one other subject, which I think it necessary to introduce here, as bearing upon the vague suspicions which are attached in this country to the Catholic Priesthood. It is one of which my accuser says much, the charge of reserve and economy. He founds it in no slight degree on what I have said on the subject in my History of the Arians, and in a note upon one of my Sermons in which I refer to it. The principle of Reserve is also advocated by an admirable writer in two numbers of the Tracts for the Times.

Now, as to the Economy itself, I leave the greater part of what I have to say to an Appendix. Here I will but say that it is founded upon the words of our Lord, "Cast not your pearls before swine"; and it was observed by the early Christians more or less in their intercourse with the heathen populations among whom they lived. In the midst of the abominable idolatries and impurities of that fearful time, they could not do otherwise. But the rule of the Economy, at least as I have explained and recommended it, did not go beyond (1) the concealing the truth when we could do so without deceit, (2) stating it only partially, and (3) representing it under the nearest form possible to a learner or inquirer, when he could not possibly understand it exactly. I conceive that to draw angels with wings is an instance of the third of these economical modes; and to avoid the question, "Do Christians believe in a Trinity?" by answering, "They believe in only one God," would be an instance of the second. As to the first, it is hardly an Economy, but comes under what is called the "Disciplina Arcani." The second and third economical modes Clement calls *lying;* meaning that a partial truth is in some sense a lie, and so also is a representative truth. And this, I think, is about the long and the short of the ground of the accusation which has been so violently urged against me, as being a patron of the Economy.

Of late years I have come to think, as I believe most writers do, that Clement meant more than I have said. I used to think he used the word "lie" as an hyperbole, but I now believe that he, as other early Fathers, thought that, under certain circumstances, it was lawful to tell a lie. This doctrine I never maintained, though I used to think, as I do now, that the theory of the subject is surrounded with considerable difficulty; and it is not strange that I should say so, considering that great English writers simply declare that in certain extreme cases, as to save life, honour, or even property, a lie is allowable. And thus I am brought to the direct question of truth, and the truthfulness of Catholic priests generally in their dealings with the world, as bearing on the general question of their honesty, and their internal belief in their religious professions.

It would answer no purpose, and it would be departing from the line of writing which I have been observing all along, if I entered into any formal discussion on the subject; what I shall do here, as I have done in the foregoing pages, is to give my own testimony on the matter in question, and there to leave it. Now first I will say, that, when I became a Catholic, nothing struck me more at once than the English out-spoken manner of the Priests. It was the same at Oscott, at Old Hall Green, at Ushaw; there was nothing of that smoothness, or mannerism, which is commonly imputed to them, and they were more natural and unaffected than many an Anglican clergyman. The many years, which have passed since, have only confirmed my first impression. I have ever found it in the priests of this Diocese; did I wish to point out a straightforward Englishman, I should instance the Bishop, who has, to our great benefit, for so many years presided over it.

And next, I was struck, when I had more opportunity of judging of the Priests, by the simple faith in the Catholic Creed and system of which they always gave evidence, and which they never seemed to feel, in any sense at all, to be a burden. And now that I have been in the Church nineteen years, I cannot recollect hearing of a single instance in England of an infidel priest. Of course there are men from time to time, who leave the Catholic Church for another religion, but I am speaking of cases, when a man keeps a fair outside to the world and is a hollow hypocrite in his heart.

I wonder that the self-devotion of our priests does not strike Protestants in this point of view. What do they gain by professing a Creed, in which, if my assailant is to be believed, they really do not believe? What is their reward for committing themselves to a life of self-restraint and toil, and after all to a premature and miserable death? The Irish fever cut off between Liverpool and Leeds thirty priests and more, young men in the flower of their days, old men who seemed entitled to some quiet time after their long toil. There was a bishop cut off in the North; but what had a man of his ecclesiastical rank to do with the drudgery and danger of sick calls, except that Christian faith and charity constrained him? Priests volunteered for the dangerous service. It was the same on the first coming of the cholera, that mysterious awe-inspiring infliction. If priests did not heartily believe in the Creed of the Church, then I will say that the remark of the Apostle had its fullest illustration:—"If in this life only we have hope in Christ, we are of all men most miserable." What could support a set of hypocrites in the presence of a deadly disorder, one of them following another in long order up the forlorn hope, and one after another perishing? And such, I may say, in its substance, is every Mission-Priest's life. He is ever ready to sacrifice himself for his people. Night and day, sick or well himself, in all weathers, off he is, on the news of a sick call. The fact of a parishioner dying without the Sacraments through his fault is terrible to him; why terrible, if he has not a deep absolute faith, which he acts upon with a free service? Protestants admire this, when they see it; but they do not seem to see as clearly, that it excludes the very notion of hypocrisy.

Sometimes, when they reflect upon it, it leads them to remark on the wonderful discipline of the Catholic priesthood; they say that no Church has so well ordered a clergy, and that in that respect it surpasses their own; they wish they could have such exact discipline among themselves. But is it an excellence which can be purchased? is it a phenomenon which depends on nothing else than itself, or is it an effect which has a cause? You cannot buy devotion at a price. "It hath never been heard of in the land of Chanaan, neither hath it been seen in Theman. The children of Agar, the merchants of Meran, none of these have known its way." What then is that wonderful charm, which makes a thousand men act all in one way, and infuses a prompt obedience to rule, as if they were under some stern military compulsion? How difficult to find an answer, unless you will allow the obvious one, that they believe intensely what they profess!

[. . .]

And now, if Protestants wish to know what our real teaching is, as on other subjects, so on that of lying, let them look, not at our books of casuistry, but at our catechisms. Works on pathology do not give the best insight into the form and the harmony of the human frame; and, as it is with the body, so is it with the mind. The Catechism of the Council of Trent was drawn up for the express purpose of providing preachers with subjects for their sermons; and, as my whole work has been a defence of myself, I may here say that I rarely preach a Sermon, but I go to this beautiful and complete Catechism to get both my matter and my doctrine. There we find the following notices about the duty of veracity:—

" 'Thou shalt not bear false witness,' &c.: let attention be drawn to two laws contained in this commandment:—the one, forbidding false witness; the other bidding, that removing all pretence and deceits, we should measure our words and deeds by simple truth, as the Apostle admonished the Ephesians of that duty in these words: 'Doing truth in charity, let us grow in Him through all things.'

"To deceive by a lie in joke or for the sake of compliment, though to no one there accrues loss or gain in consequence, nevertheless is altogether unworthy: for thus the Apostle admonishes, 'Putting aside lying, speak ye truth.' For therein is great danger of lapsing into frequent and more serious lying, and from lies in joke men gain the habit of lying, whence they gain the character of not being truthful. And thence again, in order to gain credit to their words, they find it necessary to make a practice of swearing.

"Nothing is more necessary than truth of testimony, in those things, which we neither know ourselves, nor can allowably be ignorant of, on which point there is extant that maxim of St. Augustine's; Whoso conceals the truth, and whoso puts forth a lie, each is guilty; the one because he is not willing to do a service, the other because he has a wish to do a mischief.

"It is lawful at times to be silent about the truth, but out of a court of law; for in court, when a witness is interrogated by the judge according to law, the truth is wholly to be brought out.

"Witnesses, however, must beware, lest, from over-confidence in their memory, they affirm for certain, what they have not verified.

"In order that the faithful may with more good will avoid the sin of lying, the Parish Priest shall set before them the extreme misery and turpitude of this wickedness. For, in holy writ, the devil is called the father of a lie; for, in that he did not remain in Truth, he is a liar, and the father of a lie. He will add, with the view of ridding men of so great a crime, the evils which follow upon lying; and, whereas they are innumerable, he will point out [at least] the sources and the general heads of these mischiefs and calamities, viz. 1. How great is God's displeasure and how great His hatred of a man who is insincere and a liar. 2. What security there is that a man who is specially hated by God may not be visited by the heaviest punishments. 3. What more unclean and foul, as St. James says, than . . . that a fountain by the same jet should send out sweet water and bitter? 4. For that tongue, which just now praised God, next, as far as in it lies, dishonours Him by lying. 5. In consequence, liars are shut out from the possession of heavenly beatitude. 6. That too is the worst evil of lying, that that disease of the mind is generally incurable.

"Moreover, there is this harm too, and one of vast extent, and touching men generally, that by insincerity and lying faith and truth are lost, which are the firmest bonds of human society, and, when they are lost, supreme confusion follows in life, so that men seem in nothing to differ from devils.

"Lastly, the Parish Priest will set those right who excuse their insincerity and allege the example of wise men, who, they say, are used to lie for an occasion. He will tell them, what is most true, that the wisdom of the flesh is death. He will exhort his hearers to trust in God, when they are in difficulties and straits, nor to have recourse to the expedient of a lie.

"They who throw the blame of their own lie on those who have already by a lie deceived them, are to be taught that men must not revenge themselves, nor make up for one evil by another." . . .

There is much more in the Catechism to the same effect, and it is of universal obligation; whereas the decision of a particular author in morals need not be accepted by any one.

To one other authority I appeal on this subject, which commands from me attention of a special kind, for they are the words of a Father. They will serve to bring my work to a conclusion.

"St. Philip," says the Roman Oratorian who wrote his Life, "had a particular dislike of affectation both in himself and others, in speaking, in dressing, or in any thing else.

"He avoided all ceremony which savoured of worldly compliment, and always showed himself a great stickler for Christian simplicity in every thing; so that, when he had to deal with men of worldly prudence, he did not very readily accommodate himself to them.

"And he avoided, as much as possible, having any thing to do with *two-faced persons,* who did not go simply and straightforwardly to work in their transactions.

"*As for liars, he could not endure them,* and he was *continually reminding* his spiritual children, *to avoid them as they would a pestilence.*"

These are the principles on which I have acted before I was a Catholic; these are the principles which, I trust, will be my stay and guidance to the end.

[. . .]

MATTHEW ARNOLD (1822–88)

Culture and Its Enemies (1867)

*T*his was Arnold's last lecture as Professor of Poetry in Oxford in June 1867. Under the title "Culture and Its Enemies," it was published in Cornhill Magazine *the following month and as the opening chapter of* Culture and Anarchy *two years later. For the revised edition of 1875, Arnold retitled it "Sweetness and Light," and that is how it appears in all later editions. To the modern ear (and, indeed, to many contemporaries) the phrase sounds saccharine and vapid. Originating, Arnold explains, with Jonathan Swift in his* Battle of the Books, *it derives from the image of bees who produce sweetness (honey) and light (the beeswax used in candles)—that is, beauty and intelligence, the essential components for the "perfection of human culture."*

There is much in Culture and Anarchy *to offend the modern sensibility, not only a "culture" that aspires to nothing less than perfection, but also an "anarchy" that goes well beyond the ordinary sense (the "social anarchy" of a Hyde Park riot), to the "cultural anarchy" of "doing as one likes"—and not only doing but speaking as one likes. Arnold quotes John Arthur Roebuck, a liberal member of Parliament, who declared it to be the greatness of England that everyone has the right to "say what he likes," to which Arnold retorts that culture is satisfied only if "what men say, when they may say what they like, is worth saying—has good in it, and more good than bad." His real quarrel, of course, was with Roebuck's great friend, John*

Matthew Arnold (1822–88), "Culture and Its Enemies," *Cornhill Magazine*, July 1867. Reprinted in *Culture and Anarchy* (and retitled "Sweetness and Light"), ed. J. Dover Wilson (Cambridge, 1957), pp. 43–71.

Stuart Mill, who used the expression "doing as we like" a few years earlier in the introduction to On Liberty *and made it a prime principle of his doctrine of liberty.*[1] *Mill is mentioned only once in passing in* Culture and Anarchy *(p. 221 below). But one of the great unspoken debates of Victorian England is between these two seminal works,* On Liberty *and* Culture and Anarchy.

The disparagers of culture make its motive curiosity; sometimes, indeed, they make its motive mere exclusiveness and vanity. The culture which is supposed to plume itself on a smattering of Greek and Latin is a culture which is begotten by nothing so intellectual as curiosity; it is valued either out of sheer vanity and ignorance or else as an engine of social and class distinction, separating its holder, like a badge or title, from other people who have not got it. No serious man would call this *culture,* or attach any value to it, as culture, at all. To find the real ground for the very different estimate which serious people will set upon culture, we must find some motive for culture in the terms of which may lie a real ambiguity; and such a motive the word *curiosity* gives us.

I have before now pointed out that we English do not, like the foreigners, use this word in a good sense as well as in a bad sense. With us the word is always used in a somewhat disapproving sense. A liberal and intelligent eagerness about the things of the mind may be meant by a foreigner when he speaks of curiosity, but with us the word always conveys a certain notion of frivolous and unedifying activity. In the *Quarterly Review,* some little time ago, was an estimate of the celebrated French critic, M. Sainte-Beuve, and a very inadequate estimate it in my judgment was. And its inadequacy consisted chiefly in this: that in our English way it left out of sight the double sense really involved in the word *curiosity,* thinking enough was said to stamp M. Sainte-Beuve with blame if it was said that he was impelled in his operations as a critic by curiosity, and omitting either to perceive that M. Sainte-Beuve himself, and many other people with him, would consider that this was praiseworthy and not blameworthy, or to point out why it ought really to be accounted worthy of blame and not of praise. For as there is a curiosity about intellectual matters which is futile, and merely a disease, so there is certainly a curiosity,—a desire after the things of the mind simply for their own sakes and for the pleasure of seeing them as they are,—which is, in an intelligent being, natural and laudable. Nay, and the very desire to see things as they are implies a balance and regulation of mind which is not often attained without fruitful effort, and which is the very opposite of the blind and diseased impulse of mind which is what we mean to blame when we blame curiosity. Montesquieu says: "The first motive which ought to impel us to study is the desire to augment the excellence

1. Mill, *On Liberty,* ed. Gertrude Himmelfarb ([1859] Penguin ed., London, 1974), p. 71.

of our nature, and to render an intelligent being yet more intelligent." This is the true ground to assign for the genuine scientific passion, however manifested, and for culture, viewed simply as a fruit of this passion; and it is a worthy ground, even though we let the term *curiosity* stand to describe it.

But there is of culture another view, in which not solely the scientific passion, the sheer desire to see things as they are, natural and proper in an intelligent being, appears as the ground of it. There is a view in which all the love of our neighbour, the impulses towards action, help, and beneficence, the desire for removing human error, clearing human confusion, and diminishing human misery, the noble aspiration to leave the world better and happier than we found it,—motives eminently such as are called social,—come in as part of the grounds of culture, and the main and pre-eminent part. Culture is then properly described not as having its origin in curiosity, but as having its origin in the love of perfection; it is *a study of perfection*. It moves by the force, not merely or primarily of the scientific passion for pure knowledge, but also of the moral and social passion for doing good. As, in the first view of it, we took for its worthy motto Montesquieu's words: "To render an intelligent being yet more intelligent!" so, in the second view of it, there is no better motto which it can have than these words of Bishop Wilson: "To make reason and the will of God prevail!"

Only, whereas the passion for doing good is apt to be overhasty in determining what reason and the will of God say, because its turn is for acting rather than thinking and it wants to be beginning to act; and whereas it is apt to take its own conceptions, which proceed from its own state of development and share in all the imperfections and immaturities of this, for a basis of action; what distinguishes culture is, that it is possessed by the scientific passion as well as by the passion of doing good; that it demands worthy notions of reason and the will of God, and does not readily suffer its own crude conceptions to substitute themselves for them. And knowing that no action or institution can be salutary and stable which is not based on reason and the will of God, it is not so bent on acting and instituting, even with the great aim of diminishing human error and misery ever before its thoughts, but that it can remember that acting and instituting are of little use, unless we know how and what we ought to act and to institute.

This culture is more interesting and more far-reaching than that other, which is founded solely on the scientific passion for knowing. But it needs times of faith and ardour, times when the intellectual horizon is opening and widening all round us, to flourish in. And is not the close and bounded intellectual horizon within which we have long lived and moved now lifting up, and are not new lights finding free passage to shine in upon us? For a long time there was no passage for them to make their way in upon us, and then it was of no use to think of adapting the world's action to them. Where was the hope of making reason and the will of God prevail among people who had a routine which they had christened reason and the will of God, in which they were inextricably bound, and beyond which they had no power of looking? But now the iron force of adhesion to the old routine,—social, political, religious,— has wonderfully yielded; the iron force of exclusion of all which is new has wonderfully yielded. The danger now is, not that people should obstinately refuse to allow anything but their old routine to pass for reason and the will of God, but either that they should allow some novelty or other to pass for these too easily, or else that they should underrate the importance of them alto- gether, and think it enough to follow action for its own sake, without troubling themselves to make reason and the will of God prevail therein. Now, then, is the moment for culture to be of service, culture which believes in making reason and the will of God prevail, believes in perfection, is the study and pursuit of perfection, and is no longer debarred, by a rigid invincible exclusion of whatever is new, from getting acceptance for its ideas, simply because they are new.

The moment this view of culture is seized, the moment it is regarded not solely as the endeavour to see things as they are, to draw towards a knowledge of the universal order which seems to be intended and aimed at in the world, and which it is a man's happiness to go along with or his misery to go counter to,—to learn, in short, the will of God,—the moment, I say, culture is consid- ered not merely as the endeavour to *see* and *learn* this, but as the endeavour, also, to make it *prevail,* the moral, social, and beneficent character of culture becomes manifest. The mere endeavour to see and learn the truth for our own personal satisfaction is indeed a commencement for making it prevail, a pre- paring the way for this, which always serves this, and is wrongly, therefore, stamped with blame absolutely in itself and not only in its caricature and degeneration. But perhaps it has got stamped with blame, and disparaged with the dubious title of curiosity, because in comparison with this wider endeavour of such great and plain utility it looks selfish, petty, and unprofitable.

And religion, the greatest and most important of the efforts by which the human race has manifested its impulse to perfect itself,—religion, that voice of the deepest human experience,—does not only enjoin and sanction the aim which is the great aim of culture, the aim of setting ourselves to ascertain what perfection is and to make it prevail; but also, in determining generally in what human perfection consists, religion comes to a conclusion identical with that which culture,—culture seeking the determination of this question through *all* the voices of human experience which have been heard upon it, of art, science, poetry, philosophy, history, as well as of religion, in order to give a greater fulness and certainty to its solution,—likewise reaches. Religion says: *The king-*

dom of God is within you; and culture, in like manner, places human perfection in an *internal* condition, in the growth and predominance of our humanity proper, as distinguished from our animality. It places it in the ever-increasing efficacy and in the general harmonious expansion of those gifts of thought and feeling, which make the peculiar dignity, wealth, and happiness of human nature. As I have said on a former occasion: "It is in making endless additions to itself, in the endless expansion of its powers, in endless growth in wisdom and beauty, that the spirit of the human race finds its ideal. To reach this ideal, culture is an indispensable aid, and that is the true value of culture." Not a having and a resting, but a growing and a becoming, is the character of perfection as culture conceives it; and here, too, it coincides with religion.

And because men are all members of one great whole, and the sympathy which is in human nature will not allow one member to be indifferent to the rest or to have a perfect welfare independent of the rest, the expansion of our humanity, to suit the idea of perfection which culture forms, must be a *general* expansion. Perfection, as culture conceives it, is not possible while the individual remains isolated. The individual is required, under pain of being stunted and enfeebled in his own development if he disobeys, to carry others along with him in his march towards perfection, to be continually doing all he can to enlarge and increase the volume of the human stream sweeping thitherward. And here, once more, culture lays on us the same obligation as religion, which says, as Bishop Wilson has admirably put it, that "to promote the kingdom of God is to increase and hasten one's own happiness."

But, finally, perfection,—as culture from a thorough disinterested study of human nature and human experience learns to conceive it,—is a harmonious expansion of *all* the powers which make the beauty and worth of human nature, and is not consistent with the over-development of any one power at the expense of the rest. Here culture goes beyond religion, as religion is generally conceived by us.

If culture, then, is a study of perfection, and of harmonious perfection, general perfection, and perfection which consists in becoming something rather than in having something, in an inward condition of the mind and spirit, not in an outward set of circumstances,—it is clear that culture, instead of being the frivolous and useless thing which Mr. Bright, and Mr. Frederic Harrison, and many other Liberals are apt to call it, has a very important function to fulfil for mankind. And this function is particularly important in our modern world, of which the whole civilisation is, to a much greater degree than the civilisation of Greece and Rome, mechanical and external, and tends constantly to become more so. But above all in our own country has culture a weighty part to perform, because here that mechanical character, which civilisation tends to take everywhere, is shown in the most eminent degree. Indeed nearly all the characters of perfection, as culture teaches us to fix them, meet in this country with some powerful tendency which thwarts them and sets them at defiance. The idea of perfection as an *inward* condition of the mind and spirit is at variance with the mechanical and material civilisation in esteem with us, and nowhere, as I have said, so much in esteem as with us. The idea of perfection as a *general* expansion of the human family is at variance with our strong individualism, our hatred of all limits to the unrestrained swing of the individual's personality, our maxim of "every man for himself." Above all, the idea of perfection as a *harmonious* expansion of human nature is at variance with our want of flexibility, with our inaptitude for seeing more than one side of a thing, with our intense energetic absorption in the particular pursuit we happen to be following. So culture has a rough task to achieve in this country. Its preachers have, and are likely long to have, a hard time of it, and they will much oftener be regarded, for a great while to come, as elegant or spurious Jeremiahs than as friends and benefactors. That, however, will not prevent their doing in the end good service if they persevere. And, meanwhile, the mode of action they have to pursue, and the sort of habits they must fight against, ought to be made quite clear for every one to see, who may be willing to look at the matter attentively and dispassionately.

Faith in machinery is, I said, our besetting danger; often in machinery most absurdly disproportioned to the end which the machinery, if it is to do any good at all, is to serve; but always in machinery, as if it had a value in and for itself. What is freedom but machinery? what is population but machinery? what is coal but machinery? what are railroads but machinery? what is wealth but machinery? what are, even, religious organisations but machinery? Now almost every voice in England is accustomed to speak of these things as if they were precious ends in themselves, and therefore had some of the characters of perfection indisputably joined to them. I have before now noticed Mr. Roebuck's stock argument for proving the greatness and happiness of England as she is, and for quite stopping the mouths of all gainsayers. Mr. Roebuck is never weary of reiterating this argument of his, so I do not know why I should be weary of noticing it. "May not every man in England say what he likes?"— Mr. Roebuck perpetually asks; and that, he thinks, is quite sufficient, and when every man may say what he likes, our aspirations ought to be satisfied. But the aspirations of culture, which is the study of perfection, are not satisfied, unless what men say, when they may say what they like, is worth saying,—has good in it, and more good than bad. In the same way the *Times*, replying to some foreign strictures on the dress, looks, and behaviour of the English abroad, urges that the English ideal is that every one should be free to do and to look just as he likes. But culture indefatigably tries, not to make what each raw person may like the rule by which he fashions himself; but to draw ever nearer to a sense of what is indeed beautiful, graceful, and becoming, and to get the raw person to like that.

And in the same way with respect to railroads and coal. Every one must have observed the strange language current during the late discussions as to the possible failures of our supplies of coal. Our coal, thousands of people were saying, is the real basis of our national greatness; if our coal runs short, there is an end of the greatness of England. But what *is* greatness?—culture makes us ask. Greatness is a spiritual condition worthy to excite love, interest, and admiration; and the outward proof of possessing greatness is that we excite love, interest, and admiration. If England were swallowed up by the sea to-morrow, which of the two, a hundred years hence, would most excite the love, interest, and admiration of mankind,—would most, therefore, show the evidences of having possessed greatness,—the England of the last twenty years, or the England of Elizabeth, of a time of splendid spiritual effort, but when our coal, and our industrial operations depending on coal, were very little developed? Well, then, what an unsound habit of mind it must be which makes us talk of things like coal or iron as constituting the greatness of England, and how salutary a friend is culture, bent on seeing things as they are, and thus dissipating delusions of this kind and fixing standards of perfection that are real!

Wealth, again, that end to which our prodigious works for material advantage are directed,—the commonest of commonplaces tells us how men are always apt to regard wealth as a precious end in itself; and certainly they have never been so apt thus to regard it as they are in England at the present time. Never did people believe anything more firmly than nine Englishmen out of ten at the present day believe that our greatness and welfare are proved by our being so very rich. Now, the use of culture is that it helps us, by means of its spiritual standard of perfection, to regard wealth as but machinery, and not only to say as a matter of words that we regard wealth as but machinery, but really to perceive and feel that it is so. If it were not for this purging effect wrought upon our minds by culture, the whole world, the future as well as the present, would inevitably belong to the Philistines. The people who believe most that our greatness and welfare are proved by our being very rich, and who most give their lives and thoughts to becoming rich, are just the very people whom we call Philistines. Culture says: "Consider these people, then, their way of life, their habits, their manners, the very tones of their voice; look at them attentively; observe the literature they read, the things which give them pleasure, the words which come forth out of their mouths, the thoughts which make the furniture of their minds; would any amount of wealth be worth having with the condition that one was to become just like these people by having it?" And thus culture begets a dissatisfaction which is of the highest possible value in stemming the common tide of men's thoughts in a wealthy and industrial community, and which saves the future, as one may hope, from being vulgarised, even if it cannot save the present.

Population, again, and bodily health and vigour, are things which are no-where treated in such an unintelligent, misleading, exaggerated way as in England. Both are really machinery; yet how many people all around us do we see rest in them and fail to look beyond them! Why, one has heard people, fresh from reading certain articles of the *Times* on the Registrar-General's returns of marriages and births in this country, who would talk of our large English families in quite a solemn strain, as if they had something in itself beautiful, elevating, and meritorious in them; as if the British Philistine would have only to present himself before the Great Judge with his twelve children, in order to be received among the sheep as a matter of right!

But bodily health and vigour, it may be said, are not to be classed with wealth and population as mere machinery; they have a more real and essential value. True; but only as they are more intimately connected with a perfect spiritual condition than wealth or population are. The moment we disjoin them from the idea of a perfect spiritual condition, and pursue them, as we do pursue them, for their own sake and as ends in themselves, our worship of them becomes as mere worship of machinery, as our worship of wealth or population, and as unintelligent and vulgarising a worship as that is. Every one with anything like an adequate idea of human perfection has distinctly marked this subordination to higher and spiritual ends of the cultivation of bodily vigour and activity. "Bodily exercise profiteth little; but godliness is profitable unto all things," says the author of the Epistle to Timothy. And the utilitarian Franklin says just as explicitly:—"Eat and drink such an exact quantity as suits the constitution of thy body, *in reference to the services of the mind.*" But the point of view of culture, keeping the mark of human perfection simply and broadly in view, and not assigning to this perfection, as religion or utilitarian-ism assigns to it, a special and limited character, this point of view, I say, of culture is best given by these words of Epictetus:—"It is a sign of ἀφυΐα," says he,—that is, of a nature not finely tempered,—"to give yourselves up to things which relate to the body; to make, for instance, a great fuss about exercise, a great fuss about eating, a great fuss about drinking, a great fuss about walking, a great fuss about riding. All these things ought to be done merely by the way: the formation of the spirit and character must be our real concern." This is admirable; and, indeed, the Greek word εὐφυΐα, a finely tempered nature, gives exactly the notion of perfection as culture brings us to conceive it: a harmonious perfection, a perfection in which the characters of beauty and intelligence are both present, which unites "the two noblest of things,"—as Swift, who of one of the two, at any rate, had himself all too little, most happily calls them in his *Battle of the Books*,—"the two noblest of things, *sweetness and light.*" The εὐφυής is the man who tends towards sweetness and light; the ἀφυής, on the other hand, is our Philistine. The immense spiritual significance of the Greeks is due to their having been inspired with this central and happy idea of the essential character of human perfection; and Mr. Bright's misconception of culture, as a smattering of Greek and Latin, comes itself, after all, from this wonderful significance of the Greeks having affected the very machinery of our education, and is in itself a kind of homage to it.

In thus making sweetness and light to be characters of perfection, culture is of like spirit with poetry, follows one law with poetry. Far more than on our freedom, our population, and our industrialism, many amongst us rely upon our religious organisations to save us. I have called religion a yet more important manifestation of human nature than poetry, because it has worked on a broader scale for perfection, and with greater masses of men. But the idea of beauty and of a human nature perfect on all its sides, which is the dominant idea of poetry, is a true and invaluable idea, though it has not yet had the success that the idea of conquering the obvious faults of our animality, and of a human nature perfect on the moral side,—which is the dominant idea of religion,—has been enabled to have; and it is destined, adding to itself the religious idea of a devout energy, to transform and govern the other.

The best art and poetry of the Greeks, in which religion and poetry are one, in which the idea of beauty and of a human nature perfect on all sides adds to itself a religious and devout energy, and works in the strength of that, is on this account of such surpassing interest and instructiveness for us, though it was,— as, having regard to the human race in general, and, indeed, having regard to the Greeks themselves, we must own,—a premature attempt, an attempt which for success needed the moral and religious fibre in humanity to be more braced and developed than it had yet been. But Greece did not err in having the idea of beauty, harmony, and complete human perfection, so present and paramount. It is impossible to have this idea too present and paramount; only, the moral fibre must be braced too. And we, because we have braced the moral fibre, are not on that account in the right way, if at the same time the idea of beauty, harmony, and complete human perfection, is wanting or misapprehended amongst us; and evidently it *is* wanting or misapprehended at present. And when we rely as we do on our religious organisations, which in themselves do not and cannot give us this idea, and think we have done enough if we make them spread and prevail, then, I say, we fall into our common fault of overvaluing machinery.

Nothing is more common than for people to confound the inward peace and satisfaction which follows the subduing of the obvious faults of our animality with what I may call absolute inward peace and satisfaction,—the peace and satisfaction which are reached as we draw near to complete spiritual perfection, and not merely to moral perfection, or rather to relative moral perfection. No people in the world have done more and struggled more to attain this relative moral perfection than our English race has. For no people in the world has the command to *resist the devil, to overcome the wicked one,* in the nearest and most obvious sense of those words, had such a pressing force and reality. And we have had our reward, not only in the great worldly prosperity which our obedience to this command has brought us, but also, and far more, in great inward peace and satisfaction. But to me few things are more pathetic than to see people, on the strength of the inward peace and satisfaction which their rudimentary efforts towards perfection have brought them, employ, concerning their incomplete perfection and the religious organisations within which they have found it, language which properly applies only to complete perfection, and is a far-off echo of the human soul's prophecy of it. Religion itself, I need hardly say, supplies them in abundance with this grand language. And very freely do they use it; yet it is really the severest possible criticism of such an incomplete perfection as alone we have yet reached through our religious organisations.

The impulse of the English race towards moral development and self-conquest has nowhere so powerfully manifested itself as in Puritanism. Nowhere has Puritanism found so adequate an expression as in the religious organisation of the Independents. The modern Independents have a newspaper, the *Nonconformist,* written with great sincerity and ability. The motto, the standard, the profession of faith which this organ of theirs carries aloft, is: "The Dissidence of Dissent and the Protestantism of the Protestant religion." There is sweetness and light, and an ideal of complete harmonious human perfection! One need not go to culture and poetry to find language to judge it. Religion, with its instinct for perfection, supplies language to judge it, language, too, which is in our mouths every day. "Finally, be of one mind, united in feeling," says St. Peter. There is an ideal which judges the Puritan ideal: "The Dissidence of Dissent and the Protestantism of the Protestant religion!" And religious organisations like this are what people believe in, rest in, would give their lives for! Such, I say, is the wonderful virtue of even the beginnings of perfection, of having conquered even the plain faults of our animality, that the religious organisation, which has helped us to do it can seem to us something precious, salutary, and to be propagated, even when it wears such a brand of imperfection on its forehead as this. And men have got such a habit of giving to the language of religion a special application, of making it a mere jargon, that for the condemnation which religion itself passes on the shortcomings of their religious organisations they have no ear; they are sure to cheat themselves and to explain this condemnation away. They can only be reached by the criticism which culture, like poetry, speaking a language not to be sophisticated, and resolutely testing these organisations by the ideal of a human perfection complete on all sides, applies to them.

But men of culture and poetry, it will be said, are again and again failing, and failing conspicuously, in the necessary first stage to a harmonious perfection, in the subduing of the great obvious faults of our animality, which it is the glory of these religious organisations to have helped us to subdue. True, they do often so fail. They have often been without the virtues as well as the faults of the Puritan; it has been one of their dangers that they so felt the Puritan's faults that they too much neglected the practice of his virtues. I will not, however, exculpate them at the Puritan's expense. They have often failed in morality, and morality is indispensable. And they have been punished for their failure, as the Puritan has been rewarded for his performance. They have been punished wherein they erred; but their ideal of beauty, of sweetness and light, and a human nature complete on all its sides, remains the true ideal of perfection still; just as the Puritan's ideal of perfection remains narrow and inadequate, although for what he did well he has been richly rewarded. Notwithstanding the mighty results of the Pilgrim Fathers' voyage, they and their standard of perfection are rightly judged when we figure to ourselves Shakespeare or Virgil,—souls in whom sweetness and light, and all that in human nature is most humane, were eminent,—accompanying them on their voyage, and think what intolerable company Shakespeare and Virgil would have found them! In the same way let us judge the religious organisations which we see all around us. Do not let us deny the good and the happiness which they have accomplished; but do not let us fail to see clearly that their idea of human perfection is narrow and inadequate, and that the Dissidence of Dissent and the Protestantism of the Protestant religion will never bring humanity to its true goal. As I said with regard to wealth: Let us look at the life of those who live in and for it,—so I say with regard to the religious organisations. Look at the life imaged in such a newspaper as the *Nonconformist,*—a life of jealousy of the Establishment, disputes, tea-meetings, openings of chapels, sermons; and then think of it as an ideal of a human life completing itself on all sides, and aspiring with all its organs after sweetness, light, and perfection!

Another newspaper, representing, like the *Nonconformist,* one of the religious organisations of this country, was a short time ago giving an account of the crowd at Epsom on the Derby day, and of all the vice and hideousness which was to be seen in that crowd; and then the writer turned suddenly round upon Professor Huxley, and asked him how he proposed to cure all this vice and hideousness without religion. I confess I felt disposed to ask the asker this question: and how do you propose to cure it with such a religion as yours? How is the ideal of a life so unlovely, so unattractive, so incomplete, so narrow, so far removed from a true and satisfying ideal of human perfection, as is the life of your religious organisation as you yourself reflect it, to conquer and transform all this vice and hideousness? Indeed, the strongest plea for the study of perfection as pursued by culture, the clearest proof of the actual inadequacy of the idea of perfection held by the religious organisations,—expressing, as I have said, the most widespread effort which the human race has yet made after perfection,—is to be found in the state of our life and society with these in possession of it, and having been in possession of it I know not how many hundred years. We are all of us included in some religious organisation or other; we all call ourselves, in the sublime and aspiring language of religion which I have before noticed, *children of God.* Children of God;—it is an immense pretension!—and how are we to justify it? By the works which we do, and the words which we speak. And the work which we collective children of God do, our grand centre of life, our *city* which we have builded for us to dwell in, is London! London, with its unutterable external hideousness, and with its internal canker of *publice egestas, privatim opulentia,*—to use the words which Sallust puts into Cato's mouth about Rome,—unequalled in the world! The word, again, which we children of God speak, the voice which most hits our collective thought, the newspaper with the largest circulation in England, nay, with the largest circulation in the whole world, is the *Daily Telegraph*! I say that when our religious organisations,—which I admit to express the most considerable effort after perfection that our race has yet made,—land us in no better result than this, it is high time to examine carefully their idea of perfection, to see whether it does not leave out of account sides and forces of human nature which we might turn to great use; whether it would not be more operative if it were more complete. And I say that the English reliance on our religious organisations and on their ideas of human perfection just as they stand, is like our reliance on freedom, on muscular Christianity, on population, on coal, on wealth,—mere belief in machinery, and unfruitful; and that it is wholesomely counteracted by culture, bent on seeing things as they are, and on drawing the human race onwards to a more complete, a harmonious perfection.

Culture, however, shows its single-minded love of perfection, its desire simply to make reason and the will of God prevail, its freedom from fanaticism, by its attitude towards all this machinery, even while it insists that it *is* machinery. Fanatics, seeing the mischief men do themselves by their blind belief in some machinery or other,—whether it is wealth and industrialism, or whether it is the cultivation of bodily strength and activity, or whether it is a political organisation,—or whether it is a religious organisation,—oppose with might and main the tendency to this or that political and religious organisation, or to games and athletic exercises, or to wealth and industrialism, and try violently to stop it. But the flexibility which sweetness and light give, and which is one of the rewards of culture pursued in good faith, enables a man to see that a tendency may be necessary, and even, as a preparation for something in the future, salutary, and yet that the generations or individuals who obey this tendency are sacrificed to it, that they fall short of the hope of perfection by following it; and that its mischiefs are to be criticised, lest it should take too firm a hold and last after it has served its purpose.

Mr. Gladstone well pointed out, in a speech at Paris,—and others have pointed out the same thing,—how necessary is the present great movement towards wealth and industrialism, in order to lay broad foundations of material well-being for the society of the future. The worst of these justifications is, that they are generally addressed to the very people engaged, body and soul, in the movement in question; at all events, that they are always seized with the greatest avidity by these people, and taken by them as quite justifying their life; and that thus they tend to harden them in their sins. Now, culture admits the necessity of the movement towards fortune-making and exaggerated industrialism, readily allows that the future may derive benefit from it; but insists, at the same time, that the passing generations of industrialists,—forming, for the most part, the stout main body of Philistinism,—are sacrificed to it. In the same way, the result of all the games and sports which occupy the passing generation of boys and young men may be the establishment of a better and sounder physical type for the future to work with. Culture does not set itself against the games and sports; it congratulates the future, and hopes it will make a good use of its improved physical basis; but it points out that our passing generation of boys and young men is, meantime, sacrificed. Puritanism was perhaps necessary to develop the moral fibre of the English race, Nonconformity to break the yoke of ecclesiastical domination over men's minds and to prepare the way for freedom of thought in the distant future; still, culture points out that the harmonious perfection of generations of Puritans and Nonconformists have been, in consequence, sacrificed. Freedom of speech may be necessary for the society of the future, but the young lions of the *Daily Telegraph* in the meanwhile are sacrificed. A voice for every man in his country's government may be necessary for the society of the future, but meanwhile Mr. Beales and Mr. Bradlaugh are sacrificed.

Oxford, the Oxford of the past, has many faults; and she has heavily paid for them in defeat, in isolation, in want of hold upon the modern world. Yet we in Oxford, brought up amidst the beauty and sweetness of that beautiful place, have not failed to seize one truth,—the truth that beauty and sweetness are essential characters of a complete human perfection. When I insist on this, I am all in the faith and tradition of Oxford. I say boldly that this our sentiment for beauty and sweetness, our sentiment against hideousness and rawness, has been at the bottom of our attachment to so many beaten causes, of our opposition to so many triumphant movements. And the sentiment is true, and has never been wholly defeated, and has shown its power even in its defeat. We have not won our political battles, we have not carried our main points, we have not stopped our adversaries' advance, we have not marched victoriously with the modern world; but we have told silently upon the mind of the country, we have prepared currents of feeling which sap our adversaries' position when it seems gained, we have kept up our own communications with the future. Look at the course of the great movement which shook Oxford to its centre some thirty years ago! It was directed, as any one who reads Dr. Newman's *Apology* may see, against what in one word may be called "Liberalism." Liberalism prevailed; it was the appointed force to do the work of the hour; it was necessary, it was inevitable that it should prevail. The Oxford movement was broken, it failed; our wrecks are scattered on every shore:

Quæ regio in terris nostri non plena laboris?

But what was it, this liberalism, as Dr. Newman saw it, and as it really broke the Oxford movement? It was the great middle-class liberalism, which had for the cardinal points of its belief the Reform Bill of 1832, and local self-government, in politics; in the social sphere, free-trade, unrestricted competition, and the making of large industrial fortunes; in the religious sphere, the Dissidence of Dissent and the Protestantism of the Protestant religion. I do not say that other and more intelligent forces than this were not opposed to the Oxford movement: but this was the force which really beat it; this was the force which Dr. Newman felt himself fighting with; this was the force which till only the other day seemed to be the paramount force in this country, and to be in possession of the future; this was the force whose achievements fill Mr. Lowe with such inexpressible admiration, and whose rule he was so horror-struck to see threatened. And where is this great force of Philistinism now? It is thrust into the second rank, it is become a power of yesterday, it has lost the future. A new power has suddenly appeared, a power which it is impossible yet to judge fully, but which is certainly a wholly different force from middle-class liberalism; different in its cardinal points of belief, different in its tendencies in every sphere. It loves and admires neither the legislation of middle-class Parliaments, nor the local self-government of middle-class vestries, nor the unrestricted competition of middle-class industrialists, nor the dissidence of middle-class Dissent and the Protestantism of middle-class Protestant religion. I am not now praising this new force, or saying that its own ideals are better; all I say is, that they are wholly different. And who will estimate how much the currents of feeling created by Dr. Newman's movements, the keen desire for beauty and sweetness which it nourished, the deep aversion it manifested to the hardness and vulgarity of middle-class liberalism, the strong light it turned on the

hideous and grotesque illusions of middle-class Protestantism,—who will estimate how much all these contributed to swell the tide of secret dissatisfaction
which has mined the ground under self-confident liberalism of the last thirty
years, and has prepared the way for its sudden collapse and supersession? It is in
this manner that the sentiment of Oxford for beauty and sweetness conquers,
and in this manner long may it continue to conquer!

In this manner it works to the same end as culture, and there is plenty
of work for it yet to do. I have said that the new and more democratic force
which is now superseding our old middle-class liberalism cannot yet be rightly
judged. It has its main tendencies still to form. We hear promises of its giving
us administrative reform, law reform, reform of education, and I know not
what; but those promises come rather from its advocates, wishing to make a
good plea for it and to justify it for superseding middle-class liberalism, than
from clear tendencies which it has itself yet developed. But meanwhile it has
plenty of well-intentioned friends against whom culture may with advantage
continue to uphold steadily its ideal of human perfection; that this is *an inward
spiritual activity, having for its characters increased sweetness, increased light,
increased life, increased sympathy.* Mr. Bright, who has a foot in both worlds, the
world of middle-class liberalism and the world of democracy, but who brings
most of his ideas from the world of middle-class liberalism in which he was
bred, always inclines to inculcate that faith in machinery to which, as we have
seen, Englishmen are so prone, and which has been the bane of middle-class
liberalism. He complains with a sorrowful indignation of people who "appear
to have no proper estimate of the value of the franchise"; he leads his disciples
to believe,—what the Englishman is always too ready to believe,—that the
having a vote, like the having a large family, or a large business, or large
muscles, has in itself some edifying and perfecting effect upon human nature.
Or else he cries out to the democracy,—"the men," as he calls them, "upon
whose shoulders the greatness of England rests,"—he cries out to them: "See
what you have done! I look over this country and see the cities you have built,
the railroads you have made, the manufactures you have produced, the cargoes
which freight the ships of the greatest mercantile navy the world has ever seen!
I see that you have converted by your labours what was once a wilderness, these
islands, into a fruitful garden; I know that you have created this wealth, and are
a nation whose name is a word of power throughout all the world." Why, this is
just the very style of laudation with which Mr. Roebuck or Mr. Lowe de-
bauches the minds of the middle classes, and makes such Philistines of them. It
is the same fashion of teaching a man to value himself not on what he *is,* not on
his progress in sweetness and light, but on the number of the railroads he has
constructed, or the bigness of the tabernacle he has built. Only the middle
classes are told they have done it all with their energy, self-reliance, and capital,

and the democracy are told they have done it all with their hands and sinews. But teaching the democracy to put its trust in achievements of this kind is merely training them to be Philistines to take the place of the Philistines whom they are superseding; and they too, like the middle class, will be encouraged to sit down at the banquet of the future without having on a wedding garment, and nothing excellent can then come from them. Those who know their besetting faults, those who have watched them and listened to them, or those who will read the instructive account recently given of them by one of them- selves, the *Journeyman Engineer,* will agree that the idea which culture sets before us of perfection,—an increased spiritual activity, having for its characters increased sweetness, increased light, increased life, increased sympathy,—is an idea which the new democracy needs far more than the idea of the blessedness of the franchise, or the wonderfulness of its own industrial performances.

Other well-meaning friends of this new power are for leading it, not in the old ruts of middle-class Philistinism, but in ways which are naturally alluring to the feet of democracy, though in this country they are novel and untried ways. I may call them the ways of Jacobinism. Violent indignation with the past, abstract systems of renovation applied wholesale, a new doctrine drawn up in black and white for elaborating down to the very smallest details a rational society for the future,—these are the ways of Jacobinism. Mr. Frederic Harrison and other disciples of Comte,—one of them, Mr. Congreve, is an old friend of mine, and I am glad to have an opportunity of publicly expressing my respect for his talents and character,—are among the friends of democracy who are for leading it in paths of this kind. Mr. Frederic Harrison is very hostile to culture, and from a natural enough motive; for culture is the eternal opponent of the two things which are the signal marks of Jacobinism,—its fierceness, and its addiction to an abstract system. Culture is always assigning to system- makers and systems a smaller share in the bent of human destiny than their friends like. A current in people's minds sets towards new ideas; people are dissatisfied with their old narrow stock of Philistine ideas, Anglo-Saxon ideas, or any other; and some man, some Bentham or Comte, who has the real merit of having early and strongly felt and helped the new current, but who brings plenty of narrowness and mistakes of his own into his feeling and help of it, is credited with being the author of the whole current, the fit person to be entrusted with its regulation and to guide the human race.

The excellent German historian of the mythology of Rome, Preller, relating the introduction at Rome under the Tarquins of the worship of Apollo, the god of light, healing, and reconciliation, will have us observe that it was not so much the Tarquins who brought to Rome the new worship of Apollo, as a current in the mind of the Roman people which set powerfully at that time towards a new worship of this kind, and away from the old run of Latin and Sabine religious ideas. In a similar way, culture directs our attention to the natural current there is in human affairs, and to its continual working, and will not let us rivet our faith upon any one man and his doings. It makes us see not only his good side, but also how much in him was of necessity limited and transient; nay, it even feels a pleasure, a sense of an increased freedom and of an ampler future, in so doing.

I remember, when I was under the influence of a mind to which I feel the greatest obligations, the mind of a man who was the very incarnation of sanity and clear sense, a man the most considerable, it seems to me, whom America has yet produced,—Benjamin Franklin,—I remember the relief with which, after long feeling the sway of Franklin's imperturbable commonsense, I came upon a project of his for a new version of the Book of Job, to replace the old version, the style of which, says Franklin, has become obsolete, and thence less agreeable. "I give," he continues, "a few verses, which may serve as a sample of the kind of version I would recommend." We all recollect the famous verse in our translation: "Then Satan answered the Lord and said: 'Doth Job fear God for nought?'" Franklin makes this: "Does your Majesty imagine that Job's good conduct is the effect of mere personal attachment and affection?" I well remember how, when first I read that, I drew a deep breath of relief, and said to myself: "After all, there is a stretch of humanity beyond Franklin's victorious good sense!" So, after hearing Bentham cried loudly up as the renovator of modern society, and Bentham's mind and ideas proposed as the rulers of our future, I open the *Deontology*. There I read: "While Xenophon was writing his history and Euclid teaching geometry, Socrates and Plato were talking nonsense under pretence of talking wisdom and morality. This morality of theirs consisted in words; this wisdom of theirs was the denial of matters known to every man's experience." From the moment of reading that, I am delivered from the bondage of Bentham! the fanaticism of his adherents can touch me no longer. I feel the inadequacy of his mind and ideas for supplying the rule of human society, for perfection.

Culture tends always thus to deal with the men of a system, of disciples, of a school; with men like Comte, or the late Mr. Buckle, or Mr. Mill. However much it may find to admire in these personages, or in some of them, it nevertheless remembers the text: "Be not ye called Rabbi!" and it soon passes on from any Rabbi. But Jacobinism loves a Rabbi; it does not want to pass on from its Rabbi in pursuit of a future and still unreached perfection; it wants its Rabbi and his ideas to stand for perfection, that they may with the more authority recast the world; and for Jacobinism, therefore, culture,—eternally passing onwards and seeking,—is an impertinence and an offence. But culture, just because it resists this tendency of Jacobinism to impose on us a man with limitations and errors of his own along with the true ideas of which he is the organ, really does the world and Jacobinism itself a service.

So, too, Jacobinism, in its fierce hatred of the past and of those whom it makes liable for the sins of the past, cannot away with the inexhaustible indulgence proper to culture, the consideration of circumstances, the severe judgment of actions joined to the merciful judgment of persons. "The man of culture is in politics," cries Mr. Frederic Harrison, "one of the poorest mortals alive!" Mr. Frederic Harrison wants to be doing business, and he complains that the man of culture stops him with a "turn for small fault-finding, love of selfish ease, and indecision in action." Of what use is culture, he asks, except for "a critic of new books or a professor of *belles lettres*?" Why, it is of use because, in presence of the fierce exasperation which breathes, or rather, I may say, hisses through the whole production in which Mr. Frederic Harrison asks that question, it reminds us that the perfection of human nature is sweetness and light. It is of use because, like religion,—that other effort after perfection,—it testifies that, where bitter envying and strife are, there is confusion and every evil work.

The pursuit of perfection, then, is the pursuit of sweetness and light. He who works for sweetness and light, works to make reason and the will of God prevail. He who works for machinery, he who works for hatred, works only for confusion. Culture looks beyond machinery, culture hates hatred; culture has one great passion, the passion for sweetness and light. It has one even yet greater!—the passion for making them *prevail*. It is not satisfied till we *all* come to a perfect man; it knows that the sweetness and light of the few must be imperfect until the raw and unkindled masses of humanity are touched with sweetness and light. If I have not shrunk from saying that we must work for sweetness and light, so neither have I shrunk from saying that we must have a broad basis, must have sweetness and light for as many as possible. Again and again I have insisted how those are the happy moments of humanity, how those are the marking epochs of a people's life, how those are the flowering times for literature and art and all the creative power of genius, when there is a *national* glow of life and thought, when the whole of society is in the fullest measure permeated by thought, sensible to beauty, intelligent and alive. Only it must be *real* thought and *real* beauty; *real* sweetness and *real* light. Plenty of people will try to give the masses, as they call them, an intellectual food prepared and adapted in the way they think proper for the actual condition of the masses. The ordinary popular literature is an example of this way of working on the masses. Plenty of people will try to indoctrinate the masses with the set of ideas and judgments constituting the creed of their own profession or party. Our religious and political organisations give an example of this way of working on the masses. I condemn neither way; but culture works differently. It does not try to teach down to the level of inferior classes; it does not try to win them for this or that sect of its own, with ready-made judgments and watchwords. It seeks to do away with classes; to make the best that has been thought and known in the world current everywhere; to make all men live in an atmosphere of sweetness and light, where they may use ideas, as it uses them itself, freely,— nourished, and not bound by them.

This is the *social idea;* and the men of culture are the true apostles of equality. The great men of culture are those who have had a passion for diffusing, for making prevail, for carrying from one end of society to the other, the best knowledge, the best ideas of their time; who have laboured to divest knowledge of all that was harsh, uncouth, difficult, abstract, professional, exclusive; to humanise it, to make it efficient outside the clique of the culti- vated and learned, yet still remaining the *best* knowledge and thought of the time, and a true source, therefore, of sweetness and light. Such a man was Abelard in the Middle Ages, in spite of all his imperfections; and thence the boundless emotion and enthusiasm which Abelard excited. Such were Lessing and Herder in Germany, at the end of the last century; and their services to Germany were in this way inestimably precious. Generations will pass, and literary monuments will accumulate, and works far more perfect than the works of Lessing and Herder will be produced in Germany; and yet the names of these two men will fill a German with a reverence and enthusiasm such as the names of the most gifted masters will hardly awaken. And why? Because they *humanised* knowledge; because they broadened the basis of life and intel- ligence; because they worked powerfully to diffuse sweetness and light, to make reason and the will of God prevail. With Saint Augustine they said: "Let us not leave thee alone to make in the secret of thy knowledge, as thou didst before the creation of the firmament, the division of light from darkness; let the children of thy spirit, placed in their firmament, make their light shine upon the earth, mark the division of night and day, and announce the revolution of the times; for the old order is passed, and the new arises; the night is spent, the day is come forth; and thou shalt crown the year with thy blessing, when thou shalt send forth labourers into thy harvest sown by other hands than theirs; when thou shalt send forth new labourers to new seed-times, whereof the harvest shall be not yet."

Late Victorian England

JOHN E. E. D. ACTON (1834–1902)

The History of Freedom in Antiquity (1877)

A cton is now known as the author of that memorable (and generally misquoted)
aphorism, "Power tends to corrupt and absolute power corrupts absolutely."
*Among historians he is also famous as the author of "the greatest book that never was
written," "The History of Liberty."[1] He himself spoke banteringly of that unwritten
opus as his "Madonna of the Future," a reference to Henry James's story of an artist
who devotes his life to the creation of a single masterpiece, which after his death is
revealed as a blank canvas. The essay "The History of Freedom in Antiquity" and its
sequel, "The History of Freedom in Christianity," delivered as lectures to his town
society and printed in its journal, are, in effect, the prospectus for the first volume of
that monumental unwritten history.*

*The explanation for that aborted history is obvious. Having taken the grandest
theme as his subject and having the highest standards of scholarship, Acton was
never satisfied that he had exhausted all the archives, authorities, and relevant texts.
In describing his mentor, the German historian Ignaz von Döllinger, he was writing his own epitaph: "He knew too much to write. He would not write with
imperfect materials, and to him the materials were always imperfect."[2] But there
was another problem. Acton was not only a scholarly perfectionist; he was a moral*

John E. E. D. Acton (1834–1902), "The History of Freedom in Antiquity," *Bridgnorth
Journal*, May 1877. Reprinted in Acton, *Essays on Freedom and Power*, ed. Gertrude
Himmelfarb (Boston, 1948), pp. 30–57.
1. L. M. Phillipps, *Europe Unbound* (London, 1916), p. 147n.
2. Acton, *Essays on Freedom and Power*, ed. Gertrude Himmelfarb (Boston, 1948), p. xxviii.

perfectionist as well—a moral absolutist, one might say. "The weight of opinion is against me," he announced in his inaugural lecture at Cambridge, "when I exhort you never to debase the moral currency or to lower the standard of rectitude, but to try others by the final maxim that governs your own lives, and to suffer no man and no cause to escape the undying penalty which history has the power to inflict on wrong."[3]

That double commitment, to scholarship and to morality, was a prescription for failure in one sense. But it also made for a corpus of essays and lectures that have earned Acton the status of a major historian and a perennially provocative thinker.

L iberty, next to religion, has been the motive of good deeds and the common pretext of crime, from the sowing of the seed at Athens, two thousand four hundred and sixty years ago, until the ripened harvest was gathered by men of our race. It is the delicate fruit of a mature civilisation; and scarcely a century has passed since nations, that knew the meaning of the term, resolved to be free. In every age its progress has been beset by its natural enemies, by ignorance and superstition, by lust of conquest and by love of ease, by the strong man's craving for power, and the poor man's craving for food. During long intervals it has been utterly arrested, when nations were being rescued from barbarism and from the grasp of strangers, and when the perpetual struggle for existence, depriving men of all interest and understanding in politics, has made them eager to sell their birthright for a mess of pottage, and ignorant of the treasure they resigned. At all times sincere friends of freedom have been rare, and its triumphs have been due to minorities, that have prevailed by associating themselves with auxiliaries whose objects often differed from their own; and this association, which is always dangerous, has been sometimes disastrous, by giving to opponents just grounds of opposition, and by kindling dispute over the spoils in the hour of success. No obstacle has been so constant, or so difficult to overcome, as uncertainty and confusion touching the nature of true liberty. If hostile interests have wrought much injury, false ideas have wrought still more; and its advance is recorded in the increase of knowledge, as much as in the improvement of laws. The history of institutions is often a history of deception and illusions; for their virtue depends on the ideas that produce and on the spirit that preserves them, and the form may remain unaltered when the substance has passed away.

A few familiar examples from modern politics will explain why it is that the burden of my argument will lie outside the domain of legislation. It is often said that our Constitution attained its formal perfection in 1679, when

3. Ibid., p. 25

the Habeas Corpus Act was passed. Yet Charles II succeeded, only two years later, in making himself independent of Parliament. In 1789, while the States-General assembled at Versailles, the Spanish Cortes, older than Magna Charta and more venerable than our House of Commons, were summoned after an interval of generations, but they immediately prayed the King to abstain from consulting them, and to make his reforms of his own wisdom and authority. According to the common opinion, indirect elections are a safeguard of conservatism. But all the Assemblies of the French Revolution issued from indirect elections. A restricted suffrage is another reputed security for monarchy. But the Parliament of Charles X, which was returned by 90,000 electors, resisted and overthrew the throne; while the Parliament of Louis Philippe, chosen by a Constitution of 250,000, obsequiously promoted the reactionary policy of his Ministers, and in the fatal division which, by rejecting reform, laid the monarchy in the dust, Guizot's majority was obtained by the votes of 129 public functionaries. An unpaid legislature is, for obvious reasons, more independent than most of the Continental legislatures which receive pay. But it would be unreasonable in America to send a member as far as from here to Constantinople to live for twelve months at his own expense in the dearest of capital cities. Legally and to outward seeming the American President is the successor of Washington, and still enjoys powers devised and limited by the Convention of Philadelphia. In reality the new President differs from the Magistrate imagined by the Fathers of the Republic as widely as Monarchy from Democracy, for he is expected to make 70,000 changes in the public service; fifty years ago John Quincy Adams dismissed only two men. The purchase of judicial appointments is manifestly indefensible; yet in the old French monarchy that monstrous practice created the only corporation able to resist the king. Official corruption, which would ruin a commonwealth, serves in Russia as a salutary relief from the pressure of absolutism. There are conditions in which it is scarcely a hyperbole to say that slavery itself is a stage on the road to freedom. Therefore we are not so much concerned this evening with the dead letter of edicts and of statutes as with the living thoughts of men. A century ago it was perfectly well known that whoever had one audience of a Master in Chancery was made to pay for three, but no man heeded the enormity until it suggested to a young lawyer that it might be well to question and examine with rigorous suspicion every part of a system in which such things were done. The day on which that gleam lighted up the clear, hard mind of Jeremy Bentham is memorable in the political calendar beyond the entire administration of many statesmen. It would be easy to point out a paragraph in St. Augustine, or a sentence of Grotius that outweighs in influence the Acts of fifty Parliaments, and our cause owes more to Cicero and Seneca, to Vinet and Tocqueville, than to the laws of Lycurgus or the Five Codes of France.

By liberty I mean the assurance that every man shall be protected in doing what he believes his duty against the influence of authority and majorities, custom and opinion. The State is competent to assign duties and draw the line between good and evil only in its immediate sphere. Beyond the limits of things necessary for its well-being, it can only give indirect help to fight the battle of life by promoting the influences which prevail against temptation,— religion, education, and the distribution of wealth. In ancient times the State absorbed authorities not its own, and intruded on the domain of personal freedom. In the Middle Ages it possessed too little authority, and suffered others to intrude. Modern States fall habitually into both excesses. The most certain test by which we judge whether a country is really free is the amount of security enjoyed by minorities. Liberty, by this definition, is the essential con-dition and guardian of religion; and it is in the history of the Chosen People, accordingly, that the first illustrations of my subject are obtained. The govern-ment of the Israelites was a federation, held together by no political authority, but by the unity of race and faith, and founded, not on physical force, but on a voluntary covenant. The principle of self-government was carried out not only in each tribe, but in every group of at least 120 families; and there was neither privilege of rank nor inequality before the law. Monarchy was so alien to the primitive spirit of the community that it was resisted by Samuel in that mo-mentous protestation and warning which all the kingdoms of Asia and many of the kingdoms of Europe have unceasingly confirmed. The throne was erected on a compact; and the king was deprived of the right of legislation among a people that recognized no lawgiver but God, whose highest aim in politics was to restore the original purity of the constitution, and to make its government conform to the ideal type that was hallowed by the sanctions of heaven. The inspired men who rose in unfailing succession to prophesy against the usurper and the tyrant, constantly proclaimed that the laws, which were divine, were paramount over sinful rulers, and appealed from the established authorities, from the king, the priests, and the princes of the people, to the healing forces that slept in the uncorrupted consciences of the masses. Thus the example of the Hebrew nation laid down the parallel lines on which all freedom has been won—the doctrine of national tradition and the doctrine of the higher law; the principle that a constitution grows from a root, by process of development, and not of essential change; and the principle that all political authorities must be tested and reformed according to a code which was not made by man. The operation of these principles, in unison, or in antagonism, occupies the whole of the space we are going over together.

The conflict between liberty under divine authority and the absolutism of human authorities ended disastrously. In the year 622 a supreme effort was made at Jerusalem to reform and preserve the State. The High Priest produced from the temple of Jehovah the book of the deserted and forgotten law, and both king and people bound themselves by solemn oaths to observe it. But that early example of limited monarchy and of the supremacy of law neither lasted nor spread; and the forces by which freedom has conquered must be sought elsewhere. In the very year 586, in which the flood of Asiatic despotism closed over the city which had been, and was destined again to be, the sanctuary of freedom in the East, a new home was prepared for it in the West, where, guarded by the sea and the mountains, and by valiant hearts, that stately plant was reared under whose shade we dwell, and which is extending its invincible arms so slowly and yet so surely over the civilised world.

According to a famous saying of the most famous authoress of the Continent, liberty is ancient, and it is despotism that is new. It has been the pride of recent historians to vindicate the truth of that maxim. The heroic age of Greece confirms it, and it is still more conspicuously true of Teutonic Europe. Wherever we can trace the earlier life of the Aryan nations we discover germs which favouring circumstances and assiduous culture might have developed into free societies. They exhibit some sense of common interest in common concerns, little reverence for external authority, and an imperfect sense of the function and supremacy of the State. Where the division of property and labour is incomplete there is little division of classes and of power. Until societies are tried by the complex problems of civilisation they may escape despotism, as societies that are undisturbed by religious diversity avoid persecution. In general, the forms of the patriarchal age failed to resist the growth of absolute States when the difficulties and temptations of advancing life began to tell; and with one sovereign exception, which is not within my scope to-day, it is scarcely possible to trace their survival in the institutions of later times. Six hundred years before the birth of Christ absolutism held unbounded sway. Throughout the East it was propped by the unchanging influence of priests and armies. In the West, where there were no sacred books requiring trained interpreters, the priesthood acquired no preponderance, and when the kings were overthrown their powers passed to aristocracies of birth. What followed, during many generations, was the cruel domination of class over class, the oppression of the poor by the rich, and of the ignorant by the wise. The spirit of that domination found passionate utterance in the verses of the aristocratic poet Theognis, a man of genius and refinement, who avows that he longed to drink the blood of his political adversaries. From these oppressors the people of many cities sought deliverance in the less intolerable tyranny of revolutionary usurpers. The remedy gave new shape and energy to the evil. The tyrants were often men of surprising capacity and merit, like some of those who, in the fourteenth century, made themselves lords of Italian cities; but rights secured by equal laws and by sharing power existed nowhere.

From this universal degradation the world was rescued by the most gifted of the nations. Athens, which like other cities was distracted and oppressed by a privileged class, avoided violence and appointed Solon to revise its laws. It was the happiest choice that history records. Solon was not only the wisest man to be found in Athens, but the most profound political genius of antiquity; and the easy, bloodless, and pacific revolution by which he accomplished the deliverance of his country was the first step in a career which our age glories in pursuing, and instituted a power which has done more than anything, except revealed religion, for the regeneration of society. The upper class had possessed the right of making and administering the laws, and he left them in possession, only transferring to wealth what had been the privilege of birth. To the rich, who alone had the means of sustaining the burden of public service in taxation and war, Solon gave a share of power proportioned to the demands made on their resources. The poorest classes were exempt from direct taxes, but were excluded from office. Solon gave them a voice in electing magistrates from the classes above them, and the right of calling them to account. This concession, apparently so slender, was the beginning of a mighty change. It introduced the idea that a man ought to have a voice in selecting those to whose rectitude and wisdom he is compelled to trust his fortune, his family, and his life. And this idea completely inverted the notion of human authority, for it inaugurated the reign of moral influence where all political power had depended on moral force. Government by consent superseded government by compulsion, and the pyramid which had stood on a point was made to stand upon its base. By making every citizen the guardian of his own interest Solon admitted the element of democracy into the State. The greatest glory of a ruler, he said, is to create a popular government. Believing that no man can be entirely trusted, he subjected all who exercised power to the vigilant control of those for whom they acted.

The only resource against political disorders that had been known till then was the concentration of power. Solon undertook to effect the same object by the distribution of power. He gave to the common people as much influence as he thought them able to employ, that the State might be exempt from arbitrary government. It is the essence of democracy, he said, to obey no master but the law. Solon recognised the principle that political forms are not final or inviolable, and must adapt themselves to facts; and he provided so well for the revision of his constitution, without breach of continuity or loss of stability, that for centuries after his death the Attic orators attributed to him, and quoted by his name, the whole structure of Athenian law. The direction of its growth was determined by the fundamental doctrine of Solon, that political power ought to be commensurate with public service. In the Persian war the services of the democracy eclipsed those of the Patrician orders, for the fleet that swept the Asiatics from the Aegean Sea was manned by the poorer Athenians. That class, whose valour had saved the State and had preserved European civilisation, had gained a title to increase of influence and privilege. The offices of State, which had been a monopoly of the rich, were thrown open to the poor, and in order to make sure that they should obtain their share, all but the highest commands were distributed by lot.

Whilst the ancient authorities were decaying, there was no accepted standard of moral and political right to make the framework of society fast in the midst of change. The instability that had seized on the forms threatened the very principles of government. The national beliefs were yielding to doubt, and doubt was not yet making way for knowledge. There had been a time when the obligations of public as well as private life were identified with the will of the gods. But that time had passed. Pallas, the ethereal goddess of the Athenians, and the Sun God whose oracles, delivered from the temple between the twin summits of Parnassus, did so much for the Greek nationality, aided in keeping up a lofty ideal of religion; but when the enlightened men of Greece learnt to apply their keen faculty of reasoning to the system of their inherited belief, they became quickly conscious that the conceptions of the gods corrupted the life and degraded the minds of the public. Popular morality could not be sustained by the popular religion. The moral instruction which was no longer supplied by the gods could not yet be found in books. There was no venerable code expounded by experts, no doctrine proclaimed by men of reputed sanctity like those teachers of the far East whose words still rule the fate of nearly half mankind. The effort to account for things by close observation and exact reasoning began by destroying. There came a time when the philosophers of the Porch and the Academy wrought the dictates of wisdom and virtue into a system so consistent and profound that it has vastly shortened the task of the Christian divines. But that time had not yet come.

The epoch of doubt and transition during which the Greeks passed from the dim fancies of mythology to the fierce light of science was the age of Pericles, and the endeavour to substitute certain truth for the prescriptions of impaired authorities, which was then beginning to absorb the energies of the Greek intellect, is the grandest movement in the profane annals of mankind, for to it we owe, even after the immeasurable progress accomplished by Christianity, much of our philosophy and far the better part of the political knowledge we posses. Pericles, who was at the head of the Athenian government, was the first statesman who encountered the problem which the rapid weakening of traditions forced on the political world. No authority in morals or in politics remained unshaken by the motion that was in the air. No guide could be confidently trusted; there was no available criterion to appeal to, for the means of controlling or denying convictions that prevailed among the people. The popular sentiment as to what was right might be mistaken, but it was subject to no test. The people were, for practical purposes, the seat of the knowledge of good and evil. The people, therefore, were the seat of power.

The political philosophy of Pericles consisted of this conclusion. He resolutely struck away all the props that still sustained the artificial preponderance of wealth. For the ancient doctrine that power goes with land, he introduced the idea that power ought to be so equitably diffused as to afford equal security to all. That one part of the community should govern the whole, or that one class should make laws for another, he declared to be tyrannical. The abolition of privilege would have served only to transfer the supremacy from the rich to the poor, if Pericles had not redressed the balance by restricting the right of citizenship to Athenians of pure descent. By this measure the class which formed what we should call the third estate was brought down to 14,000 citizens, and became about equal in numbers with the higher ranks. Pericles held that every Athenian who neglected to take his part in the public business inflicted an injury on the commonwealth. That none might be excluded by poverty, he caused the poor to be paid for their attendance out of the funds of the State; for his administration of the federal tribute had brought together a treasure of more than two million sterling. The instrument of his sway was the art of speaking. He governed by persuasion. Everything was decided by argument in open deliberation, and every influence bowed before the ascendancy of mind. The idea that the object of constitutions is not to confirm the predominance of any interest, but to prevent it; to preserve with equal care the independence of labour and the security of property; to make the rich safe against envy, and the poor against oppression, marks the highest level attained by the statesmanship of Greece. It hardly survived the great patriot who conceived it; and all history has been occupied with the endeavour to upset the balance of power by giving the advantage to money, land, or numbers. A generation followed that has never been equalled in talent—a generation of men whose works, in poetry and eloquence, are still the envy of the world, and in history, philosophy, and politics remain unsurpassed. But it produced no successor to Pericles, and no man was able to wield the sceptre that fell from his hand.

It was a momentous step in the progress of nations when the principle that every interest should have the right and the means of asserting itself was adopted by the Athenian Constitution. But for those who were beaten in the vote there was no redress. The law did not check the triumph of majorities or rescue the minority from the dire penalty of having been outnumbered. When the overwhelming influence of Pericles was removed, the conflict between classes raged without restraint, and the slaughter that befell the higher ranks in the Peloponnesian war gave an irresistible preponderance to the lower. The restless and inquiring spirit of the Athenians was prompt to unfold the reason of every institution and the consequences of every principle, and their Constitution ran its course from infancy to decrepitude with unexampled speed.

Two men's lives span the interval from the first admission of popular influence, under Solon, to the downfall of the State. Their history furnishes the classic example of the peril of democracy under conditions singularly favourable. For the Athenians were not only brave and patriotic and capable of generous sacrifice, but they were the most religious of the Greeks. They venerated the Constitution which had given them prosperity, and equality, and freedom, and never questioned the fundamental laws which regulated the enormous power of the Assembly. They tolerated considerable variety of opinion and great licence of speech; and their humanity towards their slaves roused the indignation even of the most intelligent partisan of aristocracy. Thus they became the only people of antiquity that grew great by democratic institutions. But the possession of unlimited power, which corrodes the conscience, hardens the heart, and confounds the understanding of monarchs, exercised its demoralising influence on the illustrious democracy of Athens. It is bad to be oppressed by a minority, but it is worse to be oppressed by a majority. For there is a reserve of latent power in the masses which, if it is called into play, the minority can seldom resist. But from the absolute will of an entire people there is no appeal, no redemption, no refuge but treason. The humblest and most numerous class of the Athenians united the legislative, the judicial, and, in part, the executive power. The philosophy that was then in the ascendant taught them that there is no law superior to that of the State—the lawgiver is above the law.

It followed that the sovereign people had a right to do whatever was within its power, and was bound by no rule of right or wrong but its own judgment of expediency. On a memorable occasion the assembled Athenians declared it monstrous that they should be prevented from doing whatever they chose. No force that existed could restrain them; and they resolved that no duty should restrain them, and that they would be bound by no laws that were not of their own making. In this way the emancipated people of Athens became a tyrant; and their government, the pioneer of European freedom, stands condemned with a terrible unanimity by all the wisest of the ancients. They ruined their city by attempting to conduct war by debate in the marketplace. Like the French Republic, they put their unsuccessful commanders to death. They treated their dependencies with such injustice that they lost their maritime Empire. They plundered the rich until the rich conspired with the public enemy, and they crowned their guilt by the martyrdom of Socrates.

When the absolute sway of numbers had endured for near a quarter of a century, nothing but bare existence was left for the State to lose; and the

Athenians, wearied and despondent, confessed the true cause of their ruin. They understood that for liberty, justice, and equal laws, it is as necessary that democracy should restrain itself as it had been that it should restrain the oligarchy. They resolved to take their stand once more upon the ancient ways, and to restore the order of things which had subsisted when the monopoly of power had been taken from the rich and had not been acquired by the poor. After a first restoration had failed, which is only memorable because Thucydides, whose judgment in politics is never at fault, pronounced it the best government Athens had enjoyed, the attempt was renewed with more experience and greater singleness of purpose. The hostile parties were reconciled, and proclaimed an amnesty, the first in history. They resolved to govern by concurrence. The laws, which had the sanction of tradition, were reduced to a code; and no act of the sovereign assembly was valid with which they might be found to disagree. Between the sacred lines of the Constitution which were to remain inviolate, and the decrees which met from time to time the needs and notions of the day, a broad distinction was drawn; and the fabric of a law which had been the work of generations was made independent of momentary variations in the popular will. The repentance of the Athenians came too late to save the Republic. But the lesson of their experience endures for all times, for it teaches that government by the whole people, being the government of the most numerous and most powerful class, is an evil of the same nature as unmixed monarchy, and requires, for nearly the same reasons, institutions that shall protect it against itself, and shall uphold the permanent reign of law against arbitrary revolutions of opinion.

Parallel with the rise and fall of Athenian freedom, Rome was employed in working out the same problems, with greater constructive sense, and greater temporary success, but ending at last in a far more terrible catastrophe. That which among the ingenious Athenians had been a development carried forward by the spell of plausible argument, was in Rome a conflict between rival forces. Speculative politics had no attraction for the grim and practical genius of the Romans. They did not consider what would be the cleverest way of getting over a difficulty, but what way was indicated by analogous cases; and they assigned less influence to the impulse and spirit of the moment, than to precedent and example. Their peculiar character prompted them to ascribe the origin of their laws to early times, and in their desire to justify the continuity of their institutions, and to get rid of the reproach of innovation, they imagined the legendary history of the kings of Rome. The energy of their adherence to traditions made their progress slow, they advanced only under compulsion of almost unavoidable necessity, and the same questions recurred often, before they were settled. The constitutional history of the Republic turns on the endeavours of the aristocracy, who claimed to be the only true Romans, to retain in their hands the power they had wrested from the kings, and of the plebeians to get an equal share in it. And this controversy, which the eager and restless Athenians went through in one generation, lasted for more than two centuries, from a time when the *plebs* were excluded from the government of the city, and were taxed, and made to serve without pay, until, in the year 286, they were admitted to political equality. Then followed one hundred and fifty years of unexampled prosperity and glory; and then, out of the original conflict which had been compromised, if not theoretically settled, a new struggle arose which was without an issue.

The mass of poorer families, impoverished by incessant service in war, were reduced to dependence on an aristocracy of about two thousand wealthy men, who divided among themselves the immense domain of the State. When the need became intense the Gracchi tried to relieve it by inducing the richer classes to allot some share in the public lands to the common people. The old and famous aristocracy of birth and rank had made a stubborn resistance, but it knew the art of yielding. The later and more selfish aristocracy was unable to learn it. The character of the people was changed by the sterner motives of dispute. The fight for political power had been carried on with the moderation which is so honourable a quality of party contests in England. But the struggle for the objects of material existence grew to be as ferocious as civil controversies in France. Repulsed by the rich, after a struggle of twenty-two years, the people, three hundred and twenty thousand of whom depended on public rations for food, were ready to follow any man who promised to obtain for them by revolution what they could not obtain by law.

For a time the Senate, representing the ancient and threatened order of things, was strong enough to overcome every popular leader that arose, until Julius Cæsar, supported by an army which he had led in an unparalleled career of conquest, and by the famished masses which he won by his lavish liberality, and skilled beyond all other men in the art of governing, converted the Republic into a monarchy by a series of measures that were neither violent nor injurious.

The Empire preserved the Republican forms until the reign of Diocletian; but the will of the Emperors was as uncontrolled as that of the people had been after the victory of the Tribunes. Their power was arbitrary even when it was most widely employed, and yet the Roman Empire rendered greater services to the cause of liberty than the Roman Republic. I do not mean by reason of the temporary accident that there were emperors who made good use of their immense opportunities, such as Nerva, of whom Tacitus says that he combined monarchy and liberty, things otherwise incompatible; or that the Empire was what its panegyrists declared it, the perfection of democracy. In truth, it was at best an ill-disguised and odious despotism. But Frederic the Great was a despot; yet he was a friend to toleration and free discussion. The Bonapartes were despotic; yet no liberal ruler was ever more acceptable to the masses of the people than the First Napoleon, after he had destroyed the Republic, in 1805, and the Third Napoleon at the height of his power in 1859. In the same way, the Roman Empire possessed merits which, at a distance, and especially at a great distance of time, concern men more deeply than the tragic tyranny which was felt in the neighbourhood of the Palace. The poor had what they had demanded in vain of the Republic. The rich fared better than during the Triumvirate. The rights of Roman citizens were extended to the people of the provinces. To the imperial epoch belong the better part of Roman literature and nearly the entire Civil Law; and it was the Empire that mitigated slavery, instituted religious toleration, made a beginning of the law of nations, and created a perfect system of the law of property. The Republic which Cæsar overthrew had been anything but a free State. It provided admirable securities for the rights of citizens; it treated with savage disregard the rights of men; and allowed the free Roman to inflict atrocious wrongs on his children, on debtors and dependants, on prisoners and slaves. Those deeper ideas of right and duty, which are not found on the tables of municipal law, but with which the generous minds of Greece were conversant, were held of little account, and the philosophy which dealt with such speculations was repeatedly proscribed, as a teacher of sedition and impiety.

At length, in the year 155, the Athenian philosopher Carneades appeared at Rome on a political mission. During an interval of official business he delivered two public orations, to give the unlettered conquerors of his country a taste of the disputations that flourished in the Attic schools. On the first day he discoursed of natural justice. On the next, he denied its existence, arguing that all our notions of good and evil are derived from positive enactment. From the time of that memorable display, the genius of the vanquished held its conquerors in thrall. The most eminent of the public men of Rome, such as Scipio and Cicero, formed their minds on Grecian models, and her jurists underwent the rigorous discipline of Zeno and Chrysippus.

If, drawing the limit in the second century, when the influence of Christianity becomes perceptible, we should form our judgment of the politics of antiquity by its actual legislation, our estimate would be low. The prevailing notions of freedom were imperfect, and the endeavours to realise them were wide of the mark. The ancients understood the regulation of power better than the regulation of liberty. They concentrated so many prerogatives in the State as to leave no footing from which a man could deny its jurisdiction or assign bounds to its activity. If I may employ an expressive anachronism, the vice of the classic State was that it was both Church and State in one. Morality was undistinguished from religion and politics from morals; and in religion, morality, and politics there was only one legislator and one authority. The State, while it did deplorably little for education, for practical science, for the indigent and helpless, or for the spiritual needs of man, nevertheless claimed the use of all his faculties and the determination of all his duties. Individuals and families, associations and dependencies were so much material that the sovereign power consumed for its own purposes. What the slave was in the hands of his master, the citizen was in the hands of the community. The most sacred obligations vanished before the public advantage. The passengers existed for the sake of the ship. By their disregard for private interests, and for the moral welfare and improvement of the people, both Greece and Rome destroyed the vital elements on which the prosperity of nations rests, and perished by the decay of families and the depopulation of the country. They survive not in their institutions, but in their ideas, and by their ideas, especially on the art of government, they are—

> The dead, but sceptred sovereigns who still rule
> Our spirits from their urns.

To them, indeed, may be tracked nearly all the errors that are undermining political society—communism, utilitarianism, the confusion between tyranny and authority, and between lawlessness and freedom.

The notion that men lived originally in a state of nature, by violence and without laws, is due to Critias. Communism in its grossest form was recommended by Diogenes of Sinope. According to the Sophists, there is no duty above expediency and no virtue apart from pleasure. Laws are an invention of weak men to rob their betters of the reasonable enjoyment of their superiority. It is better to inflict than to suffer wrong; and as there is no greater good than to do evil without fear of retribution, so there is no worse evil than to suffer without the consolation of revenge. Justice is the mask of a craven spirit; injustice is worldly wisdom; and duty, obedience, self-denial are the impostures of hypocrisy. Government is absolute, and may ordain what it pleases, and no subject can complain that it does him wrong, but as long as he can escape compulsion and punishment, he is always free to disobey. Happiness consists in obtaining power and in eluding the necessity of obedience; and he that gains a throne by perfidy and murder, deserves to be truly envied.

Epicurus differed but little from the propounders of the code of revolutionary despotism. All societies, he said, are founded on contract for mutual protection. Good and evil are conventional terms, for the thunderbolts of heaven fall alike on the just and the unjust. The objection to wrongdoing is not the act, but in its consequences to the wrongdoer. Wise men contrive laws, not to bind, but to protect themselves; and when they prove to be unprofitable they cease to be valid. The illiberal sentiments of even the most illustrious metaphysicians are disclosed in the saying of Aristotle, that the mark of the worst governments is that they leave men free to live as they please.

If you will bear in mind that Socrates, the best of the pagans, knew of no higher criterion for men, of no better guide of conduct, than the laws of each country; that Plato, whose sublime doctrine was so near an anticipation of Christianity that celebrated theologians wished his works to be forbidden, lest men should be content with them, and indifferent to any higher dogma—to whom was granted that prophetic vision of the Just Man, accused, condemned and scourged, and dying on a Cross—nevertheless employed the most splendid intellect ever bestowed on man to advocate the abolition of the family and the exposure of infants; that Aristotle, the ablest moralist of antiquity, saw no harm in making raids upon a neighbouring people, for the sake of reducing them to slavery—still more, if you will consider that, among the moderns, men of genius equal to these have held political doctrines not less criminal or absurd—it will be apparent to you how stubborn a phalanx of error blocks the paths of truth; that pure reason is as powerless as custom to solve the problem of free government; that it can only be the fruit of long, manifold, and painful experience; and that the tracing of the methods by which divine wisdom has educated the nations to appreciate and to assume the duties of freedom, is not the least part of that true philosophy that studies to

Assert eternal Providence,
And justify the ways of God to men.

But, having sounded the depth of their errors, I should give you a very inadequate idea of the wisdom of the ancients if I allowed it to appear that their precepts were no better than their practice. While statesmen and senates and popular assemblies supplied examples of every description of blunder, a noble literature arose, in which a priceless treasure of political knowledge was stored, and in which the defects of the existing institutions were exposed with unsparing sagacity. The point on which the ancients were most nearly unanimous is the right of the people to govern, and their inability to govern alone. To meet this difficulty, to give to the popular element a full share without a monopoly of power, they adopted very generally the theory of a mixed Constitution. They differed from our notion of the same thing, because modern Constitutions have been a device for limiting monarchy; with them they were invented to curb democracy. The idea arose in the time of Plato—though he repelled it—when the early monarchies and oligarchies had vanished, and it continued to be cherished long after all democracies had been absorbed in the Roman Empire. But whereas a sovereign prince who surrenders part of his authority yields to the argument of superior force, a sovereign people relinquishing its own prerogative succumbs to the influence of reason. And it has in all times proved more easy to create limitations by the use of force than by persuasion.

The ancient writers saw very clearly that each principle of government standing alone is carried to excess and provokes a reaction. Monarchy hardens into despotism. Aristocracy contracts into oligarchy. Democracy expands into the supremacy of numbers. They therefore imagined that to restrain each element by combining it with the others would avert the natural process of self-destruction, and endow the State with perpetual youth. But this harmony of monarchy, aristocracy, and democracy blended together, which was the ideal of many writers, and which they supposed to be exhibited by Sparta, by Carthage, and by Rome, was a chimera of philosophers never realised by antiquity. At last Tacitus, wiser than the rest, confessed that the mixed Constitution, however admirable in theory, was difficult to establish and impossible to maintain. His disheartening avowal is not disowned by later experience.

The experiment has been tried more often than I can tell, with a combination of resources that were unknown to the ancients—with Christianity, parliamentary government, and a free press. Yet there is no example of such a balanced Constitution having lasted a century. If it has succeeded anywhere it has been in our favoured country and in our time; and we know not yet how long the wisdom of the nation will preserve the equipoise. The Federal check was as familiar to the ancients as the Constitutional. For the type of all their Republics was the government of a city by its own inhabitants meeting in the public place. An administration embracing many cities was known to them only in the form of the oppression which Sparta exercised over the Messenians, Athens over her Confederates, and Rome over Italy. The resources which, in modern times, enabled a great people to govern itself through a single centre did not exist. Equality could be preserved only by federalism; and it occurs more often amongst them than in the modern world. If the distribution of power among the several parts of the State is the most efficient restraint on monarchy, the distribution of power among several States is the best check on democracy. By multiplying centres of government and discussion it promotes the diffusion of political knowledge and the maintenance of healthy and independent opinion. It is the protectorate of minorities, and the consecration of self-government. But although it must be enumerated among the better achievements of practical genius in antiquity, it arose from necessity, and its properties were imperfectly investigated in theory.

When the Greeks began to reflect on the problems of society, they first of all accepted things as they were, and did their best to explain and defend them. Inquiry, which with us is stimulated by doubt, began with them in wonder. The most illustrious of the early philosophers, Pythagoras, promulgated a theory for the preservation of political power in the educated class, and ennobled a form of government which was generally founded on popular ignorance and on strong class interests. He preached authority and subordination, and dwelt more on duties than on rights, on religion than on policy; and his system perished in the revolution by which oligarchies were swept away. The revolution afterwards developed its own philosophy, whose excesses I have described.

But between the two eras, between the rigid didactics of the early Pythagoreans and the dissolving theories of Protagoras, a philosopher arose who stood aloof from both extremes, and whose difficult sayings were never really understood or valued until our time. Heraclitus, of Ephesus, deposited his book in the temple of Diana. The book has perished, like the temple and the worship, but its fragments have been collected and interpreted with incredible ardour, by the scholars, the divines, the philosophers, and politicians who have been engaged the most intensely in the toil and stress of this century. The most renowned logician of the last century adopted every one of his propositions; and the most brilliant agitator among Continental Socialists composed a work of eight hundred and forty pages to celebrate his memory.

Heraclitus complained that the masses were deaf to truth, and knew not that one good man counts for more than thousands; but he held the existing order in no superstitious reverence. Strife, he says, is the source and the master of all things. Life is perpetual motion, and repose is death. No man can plunge twice into the same current, for it is always flowing and passing, and is never the same. The only thing fixed and certain in the midst of change is the universal and sovereign reason, which all men may not perceive, but which is common to all. Laws are sustained by no human authority, but by virtue of their derivation from the one law that is divine. These sayings, which recall the grand outlines of political truth which we have found in the Sacred Books, and carry us forward to the latest teaching of our most enlightened contemporaries, would bear a good deal of elucidation and comment. Heraclitus is, unfortunately, so obscure that Socrates could not understand him, and I won't pretend to have succeeded better.

If the topic of my address was the history of political science, the highest and the largest place would belong to Plato and Aristotle. The *Laws* of the one, the *Politics* of the other, are, if I may trust my own experience, the books from which we may learn the most about the principles of politics. The penetration with which those great masters of thought analysed the institutions of Greece, and exposed their vices, is not surpassed by anything in later literature; by Burke or Hamilton, the best political writers of the last century; by Tocqueville or Roscher, the most eminent of our own. But Plato and Aristotle were philosophers, studious not of unguided freedom, but of intelligent government.

They saw the disastrous effects of ill-directed striving for liberty; and they resolved that it was better not to strive for it, but to be content with a strong administration, prudently adapted to make men prosperous and happy.

Now liberty and good government do not exclude each other; and there are excellent reasons why they should go together. Liberty is not a means to a higher political end. It is itself the highest political end. It is not for the sake of a good public administration that it is required, but for security in the pursuit of the highest objects of civil society, and of private life. Increase of freedom in the State may sometimes promote mediocrity, and give vitality to prejudice; it may even retard useful legislation, diminish the capacity for war, and restrict the boundaries of Empire. It might be plausibly argued that, if many things would be worse in England or Ireland under an intelligent despotism, some things would be managed better; that the Roman government was more enlightened under Augustus and Antoninus than under the Senate, in the days of Marius or of Pompey. A generous spirit prefers that his country should be poor, and weak, and of no account, but free, rather than powerful, prosperous, and enslaved. It is better to be the citizen of a humble commonwealth in the Alps, without a prospect of influence beyond the narrow frontier, than a subject of the superb autocracy that overshadows half of Asia and of Europe. But it may be urged, on the other side, that liberty is not the sum or the substitute of all the things men ought to live for; that to be real it must be circumscribed, and that the limits of circumscription vary; that advancing civilisation invests the State with increased rights and duties, and imposes increased burdens and constraint on the subject; that a highly instructed and intelligent community may perceive the benefit of compulsory obligations which, at a lower stage, would be thought unbearable; that liberal progress is not vague or indefinite, but aims at a point where the public is subject to no restrictions but those of which it feels the advantage; that a free country may be less capable of doing much for the advancement of religion, the prevention of vice, or the relief of suffering, than one that does not shrink from confronting great emergencies by some sacrifice of individual rights, and some concentration of power; and that the supreme political object ought to be sometimes postponed to still higher moral objects. My argument involves no collision with these qualifying reflections. We are dealing, not with the effects of freedom, but with its causes. We are seeking out the influences which brought arbitrary government under control, either by the diffusion of power, or by the appeal to an authority which transcends all government, and among those influences the greatest philosophers of Greece have no claim to be reckoned.

It is the Stoics who emancipated mankind from its subjugation to despotic rule, and whose enlightened and elevated views of life bridged the chasm that separates the ancient from the Christian state, and led the way to freedom.

Seeing how little security there is that the laws of any land shall be wise or just, and that the unanimous will of a people and the assent of nations are liable to err, the Stoics looked beyond those narrow barriers, and above those inferior sanctions, for the principles that ought to regulate the lives of men and the existence of society. They made it known that there is a will superior to the collective will of man, and a law that overrules those of Solon and Lycurgus. Their test of good government is its conformity to principles that can be traced to a higher legislator. That which we must obey, that to which we are bound to reduce all civil authorities, and to sacrifice every earthly interest, is that immutable law which is perfect and eternal as God Himself, which proceeds from His nature, and reigns over heaven and earth and over all the nations.

The great question is to discover, not what governments prescribe, but what they ought to prescribe; for no prescription is valid against the conscience of mankind. Before God, there is neither Greek nor barbarian, neither rich nor poor, and the slave is as good as his master, for by birth all men are free; they are citizens of that universal commonwealth which embraces all the world, brethren of one family, and children of God. The true guide of our conduct is no outward authority, but the voice of God, who comes down to dwell in our souls, who knows all our thoughts, to whom are owing all the truth we know, and all the good we do; for vice is voluntary, and virtue comes from the grace of the heavenly spirit within.

What the teaching of that divine voice is, the philosophers who had imbibed the sublime ethics of the Porch went on to expound: It is not enough to act up to the written law, or to give all men their due; we ought to give them more than their due, to be generous and beneficent, to devote ourselves for the good of others, seeking our reward in self-denial and sacrifice, acting from the motive of sympathy and not of personal advantage. Therefore we must treat others as we wish to be treated by them, and must persist until death in doing good to our enemies, regardless of unworthiness and ingratitude. For we must be at war with evil, but at peace with men, and it is better to suffer than to commit injustice. True freedom, says the most eloquent of the Stoics, consists in obeying God. A State governed by such principles as these would have been free far beyond the measure of Greek or Roman freedom; for they open a door to religious toleration, and close it against slavery. Neither conquest nor purchase, said Zeno, can make one man the property of another.

These doctrines were adopted and applied by the great jurists of the Empire. The law of nature, they said, is superior to the written law, and slavery contradicts the law of nature. Men have no right to do what they please with their own [property], or to make profit out of another's loss. Such is the political wisdom of the ancients, touching the foundations of liberty, as we find it in its highest development, in Cicero, and Seneca, and Philo, a Jew of Alexandria.

Their writings impress upon us the greatness of the work of preparation for the Gospel which had been accomplished among men on the eve of the mission of the Apostles. St. Augustine, after quoting Seneca, exclaims: "What more could a Christian say than this Pagan has said?" The enlightened pagans had reached nearly the last point attainable without a new dispensation, when the fulness of time was come. We have seen the breadth and the splendour of the domain of Hellenic thought, and it has brought us to the threshold of a greater kingdom. The best of the later classics speak almost the language of Christianity, and they border on its spirit.

But in all that I have been able to cite from classical literature, three things are wanting,—representative government, the emancipation of the slaves, and liberty of conscience. There were, it is true, deliberative assemblies, chosen by the people; and confederate cities, of which, both in Asia and Africa, there were so many leagues, sent their delegates to sit in Federal Councils. But government by an elected Parliament was even in theory a thing unknown. It is congruous with the nature of Polytheism to admit some measure of toleration. And Socrates, when he avowed that he must obey God rather than the Athenians, and the Stoics, when they set the wise man above the law, were very near giving utterance to the principle. But it was first proclaimed and established by enactment, not in polytheistic and philosophical Greece, but in India, by Asoka, the earliest of the Buddhist kings, two hundred and fifty years before the birth of Christ.

Slavery has been, far more than intolerance, the perpetual curse and reproach of ancient civilisation, and although its rightfulness was disputed as early as the days of Aristotle, and was implicitly, if not definitely, denied by several Stoics, the moral philosophy of the Greeks and Romans, as well as their practice, pronounced decidedly in its favour. But there was one extraordinary people who, in this as in other things, anticipated the purer precept that was to come. Philo of Alexandria is one of the writers whose views on society were most advanced. He applauds not only liberty but equality in the enjoyment of wealth. He believes that a limited democracy, purged of its grosser elements, is the most perfect government, and will extend itself gradually over all the world. By freedom he understood the following of God. Philo, though he required that the condition of the slave should be made compatible with the wants and claims of his higher nature, did not absolutely condemn slavery. But he has put on record the customs of the Essenes of Palestine, a people who, uniting the wisdom of the Gentiles with the faith of the Jews, led lives which were uncontaminated by the surrounding civilisation, and were the first to reject slavery both in principle and practice. They formed a religious community rather than a State, and their numbers did not exceed 4,000. But their example testifies to how great a height religious men were able to raise their conception of society even without the succour of the New Testament, and affords the strongest condemnation of their contemporaries.

This, then, is the conclusion to which our survey brings us: there is hardly a truth in politics or in the system of the rights of man that was not grasped by the wisest of the Gentiles and the Jews, or that they did not declare with a refinement of thought and a nobleness of expression that later writers could never surpass. I might go on for hours, reciting to you passages on the law of nature and the duties of man, so solemn and religious that though they come from the profane theatre on the Acropolis, and from the Roman forum, you would deem that you were listening to the hymns of Christian churches and the discourse of ordained divines. But although the maxims of the great classic teachers, of Sophocles, and Plato, and Seneca, and the glorious examples of public virtue were in the mouths of all men, there was no power in them to avert the doom of that civilisation for which the blood of so many patriots and the genius of such incomparable writers had been wasted in vain. The liberties of the ancient nations were crushed beneath a hopeless and inevitable despotism, and their vitality was spent, when the new power came forth from Galilee, giving what was wanting to the efficacy of human knowledge to redeem societies as well as men.

It would be presumptuous if I attempted to indicate the numberless channels by which Christian influence gradually penetrated the State. The first striking phenomenon is the slowness with which an action destined to be so prodigious became manifest. Going forth to all nations, in many stages of civilisation and under almost every form of government, Christianity had none of the character of a political apostate, and in its absorbing mission to individuals did not challenge public authority. The early Christians avoided contact with the State, abstained from the responsibilities of office, and were even reluctant to serve in the army. Cherishing their citizenship of a kingdom not of this world, they despaired of an empire which seemed too powerful to be resisted and too corrupt to be converted, whose institutions, the work and the pride of untold centuries of paganism, drew their sanctions from the gods whom the Christians accounted devils, which plunged its hands from age to age in the blood of martyrs, and was beyond the hope of regeneration and foredoomed to perish. They were so much overawed as to imagine that the fall of the State would be the end of the Church and of the world, and no man dreamed of the boundless future of spiritual and social influence that awaited their religion among the race of destroyers that were bringing the empire of Augustus and of Constantine to humiliation and ruin. The duties of government were less in their thoughts than the private virtues and duties of subjects; and it was long before they became aware of the burden of power in their faith.

Down almost to the time of Chrysostom, they shrank from contemplating the obligation to emancipate the slaves.

Although the doctrine of self-reliance and self-denial, which is the foundation of political economy, was written as legibly in the New Testament as in the *Wealth of Nations,* it was not recognised until our age. Tertullian boasts of the passive obedience of the Christians. Melito writes to a pagan Emperor as if he were incapable of giving an unjust command; and in Christian times Optatus thought that whoever presumed to find fault with his sovereign exalted himself almost to the level of a god. But this political quietism was not universal. Origen, the ablest writer of early times, spoke with approval of conspiring for the destruction of tyranny.

After the fourth century the declarations against slavery are earnest and continual. And in a theological but yet pregnant sense, divines of the second century insist on liberty, and divines of the fourth century on equality. There was one essential and inevitable transformation in politics. Popular governments had existed, and also mixed and federal governments, but there had been no limited government, no State the circumference of whose authority had been defined by a force external to its own. That was the great problem which philosophy had raised, and which no statesmanship had been able to solve. Those who proclaimed the assistance of a higher authority had indeed drawn a metaphysical barrier before the governments, but they had not known how to make it real. All that Socrates could effect by way of protest against the tyranny of the reformed democracy was to die for his convictions. The Stoics could only advise the wise man to hold aloof from politics, keeping the unwritten law in his heart. But when Christ said: "Render unto Cæsar the things that are Cæsar's, and unto God the things that are God's," those words, spoken on His last visit to the Temple, three days before His death, gave to the civil power, under the protection of conscience, a sacredness it had never enjoyed, and bounds it had never acknowledged; and they were the repudiation of absolutism and the inauguration of freedom. For our Lord not only delivered the precept, but created the force to execute it. To maintain the necessary immunity in one supreme sphere, to reduce all political authority within defined limit, ceased to be an aspiration of patient reasoners, and was made the perpetual charge and care of the most energetic institution and the most universal association in the world. The new law, the new spirit, the new authority, gave to liberty a meaning and a value it had not possessed in the philosophy or in the constitution of Greece or Rome before the knowledge of the truth that makes us free.

MILLICENT GARRETT FAWCETT (1847–1929)

The Future of Englishwomen: A Reply (1878)

It is odd that Millicent Fawcett should have identified the author of the article to which she was replying as Mrs. Sutherland Orr, whereas the author had actually signed it A. Orr. Was Fawcett implying that a critic of feminism had to bear the name of her husband and that only a feminist like herself could write in her own name? In fact, Alexandra Orr was a considerable woman in her own right, even before she wrote, under the name of Mrs. Sutherland Orr, the highly regarded and often reprinted (as recently as 2006) Life and Letters of Robert Browning.[1]

Fawcett was replying, as she acknowledged, to a serious and well-reasoned argument by Orr. The "Woman's Rights" movement, Orr had conceded, might be all to the good, indeed, had already done much good for some women, but female suffrage would have unanticipated and unfortunate consequences for everyone. The demand for the suffrage, she claimed, was a product of the peculiar condition of modern society: the existence of a large class of "supernumerary" or "superfluous"— that is, unmarried—women. She did not mean these words (as Fawcett implied) in a derogatory sense; on the contrary, she portrayed these women with sympathy and dignity. Her concern was that in pursuing the interests of these "independent"

Millicent Garrett Fawcett (1847–1929), "The Future of Englishwomen: A Reply," *Nineteenth Century*, August 1878.

1. Fawcett might well have signed herself Mrs. Henry Fawcett, her husband's name carrying some weight in intellectual and public circles. (See the Introduction, p. 11, n. 24.) Mr. Sutherland Orr, on the other hand, had no public identity except as the husband of Mrs. Sutherland Orr.

women, society would weaken the familial bonds that tie husband and wife in a loving and caring relationship. If all women were married, she reasoned, female suffrage would have little ill effect, because women would exercise the vote in the common interest of both sexes. Only when there was no common interest (as was the case with unmarried women) would the domestic order, and with it the social order, become endangered. There had been and still was much need of improvement in the condition of women. "The only thing to be deprecated," she argued, "is a radical change in them"; it was all a matter of "degree."[2] To which Fawcett replied that it was precisely the "degree" of change signified by the suffrage that would benefit all women without altering the emotional bonds of marriage, let alone subverting the order of society.

M rs. Sutherland Orr has discharged a shot into the camp of what is called, for want of a better name, "the woman's movement." Hers is the serious argument of a candid antagonist, and I think that no one will desire to treat it otherwise than respectfully. It is refreshing rather than the reverse to hear on this subject something that can be called an argument. Too often our opponents base their remarks on such an observation as "Adam was first made, then Eve," and appear to believe that no one will be tempted to complete the implied analogy and say "Adam first had household suffrage, then Eve"; or "Adam first studied medicine, then Eve." But this is not the method adopted by Mrs. Orr. I will attempt to summarise her argument for the benefit of those who may have missed reading her article called "The Future of Englishwomen" in this Review for June.

Mrs. Orr says that the question of the good or evil of the emancipation of women is one of degree. It is, notwithstanding, a movement which involves not a revolution but the actual decomposition of society. So far this decomposition has only done good. The women who will be, for several generations to come, most influenced by the movement will probably be the very best of which our race is capable. "In them may be embodied the historic climax of the English race." So far the inherent "organic" characteristics of physical and moral womanhood will not have been touched by the decomposing elements of the new movement. The women brought under its influence will have a wider intellectual horizon; the range of their sympathies will be enlarged; they will have more dignity and more happiness in their lives than the average woman of the old *régime*: "their intercourse with women will be free from littleness, their manner towards men from ungraceful extremes of reserve or freedom": in a word, we shall see "the utmost expansion of which the female nature is capable." All these good results are likely to flow from the movement

2. A. Orr, "The Future of English Women," *Nineteenth Century*, June 1878, p. 1028.

if only it could be arrested at the point it has already reached. But if it continues to advance and runs its course unchecked, dire and terrible evils are to be expected from it. If female emancipation reaches its full and final attainment, "not only the power of love in women, but for either sex its possibility, will have passed away." The miserable man of the future will vainly seek the woman's love he can no longer find, and then in prophetic vision Mrs. Orr imagines that she sees "Nature, outraged and no longer to be eluded, avenging herself." The women of the future will probably refuse to bear children; or if they are mothers, their qualifications to become truly motherly mothers will be of the feeblest, and their children may be expected to be puny and miserable, alike in body, intellect, and soul. Mrs. Orr appears to attribute to this yet unborn woman of the future the views of the German philosopher, who is said to have regarded the universe as a bad joke; and she imagines that the "regenerate" woman, with a practical feminine turn, will bring one act of the farce to an end as quickly as possible. Be this movement for the emancipation of women, says Mrs. Orr, slow or rapid, indirect or direct, if it is allowed to run its whole course, the new era which it is said to inaugurate will prove the beginning of the end.

Such, as well as I have been able to gather it after two careful readings, is the argument of Mrs. Orr's article. The main flaw in it as an argument, I think, consists in her admission that the movement which she attacks is, at one and the same time, good so far as it has gone, and that it tends in its very nature to the decomposition of society. I should have thought that decomposition—that is, rottenness or decay—was bad from beginning to end, and that you could not say the process of decay is entirely good so far as it has gone. But I do not wish to dwell on this point, which after all may be construed thus: the same process which in a fruit causes it to ripen, may, if continued after a certain point, cause it to become rotten. So far, then, we may have the satisfaction of believing that from hour to hour "we ripe and ripe," and that the fatal "rot and rot," even if it comes at all, is still in the distant future.

What every one who reads Mrs. Orr's article with attention will ask is, "Where does she find the slightest foundation in actual facts for her gloomy predictions as to the effect of freedom upon Englishwomen?" There has been already much experience on which an opinion may be formed. I do not now refer to the handful of women in the upper and middle ranks of life who have made professional careers for themselves, although the fact that many of them have married and have become loving wives and tender mothers weighs for something against Mrs. Orr's argument. But they, perhaps it may be said, are exceptional. Still it is worth something to know that the power of emotion and sympathy has not been dried up in them, that it has been rather intensified and strengthened. Much more useful experience than any that can be gathered from such a limited number of cases may be found if we consider the circumstances of the women from whom the class of domestic servants are drawn. They have been for generations subjected to almost exactly the treatment which Mrs. Orr thinks would extinguish the *"organic"* and the emotional characteristics of the female sex. They have not indeed been highly educated in book learning, but they have been "independent social units." They have been free to choose their own employments, to take one situation or quit another; they are generally removed from parental control, and regard their father's house rather as a boarding house or infirmary at which they may temporarily reside; the relation that exists between parent and child among ourselves, is among them very frequently reversed. Their parents do not contribute to their income, they contribute to support their parents. They are entirely self-supporting and independent, with a career and, in a humble way, a competency of their own. Yet we do not see in them any symptom of the disappearance of the capacity of the kind of love which leads to marriage; we do not see any weakening of the family affections generally. I have often personally been struck by the considerable sacrifices servants have been ready to make for their parents, and with their motherliness to a little group of motherless brothers and sisters. In those cases in which my own servants have spoken to me about their approaching marriage, I have detected none of that harsh, unlovely drying up of the emotions, which Mrs. Orr expects to see in women of her own rank if independent professional careers are thrown open to them. Of course there are coarse, hard, unsympathetic natures in all ranks; there always have been, and it is to be feared there always will be. But is it not probable that this coarse fibre will be rendered all the more coarse by a stunted narrow life, with petty cares, and only the vulgar interests of scandal and dress to feed itself upon? This very coarseness might, if the right career were found, be the correlative of some kind of strength. One often sees that it is so in men. A man of a coarse nature would become a wild beast if he led the empty vapid life of tittle-tattle about people and clothes, to which a majority of the young ladies of England are condemned. Sheer hard work is the safety-valve of such natures. It is the safety-valve which men find, and which we wish to see available for women. Nothing, it seems to me, is so truly contrary to the emotional ideal in marriage as the social tone which condemns for women every career but marriage. Mrs. Orr is mistaken in saying that the "women's rights party," with Mr. Mill at their head, agree in regarding marriage simply as a legal contract in which the emotional element forms no important part. Certainly Mr. Mill's own marriage was a notable example to the contrary. I can only speak for myself, but I believe I represent the vast majority of women who have worked in this movement when I say that I believe that the emotional element in the marriage contract is of overwhelming importance; and that anything which puts forward the commercial view of marriage and sinks the spiritual or emotional view is degrading both to men and women. It was this belief which made many of us inclined heartily to sympathise with Mr. Herschell's bill for the abolition of breach of promise of marriage. I feel that no one, man or woman, ought to be forced into marriage by fear of social or legal penalties. That is one main reason why I should like to see honourable and honoured careers, other than marriage, open to women. That is why I should like to abolish the penalty which the law inflicts on a man who evades a promise to marry. As long as marriage is practically "Hobson's choice" for women, and as long as men are driven into marriages which they loathe by fear of an action, so long are two very powerful causes in operation which lessen the chance of marriages being of the sort that will bring enduring happiness with them. There always will be unhappy and unsuitable marriages; but it seems to me that their probability will be decreased by the means I have indicated. Mrs. Orr is herself what I must call a sinner against marriage, in the slighting way in which she speaks of single women: they are, in her language, "superfluous," "supernumerary"; they have a "mutilated existence"; if they pass through life without wishing to marry, they are "devoid of sentiment"; the whole woman's rights movement would come to an end, she says, if half a million or so of marrying men could be imported and told off in some Utopian fashion to marry all the adult single women who are asking for education, votes, and other masculine luxuries. They are clamouring, she says in effect, for their "rights"; but, whether they know it or not, they would be satisfied with husbands. As I came to these adjectives "supernumerary" and "superfluous," there arose in my mind visions of some of the noblest and best of women, whose lives are filled to the brim with useful work, well and conscientiously done, who have been free to devote themselves to this absorbing work because they have been unmarried. Are Florence Nightingale, Paulina Irby, Octavia Hill, and many others, to be cast aside, as it were, with the contemptuous adjective "superfluous," as if in marriage alone women could find an honourable career? It seems to me that a woman is or is not "superfluous" in proportion as she finds and performs useful work which the world, or some little bit of the world, wants done. "There was the work wanting to be done, and I wanting to do it," says Miss Martineau in her autobiography. Whoever can honestly say that, is not superfluous, even if she be an old maid of the most old-maidish type. Whoever cannot say it, is superfluous, even though she may have had as many husbands as the woman of Samaria.

There is something irresistibly comic in the notion which some married ladies have that their unmarried sisters are "superfluous." Charles Lamb's essay *On the Behaviour of Married People* has not yet borne its full fruit.

Every one will acknowledge that some men and women possess higher qualifications than others for making good husbands and good wives; may it not also be true that some most excellent and admirable and lovable persons are positively disqualified for the special duties of married life? I have heard a father of a family say that he judged of his boys' fitness to be husbands by the care they took of their watches: similar remarks are not infrequently made by mothers about their little girls' affection for their dolls. Is it not rather unreasonable to treat as a symptom of "social disease" the fact that some men and women have a vocation for marriage, while others, equally excellent in a different way, have none? The memoirs of Miss Charlotte Williams-Wynn, which have been lately published, contain a passage written by herself on this subject which is so much to the point that I quote it *in extenso*. The writer, it must be remembered, most justly possessed very great popularity, for in her was mingled in a remarkable degree the power of sympathy with originality and breadth of mind. Writing in the year 1846, she said:—

> Women are born wives just as men are born artists, musicians, poets. This I see, and the non-perception of it is the cause of half the uncomfortable marriages you meet with. But men and women will not content themselves with doing that which they can do—that for which they came into the world. Everybody is to do the same thing, or to set up at least for doing it. All are to speak German, all are to sing, all are to be wives! and it is quite as much of an accomplishment to be a wife as to be an artist. If we could but realise our individuality more distinctly, we should not commit these errors. I should like to have the capabilities of making a wife just as I should like to have the power of singing in church; but the talent for both has been denied me. My neighbour perhaps will possess both these talents, but have none for philosophy; and so it goes on: and if we would satisfy ourselves with reverencing our neighbours without trying to imitate them, we should all be of much more use to each other. (Pp. 74–75)

Miss Martineau is another instance of a woman with very strong affections believing herself to be naturally unfitted for married life: she also had an exceedingly high estimate of the importance of wifely duties, and explains in her autobiography why she thinks herself unfit to fulfil them.

The real difference of opinion between myself and Mrs. Orr seems to be this—that she believes that no man or woman can be at his or her best unmarried, whereas I am a humble follower of St. Paul and believe that it is best for some people to pass through life unmarried. In any case no one admits more readily than Mrs. Orr that as long as there are half a million more English women than men, and as long as polygamy is illegal and conventual institutions have only a limited popularity, so long there must necessarily be a considerable number of single women at large in our country. Starting from these undeniable facts, the question arises, is it not for the benefit of society that the women who have the greatest natural fitness for marriage should marry, whilst those who have fewer natural qualifications for the endurance and enjoyment of the special pains and pleasures of married life, should find other honourable and useful careers open to them? No society can insure that this harmonious apportionment of work to those most fitted to perform it, shall be invariable: the most that can be done is to facilitate it by removing the artificial restrictions which have so long kept women out of nearly all employments which are at once honourable and well-paid. This is really only a phase of the free-trade argument. Free-traders urge that all artificial restrictions upon commerce should be removed, because that is the only way of insuring that each country and each loyalty will occupy itself with that industry for which it has the greatest natural advantages, or the least natural disadvantages. In like manner, we say, remove the artificial restrictions which debar women from higher education and from remunerative employments (they are already free to perform, if they choose, many kinds of important unpaid work); and the play of natural forces will drive them into those occupations for which they have some natural advantage as individuals, or at least into those for which their natural disadvantages are the least overwhelming. We do not look forward to an Utopia and believe that if everything were open, no woman would make a bad choice and undertake work in which the result would prove that she was personally unfit to succeed. There is no reason whatever to suppose that in this or in any other respect women will show themselves superior in sagacity to the rest of mankind. "God Almighty made 'em to match the men," as Mrs. Poyser says; and blunders will no doubt occasionally result from the new freedom when we have got it. But, on the whole, there is no more reason for fearing that women will as a body beset those professions for which they are manifestly and physically unfit, than that free trade would cause Lancashire agriculturists to cultivate the vine, or Scottish farmers to plant the olive instead of the larch. There is one mistake which Mrs. Orr will pardon me for pointing out. She speaks in one or two places as if women had claimed to have men turned out forcibly from some employments which they are supposed to consider the exclusive field for women's labour. This is an entire error. There have been and are many demands for excluding women from various kinds of work. I never heard any woman express the slightest wish that men should be turned out of any sort of employment or occupation. The one thing that has been asked, and the one thing that is in process of being granted, is a fair field and no favour. This has been a remarkable feature of the effort, now at last successful, of women to gain entrance into the medical profession. The ladies who have conducted that struggle have invariably declined all suggestions that some back-stairs way into the profession, especially easy and especially for women, should be made. They have always fought as much against such proposals as against entire exclusion: they have, in effect, said "The preparation which men require to fit them for the profession must be equally required by women. The difficulty of the examinations is the test which the leaders of the profession have agreed upon as necessary to exclude those who are unfit; we wish to be subjected to the same test because we wish unfit women to be excluded from practising."

It will be remarked by such of Mrs. Orr's readers as are familiar with the history of the effort to open the medical profession to women, that some passages in her article would have been modified if she also had possessed a knowledge of the facts of that movement. The article has probably been written for more than a year, it may have been in type perhaps as long, and events move too rapidly to admit of such a delay without a loss of accuracy. Mrs. Orr writes:—"The facilities granted during the last session to female students of medicine are neutralised by the closing of all our hospitals against them." This was never entirely accurate, and is now, of course unintentionally, completely inaccurate. The sentence probably refers to the passing of the late Mr. Russell Gurney's Act in 1876, which enabled any of the medical licensing bodies to open their degrees to women if they wished to do so; the immediate result of that Act was the admission of five women to the Medical Register through the King and Queen's College of Physicians in Ireland. The Act, therefore, was not neutralised even at first. It is true, however, that for nearly a year after the passing of the Act there was no hospital in London, large enough to have a medical school attached to it, which would admit women students. But only a few months elapsed after the passing of the Act before negotiations were opened with the Governors of the Royal Free Hospital in Gray's Inn Road, to allow the women's medical school to be attached to it. This hospital was of the required size (more than 100 beds), and it had no male school. The negotiations were commenced in the autumn of 1876, and were brought to a successful conclusion on the 12th of June, 1877, as described in this Review for July of the same year, in an article by the Right Honourable James Stansfeld, M.P. Since that time the way into the medical profession has been open to women. It has recently been further facilitated by the action of the University of London in admitting women to its degrees, and it will be in no way impeded if the Government measure now before Parliament, "The Medical Act Amendment Bill," becomes law. A knowledge of these facts might have modified another sentence in Mrs. Orr's article, where she says:—"When once the medical profession has been thrown open to women, the question of sexual disabilities is at an end. . . . The battle for female emancipation will have been won." I wish I could agree; and yet the fact that the English people will not be dragged on, by so-called logic, into the granting of privileges which they deem inexpedient, because they have granted one which they deem expedient, is one of the surest signs of the political common sense on which we English pride ourselves. George Eliot makes Daniel Deronda say: "I think that way of arguing against a course because it may be ridden down to an absurdity would soon bring life to a standstill. It is not the logic of human action, but that of a roasting-jack, that must go on to the last turn when it has once been wound up."

Mrs. Orr seems to me to be peculiarly liable to be run away with by this "roasting-jack logic." She believes that the admission of women to medicine is the winding up of the machine, that it must now go on to the last turn, and that the last turn will literally and positively bring human life to a standstill. If the future is at all like the past history of this movement, every new claim on the part of women will have to be defended on its own merits; and the points of vantage already gained will be useful chiefly in so far as they tend to calm the imaginative horrors which many people think will flow from any new extension of liberty to women. We cannot say, or if we do, it is no good, "Women have the municipal franchise, therefore it necessarily and logically follows that they ought to have the parliamentary franchise." We have to show what good results we believe would accrue not only to women, but to the whole community, from the granting to women of this new privilege; and we can point to the experience gained of the results of their admission to the other franchises as showing that women can vote for town councillors, and can both vote for, and sit on, school boards, without ceasing to love their children or throwing every vestige of feminine propriety to the winds.

Mrs. Orr expresses the opinion that instead of striving to gain entrance to educational privileges and learned professions which have hitherto been the exclusive field of masculine enterprise, "it would be a wiser ambition on the part of women to reconquer their own sphere," and apply themselves vigorously to the better performance of household work. It will occur to many readers that this "reconquering of their own sphere" has been going on simultaneously with other movements to open to women what has hitherto been the sphere of men. Mrs. Orr admits the significance of the new-born zeal for needlework and cookery: it is not perhaps a too rash presumption to say that it has arisen mainly as an offshoot of the "women's rights" movement. The standard of women's work has been raised all round. The idea of the beauty of good work, in whatever sphere, has found its way into women's minds, and they are applying it to needlework and cookery as fast as possible. They no longer regard the fact that a certain bit of work has been done by a woman as a satisfactory reason for its being a slovenly performance.

When Mrs. Orr says "Let women reconquer their own sphere," and implies that they should devote themselves to housekeeping, and let doctoring and other masculine occupations alone, I think she does not sufficiently consider the individual cases of the women who want remunerative work. Take as an example the case of a family consisting of a father and mother and half-a-dozen daughters. The father is a professional man, two-thirds of whose income cease at his death; the mother is an active woman, and, at the time when the youngest of her daughters reaches the age of eighteen, still a vigorous house-keeper. Three of the daughters marry; one remains at home to help her mother in the management of the household. What are the others to do? How does Mrs. Orr's suggestion of "reconquering their own sphere" help them? Their own home is orderly and well governed. It is true that they may have neigh-bours and acquaintances whose homes are quite the reverse; but it is in their own home, or in none at all, that this "reconquering of their own sphere" must take place. They cannot say to a friend, nor even to an enemy: "My dear Mrs. Jellaby, I am quite distressed at the disorder of your household; I will come and put your whole establishment on a totally different footing." What generally happens in real life is that all three unmarried daughters stay at home with practically no real or sufficient occupation; they spend their time making their dresses, and endeavouring, by snipping and altering and turning, always to be in the latest fashion, and to make the 30*l.* a-year or so which they have for dress and pocket-money go as far as 35*l.* or 40*l.* This, it appears to me, is an un-healthy and unnatural existence; why should the labour of three fine, strong, active young women produce such an insignificant result? Further, they are apt to present, as time goes on, the unlovely spectacle of middle-aged spinsters aping the appearance and manners of girls of eighteen. They are eagerly and perhaps vainly hoping for marriage, which would give them a reasonable occupation and work worth doing. They are not prepared, as the *Saturday Review* says, "to judge calmly of an offer when it comes." This state of things is surely not at all conducive to the realisation of a high ideal of marriage. Let us now suppose what would have happened if these two young women had had an ambition to find some career for themselves more satisfactory than that of a third-rate dressmaker. One goes to Girton or Newnham, and thus, by getting a university training, prepares herself for the profession of teaching, and in a few years she may be earning 200*l.*, 300*l.*, or 400*l.* a-year. The other goes to the school of medicine for women; and after the proper course has been gone through and the examinations passed, she begins practice: if she has anything like a real faculty for her profession, her income will very speedily outstrip her sister's; and, moreover, she too will have found a work worthy of a rational human being—a work that calls out some of the best and noblest qualities. If either of these sisters marries after she is established in her profession, it will not be for the sake of escaping from the *ennui* of perpetual young-ladyhood. It will not be because in no other way could she find useful work to do in the world:

the chances of the marriage being happy will be improved by the fact that it was a real choice, and not a Hobson's choice, such as marriage is when other careers of usefulness are closed.

So far as present experience goes, look where one will for it, there is no evidence in support of Mrs. Orr's assertion that such careers as those I have sketched will tend to dry up the capacity of love either in men or women. It is to be inferred that Mrs. Orr does not expect to see any sign of this catastrophe at present; the judgment is yet to come. If any one is now suffering from anxiety on the subject, a glance over the Registrar-General's returns would suffice to reassure him. In estimating the probable increase of population since 1871, that official has apparently taken no cognisance of the growing importance of the women's movement. 1881 may have terrible things to reveal, but at present we cannot by any possibility conjure up the smallest alarm that Mrs. Orr's prophecy will be fulfilled either at the next census or in that of 1981. The constitution of the human character, with its mysterious affections and aspirations, is planted on too firm a foundation to be "decomposed" or turned over by the granting of more liberty to women, who after all are only a little behind their brothers in asking for it. Those who write and speak against the extension of liberty of action and conscience to men or women have always said that the change they deprecate will undermine or decompose the foundations of society. A few years pass by, the change is accomplished, and it turns out that society is not undermined or decomposed at all, but is all the healthier and more vigorous, through being possessed of a larger proportion of free citizens. The "foundations of society" are really stronger than the enemies of progress suppose; if they were not, the undermining and decomposing would have been effected long ago. It is rather irreverent perhaps, but I always feel when I hear that society will be undermined by the ballot or by household suffrage, or in France by the establishment of a Republic, that if society is in such a very delicate state, the sooner it is undermined and something stronger put in its place the better it will be. In Mr. Leslie Stephen's new *Life of Dr. Johnson* he tells how Johnson "snorted contempt when Taylor talked of breaking some small vessels if he took an emetic. 'Bah!' said the doctor, who regarded a valetudinarian as a 'scoundrel,' 'if you have so many things that will break, you had better break your neck at once, and there's an end on't.'" If the foundations of society are not strong enough to bear the extension of the parliamentary suffrage to women and the opening to them of various professional careers, many will think that there had better "be an end on't" at once. But it must be confessed that society is wronged by its would-be defenders; it is strong and vigorous still; and if it sometimes has "growing pains," these, after all, are only signs that it is still in its youth, and that the period of gradual decay has not yet set in.

I would only say in conclusion that I have purposely selected for comment those parts of Mrs. Orr's article with which I disagree: there are some parts with which I agree, and some few with which I neither agree nor disagree, because I cannot understand them. I have been reluctant to waste the time of possible readers in going over ground where I have nothing but agreement to record, and still more unwilling to comment on passages of which I cannot be sure that I understand the drift. The selection that I have made has unfortunately left me little choice but to assume a tone of hostile criticism throughout. This does not, however, truly represent my feeling towards the whole of the article. I have written as I have done because I felt it right, as a hearty sympathiser with every effort now being made to obtain a larger and a freer life for women, to show, if I could, that the way we are going is not the road to ruin that Mrs. Orr thinks it—that the whole of our aim is to hasten the time when every woman shall have the opportunity of becoming the best that her natural faculties make her capable of. In one of Oliver Cromwell's letters, he says: "It will be found an unjust and unwise jealousy to deprive a man of his natural liberty upon the supposition that he might abuse it. When he doth abuse it, judge." So I would ask that women should be judged by their use of the liberty they at present enjoy, and not by imaginary abuses of liberty of which at present the world has had no experience.

W. E. GLADSTONE (1809–98)

"Robert Elsmere": The Battle of Belief (1888)

In 1888, when he was not occupied with parliamentary affairs (he was leader of his party although not then prime minister), making speeches at home, or traveling abroad, Gladstone somehow found time to write four long scholarly essays on religion. One of these was a forty-page critique of a novel by Mrs. Humphrey Ward, Robert Elsmere. *The saga of a theological and spiritual conversion, the book was a phenomenal bestseller; in its three-volume edition, it went through seven printings in five months and soon exceeded the million-copy mark. The hero, an Oxford graduate and Anglican cleric, finding that he can no longer accept a Christianity based upon miracles, arrives at a theism that is essentially a religion of morality, with Christ—the historic, not divine Christ—figuring as an exemplary human being. Challenged by what he saw as a dangerous and heretical creed, Gladstone wrote a long critique of the book, defending a miracle-based Christianity as the only theological basis for religion itself and the only secure foundation for morality.[1]*

The author of the novel, Mrs. Ward (Mary Augusta Arnold), was an intellectual

W. E. Gladstone (1809–98), " 'Robert Elsmere': The Battle of Belief," *Nineteenth Century,* August 1888. Reprinted in Gladstone, *Later Gleanings* (New York, 1897), pp. 77–117.

1. In an interesting exchange of letters about this review, Acton (much to the surprise of Gladstone) protested that Christianity, so far from being a model for morality, was an "appalling edifice of intolerance, tyranny, cruelty" (John Morley, *The Life of William Ewart Gladstone* [New York, 1903], III, 361; Gertrude Himmelfarb, *Lord Acton: A Study in Conscience and Politics* [Chicago, 1952], pp. 167–68.)

in her own right as well as an accredited member of what has been called the "intellectual aristocracy" of Victorian England: granddaughter of Thomas Arnold and niece of Matthew Arnold, mother-in-law of the historian G. M. Trevelyan, and aunt of Julian and Aldous Huxley. She was also a great friend of such other notables as Henry James and the philosopher T. H. Green, to whom Robert Elsmere *was dedicated and who appears in the novel as Henry Grey, mentor to the hero. Apart from her twenty-odd novels, she took an active role in the founding of Somerville College (one of the two women's colleges in Oxford) as well as several settlement houses, adult education centers, and child-care centers. Like Mrs. Orr, Mrs. Ward was a prominent opponent of female suffrage; in 1908 she became the first president of the Anti-Suffrage League.*

Human nature, when aggrieved, is apt and quick in devising compensations. The increasing seriousness and strain of our present life may have had the effect of bringing about the large preference, which I understand to be exhibited in local public libraries, for works of fiction. This is the first expedient of revenge. But it is only a link in a chain. The next step is, that the writers of what might be grave books, *in esse* or *in posse,* have endeavoured with some success to circumvent the multitude. Those who have systems or hypotheses to recommend in philosophy, conduct, or religion induct them into the costume of romance. Such was the second expedient of nature, the counterstroke of her revenge. When this was done in "Télémaque," "Rasselas," or "Coelebs," it was not without literary effect. Even the last of these three appears to have been successful with its own generation. It would now be deemed intolerably dull. But a dull book is easily renounced. The more didactic fictions of the present day, so far as I know them, are not dull. We take them up, however, and we find that, when we meant to go to play, we have gone to school. The romance is a gospel of some philosophy, or of some religion; and requires sustained thought on many or some of the deepest subjects, as the only rational alternative to placing ourselves at the mercy of our author. We find that he has put upon us what is not indeed a treatise, but more formidable than if it were. For a treatise must nowhere beg the question it seeks to decide, but must carry its reader onwards by reasoning patiently from step to step. But the writer of the romance, under the convenient necessity which his form imposes, skips in thought, over undefined distances, from stage to stage, as a bee from flower to flower. A creed may (as here) be accepted in a sentence, and then abandoned in a page. But we the common herd of readers, if we are to deal with the consequences, to accept or repel the influence of the book, must, as in a problem of mathematics, supply the missing steps. Thus, in perusing as we ought a propagandist romance, we must terribly increase the pace; and it is the pace that kills.

Among the works to which the preceding remarks might apply, the most remarkable within my knowledge is "Robert Elsmere." It is indeed remarkable in many respects. It is a novel of nearly twice the length, and much more than twice the matter, of ordinary novels. It dispenses almost entirely, in the construction of what must still be called its plot, with the aid of incident in the ordinary sense. We have indeed near the close a solitary individual crushed by a waggon, but this catastrophe has no relation to the plot, and its only purpose is to exhibit a good death-bed in illustration of the great missionary idea of the piece. The *nexus* of the structure is to be found wholly in the workings of character. The assumption and the surrender of a Rectory are the most salient events, and they are simple results of what the actor has thought right. And yet the great, nay, paramount function of character-drawing, the projection upon the canvas of human beings endowed with the true forces of nature and vitality, does not appear to be by any means the master-gift of the authoress. In the mass of matter which she has prodigally expended there might obviously be retrenchment; for there are certain laws of dimension which apply to a novel, and which separate it from an epic. In the extraordinary number of personages brought upon the stage in one portion or other of the book, there are some which are elaborated with greater pains and more detail, than their relative importance seems to warrant. "Robert Elsmere" is hard reading, and requires toil and effort. Yet, if it be difficult to persist, it is impossible to stop. The prisoner on the treadmill must work severely to perform his task: but if he stops he at once receives a blow which brings him to his senses. Here, as there, it is human infirmity which shrinks; but here, as not there, the propelling motive is within. Deliberate judgment and deep interest alike rebuke a fainting reader. The strength of the book, overbearing every obstacle, seems to lie in an extraordinary wealth of diction, never separated from thought; in a close and searching faculty of social observation; in generous appreciation of what is morally good, impartially exhibited in all directions: above all in the sense of mission with which the writer is evidently possessed, and in the earnestness and persistency of purpose with which through every page and line it is pursued. The book is eminently an offspring of the time, and will probably make a deep or at least a very sensible impression; not, however, among mere novel-readers, but among those who share, in whatever sense, the deeper thought of the period.

The action begins in a Westmoreland valley, where the three young daughters of a pious clergyman are grouped around a mother infirm in health and without force of mind. All responsibility devolves accordingly upon Catherine, the eldest of the three; a noble character, living only for duty and affection. When the ear heard her, then it blessed her; and when the eye saw her, it gave witness to her. Here comes upon the scene Robert Elsmere, the eponymist and hero of the book, and the ideal, almost the idol, of the authoress.

He had been brought up at Oxford, in years when the wholesale discomfiture of the great religious movement in the University, which followed upon the secession of Cardinal Newman, had been in its turn succeeded by a new religious reaction. The youth had been open to the personal influences of a tutor, who is in the highest degree beautiful, classical, and indifferentist; and of a noble-minded rationalising teacher, whose name, Mr. Grey, is the thin disguise of another name, and whose lofty character, together with his gifts, and with the tendencies of the time, had made him a power in Oxford. But, in its action on a nature of devout susceptibilities as well as active talents, the place is stronger than the man, and Robert casts in his lot with the ministry of the Church. Let us stop at this point to notice the terms used. At St. Mary's "the sight and the experience touched his inmost feeling, and satisfied all the poetical and dramatic instincts of a passionate nature." He "carried his religious passion . . . into the service of the great positive tradition around him." This great, and commonly life-governing decision, is taken under the influence of forces wholly emotional. It is first after the step taken that we have an inkling of any reason for it. This is not an isolated phenomenon. It is a key to the entire action. The work may be summed up in this way: it represents a battle between intellect and emotion. Of right, intellect wins; and, having won, enlists emotion in its service.

Elsmere breaks upon us in Westmoreland, prepared to make the great commission the business of his life, and to spend and be spent in it to the uttermost. He is at once attracted by Catherine; attention forthwith ripens into love; and love finds expression in a proposal. But, with a less educated intelligence, the girl has a purpose of life not less determined than the youth. She believes herself to have an outdoor vocation in the glen, and above all an indoor vocation in her family, of which she is the single prop. A long battle of love ensues, fought out with not less ability, and with even greater tenacity, than the remarkable conflict of intellects, carried on by correspondence, which ended in the marriage between Mr. and Mrs. Carlyle. The resolute tension of the two minds has many phases; and a double crisis, first of refusal, secondly of acceptance. This part of the narrative, wrought out in detail with singular skill, will probably be deemed the most successful, the most normal, of the whole. It is thoroughly noble on both sides. The final surrender of Catherine is in truth an opening of the eyes to a wider view of the evolution of the individual, and of the great vocation of life; and it involves no disparagement. The garrison evacuates the citadel, but its arms have not been laid down, and its colours are flying still.

So the pair settle themselves in a family living, full of the enthusiasm of humanity, which is developed with high energy in every practical detail, and based upon the following of the Incarnate Saviour. Equipped thus far with all that renders life desirable, their union is blessed by the birth of a daughter, and everything thrives around them for the formation of an ideal parish.

But the parish is adorned by a noble old English mansion, and the mansion inhabited by a wealthy Squire, who knows little of duty, but is devoted to incessant study. As an impersonated intellect, he is abreast of all modern inquiry, and, a "Tractarian" in his youth, he has long abandoned all belief. At the outset, he resents profoundly the Rector's obtrusive concern for his neglected tenantry. But the courage of the clergyman is not to be damped by isolation, and in the case of a scandalously insanitary hamlet, after an adequate number of deaths, Mr. Wendover puts aside the screen called his agent, and rebuilds with an ample generosity. This sudden and complete surrender seems to be introduced to glorify the hero of the work, for it does not indicate any permanent change in the social ideas of Mr. Wendover, but only in his relations to his clergyman.

There is, however, made ready for him a superlative revenge. Robert has enjoyed the use of his rich library, and the two hold literary communications, but with a compact of silence on matters of belief. This treaty is honourably observed by the Squire. But the clergyman invites his fate. Mr. Wendover makes known to him a great design for a "History of Testimony," worked out through many centuries. The book speaks indeed of "the long wrestle" of the two men, and the like. But of Elsmere's wrestling there is no other trace or sign. What weapons the Rector wielded for his faith, what strokes he struck, has not even in a single line been recorded. The discourse of the Squire points out that theologians are men who decline to examine evidence, that miracles are the invention of credulous ages, that the preconceptions sufficiently explain the results. He wins in a canter. There cannot surely be a more curious contrast than that between the real battle, fought in a hundred rounds, between Elsmere and Catherine on marriage, and the fictitious battle between Elsmere and the Squire on the subject of religion, where the one side is a pæan, and the other a blank. A great creed, with the testimony of eighteen centuries at its back, cannot find an articulate word to say in its defence, and the downfall of the scheme of belief shatters also, and of right, the highly ordered scheme of life that had nestled in the Rectory of Murewell, as it still does in thousands of other English parsonages.

It is notable that Elsmere seeks, in this conflict with the Squire, no aid or counsel whatever. He encounters indeed by chance Mr. Newcome, a Ritualistic clergyman, whom the generous sympathies of the authoress place upon the roll of his friends. But the language of Mr. Newcome offers no help to his understanding. It is this:—

> Trample on yourself. Pray down the demon, fast, scourge, kill the body, that the soul may live. What are we miserable worms, that we should defy the Most High, that we should set our wretched faculties against His Omnipotence?

Mr. Newcome appears everywhere as not only a respectable but a remarkable character. But as to what he says here, how much does it amount to? Considered as a medicine for a mind diseased, for an unsettled, dislocated soul, is it less or more than pure nonsense? In the work of an insidious non-believer, it would be set down as part of his fraud. Mrs. Ward evidently gives it in absolute good faith. It is one in a series of indications, by which this gifted authoress conveys to us what appears to be her thoroughly genuine belief that historical Christianity has, indeed, broad grounds and deep roots in emotion, but in reason none whatever.

The revelation to the wife is terrible; but Catherine clings to her religion on a basis essentially akin to that of Newcome; and the faith of these eighteen centuries, and of the prime countries of the world, "Bella, immortal, benefica/Fede, ai trionfi avvezza," is dismissed without a hearing.

For my own part, I humbly retort on Robert Elsmere. Considered intellectually, his proceedings in regard to belief appear to me, from the beginning as well as in the downward process, to present dismal gaps. But the emotional part of his character is complete—nay, redundant. There is no moral weakness or hesitation. There rises up before him the noble maxim, assigned to the so-called Mr. Grey (with whom he has a consultation of foregone conclusions), "Conviction is the conscience of the mind."

He renounces his parish and his orders. He still believes in God, and accepts the historical Christ as a wonderful man, good among the good, but a *primus inter pares*. Passing through a variety of stages, he devotes himself to the religion of humanity; reconciles to the new gospel, by shoals, skilled artisans of London who had been totally inaccessible to the old one; and nobly kills himself with overwork, passing away in a final flood of light. He founds and leaves behind him the "New Christian Brotherhood" of Elgood Street; and we are at the close apprised, with enthusiastic sincerity, that this is the true effort of the race, and

> Others I doubt not, if not we,
> The issue of our toils shall see.

Who can grudge to this absolutely pure-minded and very distinguished writer the comfort of having at last found the true specific for the evils and miseries of the world? None surely who bear in mind that the Salvation Army has been known to proclaim itself the Church of the future, or who happen to know that Bunsen, when in 1841 he had procured the foundation of the bishopric of Jerusalem, suggested in private correspondence his hope that this might be the Church which would meet the glorified Redeemer at His coming.

It is necessary here to revert to the Squire. Himself the μοῖρα πεπρωμένη, the supreme arbiter of destinies in the book, he is somewhat unkindly treated; his mind at length gives way, and a darkling veil is drawn over the close. Here seems to be a little literary intolerance, something even savouring of a religious test. Robert Elsmere stopped in the downward slide at theism, and it calms and glorifies his death-bed. But the Squire had not stopped there. He had said to Elsmere, " 'You are playing into the hands of the Blacks. All this theistic philosophy of yours only means so much grist to their mill in the end.' " But the great guide is dismissed from his guiding office as summarily as all other processes are conducted, which are required by the purpose of the writer. Art everywhere gives way to purpose. Elsmere no more shows cause for his theism than he had shown it against his Christianity. Why was not Mr. Wendover allowed at least the consolations which gave a satisfaction to David Hume? [. . .]

It has been observed that the women of the book are generally drawn with more felicity than the men. As a work of art, Rose [Catherine's sister] is in my view the most successful of the women, and among the men the Squire. With the Squire Mrs. Ward is not in sympathy, for he destroys too much, and he does nothing but destroy. She cannot be in sympathy with Rose; for Rose, who is selfishly and heartlessly used, is herself selfish and heartless; with this aggrava-tion, that she has grown up in immediate contact with a noble elder sister, and yet has not caught a particle of nobleness, as well as in view of an infirm mother to whom she scarcely gives a care. On the other hand, in her Robert, who has all Mrs. Ward's affection and almost her worship, and who is clothed with a perfect panoply of high qualities, she appears to be less successful and more artificial. In the recently published correspondence of Sir Henry Taylor, who was by no means given to paradox, we are told that great earnestness of purpose and strong adhesive sympathies in an author are adverse to the freedom and independence of treatment, the disembarrassed movement of the creative hand, which are required in the supreme poetic office of projecting character on the canvas. If there be truth in this novel and interesting suggestion, we cannot wonder at finding the result exhibited in "Robert Elsmere," for never was a book written with greater persistency and intensity of purpose. Every page of its principal narrative is adapted and addressed by Mrs. Ward to the final aim which is bone of her bone and flesh of her flesh. This aim is to expel the preternatural element from Christianity, to destroy its dogmatic structure, yet to keep intact the moral and spiritual results. The Brotherhood presented to us with such sanguine hopefulness is a "Christian" brotherhood, but with a Christianity emptied of that which Christians believe to be the soul and springhead of its life. For Christianity, in the established Christian sense, is the presentation to us not of abstract dogmas for acceptance, but of a living and a Divine Person, to whom they are to be united by a vital incorporation. It is the reunion to God of a nature severed from God by sin, and the process is one, not of teaching lessons, but of imparting a new life, with its ordained equipment of gifts and powers.

It is, I apprehend, a complete mistake to suppose, as appears to be the supposition of this remarkable book, that all which has to be done with Scripture, in order to effect the desired transformation of religion, is to eliminate from it the miraculous element. Tremendous as is the sweeping process which extrudes the Resurrection, there is much else, which is in no sense miraculous, to extrude along with it. The Procession of Palms, for example, is indeed profoundly significant, but it is in no way miraculous. Yet, in any consistent history of a Robert Elsmere's Christ, there could be no Procession of Palms. Unless it be the healing of the ear of Malchus, there is not a miraculous event between the commencement of the Passion and the Crucifixion itself. Yet the notes of a superhuman majesty overspread the whole. We talk of all religions as essentially one; but what religion presents to its votaries such a tale as this? Bishop Temple, in his sermons at Rugby, has been among the later teachers who have shown how the whole behaviour of our Lord, in this extremity of His abasement, seems more than ever to transcend all human limits, and to exhibit without arguing His Divinity. The parables, again, are not less refractory than the miracles, and must disappear along with them: for what parables are there which are not built upon the idea of His unique and transcendent office? The Gospel of St. John has much less of miracle than the Synoptics; but it must of course descend from its pedestal, in all that is most its own. And what is gained by all this condemnation, until we get rid of the Baptismal formula? It is a question not of excision from the Gospels, but of tearing them into shreds. Far be it from me to deny that the parts which remain, or which remain legible, are vital parts; but this is no more than to say that there may remain vital organs of a man, after the man himself has been cut in pieces.

I have neither space nor capacity at command for the adequate discussion of the questions, which shattered the faith of Robert Elsmere: whether miracles can happen, and whether "an universal preconception" in their favour at the birth of Christianity "governing the work of all men of all schools," adequately accounts for the place which has been given to them in the New Testament, as available proofs of the Divine Mission of our Lord. But I demur on all the points to the authority of the Squire, and even of Mr. Grey.

The impossibility of miracle is a doctrine which appears to claim for its basis the results of physical inquiry. They point to unbroken sequences in material nature, and refer every phenomenon to its immediate antecedent as adequate to its orderly production. But the appeal to these great achievements of our time is itself disorderly, for it calls upon natural science to decide a question which lies beyond its precinct. There is an extraneous force of will which acts upon matter in derogation of laws purely physical, or alters the balance of those laws among themselves. It can be neither philosophical nor scientific to proclaim the impossibility of miracle, until philosophy or science shall have determined a limit, beyond which this extraneous force of will, so familiar to our experience, cannot act upon or deflect the natural order.

Next, as to that avidity for miracle, which is supposed by the omniscient Squire to account for the invention of it. Let it be granted, for argument's sake, that if the Gospel had been intended only for the Jews, they at least were open to the imputation of a biassing and blinding appetite for signs and wonders. But scarcely had the Christian scheme been established among the Jews, when it began to take root among the Gentiles. It will hardly be contended that these Gentiles, who detested and despised the Jewish race, had any predisposition to receive a religion at their hands or upon their authority. Were they then, during the century which succeeded our Lord's birth, so swayed by a devouring thirst for the supernatural as to account for the early reception, and the steady if not rapid growth, of the Christian creed among them? The statement of the Squire, which carries Robert Elsmere, is that the preconception in favour of miracles at the period "governed the work of all men of all schools." A most gross and palpable exaggeration. In philosophy the Epicurean school was atheistic, the Stoic school was ambiguously theistic, and doubt nestled in the Academy. Christianity had little direct contact with these schools, but they acted on the tone of thought, in a manner not favourable but adverse to the preconception.

Meantime the power of religion was in decay. The springs of it in the general mind and heart were weakened. A deluge of profligacy had gone far to destroy, at Rome, even the external habit of public worship; and Horace, himself an indifferentist, denounces the neglect and squalor of the temples; while further on we have the stern and emphatic testimony of Juvenal—

> Esse aliquid Manes, et subterranea regna,
> Et contum, et Stygio ranas in gurgite nigras,
> Nec pueri credunt, nisi qui nondum ære lavantur.

The age was not an age of faith, among thinking and ruling classes, either in natural or in supernatural religion. There had been indeed a wonderful "evangelical preparation" in the sway of the Greek language, in the unifying power of the Roman State and Empire, and in the utter moral failure of the grand and dominant civilisations; but not in any virgin soil, yearning for the sun, the rain, or the seed of truth.

But the Squire, treading in the footprints of Gibbon's fifteenth Chapter, leaves it to be understood that, in the appeal to the supernatural, the new religion enjoyed an exclusive as well as an overpowering advantage; that it had a patent for miracle, which none could infringe. Surely this is an error even more gross than the statement already cited about all men of all schools. The supernatural was interwoven with the entire fabric of the religion of the Roman

State, which, if weak and effete as a religious discipline, was of extraordinary power as a social institution. It stood, if not on faith, yet on nationality, on tradition, on rich endowments, on the deeply interested attachment of a powerful aristocracy, and on that policy of wide conciliation, which gave to so many creeds, less exclusive than the Christian, a cause common with its own.

[. . .]

In a concise but striking notice in the *Times* [*Robert Elsmere*] is placed in the category of "clever attacks upon revealed religion." It certainly offers us a substitute for revealed religion; and possibly the thought of the book might be indicated in these words: "The Christianity accepted in England is a good thing; but come with me, and I will show you a better."

It may, I think, be fairly described as a devout attempt, made in good faith, to simplify the difficult mission of religion in the world by discarding the supposed lumber of the Christian theology, while retaining and applying, in their undiminished breadth of scope, the whole personal, social, and spiritual morality which has now, as matter of fact, entered into the patrimony of Christendom; and, since Christendom is the dominant power of the world, into the patrimony of our race. It is impossible indeed to conceive a more religious life than the later life of Robert Elsmere, in his sense of the word religion. And that sense is far above the sense in which religion is held, or practically applied, by great multitudes of Christians. It is, however, a new form of religion. The question is, can it be actually and beneficially substituted for the old one? It abolishes, of course, the whole authority of Scripture. It abolishes also Church, priesthood or ministry, sacraments, and the whole established machinery which trains the Christian as a member of a religious society. These have been regarded by fifty generations of men as wings of the soul. It is still required of us by Mrs. Ward to fly, and to fly as high as ever; but it is to fly without wings. For baptism, we have a badge of silver, and inscription in a book. For the Eucharist there is at an ordinary meal a recital of the fragment, "This do in remembrance of Me." The children respond, "Jesus, we remember Thee always." It is hard to say that prayer is retained. In the Elgood Street service "it is rather an act of adoration and faith, than a prayer properly so called," and it appears that memory and trust are the instruments on which the individual is to depend, for maintaining his communion with God. It would be curious to know how the New Brotherhood is to deal with the great mystery of marriage, perhaps the truest touchstone of religious revolution.

It must be obvious to every reader that in the great duel between the old faith and the new, as it is fought in "Robert Elsmere," there is a great inequality in the distribution of the arms. Reasoning is the weapon of the new scheme; emotion the sole resource of the old. Neither Catherine nor Newcome have a word to say beyond the expression of feeling; and it is when he has adopted the negative side that the hero himself is fully introduced to the faculty of argument. This is a singular arrangement, especially in the case of a writer who takes a generous view of the Christianity that she only desires to supplant by an improved device. The explanation may be simple. There are abundant signs in the book that the negative speculatists have been consulted if not ransacked; but there is nowhere a sign that the authoress has made herself acquainted with the Christian apologists, old or recent; or has weighed the evidences derivable from the Christian history; or has taken measure of the relation in which the doctrines of grace have historically stood to the production of the noblest, purest, and greatest characters of the Christian ages. If such be the case, she has skipped lightly (to put it no higher) over vast mental spaces of literature and learning relevant to the case, and has given sentence in the cause without hearing the evidence.

It might perhaps be not unjust to make a retort upon the authoress, and say that while she believes herself simply to be yielding obedience to reason, her movement is in reality impelled by bias. We have been born into an age when, in the circles of literature and science, there is a strong anti-dogmatic leaning, a prejudice which may largely intercept the action of judgment. Partly because belief has its superstitions, and the detection of these superstitions opens the fabric to attack, like a breach in the wall of a fortress when at a given point it has been stuffed with unsound material. Partly because the rapidity of the movement of the time predisposes the mind to novelty. Partly because the multiplication of enjoyments, through the progress of commerce and invention, enhances the materialism of life, strengthens by the forces of habit the hold of the seen world upon us, and leaves less both of brain power and of heart power available for the unseen. Enormous accretion of wealth is no more deprived of its sting now, than it was when Saint Paul penned his profoundly penetrating admonition to Timothy. And when, under the present conditions, it happens that the environment of personal association represents either concentrated hostility or hopeless diversity in religion, there may be hardly a chance for firm and measured belief. What we find to be troublesome, yet from some inward protest are not prepared wholly to reject, we like to simplify and reduce; and the instances of good and devoted men who are averse to dogma, more frequent than usual in this age, are powerful to persuade us that in lightening the cargo we are really securing the safe voyage of the ship. "About dogma we hear dispute, but the laws of high social morality no speculation is disposed to question. Why not get rid of the disputable, and concentrate all our strength on grasping the undisputed?" We may by a little wresting quote high authority for this recommendation. "Whereto we have already attained . . . let us mind the same thing. . . . And if in anything ye be otherwise minded, God shall reveal even this unto you." It is not difficult to conceive how, under the action of causes with which the time abounds, pure and lofty minds, wholly guiltless of the intention to impair or lower the motive forces of Christianity, may be led into the snare, and may even conceive a process in itself destructive to be, on the contrary, conservative and reparatory.

But it is a snare none the less. And first let us recollect, when we speak of renouncing Christian dogma, what it is that we mean. The germ of it as a system lies in the formula, "Baptising them in the name of the Father, and of the Son, and of the Holy Ghost." This was speedily developed into the substance of the Apostles' Creed: the Creed which forms our confession of individual faith, in baptism and on the bed of death. Now belief in God, which forms (so to speak) the first great limb of the Creed, is strictly a dogma, and is on no account, according to Mrs. Ward, to be surrendered. But the second and greatest portion of the Creed contains twelve propositions, of which nine are matters of fact, and the whole twelve have for their office the setting forth to us of a Personage, to whom a great dispensation has been committed. The third division of the Creed is more dogmatic, but it is bound down like the second to earth and fact by the article of the Church, a visible and palpable institution. The principal purely dogmatic part of this great document is the part which is to be retained. And we, who accept the Christian story, are entitled to say, that to extrude from a history, tied to strictly human facts, that by which they become a standing channel of organic connection between Deity and humanity, is not presumptively a very hopeful mode of strengthening our belief in God, thus deprived of its props and accessories. The chasm between deity and the human soul, over which the scheme of Redemption has thrown a bridge, again yawns beneath our feet, in all its breadth and depth.

Although the Divinity of Christ is not put prominently forward in this book, but rather the broader objection to supernatural manifestations, yet it will be found to be the real hinge of the entire question. For, if Christ be truly God, few will deny that the exceptional incidents, which follow in the train of His appearance upon earth, raise, in substance, no new difficulty. Is it true, then, that Christians have been so divided on this subject as to promise us a return of peace and progress by its elimination?

To answer this question rightly, we must not take the humour of this or that particular time or country, but must regard the Christian system in its whole extension, and its whole duration. So regarding it, we shall find that the assertion, far from being true, is glaringly untrue. The truth in rude outline is surely this. That when the Gospel went out into the world, the greatest of all the groups of controversies, which progressively arose within its borders, was that which concerned the true nature of the Object of worship. That these controversies ran through the most important shapes, which have been known to the professing Church of later years, and through many more. That they rose, especially in the fourth century, to such a height, amidst the conflict of councils, popes, and theologians, that the private Christian was too often like the dove wandering over the waters, and seeking in vain a resting-place for the sole of his foot. That the whole mind and heart of the Church were given, in their whole strength and through a lengthened period, to find some solution of these controversies. That many generations passed before Arianism wholly ceased to be the basis of Christian profession in spots or sections of Christendom, but not so long before the central thought of the body as a whole had come to be fixed in the form of what has ever since, and now for over fourteen hundred years, been known as the orthodox belief. The authority of this tradition, based upon the Scriptures, has through all that period been upheld at the highest point to which a marvellous continuity and universality could raise it. It was not impeached by the questioning mind of the thirteenth century. The scientific revolution, which opened to us the antipodes and the solar system, did not shake it. The more subtle dangers of the Renascence were dangers to Christianity as a whole, but not to this great element of Christianity as a part. And when the terrible struggles of the Reformation stirred every coarse human passion as well as every fond religious interest into fury, even then the Nicene belief, as Möhler in his "Symbolik" has so well observed, sat undisturbed in a region elevated above the controversies of the time; which only touched it at points so exceptional, and comparatively so obscure, as not appreciably to qualify its majestic authority. A Christianity without Christ is no Christianity; and a Christ not divine is one other than the Christ on whom the souls of Christians have habitually fed. What virtue, what piety, have existed outside of Christianity, is a question totally distinct. But to hold that, since the great controversy of the early time was wound up at Chalcedon, the question of our Lord's Divinity (which draws after it all that Robert Elsmere would excide), has generated the storms of the Christian atmosphere, would be simply an historical untruth. How then is the work of peace to be promoted by the excision from our creed of that central truth on which we are generally agreed?

The onward movement of negation in the present day has presented perhaps no more instructive feature than this, that the Unitarian persuasion has, in this country at least, by no means thriven upon it. It might have been thought that, in the process of dilapidation, here would have been a point at which the receding tide of belief would have rested at any rate for a while. But instead of this, we are informed that the numbers of professed Unitarians have increased less than those of other communions, and less than the natural growth of the population. And we find Mrs. Ward herself describing the old

Unitarian scheme as one wholly destitute of logic; but in what respect she improves upon it I have not yet perceived.

In order to invest any particular propagandism with a show of presumptive title to our acceptance, its author should be able to refer it to some standard of appeal which will show that it has foundations otherwise than in mere private judgment or active imagination. The books of the New Testament I understand to be, for Mrs. Ward, of no value except for the moral precepts they contain. Still less may we invoke the authority of the Old Testament, where the ethical picture is more chequered. She finds no spell in the great moral miracle (so to phrase it) of the Psalms; nor in the marvellous *propaideia* of the Jewish history, so strikingly confirmed by recent research; in the Levitical law, the prophetic teaching, the entire dispensation of temporal promise and of religious worship and instruction, by which the Hebrew race was kept in social isolation through fifteen centuries, as a cradle for the Redeemer that was to come. She is not awakened by the Christian more than by the Jewish history. No way to her assent is opened by the great victory of the world's babes and striplings over its philosophers and scholars, and the serried array of emperors, aristocracies, and statesmen, with their elaborate apparatus of organised institutions. All this cogent mass of human testimony is rendered, I admit, on behalf not of a vague and arbitrary severance of Christian morals from the roots which have produced them, but of what we term the Christian dogma, that is to say, of belief in God supplemented and brought home by the great fact of Redemption, and of the provision made through the Church of Christ for the perpetual conservation and application of its living powers.
[. . .]

It is sometimes possible to trace peculiar and marked types of human character with considerable precision to their causes. Take, for instance, the Spartan type of character, in its relation to the legislation attributed to Lycurgus. Or take, again, the Jewish type, such as it is presented to us both by the ancient and the later history, in its relation to the Mosaic law and institutions. It would surely have been a violent paradox, in either of these cases, to propose the abolition of the law, and to assert at the same time that the character would continue to be exhibited, not only sporadically and for a time, but normally and in permanence.

These were restricted, almost tribal, systems. Christianity, though by no means less peculiar, was diffusive. It both produced a type of character wholly new to the Roman world, and it fundamentally altered the laws and institutions, the tone, temper, and tradition of that world. For example, it changed profoundly the relation of the poor to the rich, and the almost forgotten obligations of the rich to the poor. It abolished slavery, abolished human sacrifice, abolished gladiatorial shows, and a multitude of other horrors. It restored the position of woman in society. It proscribed polygamy; and put down divorce, absolutely in the West, though not absolutely in the East. It made peace, instead of war, the normal and presumed relation between human societies. It exhibited life as a discipline everywhere and in all its parts, and changed essentially the place and function of suffering in human experience. Accepting the ancient morality as far as it went, it not only enlarged but transfigured its teaching, by the laws of humility and of forgiveness, and by a law of purity perhaps even more new and strange than these. Let it be understood that I speak throughout not of such older religion as may have subsisted in the lowly and unobserved places of human life, but of what stamped the character of its strongholds; of the elements which made up the main and central currents of thought, action, and influence, in those places, and in those classes, which drew the rest of the world in their train. All this was not the work of a day, but it was the work of powers and principles which persistently asserted themselves in despite of controversy, of infirmity, and of corruption in every form; which reconstituted in life and vigour a society found in decadence; which by degrees came to pervade the very air we breathe; and which eventually have beyond all dispute made Christendom the dominant portion, and Christianity the ruling power, of the world. And all this has been done, not by eclectic and arbitrary fancies, but by the creed of the Homoousion, in which the philosophy of modern times sometimes appears to find a favourite theme of ridicule. But it is not less material to observe that the whole fabric, social as well as personal, rests on the new type of individual character which the Gospel brought into life and action: enriched and completed without doubt from collateral sources which made part of the "Evangelical preparation," but in its central essence due entirely to the dispensation, which had been founded and wrought out in the land of Judæa, and in the history of the Hebrew race. What right have we to detach, or to suppose we can detach, this type of personal character from the causes out of which as matter of history it has grown, and to assume that without its roots it will thrive as well as with them?

For Mrs. Ward is so firmly convinced, and so affectionately sensible, of the exquisite excellence of the Christian type that she will permit no abatement from it, though she thinks it can be cast in a mould which is human as well as, nay, better than, in one which is divine. Nor is she the first person who, in renouncing the Christian tradition, has reserved her allegiance to Christian morals and even sought to raise their standard. We have, for instance, in America, not a person only, but a society, which, while trampling on the Divinity and Incarnation of Christ, not only accepts His rule of life, but pushes evangelical counsels into absolute precepts, and insists upon them as the rule of life for all who seek, instead of abiding in the "lower floor churches," to be

Christians indeed. "The fundamental principles of Shakerism" are "virgin purity, non-resistance, peace, equality of inheritance, and unspottedness from the world." The evidence of travellers appears to show that the ideal of these projectors has to a certain degree been realised; nor can we know for how many years an eccentric movement of this kind will endure the test of time without palpably giving way. The power of environment, and the range of idiosyncrasy, suffice to generate, especially in dislocating times, all sorts of abnormal combinations, which subsist, in a large degree, upon forces not their own, and so impose themselves, with a show of authority, upon the world.

Let us return to the point. The Christian type is the product and the property of the Christian scheme. No, says the objector, the improvements which we witness are the offspring of civilisation. It might be a sufficient answer to point out that the civilisation before and around us is a Christian civilisation. What civilisation could do without Christianity for the greatest races of mankind, we know already. Philosophy and art, creative genius and practical energy, had their turn before the Advent; and we can register the results. I do not say that the great Greek and Roman ages lost—perhaps even they improved—the ethics of *meum* and *tuum,* in the interests of the leisured and favoured classes of society, as compared with what those ethics had been in archaic times. But they lost the hold which some earlier races within their sphere had had of the future life. They degraded, and that immeasurably, the position of woman. They effaced from the world the law of purity. They even carried indulgence to a worse than bestial type; and they gloried in the achievement. Duty and religion, in the governing classes and the governing places, were absolutely torn asunder; and self-will and self-worship were established as the unquestioned rule of life. It is yet more important to observe that the very qualities which are commended in the Beatitudes, and elsewhere in the Sermon on the Mount, and which form the base of the character specifically Christian, were for the Greek and the Roman mind the objects of contempt. From the history of all that has lain within the reach of the great Mediterranean basin, not a tittle of encouragement can be drawn for the ideas of those, who would surrender the doctrines of Christianity and yet retain its moral and spiritual fruits.

Does then that severance, unsustained by authority or by experience, commend itself at any single point by an improved conformity with purely abstract principles of philosophy? and is the new system better adapted to the condition and the needs of human nature, than the old? Does it better correspond with what an enlightened reason would dictate as the best provision for those needs? Does it mitigate, or does it enhance, the undoubted difficulties of belief? And if the answer must be given in the negative to both these inquiries, how are we to account for the strange phenomenon which exhibits to us persons sincerely, nay painfully, desirous of seeing Divine government more and more accepted in the world, yet enthusiastically busied in cutting away the best among the props, by which that government has been heretofore sustained?

As regards the first of these three questions, it is to be observed that, while the older religions made free use of prodigy and portent, they employed these instruments for political rather than moral purposes; and it may be doubted whether the sum total of such action tended to raise the standard of life and thought. The general upshot was that the individual soul felt itself very far from God. Our bedimmed eye could not perceive His purity; and our puny reach could not find touch of His vastness. By the scheme of Redemption, this sense of distance was removed. The divine perfections were reflected through the medium of a perfect humanity, and were thus made near, familiar, and liable to love. The great all-pervading law of human sympathy became directly available for religion, and in linking us to the Divine Humanity, linked us by the same act to God. And this not for rare and exceptional souls alone, but for the common order of mankind. The direct contact, the interior personal communion of the individual with God was re-established: for human faculties, in their normal action, could now appreciate, and approach to, what had previously been inappreciable and unapproachable. Surely the system I have thus rudely exhibited was ideally a great philosophy, as well as practically an immeasurable boon. To strike out the redemptive clauses from the scheme is to erase the very feature by which it essentially differed from all other schemes; and to substitute a didactic exhibition of superior morality, with the rays of an example in the preterite tense, set by a dead man in Judæa, for that scheme of living forces, by which the powers of a living Saviour's humanity are daily and hourly given to man, under a charter which expires only with the world itself. Is it possible here to discern, either from an ideal or from a practical point of view, anything but depletion and impoverishment, and the substitution of a spectral for a living form?

If we proceed to the second question, the spectacle, as it presents itself to me, is stranger still. Although we know that James Mill, arrested by the strong hand of Bishop Butler, halted rather than rested for a while in theism on his progress towards general negation, yet his case does not supply, nor can we draw from other sources, any reason to regard such a position as one which can be largely and permanently held against that relentless force of logic, which is ever silently at work to assert and to avenge itself. The theist is confronted, with no breakwater between, by the awful problem of moral evil, by the mystery of pain, by the apparent anomalies of waste and of caprice on the face of creation; and not least of all by the fact that, while the moral government of the world is founded on the free agency of man, there are in multitudes of cases environing circumstances independent of his will which seem to deprive that agency, called free, of any operative power adequate to contend against them. In this bewildered state of things, in this great enigma of the world, "Who is this that cometh from Edom, with dyed garments from Bozrah? . . . Wherefore art thou red in thine apparel, and thy garments like him that treadeth in the winefat?" There has come upon the scene the figure of a Redeemer, human and divine. Let it be granted that the Incarnation is a marvel wholly beyond our reach, and that the miracle of the Resurrection to-day gives serious trouble to some fastidious intellects. But the difficulties of a baffled understanding, lying everywhere around us in daily experience, are to be expected from its limitations; not so the shocks encountered by the moral sense. Even if the Christian scheme slightly lengthened the immeasurable catalogue of the first, this is dust in the balance compared with the relief it furnishes to the second; in supplying the most powerful remedial agency ever known, in teaching how pain may be made a helper, and evil transmuted into good; and in opening clearly the vision of another world, in which we are taught to look for yet larger counsels of the Almighty wisdom. To take away, then, the agency so beneficent, which has so softened and reduced the moral problems that lie thickly spread around us, and to leave us face to face with them in all their original rigour, is to enhance and not to mitigate the difficulties of belief.

Lastly, it is not difficult to understand why those who prefer the Pagan ideal, or who cannot lay hold on the future world, or who labour under still greater disadvantages, should put aside as a whole the gospel of God manifest in the flesh. But Mrs. Ward is none of these; and it is far harder to comprehend the mental attitude, or the mental consistency at least, of those who like her desire to retain what was manifested, but to thrust aside the manifesting Person, and all that His living personality entails: or, if I may borrow an Aristotelian figure, to keep the accidents and discard the substance. I cannot pretend to offer a solution of this hard riddle. But there is one feature which almost uniformly marks writers whose mind as in this case is of a religions tone, or who do not absolutely exclude religion, while they reject the Christian dogma and the authority of Scripture. They appear to have a very low estimate both of the quantity and the quality of sin: of its amount, spread like a deluge over the world, and of the subtlety, intensity, and virulence of its nature. I mean a low estimate as compared with the mournful denunciations of the sacred writings, or with the language especially of the later Christian Confessions. Now let it be granted that, in interpreting those Confessions, we do not sufficiently allow for the enormous differences among human beings—differences both of original disposition, and of ripened character. We do not sufficiently take account of the fact that, while disturbance and degradation have so heavily affected the mass, there are a happy few on whom nature's degeneracy has but lightly laid its hand. In the biography of the late Dr. Marsh we have an illustration apt for my purpose. His family was straitly Evangelical. He underwent what he deemed to be conversion. A like-minded friend congratulated his mother on the work of Divine grace in her son. But, in the concrete, she mildly resented the remark, and replied that in truth "Divine grace would find very little to do in her son William."

In the novel of "The Unclassed" by the author of "Thyrza," which like "Robert Elsmere" is of the didactic and speculative class, the leading man-character, when detailing his mental history, says that "sin" has never been for him a word of weighty import. So ingenuous a confession is not common. I remember but one exception to the rule that the negative writers of our own day have formed, or at least have exhibited, a very feeble estimate of the enormous weight of sin, as a factor in the condition of man and of the world. That exception is Amiel. Mrs. Ward has prefixed to her translation of his remarkable and touching work an Introduction from which I make the following extract:—

> His Calvinistic training lingers long in him; and what detaches him from the Hegelian school, with which he has much in common, is his own stronger sense of personal need, his preoccupation with the idea of sin. He speaks (says M. Renan contemptuously) of sin, of salvation, of redemption and conversion, as if these things were realities. He asks me, "What does M. Renan make of sin? 'Eh bien, je crois que je le supprime.'"

The closing expression is a happy one: sin is for the most part suppressed.

We are bound to believe, and I for one do believe, that in many cases the reason why the doctrines of grace, so profoundly embedded in the Gospel, are dispensed with by the negative writers of the day, is in many cases because they have not fully had to feel the need of them: because they have not travelled with St. Paul through the dark valley of agonising conflict, or with Dante along the circles downward and the hill upward; because, having to bear a smaller share than others of the common curse and burden, they stagger and falter less beneath its weight.

But ought they not to know that they are physicians, who have not learned the principal peril of the patient's case, and whose prescription accordingly omits the main requisite for a cure? For surely in this matter there should be no mistake. As the entire Levitical institutions seem to have been constructed to impress upon the Hebrew mind a deep and definite idea of sin, we find in the New Testament that that portion of our Lord's work was so to speak ready-made. But He placed it at the foundation of His great design for the future. "When the Comforter is come, He will reprove the world of sin, and of righteousness, and of judgment." Mrs. Ward seeks, and even with enthusiasm, to "make for righteousness"; but the three terms compose an organic whole, and if a part be torn away the residue will bleed to death. For the present, however, we have only to rest in the real though but partial consolation that, if the ancient and continuous creed of Christendom has slipped away from its place in Mrs. Ward's brilliant and subtle understanding, it has nevertheless by no means lost a true, if unacknowledged, hold upon the inner sanctuary of her heart.

BEATRICE WEBB (NÉE POTTER) (1858–1943)

Pages from a Work-Girl's Diary (1888)

*T*here are fascinating anomalies in Beatrice Webb's life: a socialist, activist, and
prominent woman writer who was opposed to women's suffrage; a romantic
who married the notably unromantic and ill-favored ("hideous," she said of a
photograph of him) Sidney Webb, explaining that she did not love him, that "it is
the head only that I am marrying," and then went on to a long and happy marriage;
a "divided personality," as she once described herself—a "normal woman" who
sought happiness in love and marriage, and an independent spirit who wanted to
exercise the "free activity of 'a clear and analytic mind.'"[1] It was the latter persona,
Beatrice Potter, who undertook an "apprenticeship" in social research that resulted
in a remarkable chapter in the first volume of Charles Booth's Life and Labour of
the People of London *(1889), a sympathetic, even admiring account of the impoverished yet self-reliant, industrious, and entrepreneurial Jewish community of
London's East End.*

"Pages from a Work-Girl's Diary," *on her personal experience in the East End,
was, Webb later ironically said, her "one and only literary 'success.'"[2] But it had a
troubling history. Before it appeared, she was called to testify before a House of Lords
Committee on sweatshops, and she inadvertently gave the impression that she had
worked twelve hours a day for three weeks. In fact, she had worked only two full*

Beatrice Webb (née Potter) (1858–1943), "Pages from a Work-Girl's Diary," *Nineteenth
Century*, September 1888.
1. Beatrice Webb, *My Apprenticeship* ([1926] Penguin ed., London, 1971), p. 284.
2. Ibid, p. 323.

days in one shop and a few hours in others. For various reasons, it proved difficult to make the correction, and she was so conscience-stricken that, according to her biographer, she had "bouts of suicidal depression."³ That mood did not last long, for she soon recovered, resuming her work with Booth, getting involved with the cooperative movement, and finally, in January 1890, meeting "the other one," "the little figure with a big head" who was to become "the man of my destiny," the "predominant partner of the firm of Webb."⁴

I t is midday. The sun's rays beat fiercely on the crowded alleys of the Jewish settlement: the air is moist from the heavy rains. An unsavoury steam rises from the down-trodden slime of the East End streets and mixes with the stronger odours of the fried fish, the decomposing vegetables, and the second-hand meat which assert their presence to the eyes and nostrils of the passers-by.

For a brief interval the "whirr" of the sewing-machines and the muffled sound of the presser's iron have ceased. Machinists and pressers, well-clothed and decorated with heavy watch-chains; Jewish girls with flashy hats, full figures, and large bustles; furtive-eyed Polish immigrants with their pallid faces and crouching forms; and here and there poverty-stricken Christian women— all alike hurry to and from the midday meal; while the labour-masters, with their wives and daughters, sit or lounge round about the house-door, and exchange notes on the incompetency of "season hands," the low price of work, the blackmail of shop foremen, or discuss the more agreeable topic of the last "deal" in Petticoat Lane and the last venture on racehorses.

Jostled on and off the pavement, I wander on and on, seeking work. Hour after hour I have paced the highways and byways of the London Ghetto. No bills up except for a "good tailoress," and at these places I dare not apply, for I feel myself an impostor, and as yet my conscience and my fingers are equally unhardened. Each step I take I am more faint-hearted and more weary in body and limb. At last, in sheer despair, I summon up my courage. In a window the usual bill, but seated on the doorstep a fat cheerful-looking daughter of Israel, who seems to invite application.

"Do you want a plain 'and?" say I, aping ineffectually a work-woman's manner and accent, and attaining only supreme awkwardness.

The Jewess glances quickly, first at my buttonless boots, then at my short but already bedraggled skirt, upwards along the straight line of my ill-fitting coat, to the tumbled black bonnet which sits ill at ease over an unkempt twist of hair.

"No," is the curt reply.

---

3. *Letters of Sidney and Beatrice Webb,* ed. Norman Mackenzie (Cambridge, Eng., 1978), I, 65.
4. *My Apprenticeship,* p. 398.

"I can do all except buttonholes," I insist in a more natural tone.

She looks at my face and hesitates. "Where have you worked?"

"In the country," I answer vaguely.

She turns her head slowly towards the passage of the house. "Rebecca, do you want a hand?"

"Suited an hour ago," shouts back Rebecca.

"There, there, you see," remarks the Jewess in a deprecating and kindly voice as her head sinks into the circles of fat surrounding it. "You will find plenty of bills in the next street; no fear of a decent young person, as knows her work, staying out o' door this time of year"; and then, turning to the woman by her side: "It's rare tho' to find one as does. In these last three days, if we've sat down one, we've sat a dozen to the table, and not a woman amongst them as knows how to baste out a coat fit for the machine."

Encouraged by these last words I turn round and trudge on. I ask at every house with a bill up, but always the same scrutinising glance at my clothes and the fatal words, "We are suited!"

Is it because it is the middle of the week, or because they think I'm not genuine? think I. And at the next shop window I look nervously at my reflection, and am startled at my utterly forlorn appearance—destitute enough to be "sweated" by any master.

"Sure, there's not much on 'er back to take to the h'old uncle," remarks an Irish servant to her mistress, as I turn away from the last house advertising for a "good tailoress."

I feel horribly sick and ill; and I am so painfully conscious of my old clothes that I dare not ask for refreshment at an eating-house or even at a public. Any way I will have air, so I drag one foot after another into the Hackney thoroughfare. Straight in front of me, in a retail slop-shop of the lowest description, I see a large placard: "Trouser and Vest Hands Wanted Immediately." In another moment I am within a large workroom crowded with women and girls as ill-clothed as myself. At the head of a long table, examining finished garments, stands a hard-featured, shrewd-looking Jewess, in a stamped cotton velvet and with a gold-rimmed eyeglass.

"Do you want trouser hands?"

"Yes we do—indoor."

"I'm a trouser finisher."

The Jewess examines me from head to foot. My standard of dress suits her. "Call at eight o'clock to-morrow morning." And she turns from me to look over a pair of trousers handed up the table.

"What price do you pay?" say I with firmness.

"Why, according to the work done, to be sure. All prices," she answers laconically.

"Then to-morrow at eight." And I leave the shop hurriedly to escape that hard gaze of my future mistress. Again in the open street: the dazed-headiness, the dragging back-ache, and the sore feet—all the physical ills and moral depressions of the out o' work—seem suddenly swept away. At length, after this weary pilgrimage, I have secured work. The cool evening breeze, the picturesque life and stirring activity of the broad highway, even the sounds and sights of East London, add to my feeling of intense exhilaration. Only one drawback to perfect content: *Can* I "finish" trousers?

At a few minutes past eight the following morning I am standing in front of "MOSES AND SON. CHEAP CLOTHING." In the window two shop-boys are arranging the show garments: coats and vests (sold together) 17s. to 22s.; trousers from 4s. 6d. up to 11s. 6d.

"Coats evidently made out: I wonder where and at what price?" ponders the investigator as the work-girl loiters at the door.

"You'd better come in," says the friendly voice of a fellow worker as she brushes past me. "You're a new-comer; the missus will expect you to be there sharp."

I follow her into the retail shop and thence through a roughly made wooden door. The workroom is long and irregularly shaped, somewhat low and dark near the entrance, but expanding into a lofty skylight at the further end. The walls are lined with match-boarding; in a prominent place, framed and under glass, hang the *Factory and Workshop Regulations.* Close by the door, and well within reach of the gas-stove (used for heating irons), two small but high tables serve the pressers: a long low plank table, furnished with a wooden rail for the feet, forms on either side of it, chairs top and bottom, runs lengthways for the trouser finishers; a high table for the basters; and, directly, under the skylight, two other tables for machinists and vest hands complete the furniture of the room. Through an open door, at the extreme end of the workshop, you can see the private kitchen of the Moses family, and beyond, in a very limited backyard, an outhouse, and, near to it, a tap and sink for the use of all the inmates of the establishment.

Some thirty women and girls are crowding in. The first arrivals hang bonnets and shawls on the scanty supply of nails jotted here and there along the wooden partition separating the front shop from the workroom; the later comers shed their outdoor garments in various corners. There is a general Babel of voices as each "hand" settles down in front of the bundle of work and the old tobacco or candle box that holds the cottons, twist, gimp, needles, thimble, and scissors belonging to her. They are all English or Irish women, with the exception of some half-dozen well-dressed "young ladies" (daughters of the house), one of whom acts as forewoman, while the others are already at work on the vests. The "missus" is still at breakfast. A few minutes after the half-hour the two pressers (English lads are the only men employed) saunter lazily into the room, light up the gas jet, and prepare the irons.

The forewoman calls for a pair of trousers, already machined, and hands them to me. I turn them over and over, puzzled to know where to begin. The work is quite different from that of the *bespoke* shop, at which I was trained— much coarser and not so well arranged. Besides, I have no cotton, thread, twist, or gimp. The woman next me explains: "You'll 'ave to bring trimmings; we h'aint supplied with them things y'ere; but I'll lend you some, jist to set off with."

"What ought I to buy?" I ask, feeling rather helpless.

At this moment the "missus" sweeps into the room. She is a big woman, enormously developed in the hips and thighs; she has strongly marked Jewish features, and, I see now, she is blind of one eye. The sardonic and enigmatical expression of her countenance puzzles me with its far-off associations, until I remember the caricatures, sold in City shops for portraits, of the great Disraeli. Her hair is crisp and oily—once jet black, now, in places, gray—it twists itself in scanty locks over her forehead. The same stamped cotton velvet, of a large flowery pattern, that she wore yesterday; a heavy watch-chain, plentiful supply of rings, and a spotlessly clean apron.

"Good-morning to you," she says graciously to the whole assembly as she walks round our table towards my seat. "Sarah, have you given this young person some work?"

"Yes," replies Sarah; "fourpence halfpenny's."

"I have not got any trimmings. I did not know that I had to supply them. Where I worked before they were given," I ejaculate humbly.

"That's easily managed; the shop's just round the corner— Or, Sarah," she calls across the table, "you're going out—just get the young person her trimmings. The lady next you will tell you what you want," she adds in a lower tone, bending over between us.

The "lady" next me is already my friend. She is a neat and respectable married woman with a look of conscious superiority to her surroundings. Like all the trouser hands she is paid by the piece; but in spite of this she is ready to give me up time in explaining how I am to set about my work.

"You'll feel a bit strange the first day. 'Ave you been long out o' work?"

"Yes," I answer abruptly.

"Ah! that accounts for you're being a bit awkward-like. One's fingers feel like so many thumbs after a slack time."

And certainly mine do. I feel nervous, and very much on trial. The growing heat of the room, the form so crowded that one must sit sideways to secure even a limited freedom for one's elbows; the general strangeness of my position—all these circumstances unite to incapacitate a true hater of needlework for even the roughest of sewing. However, happily for me no one pays me much attention. As the morning wears on, the noise increases. The two pressers have worked up their spirits, and a lively exchange of chaff and bad language is thrown from the two lads at the pressing (immediately behind us) to the girls round our table. Offers of kisses, sharp despatches to the devil and his abode, a constant and meaningless use of the inevitable adjective, form the staple of the conversation between the pressers and the younger hands; while the elder women whisper scandal and news in each other's ears. From the further end of the room catches of music-hall songs break into the monotonous whirr of the sewing-machine. The somewhat crude and un-rhythmical chorus—

> Why should not the girls have freedom now and then?
> And if a girl likes a man, why should she not propose?
> Why should the little girls always be led by the nose?

seems the favourite refrain, and, judging from the gusto with which it is repeated, expresses the dominant sentiment of the work-girls. Now and again the mistress shouts out, "Sing in time, girls; I don't mind your singing, but sing in time." There is a free giving and taking of each other's trimmings, a kindly and general supervision of each other's work—altogether a hearty geniality of a rough sort. The enigmatical and sardonic-looking Jewess sits at the upper end of our table, scans the finished garment through her gold-rimmed eyeglass, encourages or scolds as befits the case; or, screwing up her blind eye, joins in the chatter and broad-witted talk of the work-women immediately surrounding her.

"The missus 'as sixteen children," remarks my friend Mrs. Long confidentially—"h'eight by Mr. Moses, and h'eight by the master she buried years ago. All them girls at the bottom table ar' 'er daughters."

"They are a nice-looking set," say I, in a complimentary tone.

"Yes, it's a pity some of the girls in the shop h'ain't like them," mutters my respectable friend. "They're an awful bad lot, some of them. Why, bless you, that young person as is laughing and joking with the pressers jist be'ind us"— and here follow horrible details of the domestic vice and unnatural crime which disgrace the so-called "Christian" life of East London.

"Eh, eh!" joins in the woman next her, with a satisfied sniff at the scandal (a regular woman of the slums, with nose and skin patched by drink), "it's h'ill thinking of what you may 'ave to touch in these sort of places."

"Well to be sure," rejoins Mrs. Long, nettled both by the tone of superiority and by the unwarranted interruption of her disreputable neighbour. "I've worked at this same place for h'eight years and never yet 'ave I 'ad words with anyone. There's reg'ler work the week round, and reg'ler pay on a Saturday;

and y're money kept for you, if you 'appen to be a-cleaning. There's no need to mix y'rself up with them whose look you don't like," she adds, with just a perceptible edging away from the slum woman, as if to emphasise her words—"there's some of all sorts y'ere."

"H'I'm one of that sort," blusters the woman of the slums, "that h'answers a person back when they call me "bl——y names. H'I'll give the last word to no one."

"I don't choose to 'old conversation wi' the like of they," says Mrs. Long, pursing up her thin lips as if to end this undesired intercourse: "it h'ain't as if *I* 'ad to work for my living. My 'usband's in reg'ler work; it's only for the hextras like that I work, and jist for them times, per'aps a month the 'ole year through, that the building trade's slack."

This effectually silences the woman of the slums. Her husband, alas! comes home drunk every night and spends the irregularly earned pence lounging about the publics (so I am afterwards informed by Mrs. Long). She has an ill-favoured daughter by her side, with a black eye and a swollen face, with whom she exchanges work and bad language and shares greasy victuals.

"One o'clock," shouts a shrill boy's voice.

"Stop work," orders the mistress.

"I wish I might finish this bit," I say pathetically to my friend, painfully conscious of the shortcoming in the quantity if not in the quality of my work.

"You mustn't; it's the dinner hour."

The pressers are already off, the mistress and her daughters retire into the kitchen: the greater number of women and girls turn out into the street, while one or two pulls baskets from under the table, spread out before them, on dirty newspapers, cracked mugs, bits of bread and butter, cold sausage or salt fish; and lift, from off the gas-stove, the tin teapot wherein their drink has been stewing since the early morning. Heartily thankful for a breath of fresh air and a change from my cramped posture, I wander up and down the open street, and end my "dinner hour" by turning into a clean shop for a bun and a fresh cup of tea. Back again at two.

"You must work sharper than this," remarks the mistress, who is inspecting my work. I colour up and tremble perceptibly as I meet the scrutinising gaze of the hard-featured Jewess. She looks into my eyes with a comically puzzled expression, and adds in a gentler voice: "You must work a little quicker for your own sake. We've had worse buttonholes than these, but it don't look as if you'd been 'customed to much work."

But now the drama of the day begins. The two pressers saunter in ten minutes after the hour. This brings down upon them the ire of the Jewess. They, however, seem masters of the situation, for they answer her back in far choicer language than that in which they were addressed—language which I fear (even in a private diary) I could hardly reproduce; they assert their right to come when they choose; they declare that if they want a day off they "will see her to the devil and take it"; and lastly, as a climax to all insults, they threaten her with the "factory man," and taunt her with gambling away on racehorses the money she "sweats" out of them.

At these last words the enigmatical and sardonic expression of the Jewess changes into one of out-bursting rage. All resemblance to the City caricatures of that great passionless spirit vanishes. The deep furrows extending from just above the nostril to the corner of the mouth—lines which must surely express some race experience of the children of Israel—open out into one universal bubble of human fury. A perfect volley of oaths fly in quick succession between the principal combatants; while woman after woman joins in the fray, taking the missus's side against the pressers. The woman of the slums actually rises in her seat and prepares to use her fists; while her daughter seizes the opportunity to empty the small bottle of brandy hidden under her mother's trimmings. Mrs. Long purses up her thin lips still more tightly, and looks down steadily at her work. At this critical point—enter the master.

Mr. Moses is a corpulent, well-dressed English Jew. His face is heavy and sensual, his eyes sheepish, his reputation among his wife's "hands" none of the best. At this moment, his one desire is to keep the Queen's peace in his establishment. I suspect, also, from the sleepy viciousness of his expression, that he himself suffers occasionally from the missus's forcible tongue; and with this bevy of women shouting on all sides he feels the masculine side of the question. Any way, he is inclined to take a strictly impartial view of the row. "Sit down, Mrs. Jones," he shouts to the woman of the slums—"sit you down, or you and that —— daughter of yours leave the shop this very instant. Now, lads, just you be quiet; go on with your work and don't speak to my wife." And then, turning to his wife, in a lower tone—"Why won't you leave them alone and not answer them?" and the rest of his speech we cannot hear; but, judging from the tone and the look, it takes the form of deprecating expostulation. I catch the words "push of work" and "season hands."

"Why, if you were only a bit of a man," cries the mistress, raising her voice so that all may hear, "you'd throw those two bl——y rascals out. I'd throw them out at any price, if I were a woman's husband. The idea of saying how I spend my money—what's that to him? And that Jo says he'll call the factory man in. He may call the devil in (and he's welcome)—the only person as he'll notice will be himself. The idea of him saying that I spend my money on horses; as if I couldn't spend money on anything I like. As if you wouldn't give me money as I earn, when I asks you, Mr. Moses," gasps the Jewess, as she looks threateningly at her partner, "and never ask where it goes to." The betting on horses is evidently a sore point.

"It isn't their business what you do with your money," rejoins the master soothingly. "But just let them alone, and tell those girls to be quiet. It's more than half the girls' fault—they're always at the fellows," he adds, anxious to shift the blame into a safe quarter.

The storm lulls, and Mr. Moses returns into the front shop. But the anger of the Jewess is not yet exhausted. A stray word, and the quick firing of abusive language between the mistress and the pressers begins afresh; though this time the women, awed by the master's interference, are silent. The tall weak-looking young man, Jo by name, shouts the longest and loudest; but, as Mrs. Long whispers to me without raising her eyes from her work, "It's 'Arry as makes the bullets—jist listen to 'im—but it's Jo as fires 'em!"

At last it subsides. Women (outdoor hands) troop in with bundles of finished trousers. The bubbling rage of the injured woman yields to the keen-eyed supervision of the profit-making Jewess. "I'd have nothing but indoor hands, if I knew where to find them and had a room to put them into," she mutters to Esther as she turns over garment after garment. "Just look at this work, it's all soap! Call again on Monday morning, Mrs. Smith. But mind it *is* Monday and not Tuesday morning. You understand English, don't you?— Monday morning."

A small boy creeps into the shop laden with unfinished work. "What d'you say to this, Sarah? Mrs. Hall sends word she was washing on Monday, cleaning on Tuesday, and I suppose playing the devil on Wednesday, for here's Thursday, with shop day to-morrow, and the work's untouched. Now, girls, be quick with your work," continues the mistress as she throws the bundle on to our table—"all this to be done extra before Friday. Perkins won't wait for no one!"

"The name of a wholesale shipping firm; so she works for export as well as for retail and pays same price for both," inwardly notes the investigator as she glances at the shoddy garments. (The work-girl meanwhile pushes her needle into her thumb-nail, and in her agony digs her elbow into her neighbour's half-turned back, which causes a cannonade all round the table.)

"Law! how awkward she still be," growls the woman of the slums, anxious to pick a quarrel and vent her unspent wrath.

At length teatime breaks the working-day. Pence have already been collected for the common can of milk; innumerable teapots are lifted off the gas-stove, small parcels of bread and butter, with a relish or a sweet, are everywhere unrolled. My neighbours, on either side, offer me tea, which I resolutely refuse. The mistress sips her cup at the head of the table. The obnoxious pressers have left for the half-hour. Her feelings break out—

"Pay them 5s. a day to abuse you! As if I couldn't spend my money on what I like; and as if Mr. Moses would ever ask—I'd like to see him ask me—how the money'd gone!"

All the women sympathise with her and vie with each other in abusing the absent pressers.

"It's h'awful, their language," cries the slum woman; "if I were the missus, I'd give the bl——y scoundrels tit for tat. Whativer's the use of bein' a missus if you've got to 'old in y're tongue?"

"As for the factory man," continues the irate Jewess, turning to the other sore point, "just fancy threatening me with him! Why they ar'n't fit to work in a respectable shop; they're d——d spies. I'd throw them out, if it cost me 100*l.* And if Mr. Moses were half a man, he'd do it too."

At the word spy, I feel rather hot; but conscious of the innocence of my object, I remark, "You have nothing to fear from the factory inspector; you keep the regulations exactly."

"I don't deny," she answers quite frankly, "that if we're pressed for work I turn the girls upstairs; but it isn't once in three months I do it; and it all tells for their good."

Two hours afterwards, and I have finished my second pair. "This won't do," she says as she looks over both pairs together. "Here, take and undo the band of that one; I'll set this one to rights. Better have respectable persons who know little to work here than blaguards who know a lot—and a deal too much," she mutters, smarting over the taunts of the "factory man" and the money laid on horses.

"Eight o'clock by the Brewery clock," cries the shrill voice.

"Ten minutes to," shouts the missus, looking at her watch. "However, it ain't worth while breaking the law for a few minutes. Stop work."

This is most welcome to me. The heat since the gas has been lit is terrific, my fingers are horribly sore, and my back aches as if it would break. The women bundle up their work; one or two take it home. Everyone leaves her trimmings on the table, with scissors and thimble. Outside, the freshness of the evening air, the sensation of free movement, and rest to the weary eyes and fingers constitute the keenest physical enjoyment I have ever yet experienced.

Friday morning, and I am hopelessly tired. Jammed between my two neighbours, with the garment of hard shoddy stuff on my knee, and with the whole day's work before me, I feel on the brink of deep disgrace as a work-girl. I am "shaky like all over," my fingers, worn in places into holes, refuse to push the thick needle through the objectionable substance; damp hands (the more I rub them in my apron the damper they become) stretch the thin linings out of place; my whole energy is riveted on my work, with the discouraging result that it becomes worse and worse. Mrs. Long works silently by my side at high pressure to bring a pair of "ordered" trousers in to time. And she begins to scent dismissal.

"I keeps myself to myself," she told me yesterday. "Down y're they're all a-going down 'ill; except them Jews as is going hup." And to-day she applies her theory strictly, and is unwilling to "mix herself up" with even a respectable failure. So I bungle on without help until I have finished after a fashion.

"This will never do," angrily remarks the mistress. And then, perceiving the culprit by her side, she adds sternly: "This won't do—this work won't suit me; you want to go and learn somewhere first. This will never do—this won't suit me," she repeats slowly as she pulls the work to pieces. She dismisses me from her side with a wave of her eyeglass, as if to say, "It's no good answering me back again."

Without a word I arrange my trimmings ready to depart if the missus persists.

Is it over-fatigue, or is it the perfect realisation of my position as a disgraced work-girl? An ominous lump rises in my throat, and my eyes fill with tears. There is a dead silence. The younger hands look up from their work sympathetically; Mrs. Long, with her head down, stitches on steadily; the woman of the slums gazes on me with bleared expression of mingled stupor and pity; fumbles underneath her work on the table and pushes something towards me. I hear the rattle of the brandy-bottle against the scissors as I see the old tobacco-box that holds her trimmings advancing towards me. Meanwhile the Jewess has screwed up her left eye and is looking at me through her eyeglass. The deep furrows of inherited experience again relax in favour of personal feeling. But this time it is human kindness instead of human fury. She beckons to me. In a second I am by her side.

"I'll see what I can do with you. If you like to stay and work on threepence-halfpennies, the same as I give to outdoor hands, you can take better work when you're fit for it. I'm sure I don't want to be hard on any decent young person as is trying to earn her living in a respectable way. There ain't so many respectable persons in the world that we can afford to starve 'em," the Jewess adds, casting an angry glance at the pressers. "Sarah, give her a pair of threepence-halfpennies. I'll alter these for you. You sit between those two young ladies and they'll show you. You must help one another," she says to the girls as they make room for me; "tho' of course they all come here to make their own living; you can't expect them to teach you for ever."

The girl who takes me under her especial charge is a respectably dressed and delicate-looking young woman, with none of the rowdy slovenliness or tarnished finery of the typical Gentile girl of East London. Slightly made, with a pale, weary face, she looks at least thirty (she tells me she is only just nineteen);

she stitches silently, and seems hardly conscious of the boisterous life of her fellow-workers; but instead of Mrs. Long's air of ever-present superiority, her form, face, manner, denote physical depression, lit up now and again by the dreamy consciousness of another world beyond the East End workroom.

"You'll soon learn," she says kindly; "you must watch me fix this, and then you can do the next yourself."

Directed and encouraged by her kindness, I work on, in a calmer frame of mind, listening to the conversation of my neighbours. Among the younger hands who sit at this end of the table it chiefly concerns the attraction of the rival music-halls, or the still more important question of the presents and attentions of their different "blokes." For monotonous work and bad food have not depressed the physical energies of these young women. With warm hearts, with overflowing good nature, with intellects keenly alive to the varied sights of East London, these genuine daughters of the people brim over with the frank enjoyment of low life. During the day their fingers and eyes are fully occupied; in the evenings, on holidays, in the slack season, their thoughts rush out and gather in the multitudinous excitements of the East End streets; while their feelings unburden themselves in the pleasure of promiscuous love-making. You cannot accuse them of immorality, for they have no consciousness of sin. The veneer of morality, the hidden but secretly self-conscious vice of that little set that styles itself "London society" (in the city of millions!) are unknown to them. They live in the Garden of Eden of uncivilised life; as yet they have not tasted the forbidden fruit of the Tree of the Knowledge of Good and Evil, and the heaven and hell of an awakened conscience are alike undreamt of. There is only one Fall possible to them—drink, leading slowly but inevitably to the drunkard's death.

"I say, Milly," shouts one to the other, "you tell that bl——y brother of yours that I waits 'alf an 'our for 'im houtside the Paragon last night. I'll be blessed before I serves as 'is Round the Corner ag'in. 'Owever, at last, I says to myself, 'a watched kittle niver biles,' so I walks in by myself. The dressin' there is grand," she adds enthusiastically.

"Eh! but you sh'd see the piece they're running at the Standard!" rejoins Milly. "Jim's promised to take me up to one of them grand places up West next Saturday. Will you come along? I'll git Tom to come. You'll want to be a making of it up by that time. Tom's in reg'lar work and a rare catch h'as a sweet'eart," laughs the sister of the faithless swain.

"It's too much trouble to go up West," answers the girl, anxious to prove her indifference to Tom's attentions. "I don't care to turn h'out 'fore 'alf-past nine. It takes a full hour to clean up and git a bit of supper, and that leaves three hours for our houting like; for mother don't hexpect us back 'fore 'alf-past twelve. But I don't say I wouldn't come, as it's the 'alf day, if Tom's very pressin'," she continues. "I've 'eard it said them grand ladies as sits in the boxes and the stalls 'as low dresses on, like so many h'actrices, and h'it's as good h'as a play jist to look on 'em. So 'Arry told me, and 'e's a rare 'un for liking the look of them lords and ladies as lives up there."

The pale, weary girl stitches silently by my side. She works harder than the others—finished four pair yesterday and hopes to finish the same to-day. "Are you chapel?" she asks presently.

"Yes," I reply, attending more to the spirit than to the letter of her question.

"Do you belong to the Army?" she says inquiringly, glancing at my plain grey dress, and no doubt remembering my close black bonnet.

"No," I answer, "do you?"

She shakes her head: "They've tried to get me to join since I've been in London. But we're a quieter set than they. Mother and I have only been in London these two years since father's death," she adds in an explanatory tone. "Mother's a skilled vest hand; not this sort of work—she wouldn't look at this. She can make 2*l.* a week in good times; but now her eyesight's going fast. And it isn't much as I earn. I was brought up to teaching."

"And why did you not go on with it?"

"I failed in the first examination. Then father died, and mother heard there were skilled hands wanted in London, so we left our home. But I've found a Bible-class in our street and I teaches there twice a week. That and the chapel on a Sunday is like a bit of the old home." The work-girl sighs, and the far-off look of "another world" gleams in the clear depths of her grey eyes. "If you're going out for the dinner-hour, I might show you the chapel and the class-room," she adds with hesitating gentleness; "are you going home for dinner?"

"No, I shall get a cup of tea at Lockhart's, and a bun."

"Why, you've niver a-goin' to dine off that!" cries the girl on my other side. And there is a whispering all round the table. Only a cup of tea and a bun means great poverty.

"You 'ad no tea last evening," continues the same girl; "now you must take a cup o' mine this afternoon."

The hours of the day pass away quietly in work. There are no words between the mistress and the pressers, and the workshop life becomes monotonous. During the interval between dinner and tea a golden-haired young lady (married daughter of the Jewess), beautifully gloved and bonneted, covered with jewels, but with a somewhat unseasonable tippet of sable-tails, enters the workroom. She seats herself by her mother at the head of the table and chats confidentially. I hear the names of various racehorses and of forthcoming races. Apparently her husband belongs to the genus of "betting men," and, judging from her dress, he is a successful one. The mistress is in high good humour. At teatime she turns to me:

"Now, I'm very much interested in you; there is something in your face that's uncommon, and your voice too, that's odd—no word higher than another. The woman here will tell you, if I hadn't taken a fancy to your face and your voice I should have bundled you out long ago. Now what have you been?" she continues with gracious inquisitiveness.

"I hadn't to work when my father was in work," I answer with literal truthfulness.

"A tidy-looking young person like you ought to get some respectable man to marry her—like my daughter here; you're more fit for that than to be making your own living in this sort of place. But, since you have come, I'll see what I can do with you. Come, you're getting on nicely," she says encouragingly, as she looks over my work.

I am drinking the cup of tea forced on me by my neighbour. The pale, weary girl is munching her bread and butter.

"Won't you have some?" she says, as she pushes the paper towards me.

"No, thank you," I answer.

"Sure?" and without more to do she lays a thick slice in my lap and turns away to avoid my thanks. A little bit of human kindness that goes to the heart and brings tears into the eyes of the investigator.

Work begins again. My friend has finished her third piece and is waiting for the fourth. She covers her head with her hands as she bends backward to rest the strained figure. In her grey eyes there is a look of intense weariness— weariness of body and mind. Another pair is handed to her and she begins again. She is a quick worker; but, work as hard as she may, she cannot clear much over 1s. a day after she has paid for trimmings. (A shilling a day is about the price of unskilled woman's labour.)

Another two hours and I say good-night.

"I'll be married in a week" are the last words I hear passing from Jo to Harry, "and then my wife shall keep me."

"I'll go to the bl—y workhouse," jokes Harry, "if I don't get a gal to keep me. I won't sweat here any longer for 5s. a day."

OSCAR WILDE (1854–1900)

The Soul of Man under Socialism (1891)

*T*his is not the *"decadent"* Oscar Wilde—*facetious, foppish, scandalous. It is the "earnest" Wilde—passionate, epigrammatic, serious even when (especially when) sounding paradoxical. This long essay, his last, was provoked by a speech by George Bernard Shaw that Wilde happened to attend. Repelled by Shaw's economic and collectivist socialism, Wilde proposed a quite different kind of socialism, anarchic and individualistic. Shaw, in turn, dismissed Wilde's essay as witty and entertaining but having nothing to do with socialism. He was especially scornful, Shaw's biographer Hesketh Pearson reports, of such statements by Wilde as, "If the Socialism is Authoritarian; if there are Governments armed with economic power as they are now with political power; if, in a word, we are to have Industrial Tyrannies, then the last state of man will be worse than the first." Or, "It is to be regretted that a portion of our community should be practically in slavery, but to propose to solve the problem by enslaving the entire community is childish."* [1]

Half a century later, perhaps as a rebuke to Shaw, who was a fervent admirer of Stalin and the Soviet Union, Pearson pronounced Wilde's essay "one of the greatest in the language," provoking "more thought among the young of two generations than anything else written in that period . . . a sort of bible among the youthful

Oscar Wilde (1854–1900), "The Soul of Man under Socialism," *Fortnightly Review,* February 1891. Reprinted in *Complete Works of Oscar Wilde,* ed. Robert Ross (New York, 1921), pp. 46–86.
1. Hesketh Pearson, introduction to Oscar Wilde, *De Profundis and Other Writings* ([1954] London, 1982), p. 16.

rebellious spirits of nations whose governments frowned upon free thought, especially in Tsarist Russia, where copies were mysteriously printed, furtively circulated, and carefully concealed from authority." [2] *Pearson may have overstated the influence of Wilde's essay, but not his remarkable prescience in cautioning against an "authoritarian" socialism that few other people, still less other socialists, conceived of at the time.*

The chief advantage that would result from the establishment of Socialism is, undoubtedly, the fact that Socialism would relieve us from that sordid necessity of living for others which, in the present condition of things, presses so hardly upon almost everybody. In fact, scarcely any one at all escapes.

Now and then, in the course of the century, a great man of science, like Darwin; a great poet, like Keats; a fine critical spirit, like M. Renan; a supreme artist, like Flaubert, has been able to isolate himself, to keep himself out of reach of the clamorous claims of others, to stand "under the shelter of the wall," as Plato puts it, and so to realise the perfection of what was in him, to his own incomparable gain, and to the incomparable and lasting gain of the whole world. These, however, are exceptions. The majority of people spoil their lives by an unhealthy and exaggerated altruism—are forced, indeed, so to spoil them. They find themselves surrounded by hideous poverty, by hideous ugliness, by hideous starvation. It is inevitable that they should be strongly moved by all this. The emotions of man are stirred more quickly than man's intelligence; and, as I pointed out some time ago in an article on the function of criticism, it is much more easy to have sympathy with suffering than it is to have sympathy with thought. Accordingly, with admirable though misdirected intentions, they very seriously and very sentimentally set themselves to the task of remedying the evils that they see. But their remedies do not cure the disease: they merely prolong it. Indeed, their remedies are part of the disease.

They try to solve the problem of poverty, for instance, by keeping the poor alive; or, in the case of a very advanced school, by amusing the poor.

But this is not a solution: it is an aggravation of the difficulty. *The proper aim is to try and re-construct society on such a basis that poverty will be impossible.* And the altruistic virtues have really prevented the carrying out of this aim. Just as the worst slave-owners were those who were kind to their slaves, and so prevented the horror of the system being realised by those who suffered from it, and understood by those who contemplated it, so, in the present state of things in England, the people who do most harm are the people who try to do most good; and at last we have had the spectacle of men who have really studied the problem and know the life—educated men who live in the East-End—coming

---

2. Ibid., p. 15.

forward and imploring the community to restrain its altruistic impulses of charity, benevolence and the like. They do so on the ground that such charity degrades and demoralises. They are perfectly right. Charity creates a multitude of sins.

There is also this to be said. It is immoral to use private property in order to alleviate the horrible evils that result from the institution of private property. It is both immoral and unfair.

Under Socialism all this will, of course, be altered. There will be no people living in fetid dens and fetid rags, and bringing up unhealthy, hunger-pinched children in the midst of impossible and absolutely repulsive surroundings. The security of society will not depend, as it does now, on the state of the weather. If a frost comes we shall not have a hundred thousand men out of work, tramping about the streets in a state of disgusting misery, or whining to their neighbours for aims, or crowding round the doors of loathsome shelters to try and secure a hunch of bread and a night's unclean lodging. Each member of the society will share in the general prosperity and happiness of the society, and if a frost comes no one will practically be anything the worse.

Upon the other hand, *Socialism itself will be of value simply because it will lead to Individualism.*

Socialism, Communism, or whatever one chooses to call it, by converting private property into public wealth, and substituting co-operation for competition, will restore society to its proper condition of a thoroughly healthy organism, and ensure the material well-being of each member of the community. It will, in fact, give Life its proper basis and its proper environment. But for the full development of Life to its highest mode of perfection something more is needed. What is needed is Individualism. If the Socialism is Authoritarian; if there are Governments armed with economic power as they are now with political power; if, in a word, we are to have Industrial Tyrannies, then the last state of man will be worse than the first. At present, in consequence of the existence of private property, a great many people are enabled to develop a certain very limited amount of Individualism. They are either under no necessity to work for their living, or are enabled to choose the sphere of activity that is really congenial to them and gives them pleasure. These are the poets, the philosophers, the men of science, the men of culture—in a word, the real men, the men who have realised themselves, and in whom all Humanity gains a partial realisation. Upon the other hand, there are a great many people who, having no private property of their own, and being always on the brink of sheer starvation, are compelled to do the work of beasts of burden, to do work that is quite uncongenial to them, and to which they are forced by the peremptory, unreasonable, degrading Tyranny of want. These are the poor, and amongst them there is no grace of manner, or charm of speech, or civilisation, or culture, or refinement in pleasures, or joy of life. From their collective force Humanity gains much in material prosperity. But it is only the material result that it gains, and the man who is poor is in himself absolutely of no importance. He is merely the infinitesimal atom of a force that, so far from regarding him, crushes him: indeed, prefers him crushed, as in that case he is far more obedient.

Of course, it might be said that the Individualism generated under conditions of private property is not always, or even as a rule, of a fine or wonderful type, and that the poor, if they have not culture and charm, have still many virtues. Both these statements would be quite true. The possession of private property is very often extremely demoralising, and that is, of course, one of the reasons why Socialism wants to get rid of the institution. In fact, property is really a nuisance. Some years ago people went about the country saying that property has duties. They said it so often and so tediously that, at last, the Church has begun to say it. One hears it now from every pulpit. It is perfectly true. Property not merely has duties, but has so many duties that its possession to any large extent is a bore. It involves endless claims upon one, endless attention to business, endless bother. If property had simply pleasures we could stand it; but its duties make it unbearable. In the interest of the rich we must get rid of it. The virtues of the poor may be readily admitted, and are much to be regretted. We are often told that the poor are grateful for charity. Some of them are, no doubt, *but the best amongst the poor are never grateful.* They are ungrateful, discontented, disobedient and rebellious. They are quite right to be so. Charity they feel to be a ridiculously inadequate mode of partial restitution, or a sentimental dole, usually accompanied by some impertinent attempt on the part of the sentimentalist to tyrannise over their private lives. Why should they be grateful for the crumbs that fall from the rich man's table? They should be seated at the board, and are beginning to know it. As for being discontented, a man who would not be discontented with such surroundings and such a low mode of life would be a perfect brute. Disobedience, in the eyes of any one who has read history, is man's original virtue. It is through disobedience that progress has been made, through disobedience and through rebellion. Sometimes the poor are praised for being thrifty. But to recommend thrift to the poor is both grotesque and insulting. It is like advising a man who is starving to eat less. For a town or country labourer to practise thrift would be absolutely immoral. Man should not be ready to show that he can live like a badly fed animal. He should decline to live like that, and should either steal or go on the rates, which is considered by many to be a form of stealing. As for begging, it is safer to beg than to take, but it is finer to take than to beg. No: a poor man who is ungrateful, unthrifty, discontented and rebellious is probably a real personality, and has much in him. He is at any rate a healthy protest. As for the virtuous poor, one can pity them, of course, but one cannot possibly admire them. They have made private terms with the enemy, and sold their birthright for very bad pottage. They must also be extraordinarily stupid. I can quite understand a man accepting laws that protect private property, and admit of its accumulation, as long as he himself is able under those conditions to realise some form of beautiful and intellectual life. But it is almost incredible to me how a man whose life is marred and made hideous by such laws can possibly acquiesce in their continuance.

However, the explanation is not really difficult to find. It is simply this. Misery and poverty are so absolutely degrading, and exercise such a paralysing effect over the nature of men, that no class is ever really conscious of its own suffering. They have to be told of it by other people, and they often entirely disbelieve them. What is said by great employers of labour against agitators is unquestionably true. Agitators are a set of interfering, meddling people, who come down to some perfectly contented class of the community and sow the seeds of discontent amongst them. That is the reason why agitators are so absolutely necessary. Without them, in our incomplete state, there would be no advance towards civilisation. Slavery was put down in America, not in consequence of any action on the part of slaves, or even any express desire on their part that they should be free. It was put down entirely through the grossly illegal conduct of certain agitators in Boston and elsewhere, who were not slaves themselves, nor owners of slaves, nor had anything to do with the question really. It was, undoubtedly, the Abolitionists who set the torch alight, who began the whole thing. And it is curious to note that from the slaves themselves they received, not merely very little assistance, but hardly any sympathy even; and when at the close of the war the slaves found themselves free, found themselves indeed so absolutely free that they were free to starve, many of them bitterly regretted the new state of things. To the thinker, the most tragic fact in the whole of the French Revolution is not that Marie Antoinette was killed for being a queen, but that the starved peasant of the Vendee voluntarily went out to die for the hideous cause of feudalism.

It is clear, then, that no Authoritarian Socialism will do. For, while under the present system a very large number of people can lead lives of a certain amount of freedom and expression and happiness, under an industrial barrack system, or a system of economic tyranny, nobody would be able to have any such freedom at all. It is to be regretted that a portion of our community should be practically in slavery, but to propose to solve the problem by enslaving the entire community is childish. Every man must be left quite free to choose his own work. No form of compulsion must be exercised over him. If there is, his work will not be good for him, will not be good in itself, and will not be good for others. And by work I simply mean activity of any kind.

I hardly think that any Socialist, nowadays, would seriously propose that an inspector should call every morning at each house to see that each citizen rose up and did manual labour for eight hours. Humanity has got beyond that stage, and reserves such a form of life for the people whom, in a very arbitrary manner, it chooses to call criminals. But I confess that many of the socialistic views that I have come across seem to me to be tainted with ideas of authority, if not of actual compulsion. Of course authority and compulsion are out of the question. All association must be quite voluntary. *It is only in voluntary association that man is fine.*

But it may be asked how Individualism, which is now more or less dependent on the existence of private property for its development, will benefit by the abolition of such private property. The answer is very simple. It is true that, under existing conditions, a few men who have had private means of their own, such as Byron, Shelley, Browning, Victor Hugo, Baudelaire, and others, have been able to realise their personality more or less completely. Not one of these men ever did a single day's work for hire. They were relieved from poverty. They had an immense advantage. The question is whether it would be for the good of Individualism that such an advantage should be taken away. Let us suppose that it is taken away. What happens then to Individualism? How will it benefit?

It will benefit in this way. Under the new conditions Individualism will be far freer, far finer and far more intensified than it is now. I am not talking of the great imaginatively-realised individualism of such poets as I have mentioned, but of the great actual Individualism latent and potential in mankind generally. For the recognition of private property has really harmed Individualism, and obscured it, by confusing a man with what he possesses. It has led Individualism entirely astray. It has made gain not growth its aim. So that man thought that the important thing was to have, and did not know that the important thing is to be. *The true perfection of man lies, not in what man has, but in what man is.* Private property has crushed true Individualism, and set up an Individualism that is false. It has debarred one part of the community from being individual by starving them. It has debarred the other part of the community from being individual, by putting them on the wrong road and encumbering them. Indeed, so completely has man's personality been absorbed by his possessions that the English law has always treated offences against a man's property with far more severity than offences against his person, and property is still the test of complete citizenship. The industry necessary for the making [of] money is also very demoralising. In a community like ours, where property confers immense distinction, social position, honour, respect, titles, and other pleasant things of the kind, man, being naturally ambitious, makes it his aim to accumulate this property, and goes on wearily and tediously accumulating it long after he has got far more than he wants, or can use, or enjoy, or perhaps even know of. Man will kill himself by over-work in order to secure property, and really, considering the enormous advantages that property brings, one is hardly surprised. One's regret is that society should be constructed on such a basis that man has been forced into a groove in which he cannot freely develop what is wonderful, and fascinating, and delightful in him—in which, in fact, he misses the true pleasure and joy of living. He is also, under existing conditions, very insecure. An enormously wealthy merchant may be—often is—at every moment of his life at the mercy of things that are not under his control. If the wind blows an extra point or so, or the weather suddenly changes, or some trivial thing happens, his ship may go down, his speculations may go wrong, and he finds himself a poor man, with his social position quite gone. Now, nothing should be able to harm a man except himself. Nothing should be able to rob a man at all. What a man really has, is what is in him. What is outside of him should be a matter of no importance.

With the abolition of private property, then, we shall have true beautiful, healthy Individualism. Nobody will waste his life in accumulating things and the symbols for things. One will live. To live is the rarest thing in the world. Most people exist, that is all.

[. . .]

It will be a marvellous thing—the true personality of man—when we see it. It will grow naturally and simply, flower-like, or as a tree grows. It will not be at discord. It will never argue or dispute. It will not prove things. It will know everything. And yet it will not busy itself about knowledge. It will have wisdom. Its value will not be measured by material things. It will have nothing. And yet it will have everything, and whatever one takes from it, it will still have, so rich will it be. It will not be always meddling with others, or asking them to be like itself. It will love them because they will be different. And yet while it will not meddle with others it will help all, as a beautiful thing helps us, by being what it is. The personality of man will be very wonderful. It will be as wonderful as the personality of a child.

In its development it will be assisted by Christianity, if men desire that; but if men do not desire that, it will develop none the less surely. For it will not worry itself about the past, nor care whether things happened or did not happen. Nor will it admit any laws but its own laws; nor any authority but its own authority. Yet it will love those who sought to intensify it, and speak often of them. And of these Christ was one.

"Know Thyself" was written over the portal of the antique world. Over the portal of the new world, "Be Thyself" shall be written. And the message of Christ to man was simply "Be thyself." That is the secret of Christ.

[. . .]

Yes; there are suggestive things in Individualism. Socialism annihilates family life, for instance. With the abolition of private property, marriage in its present form must disappear. This is part of the programme. Individualism accepts this and makes it fine. It converts the abolition of legal restraint into a form of freedom that will help the full development of personality, and make the love of man and woman more wonderful, more beautiful, and more ennobling. Jesus knew this. He rejected the claims of family life, although they existed in his day and community in a very marked form. "Who is my mother? Who are my brothers?" he said, when he was told that they wished to speak to him. When one of his followers asked leave to go and bury his father, "Let the dead bury the dead," was his terrible answer. He would allow no claim whatsoever to be made on personality.

And so he who would lead a Christlike life is he who is perfectly and absolutely himself. He may be a great poet, or a great man of science; or a young student at a University, or one who watches sheep upon a moor; or a maker of dramas, like Shakespeare, or a thinker about God, like Spinoza; or a child who plays in a garden, or a fisherman who throws his nets into the sea. It does not matter what he is, as long as he realises the perfection of the soul that is within him. All imitation in morals and in life is wrong. Through the streets of Jerusalem at the present day crawls one who is mad and carries a wooden cross on his shoulders. He is a symbol of the lives that are marred by imitation. Father Damien was Christlike when he went out to live with the lepers, because in such service he realised fully what was best in him. But he was not more Christlike than Wagner, when he realised his soul in music; or than Shelley, when he realised his soul in song. There is no one type for man. There are as many perfections as there are imperfect men. And while to the claims of charity a man may yield and yet be free, to the claims of conformity no man may yield and remain free at all.

Individualism, then, is what through Socialism we are to attain to. As a natural result the State must give up all idea of government. It must give it up because, as a wise man once said many centuries before Christ, there is such a thing as leaving mankind alone; there is no such thing as governing mankind. *All modes of government are failures.* Despotism is unjust to everybody, including the despot, who was probably made for better things. Oligarchies are unjust to the many, and ochlocracies are unjust to the few. High hopes were once formed of democracy; but democracy means simply the bludgeoning of the people by the people for the people. It has been found out. I must say that it was high time, for all authority is quite degrading. It degrades those who exercise it, and degrades those over whom it is exercised. When it is violently, grossly and cruelly used, it produces a good effect, by creating, or at any rate bringing out, the spirit of revolt and individualism that is to kill it. When it is used with a certain amount of kindness, and accompanied by prizes and rewards, it is dreadfully demoralising. People, in that case, are less conscious of the horrible pressure that is being put on them, and so go through their lives in a sort of coarse comfort, like petted animals, without ever realising that they are probably thinking other people's thoughts, living by other people's standards, wearing practically what one may call other people's second-hand clothes, and never being themselves for a single moment. "He who would be free," says a fine thinker, "must not conform." And authority, by bribing people to conform, produces a very gross kind of over-fed barbarism amongst us.

With authority, punishment will pass away. This will be a great gain—a gain, in fact, of incalculable value. As one reads history, not in the expurgated editions written for schoolboys and passmen, but in the original authorities of each time, one is absolutely sickened, not by the crimes that the wicked have committed, but by the punishments that the good have inflicted; *and a community is infinitely more brutalised by the habitual employment of punishment, than it is by the occasional occurrence of crime.* It obviously follows that the more punishment is inflicted the more crime is produced, and most modern legislation has clearly recognised this, and has made it its task to diminish punishment as far as it thinks it can. Wherever it has really diminished it, the results have always been extremely good. The less punishment, the less crime. When there is no punishment at all, crime will either cease to exist, or if it occurs, will be treated by physicians as a very distressing form of dementia, to be cured by care and kindness. For what are called criminals nowadays are not criminals at all. Starvation, and not sin, is the parent of modern crime. That indeed is the reason why our criminals are, as a class, so absolutely uninteresting from any psychological point of view. They are not marvellous Macbeths and terrible Vautrins. They are merely what ordinary, respectable, commonplace people would be if they had not got enough to eat. When private property is abolished there will be no necessity for crime, no demand for it; it will cease to exist. Of course all crimes are not crimes against property, though such are the crimes that the English law, valuing what a man has more than what a man is, punishes with the harshest and most horrible severity, if we except the crime of murder, and regard death as worse than penal servitude, a point on which our criminals, I believe, disagree. But though a crime may not be against property, it may spring from the misery and rage and depression produced by our wrong system of property-holding, and so, when that system is abolished, will disappear. When each member of the community has sufficient for his wants, and is not interfered with by his neighbour, it will not be an object of any interest to him to interfere with any one else. Jealousy, which is an extraordinary source of crime in modern life, is an emotion closely bound up with our conceptions of property, and under Socialism and Individualism will die out. It is remarkable that in communistic tribes jealousy is entirely unknown.

Now as the State is not to govern, it may be asked what the State is to do. The State is to be a voluntary association that will organise labour, and be the manufacturer and distributor of necessary commodities. *The State is to make what is useful. The individual is to make what is beautiful.* And as I have mentioned the word labour, I cannot help saying that a great deal of nonsense is being written and talked nowadays about the dignity of manual labour. There is nothing necessarily dignified about manual labour at all, and most of it is absolutely degrading. It is mentally and morally injurious to man to do anything in which he does not find pleasure, and many forms of labour are quite pleasureless activities, and should be regarded as such. To sweep a slushy crossing for eight hours on a day when the east wind is blowing is a disgusting occupation. To sweep it with mental, moral or physical dignity seems to me to be impossible. To sweep it with joy would be appalling. Man is made for something better than disturbing dirt. All work of that kind should be done by a machine.

And I have no doubt that it will be so. Up to the present, man has been, to a certain extent, the slave of machinery, and there is something tragic in the fact that as soon as man had invented a machine to do his work he began to starve. This, however, is, of course, the result of our property system and our system of competition. One man owns a machine which does the work of five hundred men. Five hundred men are, in consequence, thrown out of employment, and having no work to do, become hungry and take to thieving. The one man secures the produce of the machine and keeps it, and has five hundred times as much as he should have, and probably, which is of much more importance, a great deal more than he really wants. Were that machine the property of all, every one would benefit by it. It would be an immense advantage to the community. All unintellectual labour, all monotonous, dull labour, all labour that deals with dreadful things, and involves unpleasant conditions, must be done by machinery. Machinery must work for us in coal mines, and do all sanitary services, and be the stoker of steamers, and clean the streets, and run messages on wet days, and do anything that is tedious or distressing. *At present machinery competes against man. Under proper conditions machinery will serve man.*
[. . .]

Now, I have said that the community by means of organisation of machinery will supply the useful things, and that the beautiful things will be made by the individual. This is not merely necessary, but it is the only possible way by which we can get either the one or the other. An individual who has to make things for the use of others, and with reference to their wants and their wishes, does not work with interest, and consequently cannot put into his work what is best in him. Upon the other hand, whenever a community or a powerful section of a community, or a government of any kind, attempts to dictate to the artist what he is to do, Art either entirely vanishes, or becomes stereotyped, or degenerates into a low and ignoble form of craft. *A work of art is the unique result of a unique temperament. Its beauty comes from the fact that the author is what he is. It has nothing to do with the fact that other people want what they want.* Indeed, the moment that an artist takes notice of what other people want, and tries to supply the demand, he ceases to be an artist, and becomes a dull or an amusing craftsman, an honest or a dishonest tradesman. He has no further claim to be considered as an artist. *Art is the most intense mode of individualism that the world has known.* I am inclined to say that it is the only real mode of individualism that the world has known. Crime, which, under certain conditions, may seem to have created individualism, must take cognisance of other people and interfere with them. It belongs to the sphere of action. But alone, without any reference to his neighbours, without any interference, the artist can fashion a beautiful thing; and if he does not do it solely for his own pleasure, he is not an artist at all.

And it is to be noted that it is the fact that Art is this intense form of individualism that makes the public try to exercise over it an authority that is as immoral as it is ridiculous, and as corrupting as it is contemptible. It is not quite their fault. The public has always, and in every age, been badly brought up. They are continually asking Art to be popular, to please their want of taste, to flatter their absurd vanity, to tell them what they have been told before, to show them what they ought to be tired of seeing, to amuse them when they feel heavy after eating too much, and to distract their thoughts when they are wearied of their own stupidity. *Now Art should never try to be popular. The public should try to make itself artistic.* There is a very wide difference. If a man of science were told that the results of his experiments, and the conclusions that he arrived at, should be of such a character that they would not upset the received popular notions on the subject, or disturb popular prejudice, or hurt the sensibilities of people who knew nothing about science; if a philosopher were told that he had a perfect right to speculate in the highest spheres of thought, provided that he arrived at the same conclusions as were held by those who had never thought in any sphere at all—well, nowadays the man of science and the philosopher would be considerably amused. Yet it is really a very few years since both philosophy and science were subjected to brutal popular control, to authority in fact—the authority of either the general ignorance of the community, or the terror and greed for power of an ecclesiastical or governmental class. Of course, we have to a very great extent got rid of any attempt on the part of the community, or the Church, or the Government, to interfere with the individualism of speculative thought, but the attempt to interfere with the individualism of imaginative art still lingers. In fact, it does more than linger: it is aggressive, offensive, and brutalising.

In England, the arts that have escaped best are the arts in which the public takes no interest. Poetry is an instance of what I mean. We have been able to have fine poetry in England because the public does not read it, and consequently does not influence it. The public likes to insult poets because they are individual, but once they have insulted them they leave them alone. In the case of the novel and the drama, arts in which the public does take an interest, the result of the exercise of popular authority has been absolutely ridiculous. No country produces such badly written fiction, such tedious, common work in the novel-form, such silly, vulgar plays as in England. It must necessarily be so. The popular standard is of such a character that no artist can get to it. It is at once too easy and too difficult to be a popular novelist. It is too easy, because the requirements of the public as far as plot, style, psychology, treatment of life and treatment of literature are concerned, are within the reach of the very meanest capacity and the most uncultivated mind. It is too difficult, because to meet such requirements the artist would have to do violence to his temperament, would have to write not for the artistic joy of writing, but for the amusement of half-educated people, and so would have to suppress his individualism, forget his culture, annihilate his style, and surrender everything that is valuable in him. In the case of the drama, things are a little better: the theatre-going public likes the obvious, it is true, but it does not like the tedious; and burlesque and farcical comedy, the two most popular forms, are distinct forms of art. Delightful work may be produced under burlesque and farcical conditions, and in work of this kind the artist in England is allowed very great freedom. It is when one comes to the higher forms of the drama that the result of popular control is seen. The one thing that the public dislikes is novelty. Any attempt to extend the subject-matter of art is extremely distasteful to the public; and yet the vitality and progress of art depend in a large measure on the continual extension of subject-matter. The public dislikes novelty because it is afraid of it. It represents to them a model of Individualism, an assertion on the part of the artist that he selects his own subject, and treats it as he chooses. The public is quite right in its attitude. Art is Individualism, and Individualism is a disturbing and disintegrating force. Therein lies its immense value. For what it seeks to disturb is monotony of type, slavery of custom, tyranny of habit, and the reduction of man to the level of a machine. In Art, the public accepts what has been, because they cannot alter it, not because they appreciate it. They swallow their classics whole, and never taste them. They endure them as the inevitable, and, as they cannot mar them, they mouth about them. Strangely enough, or not strangely, according to one's own views, this acceptance of the classics does a great deal of harm. The uncritical admiration of the Bible and Shakespeare in England is an instance of what I mean. With regard to the Bible, considerations of ecclesiastical authority enter into the matter, so that I need not dwell upon the point.

But in the case of Shakespeare it is quite obvious that the public really sees neither the beauties nor the defects of his plays. If they saw the beauties, they would not object to the development of the drama; and if they saw the defects, they would not object to the development of the drama either. *The fact is, the public makes use of the classics of a country as a means of checking the progress of Art.* They degrade the classics into authorities. They use them as bludgeons for preventing the free expression of Beauty in new forms. They are always asking a writer why he does not write like somebody else, or a painter why he does not paint like somebody else, quite oblivious of the fact that if either of them did anything of the kind he would cease to be an artist. A fresh mode of Beauty is absolutely distasteful to them, and whenever it appears they get so angry and bewildered that they always use two stupid expressions—one is that the work of art is grossly unintelligible; the other, that the work of art is grossly immoral. [. . .]

In old days men had the rack. Now they have the press. That is an improvement certainly. But still it is very bad, and wrong, and demoralising. Somebody—was it Burke?—called journalism the fourth estate. That was true at the time, no doubt. But at the present moment it really is the only estate. It has eaten up the other three. The Lords Temporal say nothing, the Lords Spiritual have nothing to say, and the House of Commons has nothing to say and says it. We are dominated by Journalism. In America the President reigns for four years, and Journalism governs for ever and ever. Fortunately in America journalism has carried its authority to the grossest and most brutal extreme. As a natural consequence it has begun to create a spirit of revolt. People are amused by it, or disgusted by it, according to their temperaments. But it is no longer the real force it was. It is not seriously treated. In England, Journalism, not, except in a few well-known instances, having been carried to such excesses of brutality, is still a great factor, a really remarkable power. The tyranny that it proposes to exercise over people's private lives seems to me to be quite extraordinary. *The fact is, that the public has an insatiable curiosity to know everything, except what is worth knowing.* Journalism, conscious of this, and having tradesmanlike habits, supplies their demands. In centuries before ours the public nailed the ears of journalists to the pump. That was quite hideous. In this century journalists have nailed their own ears to the keyhole. That is much worse. And what aggravates the mischief is that the journalists who are most to blame are not the amusing journalists who write for what are called Society papers. The harm is done by the serious, thoughtful, earnest journalists, who solemnly, as they are doing at present, will drag before the eyes of the public some incident in the private life of a great statesman, of a man who is a leader of political thought as he is a creator of political force, and invite the public to discuss the incident, to exercise authority in the matter, to give their views, and not merely to give their views, but to carry them into action, to dictate to the man upon all other points, to dictate to his party, to dictate to his country, in fact to make themselves ridiculous, offensive and harmful. The private lives of men and women should not be told to the public. The public has nothing to do with them at all. In France they manage these things better. There they do not allow the details of the trials that take place in the divorce courts to be published for the amusement or criticism of the public. All that the public is allowed to know is that the divorce has taken place and was granted on petition of one or other or both of the married parties concerned. In France, in fact, they limit the journalist, and allow the artist almost perfect freedom. *Here we allow absolute freedom to the journalist, and entirely limit the artist.* English public opinion, that is to say, tries to constrain and impede and warp the man who makes things that are beautiful in effect, and compels the journalist to retail things that are ugly, or disgusting, or revolting in fact, so that we have the most serious journalists in the world and the most indecent newspapers.

[. . .]

It is evident, then, that all authority in such things is bad. People sometimes inquire what form of government is most suitable for an artist to live under. To this question there is only one answer. *The form of government that is most suitable to the artist is no government at all.* Authority over him and his art is ridiculous. It has been stated that under despotisms artists have produced lovely work. This is not quite so. Artists have visited despots, not as subjects to be tyrannised over, but as wandering wonder-makers, as fascinating vagrant personalities, to be entertained and charmed and suffered to be at peace, and allowed to create. There is this to be said in favour of the despot, that he, being an individual, may have culture, while the mob, being a monster, has none. One who is an Emperor and King may stoop down to pick up a brush for a painter, but when the democracy stoops down it is merely to throw mud. And yet the democracy have not so far to stoop as the emperor. In fact, when they want to throw mud they have not to stoop at all. But there is no necessity to separate the monarch from the mob; all authority is equally bad.

There are three kinds of despots. There is the despot who tyrannises over the body. There is the despot who tyrannises over the soul. There is the despot who tyrannises over soul and body alike. The first is called the Prince. The second is called the Pope. The third is called the People. The Prince may be cultivated. Many Princes have been. Yet in the Prince there is danger. One thinks of Dante at the bitter feast in Verona, of Tasso in Ferrara's madman's cell. It is better for the artist not to live with Princes. The Pope may be cultivated. Many Popes have been; the bad Popes have been. The bad Popes loved Beauty, almost as passionately, nay, with as much passion as the good Popes hated Thought. To the wickedness of the Papacy humanity owes much. The goodness of the Papacy owes a terrible debt to humanity. Yet, though the Vatican has kept the rhetoric of its thunders and lost the rod of its lightning, it is better for the artist not to live with Popes. It was a Pope who said of Cellini to a conclave of Cardinals that common laws and common authority were not made for men such as he; but it was a Pope who thrust Cellini into prison, and kept him there till he sickened with rage, and created unreal visions for himself, and saw the gilded sun enter his room, and grew so enamoured of it that he sought to escape, and crept out from tower to tower, and falling through dizzy air at dawn, maimed himself, and was by a vine-dresser covered with vine leaves, and carried in a cart to one who, loving beautiful things, had care of him. There is danger in Popes. And as for the People, what of them and their authority? Perhaps of them and their authority one has spoken enough. Their authority is a thing blind, deaf, hideous, grotesque, tragic, amusing, serious and obscene. It is impossible for the artist to live with the People. All despots bribe. The people bribe and brutalise. Who told them to exercise authority? They were made to live, to listen, and to love. Some one has done them a great wrong. They have marred themselves by imitation of their inferiors. They have taken the sceptre of the Prince. How should they use it? They have taken the triple tiara of the Pope. How should they carry its burden? They are as a clown whose heart is broken. They are as a priest whose soul is not yet born. Let all who love Beauty pity them. Though they themselves love not Beauty, yet let them pity themselves. Who taught them the trick of tyranny?

There are many other things that one might point out. One might point out how the Renaissance was great, because it sought to solve no social problem, and busied itself not about such things, but suffered the individual to develop freely, beautifully and naturally, and so had great and individual artists, and great and individual men. One might point out how Louis xiv., by creating the modern state, destroyed the individualism of the artist, and made things monstrous in their monotony of repetition, and contemptible in their conformity to rule, and destroyed throughout all France all those fine freedoms of expression that had made tradition new in beauty, and new modes one with antique form. But the past is of no importance. The present is of no importance. It is with the future that we have to deal. For the past is what man should not have been. The present is what man ought not to be. The future is what artists are.

It will, of course, be said that such a scheme as is set forth here is quite unpractical, and goes against human nature. This is perfectly true. It is unpractical, and it goes against human nature. This is why it is worth carrying out, and that is why one proposes it. For what is a practical scheme? *A practical scheme is either a scheme that is already in existence, or a scheme that could be carried out under existing conditions.* But it is exactly the existing conditions that one objects to; and any scheme that could accept these conditions is wrong and foolish. The conditions will be done away with, and human nature will change. The only thing that one really knows about human nature is that it changes. Change is the one quality we can predicate of it. The systems that fail are those that rely on the permanency of human nature, and not on its growth and development. The error of Louis XIV. was that he thought human nature would always be the same. The result of his error was the French Revolution. It was an admirable result. All the results of the mistakes of governments are quite admirable.

[. . .]

The evolution of man is slow. The injustice of men is great. It was necessary that pain should be put forward as a mode of self-realisation. Even now, in some places in the world, the message of Christ is necessary. No one who lived in modern Russia could possibly realise his perfection except by pain. A few Russian artists have realised themselves in Art, in a fiction that is mediæval in character, because its dominant note is the realisation of men through suffering. But for those who are not artists, and to whom there is no mode of life but the actual life of fact, pain is the only door to perfection. A Russian who lives happily under the present system of government in Russia must either believe that man has no soul, or that, if he has, it is not worth developing. A Nihilist who rejects all authority, because he knows authority to be evil, and who welcomes all pain, because through that he realises his personality, is a real Christian. To him the Christian ideal is a true thing.

And yet, Christ did not revolt against authority. He accepted the imperial authority of the Roman Empire and paid tribute. He endured the ecclesiastical authority of the Jewish Church, and would not repel its violence by any violence of his own. He had, as I said before, no scheme for the re-construction of society. But the modern world has schemes. It proposes to do away with poverty and the suffering that it entails. It desires to get rid of pain and the suffering that pain entails. It trusts to Socialism and to Science as its methods. What it aims at is an Individualism expressing itself through joy. This Individualism will be larger, fuller, lovelier than any Individualism has ever been. Pain is not the ultimate mode of perfection. It is merely provisional and a protest. It has reference to wrong, unhealthy, unjust surroundings. When the wrong, and the disease and the injustice are removed, it will have no further place. It will have done its work. It was a great work, but it is almost over. Its sphere lessens every day.

Nor will man miss it. *For what man has sought for is, indeed, neither pain nor pleasure, but simply Life.* Man has sought to live intensely, fully, perfectly. When he can do so without exercising restraint on others, or suffering it ever, and his activities are all pleasurable to him, he will be saner, healthier, more civilised, more himself. Pleasure is Nature's test, her sign of approval. When man is happy, he is in harmony with himself and his environment. The new Individualism, for whose service Socialism, whether it wills it or not, is working, will be perfect harmony. It will be what the Greeks sought for, but could not, except in Thought, realise completely, because they had slaves, and fed them; it will be what the Renaissance sought for, but could not realise completely, except in Art, because they had slaves, and starved them. It will be complete, and through it each man will attain to his perfection. The new Individualism is the new Hellenism.

T. H. HUXLEY (1825–95)

Evolution and Ethics (1893)

*H*uxley's was the second in the prestigious series of Romanes Lectures at Oxford, the first having been delivered by Gladstone the previous year. The choice of Gladstone was especially odd in view of the conditions laid down by George Romanes: a prohibition of any discussion of politics and religion, the very subjects about which Gladstone was most passionate. As skilled a rhetorician as a politician, Gladstone managed to address his theme, "Medieval Universities," while skirting any explicit (although not implicit) mention of religion.

Huxley also had to perform an "egg-dance," as he said, on the subject of "Evolution and Ethics." Before delivering the lecture, he had repeatedly to reassure Romanes that there was "no allusion to politics" in it and that his only reference to religion was to Buddhism, and this only to the "speculative and ethical side" of it. [1] In fact, politics did appear, if not overtly, because his good friend Herbert Spencer had politicized evolution itself in the form of Social Darwinism, making the "struggle for existence" the proper basis for society—a doctrine Huxley had criticized at some length five years earlier in his essay of that title. Although his Romanes Lecture did not mention Spencer by name, Huxley clearly had him in mind when

T. H. Huxley (1825–95), "Evolution and Ethics," Romanes Lecture, 1893, published as a pamphlet. Reprinted in Huxley, *Evolution and Ethics and Other Essays* (New York, 1898), pp. 46–86.
1. Leonard Huxley, *Life and Letters of Thomas Henry Huxley* (London, 1903), III, 296, 293.

he spoke of the "fanatical individualism of our time [that] attempts to apply the analogy of cosmic nature to society."

"Evolution and Ethics" might more accurately have been titled "Evolution versus Ethics," the ethical progress of society depending not on imitating the evolutionary process but precisely on combating it. Huxley himself described it as "a very orthodox discourse on the text, 'Satan, the Prince of the world,'" a warning against sanctioning in society the evils of nature. [2] The following year, reprinting the essay, he prefaced it with a "Prolegomena" reaffirming the theory of evolution as an explanation for the evolution of species, rather than a prescription for mankind.

T here is a delightful child's story, known by the title of "Jack and the Beanstalk," with which my contemporaries who are present will be familiar. But so many of our grave and reverend juniors have been brought up on severer intellectual diet, and, perhaps, have become acquainted with fairyland only through primers of comparative mythology, that it may be needful to give an outline of the tale. It is a legend of a bean-plant, which grows and grows until it reaches the high heavens and there spreads out into a vast canopy of foliage. The hero, being moved to climb the stalk, discovers that the leafy expanse supports a world composed of the same elements as that below, but yet strangely new; and his adventures there, on which I may not dwell, must have completely changed his views of the nature of things; though the story, not having been composed by, or for, philosophers, has nothing to say about views.

My present enterprise has a certain analogy to that of the daring adventurer. I beg you to accompany me in an attempt to reach a world which, to many, is probably strange, by the help of a bean. It is, as you know, a simple, inert-looking thing. Yet, if planted under proper conditions, of which sufficient warmth is one of the most important, it manifests active powers of a very remarkable kind. A small green seedling emerges, rises to the surface of the soil, rapidly increases in size and, at the same time, undergoes a series of metamorphoses which do not excite our wonder as much as those which meet us in legendary history, merely because they are to be seen every day and all day long.

By insensible steps, the plant builds itself up into a large and various fabric of root, stem, leaves, flowers, and fruit, every one moulded within and without in accordance with an extremely complex but, at the same time, minutely defined pattern. In each of these complicated structures, as in their smallest constituents, there is an immanent energy which, in harmony with that resident in all the others, incessantly works towards the maintenance of the whole and the efficient performance of the part which it has to play in the economy of nature. But no sooner has the edifice, reared with such exact elaboration,

---

2. Ibid., III, 299, 301.

attained completeness, than it begins to crumble. By degrees, the plant withers and disappears from view, leaving behind more or fewer apparently inert and simple bodies, just like the bean from which it sprang; and, like it, endowed with the potentiality of giving rise to a similar cycle of manifestations.

Neither the poetic nor the scientific imagination is put to much strain in the search after analogies with this process of going forth and, as it were, returning to the starting-point. It may be likened to the ascent and descent of a slung stone, or the course of an arrow along its trajectory. Or we may say that the living energy takes first an upward and then a downward road. Or it may seem preferable to compare the expansion of the germ into the full-grown plant, to the unfolding of a fan, or to the rolling forth and widening of a stream; and thus to arrive at the conception of "development," or "evolution." Here as elsewhere, names are "noise and smoke"; the important point is to have a clear and adequate conception of the fact signified by a name. And, in this case, the fact is the Sisyphæan process, in the course of which, the living and growing plant passes from the relative simplicity and latent potentiality of the seed to the full epiphany of a highly differentiated type, thence to fall back to simplicity and potentiality.

The value of a strong intellectual grasp of the nature of this process lies in the circumstances that what is true of the bean is true of living things in general. From very low forms up to the highest—in the animal no less than in the vegetable kingdom—the process of life presents the same appearance of cyclical evolution. Nay, we have but to cast our eyes over the rest of the world and cyclical change presents itself on all sides. It meets us in the water that flows to the sea and returns to the springs; in the heavenly bodies that wax and wane, go and return to their places; in the inexorable sequence of the ages of man's life; in that successive rise, apogee, and fall of dynasties and of states which is the most prominent topic of civil history.

As no man fording a swift stream can dip his foot twice into the same water, so no man can, with exactness, affirm of anything in the sensible world that it is. As he utters the words, nay, as he thinks them, the predicate ceases to be applicable; the present has become the past; the "is" should be "was." And the more we learn of the nature of things, the more evident is it that what we call rest is only unperceived activity; that seeming peace is silent but strenuous battle. In every part, at every moment, the state of the cosmos is the expression of a transitory adjustment of contending forces; a scene of strife, in which all the combatants fall in turn. What is true of each part, is true of the whole. Natural knowledge tends more and more to the conclusion that "all the choir of heaven and furniture of the earth" are the transitory forms of parcels of cosmic substance wending along the road of evolution, from nebulous potentiality, through endless growths of sun and planet and satellite; through all varieties of matter; through infinite diversities of life and thought; possibly, through modes of being of which we neither have a conception, nor are competent to form any, back to the indefinable latency from which they arose. Thus the most obvious attribute of the cosmos is its impermanence. It assumes the aspect not so much of a permanent entity as of a changeful process, in which naught endures save the flow of energy and the rational order which pervades it.

We have climbed our bean-stalk and have reached a wonderland in which the common and the familiar become things new and strange. In the exploration of the cosmic process thus typified, the highest intelligence of man finds inexhaustible employment; giants are subdued to our service; and the spiritual affections of the contemplative philosopher are engaged by beauties worthy of eternal constancy.

But there is another aspect of the cosmic process, so perfect as a mechanism, so beautiful as a work of art. Where the cosmopoietic energy works through sentient beings, there arises, among its other manifestations, that which we call pain or suffering. This baleful product of evolution increases in quantity and in intensity, with advancing grades of animal organization, until it attains its highest level in man. Further, the consummation is not reached in man, the mere animal; nor in man, the whole or half savage; but only in man, the member of an organized polity. And it is a necessary consequence of his attempt to live in this way; that is, under those conditions which are essential to the full development of his noblest powers.

Man, the animal, in fact, has worked his way to the headship of the sentient world, and has become the superb animal which he is, in virtue of his success in the struggle for existence. The conditions having been of a certain order, man's organization has adjusted itself to them better than that of his competitors in the cosmic strife. In the case of mankind, the self-assertion, the unscrupulous seizing upon all that can be grasped, the tenacious holding of all that can be kept, which constitute the essence of the struggle for existence, have answered. For his successful progress, throughout the savage state, man has been largely indebted to those qualities which he shares with the ape and the tiger; his exceptional physical organization; his cunning, his sociability, his curiosity, and his imitativeness; his ruthless and ferocious destructivenes when his anger is roused by opposition.

But, in proportion as men have passed from anarchy to social organization, and in proportion as civilization has grown in worth, these deeply in-grained serviceable qualities have become defects. After the manner of success-ful persons, civilized man would gladly kick down the ladder by which he has climbed. He would be only too pleased to see "the ape and tiger die." But they decline to suit his convenience; and the unwelcome intrusion of these boon companions of his hot youth into the ranged existence of civil life adds pains and griefs, innumerable and immeasurably great, to those which the cosmic process necessarily brings on the mere animal. In fact, civilized man brands all these ape and tiger promptings with the name of sins; he punishes many of the acts which flow from them as crimes; and, in extreme cases, he does his best to put an end to the survival of the fittest of former days by axe and rope.

I have said that civilized man has reached this point; the assertion is perhaps too broad and general; I had better put it that ethical man has attained thereto. The science of ethics professes to furnish us with a reasoned rule of life; to tell us what is right action and why it is so. Whatever differences of opinion may exist among experts, there is a general consensus that the ape and tiger methods of the struggle for existence are not reconcilable with sound ethical principles.

The hero of our story descended the bean-stalk, and came back to the common world, where fare and work were alike hard; where ugly competitors were much commoner than beautiful princesses; and where the everlasting battle with self was much less sure to be crowned with victory than a turn-to with a giant. We have done the like. Thousands upon thousands of our fellows, thousands of years ago, have preceded us in finding themselves face to face with the same dread problem of evil. They also have seen that the cosmic process is evolution; that it is full of wonder, full of beauty, and, at the same time, full of pain. They have sought to discover the bearing of these great facts on ethics; to find out whether there is, or is not, a sanction for morality in the ways of the cosmos.

Theories of the universe, in which the conception of evolution plays a leading part, were extant at least six centuries before our era. Certain knowledge of them, in the fifth century, reaches us from localities as distant as the valley of the Ganges and the Asiatic coasts of the Aegean. To the early philosophers of Hindostan, no less than to those of Ionia, the salient and characteristic feature of the phenomenal world was its changefulness; the unresting flow of all things, through birth to visible being and thence to not being, in which they could discern no sign of a beginning and for which they saw no prospect of an ending. It was no less plain to some of these antique forerunners of modern philosophy that suffering is the badge of all the tribe of sentient things; that it is no accidental accompaniment, but an essential constituent of the cosmic process. The energetic Greek might find fierce joys in a world in which "strife is father and king"; but the old Aryan spirit was subdued to quietism in the Indian sage; the mist of suffering which spread over humanity hid everything else from his view; to him life was one with suffering and suffering with life.

In Hindostan, as in Ionia, a period of relatively high and tolerably stable civilization had succeeded long ages of semi-barbarism and struggle. Out of wealth and security had come leisure and refinement, and, close at their heels, had followed the malady of thought. To the struggle for bare existence, which never ends, though it may be alleviated and partially disguised for a fortunate few, succeeded the struggle to make existence intelligible and to bring the order of things into harmony with the moral sense of man, which also never ends, but, for the thinking few, becomes keener with every increase of knowledge and with every step towards the realization of a worthy ideal of life.

Two thousand five hundred years ago, the value of civilization was as apparent as it is now; then, as now, it was obvious that only in the garden of an orderly polity can the finest fruits humanity is capable of bearing be produced. But it had also become evident that the blessings of culture were not unmixed. The garden was apt to turn into a hothouse. The stimulation of the senses, the pampering of the emotions, endlessly multiplied the sources of pleasure. The constant widening of the intellectual field indefinitely extended the range of that especially human faculty of looking before and after, which adds to the fleeting present those old and new worlds of the past and the future, wherein men dwell the more the higher their culture. But that very sharpening of the sense and that subtle refinement of emotion, which brought such a wealth of pleasures, were fatally attended by a proportional enlargement of the capacity for suffering; and the divine faculty of imagination, while it created new heavens and new earths, provided them with the corresponding hells of futile regret for the past and morbid anxiety for the future. Finally, the inevitable penalty of over-stimulation, exhaustion, opened the gates of civilization to its great enemy, ennui; the stale and flat weariness when man delights not, nor woman either; when all things are vanity and vexation; and life seems not worth living except to escape the bore of dying.

Even purely intellectual progress brings about its revenges. Problems settled in a rough and ready way by rude men, absorbed in action, demand renewed attention and show themselves to be still unread riddles when men have time to think. The beneficent demon, doubt, whose name is Legion and who dwells amongst the tombs of old faiths, enters into mankind and thenceforth refuses to be cast out. Sacred customs, venerable dooms of ancestral wisdom, hallowed by tradition and professing to hold good for all time, are put to the question. Cultured reflection asks for their credentials; judges them by its own standards; finally, gathers those of which it approves into ethical systems, in which the reasoning is rarely much more than a decent pretext for the adoption of foregone conclusions.

One of the oldest and most important elements in such systems is the conception of justice. Society is impossible unless those who are associated agree to observe certain rules of conduct towards one another; its stability depends on the steadiness with which they abide by that agreement; and, so far as they waver, that mutual trust which is the bond of society is weakened or destroyed. Wolves could not hunt in packs except for the real, though unexpressed, understanding that they should not attack one another during the chase. The most rudimentary polity is a pack of men living under the like tacit, or expressed, understanding; and having made the very important advance upon wolf society, that they agree to use the force of the whole body against individuals who violate it and in favour of those who observe it. This observance of a common understanding, with the consequent distribution of punishments and rewards according to accepted rules, received the name of justice, while the contrary was called injustice. Early ethics did not take much note of the animus of the violator of the rules. But civilization could not advance far, without the establishment of a capital distinction between the case of involuntary and that of wilful misdeed; between a merely wrong action and a guilty one. And, with increasing refinement of moral appreciation, the problem of desert, which arises out of this distinction, acquired more and more theoretical and practical importance. If life must be given for life, yet it was recognized that the unintentional slayer did not altogether deserve death; and, by a sort of compromise between the public and the private conception of justice, a sanctuary was provided in which he might take refuge from the avenger of blood.

The idea of justice thus underwent a gradual sublimation from punishment and reward according to acts, to punishment and reward according to desert; or, in other words, according to motive. Righteousness, that is, action from right motive, not only became synonymous with justice, but the positive constituent of innocence and the very heart of goodness.

Now when the ancient sage, whether Indian or Greek, who had attained to this conception of goodness, looked the world, and especially human life, in the face, he found it as hard as we do to bring the course of evolution into harmony with even the elementary requirements of the ethical ideal of the just and the good.

If there is one thing plainer than another, it is that neither the pleasures nor the pains of life, in the merely animal world, are distributed according to desert; for it is admittedly impossible for the lower orders of sentient beings to deserve either the one or the other. If there is a generalization from the facts of human life which has the assent of thoughtful men in every age and country, it is that the violator of ethical rules constantly escapes the punishment which he deserves; that the wicked flourishes like a green bay tree, while the righteous begs his bread; that the sins of the fathers are visited upon the children; that, in the realm of nature, ignorance is punished just as severely as wilful wrong; and that thousands upon thousands of innocent beings suffer for the crime, or the unintentional trespass of one.

Greek and Semite and Indian are agreed upon this subject. The book of Job is at one with the "Works and Days" and the Buddhist Sutras; the Psalmist and the Preacher of Israel, with the Tragic Poets of Greece. What is a more common motive of the ancient tragedy in fact, than the unfathomable injustice of the nature of things; what is more deeply felt to be true than its presentation of the destruction of the blameless by the work of his own hands, or by the fatal operation of the sins of others? Surely Oedipus was pure of heart; it was the natural sequence of events—the cosmic process—which drove him, in all innocence, to slay his father and become the husband of his mother, to the desolation of his people and his own headlong ruin. Or to step, for a moment, beyond the chronological limits I have set myself, what constitutes the sempiternal attraction of Hamlet but the appeal to deepest experience of that history of a no less blameless dreamer, dragged, in spite of himself, into a world out of joint; involved in a tangle of crime and misery, created by one of the prime agents of the cosmic process as it works in and through man?

Thus, brought before the tribunal of ethics, the cosmos might well seem to stand condemned. The conscience of man revolted against the moral indifference of nature, and the microcosmic atom should have found the illimitable macrocosm guilty. But few, or none, ventured to record that verdict.

In the great Semitic trial of this issue, Job takes refuge in silence and submission; the Indian and the Greek, less wise perhaps, attempt to reconcile the irreconcilable and plead for the defendant. To this end, the Greeks invented Theodicies; while the Indians devised what, in its ultimate form, must rather be termed a Cosmodicy. For, though Buddhism recognizes gods many and lords many, they are products of the cosmic process; and transitory, however long enduring, manifestations of its eternal activity. In the doctrine of transmigration, whatever its origin, Brahminical and Buddhist speculation found, ready to hand, the means of constructing a plausible vindication of the ways of the cosmos to man. If this world is full of pain and sorrow; if grief and evil fall, like the rain, upon both the just and the unjust; it is because, like the rain, they are links in the endless chain of natural causation by which past, present, and future are indissolubly connected; and there is no more injustice in the one case than in the other. Every sentient being is reaping as it has sown; if not in this life, then in one or other of the infinite series of antecedent existences of which it is the latest term. The present distribution of good and evil is, therefore, the algebraical sum of accumulated positive and negative deserts; or, rather, it depends on the floating balance of the account. For it was not thought necessary that a complete settlement should ever take place. Arrears might stand over as a sort of "hanging gale"; a period of celestial happiness just earned might be succeeded by ages of torment in a hideous nether world, the balance still overdue for some remote ancestral error.

Whether the cosmic process looks any more moral than at first, after such a vindication, may perhaps be questioned. Yet this plea of justification is not less plausible than others; and none but very hasty thinkers will reject it on the ground of inherent absurdity. Like the doctrine of evolution itself, that of transmigration has its roots in the world of reality; and it may claim such support as the great argument from analogy is capable of supplying.

Everyday experience familiarizes us with the facts which are grouped under the name of heredity. Every one of us bears upon him obvious marks of his parentage, perhaps of remoter relationships. More particularly, the sum of tendencies to act in a certain way, which we call "character," is often to be traced through a long series of progenitors and collaterals. So we may justly say that this "character"—this moral and intellectual essence of a man—does veritably pass over from one fleshly tabernacle to another, and does really transmigrate from generation to generation. In the new-born infant, the character of the stock lies latent, and the Ego is little more than a bundle of potentialities. But, very early, these become actualities; from childhood to age they manifest themselves in dulness or brightness, weakness or strength, viciousness or uprightness; and with each feature modified by confluence with another character, if by nothing else, the character passes on to its incarnation in new bodies.

The Indian philosophers called character, as thus defined, "karma." It is this karma which passed from life to life and linked them in the chain of transmigrations; and they held that it is modified in each life, not merely by confluence of parentage, but by its own acts. They were, in fact, strong believers in the theory, so much disputed just at present, of the hereditary transmission of acquired characters. That the manifestation of the tendencies of a character may be greatly facilitated, or impeded, by conditions, of which self-discipline, or the absence of it, are among the most important, is indubitable; but that the character itself is modified in this way is by no means so certain; it is not so sure that the transmitted character of an evil liver is worse, or that of a righteous man better, than that which he received. Indian philosophy, however, did not admit of any doubt on this subject; the belief in the influence of conditions, notably of self-discipline, on the karma was not merely a necessary postulate of its theory of retribution, but it presented the only way of escape from the endless round of transmigrations.

[. . .]

Let us now set our faces westwards, towards Asia Minor and Greece and Italy, to view the rise and progress of another philosophy, apparently independent, but no less pervaded by the conception of evolution.

The sages of Miletus were pronounced evolutionists; and, however dark may be some of the sayings of Heracleitus of Ephesus, who was probably a contemporary of Gautama, no better expressions of the essence of the modern doctrine of evolution can be found than are presented by some of his pithy aphorisms and striking metaphors. Indeed, many of my present auditors must have observed that, more than once, I have borrowed from him in the brief exposition of the theory of evolution with which this discourse commenced.

But when the focus of Greek intellectual activity shifted to Athens, the leading minds concentrated their attention upon ethical problems. Forsaking the study of the macrocosm for that of the microcosm, they lost the key to the thought of the great Ephesian, which, I imagine, is more intelligible to us than it was to Socrates, or to Plato. Socrates, more especially, set the fashion of a kind of inverse agnosticism, by teaching that the problems of physics lie beyond the reach of the human intellect; that the attempt to solve them is essentially vain; that the one worthy object of investigation is the problem of ethical life; and his example was followed by the Cynics and the later Stoics. Even the comprehensive knowledge and the penetrating intellect of Aristotle failed to suggest to him that in holding the eternity of the world, within its present range of mutation, he was making a retrogressive step. The scientific heritage of Heracleitus passed into the hands neither of Plato nor of Aristotle, but into those of Democritus. But the world was not yet ready to receive the great conceptions of the philosopher of Abdera. It was reserved for the Stoics to return to the track marked out by the earlier philosophers; and, professing themselves disciples of Heracleitus, to develop the idea of evolution systematically. In doing this, they not only omitted some characteristic features of their master's teaching, but they made additions altogether foreign to it. One of the most influential of these importations was the transcendental theism which had come into vogue. The restless, fiery energy, operating according to law, out of which all things emerge and into which they return, in the endless successive cycles of the great year; which creates and destroys worlds as a wanton child builds up, and anon levels, sand castles on the seashore; was metamorphosed into a material world-soul and decked out with all the attributes of ideal Divinity; not merely with infinite power and transcendent wisdom, but with absolute goodness.

The consequences of this step were momentous. For if the cosmos is the effect of an immanent, omnipotent, and infinitely beneficent cause, the existence in it of real evil, still less of necessarily inherent evil, is plainly inadmissible. Yet the universal experience of mankind testified then, as now, that, whether we look within us or without us, evil stares us in the face on all sides; that if anything is real, pain and sorrow and wrong are realities.

[...]

But the attempt of the Stoics to blind themselves to the reality of evil, as a necessary concomitant of the cosmic process, had less success than that of the Indian philosophers to exclude the reality of good from their purview. Unfortunately, it is much easier to shut one's eyes to good than to evil. Pain and sorrow knock at our doors more loudly than pleasure and happiness; and the prints of their heavy footsteps are less easily effaced. Before the grim realities of practical life the pleasant fictions of optimism vanished. If this were the best of all possible worlds, it nevertheless proved itself a very inconvenient habitation for the ideal sage.

The stoical summary of the whole duty of man, "Live according to nature," would seem to imply that the cosmic process is an exemplar for human conduct. Ethics would thus become applied Natural History. In fact, a confused employment of the maxim, in this sense, has done immeasurable mischief in later times. It has furnished an axiomatic foundation for the philosophy of philosophasters and for the moralizing of sentimentalists. But the Stoics were, at bottom, not merely noble, but sane, men; and if we look closely into what they really meant by this ill-used phrase, it will be found to present no justification for the mischievous conclusions that have been deduced from it.

In the language of the Stoa, "Nature" was a word of many meanings. There was the "Nature" of the cosmos and the "Nature" of man. In the latter, the animal "nature," which man shares with a moiety of the living part of the cosmos, was distinguished from a higher "nature." Even in this higher nature there were grades of rank. The logical faculty is an instrument which may be turned to account for any purpose. The passions and the emotions are so closely tied to the lower nature that they may be considered to be pathological, rather than normal, phenomena. The one supreme, hegemonic, faculty, which constitutes the essential "nature" of man, is most nearly represented by that which, in the language of a later philosophy, has been called the pure reason. It is this "nature" which holds up the ideal of the supreme good and demands absolute submission of the will to its behests. It is this which commands all men to love one another, to return good for evil, to regard one another as fellow-citizens of one great state. Indeed, seeing that the progress towards perfection of a civilized state, or polity, depends on the obedience of its members to these commands, the Stoics sometimes termed the pure reason the "political" nature. Unfortunately, the sense of the adjective has undergone so much modification, that the application of it to that which commands the sacrifice of self to the common good would now sound almost grotesque.

But what part is played by the theory of evolution in this view of ethics? So far as I can discern, the ethical system of the Stoics, which is essentially intuitive, and reverences the categorical imperative as strongly as that of any later moralists, might have been just what it was if they had held any other theory; whether that of special creation, on the one side, or that of the eternal existence of the present order, on the other. To the Stoic, the cosmos had no importance for the conscience, except in so far as he chose to think it a pedagogue to virtue. The pertinacious optimism of our philosophers hid from them the actual state of the case. It prevented them from seeing that cosmic nature is no school of virtue, but the headquarters of the enemy of ethical nature. The logic of facts was necessary to convince them that the cosmos works through the lower nature of man, not for righteousness, but against it. And it finally drove them to confess that the existence of their ideal "wise man" was incompatible with the nature of things; that even a passable approximation to that ideal was to be attained only at the cost of renunciation of the world and mortification, not merely of the flesh, but of all human affections. The state of perfection was that "apatheia" in which desire, though it may still be felt, is powerless to move the will, reduced to the sole function of executing the commands of pure reason. Even this residuum of activity was to be regarded as a temporary loan, as an efflux of the divine world-pervading spirit, chafing at its imprisonment in the flesh, until such time as death enabled it to return to its source in the all-pervading logos.

I find it difficult to discover any very great difference between Apatheia and Nirvana, except that stoical speculation agrees with pre-Buddhistic philosophy, rather than with the teachings of Gautama, in so far as it postulates a permanent substance equivalent to "Brahma" and "Atman"; and that, in stoical practice, the adoption of the life of the mendicant cynic was held to be more a counsel of perfection than an indispensable condition of the higher life.

Thus the extremes touch. Greek thought and Indian thought set out from ground common to both, diverge widely, develop under very different physical and moral conditions, and finally converge to practically the same end.

The Vedas and the Homeric epos set before us a world of rich and vigorous life, full of joyous fighting men

> That ever with a frolic welcome took
> The thunder and the sunshine . . .

and who were ready to brave the very Gods themselves when their blood was up. A few centuries pass away, and under the influence of civilization the descendants of these men are "sicklied o'er with the pale cast of thought"— frank pessimists, or, at best, make-believe optimists. The courage of the warlike stock may be as hardly tried as before, perhaps more hardly, but the enemy is self. The hero has become a monk. The man of action is replaced by the quietist, whose highest aspiration is to be the passive instrument of the divine Reason. By the Tiber, as by the Ganges, ethical man admits that the cosmos is too strong for him; and, destroying every bond which ties him to it by ascetic discipline, he seeks salvation in absolute renunciation.

Modern thought is making a fresh start from the base whence Indian and Greek philosophy set out; and, the human mind being very much what it was six-and-twenty centuries ago, there is no ground for wonder if it presents indications of a tendency to move along the old lines to the same results.

We are more than sufficiently familiar with modern pessimism, at least as a speculation; for I cannot call to mind that any of its present votaries have sealed their faith by assuming the rags and the bowl of the mendicant Bhikku, or the cloak and the wallet of the Cynic. The obstacles placed in the way of sturdy vagrancy by an unphilosophical police have, perhaps, proved too formidable for philosophical consistency. We also know modern speculative optimism, with its perfectibility of the species, reign of peace, and lion and lamb transformation scenes; but one does not hear so much of it as one did forty years ago; indeed, I imagine it is to be met with more commonly at the tables of the healthy and wealthy, than in the congregations of the wise. The majority of us, I apprehend, profess neither pessimism nor optimism. We hold that the world is neither so good, nor so bad, as it conceivably might be; and, as most of us have reason, now and again, to discover that it can be. Those who have failed to experience the joys that make life worth living are, probably, in as small a minority as those who have never known the griefs that rob existence of its savour and turn its richest fruits into mere dust and ashes.

Further, I think I do not err in assuming that, however diverse their views on philosophical and religious matters, most men are agreed that the proportion of good and evil in life may be very sensibly affected by human action. I never heard anybody doubt that the evil may be thus increased, or diminished; and it would seem to follow that good must be similarly susceptible of addition or subtraction. Finally, to my knowledge, nobody professes to doubt that, so far forth as we possess a power of bettering things, it is our paramount duty to use it and to train all our intellect and energy to this supreme service of our kind.

Hence the pressing interest of the question, to what extent modern progress in natural knowledge, and, more especially, the general outcome of that progress in the doctrine of evolution, is competent to help us in the great work of helping one another?

The propounders of what are called the "ethics of evolution," when the "evolution of ethics" would usually better express the object of their speculations, adduce a number of more or less interesting facts and more or less sound arguments, in favour of the origin of the moral sentiments, in the same way as other natural phenomena, by a process of evolution. I have little doubt, for my own part, that they are on the right track; but as the immoral sentiments have no less been evolved, there is, so far, as much natural sanction for the one as the other. The thief and the murderer follow nature just as much as the philanthropist. Cosmic evolution may teach us how the good and the evil tendencies of man may have come about; but, in itself, it is incompetent to furnish any better reason why what we call good is preferable to what we call evil than we had before. Some day, I doubt not, we shall arrive at an understanding of the evolution of the æsthetic faculty; but all the understanding in the world will neither increase nor diminish the force of the intuition that this is beautiful and that is ugly.

There is another fallacy which appears to me to pervade the so-called "ethics of evolution." It is the notion that because, on the whole, animals and plants have advanced in perfection of organization by means of the struggle for existence and the consequent "survival of the fittest"; therefore men in society, men as ethical beings, must look to the same process to help them towards perfection. I suspect that this fallacy has arisen out of the unfortunate ambiguity of the phrase "survival of the fittest." "Fittest" has a connotation of "best"; and about "best" there hangs a moral flavour. In cosmic nature, however, what is "fittest" depends upon the conditions. Long since, I ventured to point out that if our hemisphere were to cool again, the survival of the fittest might bring about, in the vegetable kingdom, a population of more and more stunted and humbler and humbler organisms, until the "fittest" that survived might be nothing but lichens, diatoms, and such microscopic organisms as those which give red snow its colour; while, if it became hotter, the pleasant valleys of the Thames and Isis might be uninhabitable by any animated beings save those that flourish in a tropical jungle. They, as the fittest, the best adapted to the changed conditions, would survive.

Men in society are undoubtedly subject to the cosmic process. As among other animals, multiplication goes on without cessation, and involves severe competition for the means of support. The struggle for existence tends to eliminate those less fitted to adapt themselves to the circumstances of their existence. The strongest, the most self-assertive, tend to tread down the weaker. But the influence of the cosmic process on the evolution of society is the greater the more rudimentary its civilization. Social progress means a checking of the cosmic process at every step and the substitution for it of another, which may be called the ethical process; the end of which is not the survival of those who may happen to be the fittest, in respect of the whole of the conditions which obtain, but of those who are ethically the best.

As I have already urged, the practice of that which is ethically best—what we call goodness or virtue—involves a course of conduct which, in all respects, is opposed to that which leads to success in the cosmic struggle for existence. In place of ruthless self-assertion it demands self-restraint; in place of thrusting aside, or treading down, all competitors, it requires that the individual shall not merely respect, but shall help his fellows; its influence is directed, not so much to the survival of the fittest, as to the fitting of as many as possible to survive. It repudiates the gladiatorial theory of existence. It demands that each man who enters into the enjoyment of the advantages of a polity shall be mindful of his debt to those who have laboriously constructed it; and shall take heed that no act of his weakens the fabric in which he has been permitted to live. Laws and moral precepts are directed to the end of curbing the cosmic process and reminding the individual of his duty to the community, to the protection and influence of which he owes, if not existence itself, at least the life of something better than a brutal savage.

It is from neglect of these plain considerations that the fanatical individualism of our time attempts to apply the analogy of cosmic nature to society. Once more we have a misapplication of the stoical injunction to follow nature; the duties of the individual to the state are forgotten, and his tendencies to self-assertion are dignified by the name of rights. It is seriously debated whether the members of a community are justified in using their combined strength to constrain one of their number to contribute his share to the maintenance of it; or even to prevent him from doing his best to destroy it. The struggle for existence, which has done such admirable work in cosmic nature, must, it appears, be equally beneficent in the ethical sphere. Yet if that which I have insisted upon is true; if the cosmic process has no sort of relation to moral ends; if the imitation of it by man is inconsistent with the first principles of ethics; what becomes of this surprising theory?

Let us understand, once for all, that the ethical progress of society depends, not on imitating the cosmic process, still less in running away from it, but in combating it. It may seem an audacious proposal thus to pit the microcosm against the macrocosm and to set man to subdue nature to his higher ends; but I venture to think that the great intellectual difference between the ancient times with which we have been occupied and our day, lies in the solid foundation we have acquired for the hope that such an enterprise may meet with a certain measure of success.

The history of civilization details the steps by which men have succeeded in building up an artificial world within the cosmos. Fragile reed as he may be, man, as Pascal says, is a thinking reed: there lies within him a fund of energy, operating intelligently and so far akin to that which pervades the universe, that it is competent to influence and modify the cosmic process. In virtue of his intelligence, the dwarf bends the Titan to his will. In every family, in every polity that has been established, the cosmic process in man has been restrained and otherwise modified by law and custom; in surrounding nature, it has been similarly influenced by the art of the shepherd, the agriculturalist, the artisan.

As civilization has advanced, so has the extent of this interference increased; until the organized and highly developed sciences and arts of the present day have endowed man with a command over the course of non-human nature greater than that once attributed to the magicians. The most impressive, I might say startling, of these changes have been brought about in the course of the last two centuries; while a right comprehension of the process of life and of the means of influencing its manifestations is only just dawning upon us. We do not yet see our way beyond generalities; and we are befogged by the obtrusion of false analogies and crude anticipations. But Astronomy, Physics, Chemistry, have all had to pass through similar phases, before they reached the stage at which their influence became an important factor in human affairs. Physiology, Psychology, Ethics, Political Science, must submit to the same ordeal. Yet it seems to me irrational to doubt that, at no distant period, they will work as great a revolution in the sphere of practice.

The theory of evolution encourages no millennial anticipations. If, for millions of years, our globe has taken the upward road, yet, some time, the summit will be reached and the downward route will be commenced. The most daring imagination will hardly venture upon the suggestion that the power and the intelligence of man can ever arrest the procession of the great year.

Moreover, the cosmic nature born with us and, to a large extent, necessary for our maintenace, is the outcome of millions of years of severe training, and it would be folly to imagine that a few centuries will suffice to subdue its masterfulness to purely ethical ends. Ethical nature may count upon having to reckon with a tenacious and powerful enemy as long as the world lasts. But, on the other hand, I see no limit to the extent to which intelligence and will, guided by sound principles of investigation, and organized in common effort, may modify the conditions of existence, for a period longer than that now covered by history. And much may be done to change the nature of man himself. The intelligence which has converted the brother of the wolf into the faithful guardian of the flock ought to be able to do something towards curbing the instincts of savagery in civilized men.

But if we may permit ourselves a larger hope of abatement of the essential evil of the world than was possible to those who, in the infancy of exact knowledge, faced the problem of existence more than a score of centuries ago, I deem it an essential condition of the realization of that hope that we should cast aside the notion that the escape from pain and sorrow is the proper object of life.

We have long since emerged from the heroic childhood of our race, when good and evil could be met with the same "frolic welcome"; the attempts to escape from evil, whether Indian or Greek, have ended in flight from the battle-field; it remains to us to throw aside the youthful overconfidence and the no less youthful discouragement of nonage. We are grown men, and must play the man.

> strong in will
> To strive, to seek, to find, and not to yield,

cherishing the good that falls in our way, and bearing the evil, in and around us, with stout hearts set on diminishing it. So far, we all may strive in one faith towards one hope:

> It may be that the gulfs will wash us down,
> It may be we shall touch the Happy Isles,
>
> . . . but something ere the end,
> Some work of noble note may yet be done. [Tennyson]